Performing Post-Tariqa Sufism

This ethnographic research project examines the generation of post-tariqa *Tasavvuf* (Sufism: a spiritual practice and philosophy recognised as the inner dimension of Islam) in a variety of private, semi-public, public, secular and sacred urban spaces in present-day Turkey.

Through extensive field research in minority Sufi communities, this book investigates how devotees of specific orders maintain, adapt, mobilise, and empower their beliefs and values through embodied acts of their Sufi followers. Using an ethnographic methodology and theories derived from performance studies, Esra Çizmeci examines the multiple ways in which the post-tariqa *Mevlevi* and *Rifai* practice is formed in present-day Turkey, such as through the authority of the spiritual teacher; the individual and collective performance of Sufi rituals; *nefs* (self) training; and, most importantly, the practice of Sufi doctrines in everyday life through the production of sacred spaces. Drawing on the theories of performance, she examines how the Sufi way of living and spaces are created anew in the process of each devotee's embodied action.

This book is informed by theories in performance studies, anthropology, religious studies, and cultural studies and places current Sufi practices in a historical perspective.

Esra Çizmeci is a performance studies scholar and an ethnographer. Her research interests include performance in the everyday, performance for actors and non-actors, Islam and performance, performance theory and ethnographic methods, the study of minority cultures as well as community performance.

Routledge Advances in Theatre & Performance Studies

This series is our home for cutting-edge, upper-level scholarly studies and edited collections. Considering theatre and performance alongside topics such as religion, politics, gender, race, ecology, and the avant-garde, titles are characterized by dynamic interventions into established subjects and innovative studies on emerging topics.

Boundaries of Violence in Early Modern England
Samantha Dressel and Matthew Carter

Bourdieu in the Studio
Decolonising and Decentering Actor Training through Ludic Activism
Evi Stamatiou

Ethical Agility in Dance
Rethinking Technique in British Contemporary Dance
Noyale Colin, Catherine Seago, Kathryn Stamp

At the Threshold
Contemporary Theatre, Art, and Music of Iran
Rana Esfandiary

Gut Knowledges
Culinary Performance and Activism in the Post-Truth Era
Kristin Hunt

Butoh, as Heard by a Dancer
Dominique Savitri Bonarjee

Performing Post-Tariqa Sufism
Making Sacred Space with *Mevlevi* and *Rifai Zikir* in Turkey
Esra Çizmeci

For more information about this series, please visit: www.routledge.com/Routledge-Advances-in-Theatre-Performance-Studies/book-series/RATPS

Performing Post-Tariqa Sufism
Making Sacred Space with *Mevlevi* and *Rifai Zikir* in Turkey

Esra Çizmeci

LONDON AND NEW YORK

First published 2024
by Routledge
4 Park Square, Milton Park, Abingdon, Oxon OX14 4RN

and by Routledge
605 Third Avenue, New York, NY 10158

Routledge is an imprint of the Taylor & Francis Group, an informa business

© 2024 Esra Çizmeci

The right of Esra Çizmeci to be identified as author of this work has been asserted in accordance with sections 77 and 78 of the Copyright, Designs and Patents Act 1988.

All rights reserved. No part of this book may be reprinted or reproduced or utilised in any form or by any electronic, mechanical, or other means, now known or hereafter invented, including photocopying and recording, or in any information storage or retrieval system, without permission in writing from the publishers.

Trademark notice: Product or corporate names may be trademarks or registered trademarks, and are used only for identification and explanation without intent to infringe.

British Library Cataloguing-in-Publication Data
A catalogue record for this book is available from the British Library

Library of Congress Cataloging-in-Publication Data
Names: Çizmeci, Esra, author.
Title: Performing post-tariqa Sufism : making sacred space with Mevlevi and Rifai zikir in Turkey / Esra Çizmeci.
Description: 1. | New York : Routledge, 2023. | Series: Routledge advances in theatre & performance studies | Includes bibliographical references and index.
Identifiers: LCCN 2023026299 (print) | LCCN 2023026300 (ebook) | ISBN 9780367632694 (hardback) | ISBN 9780367633301 (paperback) | ISBN 9781003118589 (ebook)
Subjects: LCSH: Sufism—Turkey. | Mevleviyeh—Turkey. | Rifāʿīyah—Turkey.
Classification: LCC BP188.8.T9 C59 2023 (print) | LCC BP188.8.T9 (ebook) | DDC 297.409561—dc23/eng/20230705
LC record available at https://lccn.loc.gov/2023026299
LC ebook record available at https://lccn.loc.gov/2023026300

ISBN: 978-0-367-63269-4 (hbk)
ISBN: 978-0-367-63330-1 (pbk)
ISBN: 978-1-003-11858-9 (ebk)

DOI: 10.4324/9781003118589

Typeset in Sabon
by Apex CoVantage, LLC

Contents

Introduction: Post-Tariqa Sufi Space in Turkey   1

PART ONE
Restoring   35

1   Historical Perspectives: Post-Tariqa *Mevlevi* Devotion   37

2   Designing a Post-Tariqa Communal Sufi Training   70

PART TWO
Transmitting   95

3   Whirling "Anytime and AnyPlace"   97

PART THREE
Transforming   125

4   Sacralisation of the Body and Mind   127

5   World as Manyness of Reality   149

Conclusion   188

Bibliography   *195*
Index   *221*

Introduction
Post-Tariqa Sufi Space in Turkey

The first time I attended a Sufi[1] ritual gathering was at a newly renovated *Mevlevi*[2] lodge in Istanbul. As most of the lodges in Turkey, that year, Yenikapı *Mevlevi* lodge was not open to everyday use and lodging for the *Mevlevi* dervishes (known in the West as whirling dervishes) due to 1925 legal restrictions (prohibiting any activity in Sufi sites) and reclassification of the *Mevlevi* lodges.[3] All the historical *Mevlevi* lodges were either functioning as museums or were under renovation if not abandoned by government officials. Although I knew that the religious landscape of Turkey has been transforming with the actions of the *Adalet ve Kalkınma Partisi* (Justice and Development Party—JDP) turning a blind eye to the activities of many Sufi orders,[4] *Mevlevi* dervishes were only allowed to use the lodges for the performance of the ceremony as tourist attraction. The government was only supporting *Mevlevi* ritual gatherings to promote tourism. I remember devotees stating that they were in the lodge only for specific activities allowed by the Ministry of Tourism and Culture and that the government was not allowing them to use the spaces for lodging or regular worship. However, they also expressed without fear that they were in the lodge to worship. *Mevlevis* performed the whirling ritual simultaneously as tourist attraction and worship. After that day, two contrasting images stayed with me. One was the cold and deserted corridors of the renovated building. The other was the crying sound of the reed flute along with the sense of devotion that *semazens* (whirling dervishes) conveyed when they crossed their arms on their chests signifying God's unity. As time passed during the initial months of my fieldwork, I was starting to see how the lodge gained meaning with the devotees whirling and singing. Since then, whenever I need to talk about *Sema* as a *Mevlevi zikir* in my performance classes or at conferences, I often recall that initial gaze of how the newly renovated building transformed with *semazens*' white robes rising in unison as they whirled their arms open, right hand directed towards the sky and left hand turned towards the earth (representing *Mevlevi* dervishes' willingness to convey God's unity to those witnessing the *Sema*). It was the *semazens*' performances of remembrance (*zikir*), including the sense of concentration achieved as *semazens* embodied God's unity, the execution of the whirling ritual and the singing of the

DOI: 10.4324/9781003118589-1

liturgical actions,[5] that gave meaning to the cold paint-smelling corridors of the newly renovated *Mevlevi* lodge.

During the preliminary phases of my fieldwork, I had epiphanies about how these initial meetings with the *Mevlevi* dervishes at the lodge had also been my first encounters with Turks who were practising Muslims in Turkey. My childhood memories growing up in İzmir (a city recognised for its Westernised and secular values) were guiding me as I questioned my position as a researcher coming from a family that disapproved Islam's visibility in public. As I come from a secular Turkish family (also immigrants that had moved from former Yugoslavia in the 1920s), who have regarded religion as a threat to the safety and freedom of the Turkish Republic, growing up, I did not learn about Islam. Although my family members and I had national identity cards that included a mandatory section about religious affiliation, declaring our faith as Islam, according to my mom, I was not necessarily Muslim. Growing up, I could research and learn about different religions and in time choose one, several or none. I knew I was free to choose any belief system and at that time, I was interested in my best friend's religion, Judaism. This, I recall, was probably due to the synagogue located right across my family home in Izmir and that I wanted to spend time in there with my best friend. At the time, my best friend's synagogue was a mystery that I needed to solve.

Due to safety regulations, I was not allowed to enter the synagogue to attend the gatherings, and I was very curious about the events my best friend was attending on the weekends. My best friend was fond of attending a variety of religious gatherings at the synagogue on the weekends. Therefore, on Saturdays, I would have to content myself with sitting by the window watching her and her family entering the synagogue in their elaborate outfits looking tidy and modest. I did not know back then that my attention was growing due to my curiosity about the image of a synagogue that was created by the stories told by my Jewish friend. I remember asking her in curiosity to describe the synagogue to me and her trying to illustrate the space by talking about her and other members' actions and behaviours in classes, dance parties and a variety of other gatherings organised on the weekends. Her descriptions would make me imagine the sense of togetherness and playfulness in the space instead of the architecture or how the space looked. I remember her saying that it was just a room but the activities were fun. They played. They danced. They sang. In my imagination, the synagogue was people performing a variety of fun rituals. Years later, visiting many Sufi lodges as a researcher and remembering my interest in my best friend's synagogue, I realised how my interest in Sufism lies beyond the aesthetic qualities of the Sufi ritual. I was interested in analysing how, with their embodied acts, *Mevlevi* and *Rifai* (known in the West as howling dervishes) devotees restored and transmitted their beliefs and values and gave meaning to the spaces they use for Sufi gatherings.

My memories with my Jewish best friend were full of little enlightening stories about devotion and use of sacred space. Listening to my friend talking, I also remember questioning why I and my family did not have a similar religious space to attend such fun gatherings. My grandmother, who also was not a practising Muslim, would often explain how why we do not attend mosques because they were spaces used solely for conservative male devotees' prayer. Years later, when I witnessed how *Rifai* devotees organise a variety of gatherings in an old wooden house (organised as their sacred space), I truly comprehended what the synagogue meant for my best friend and her family. Whether it was a synagogue or a Sufi lodge, it was devotees' actions that sacralised these worship sites. During fieldwork, I have come to understand how performance and sacred space production were at the core of most religious life. Elif, a devotee I met at the Yenikapı lodge, once said:

> [W]e usually gather in our private homes to whirl . . . , all we need is a large room . . . but it also feels nice to be here in a historical *semahane* [a ritual hall designed specifically for the whirling ritual] that once belonged to beloved [*Mevlevi*] mystics.[6]

Contrary to how Muslims use the mosques in Turkey (in which male and female devotees have not been allowed to occupy the same prayer spaces), *Mevlevis* and *Rifais*, discussed in this book, use their embodied acts to transform their private homes to multipurpose sacred sites available for mixed gender social gatherings. While many Muslims tend to only occupy mosques during prayer times, separating non-worship time (with family and friends) from prayer time (performing *namaz* and listening to *imam*'s readings of the Quran), *Rifais* I have met during my fieldwork have also combined non-worship leisure activities with prayer time and produced their sacred sites as multilayered spaces of learning, celebrating, dancing, singing, lodging and creating art. This book is about how and why *Mevlevis* and *Rifais* use their embodied acts (variety of *zikir* rituals, including *Mevlevi* whirling, poetry readings, vocalising Sufi hymns, and repeating God's names individually and as a group) to produce such multilayered post-tariqa[7] *Rifai* and *Mevlevi* spaces. I will discuss how by transforming private homes into such multilayered sacred sites, devotees seek to overcome the sense of isolation they have been experiencing due to 1925 legal restrictions and restore *Mevlevi* and *Rifai* Sufism as a post-tariqa devotional practice. Between 2010 and 2021, I attended a variety of *Rifai* and *Mevlevi* gatherings in Istanbul, Izmir, Çanakkale, Yalova and Konya and realised how performance (embodiment of *zikir*) is at the core of these devotees' generation of post-tariqa Sufi practice and production of post-tariqa sacred Sufi space. Although some of them (usually more doctrinal ones) would not use the word "performance" to define their rituals, classes and/or practice of everyday life, through their private and public experience of a variety of ritual performances, public speeches, tourist attractions, classes, workshops, etc., some devotees begun to redefine their ritual performances as "doing" and "sharing doing."[8] It is also possible to witness devotees who use performance in an intentional way to transmit their

4 *Introduction*

Sufi values and transform a variety of private spaces into sacred sites (halls, rooms, houses, culture centres) for themselves and for their visitors.

The appeal of the chapters in this book is that many of them provide, for the first time, detailed accounts of certain post-tariqa *Mevlevi* and *Rifai* formations gathered through full participant observation and co-performance (studying the culture by taking a role and getting involved in their rituals and everyday life actions, such as cleaning, cooking, teaching, serving dinner and reading poetry with them). I take every embodied act executed by the devotees, including tourist attractions, classes, workshops, *sohbets* (talks), service training and presentations of self in everyday life (daily actions and interactions) as performance. By focusing on *Mevlevi* practice in a variety of commodified spaces and *Rifai* practice in specific non-commodified secluded spaces, this book evaluates how while trying to preserve certain traditional Sufi practices, some of these groups and individuals embody certain qualities of "new religious movements,"[9] such as focusing on alternative ways of seeking the divine. Their eclectic and pluralistic nature inspires a sense of trust in diversity in that they are able to use their embodied acts to combine and modify certain doctrines and practices. Devotees contemplate and transform the position of the spiritual teacher (sheikh), *zikir* ceremonies, training of *nefs* (translated as self, soul, mind or ego), the representation of universal and multi-cultural ideas and the embodiment of other Sufi teachings in everyday life. Using an ethnographic methodology and theories derived from performance studies, I examine the multiple ways the *Mevlevi* and *Rifai* post-tariqa devotional life is formed in temporary and permanent sacred spaces.

Performance as an Object of Study

Mevlevis and *Rifais* discussed in this book perceive that the aim of their Sufi practice is to perform *zikir* (remembrance of God) at all times, train *nefs* (translated as self, soul, mind or ego), become a *kamil* (translated as mature, wise, competent and perfect) *insan* (human being) and embody God's unity. Devotees discuss Sufism as a journey taken to comprehend and embody God's unity. They also depict their rituals as a spiritual journey to move and stay close to God. For these devotees, *zikir* is a meditation that they seek to perform to remember God. Sufi devotees perform a variety of rituals, such as *sema ceremony, sohbet, burhan, çile, service* and other *zikir* ceremonies, all as different forms of teaching oneself to remember God at all times and realise God's unity. They believe that all of the living and non-living things are part of God's unity as manyness of reality (that all things are different from one another yet their true self is united in God). It is their ultimate goal to realise this oneness. This theory (of unity) for them means acquiring the ability to stay in harmony with all of God's creation. Constantly studying to remember and embody this sense of unity is considered the core of their Sufi faith.

With this perception of unity, they seek to learn disciplining oneself (*nefs* training) in order to be aware of one's shortcomings such as anger, greed, pride or any aspect that keeps a human being from knowing one's true self. To train *nefs* is to know oneself in all aspects. Devotees tend to explain that a strong sense of awareness of self is key to training the mind (*nefs*) and to becoming a *kamil insan*. Devotees often refer to individuals who have achieved such states of awareness as *kamil insan*. For a *kamil insan*, as elderly devotees often explain, nothing is more important than realising His unity and staying on the journey of realisation. The state of realisation, according to devotees, is not a termination of practice, rather a journey that never ends. In order to stay on the journey of realisation, even Sufi masters (who are considered *kamil insan*) seek to meditate at all times by repeating God's Quranic names and continue their training. As many devotees say, "one never knows when a person will go astray."[10] To embody unity, devotees practice *zikir* and perceive all of their rituals, including the well-known whirling dervish ceremonies and rituals that are everyday actions and behaviours, as different forms of practising remembrance. Aside from the more obvious performances such as the whirling ritual that devotees execute in public, it is this sense of seeking to embody remembrance at all times (even when performing everyday tasks in ordinary life) that makes performance of *zikir* (doing and sharing remembrance) the heart of Sufi practice. For devotees, performance of *zikir*, with all its forms (remembering through speaking, dancing, singing, etc.), is also about restoring Sufi practice and Sufi space (Part One), transmitting Sufi beliefs and values "anytime and anyplace" (Part Two) and transforming the mind and the world (Part Three). All the chapters in this book discuss different ways post-tariqa Sufi practice is restored, transmitted and transformed with the performance of *zikir* (different ways devotees do and share their practice of remembrance).

To examine post-tariqa Sufi everyday life, this book focuses on specific *Rifai* and *Mevlevi* groups and takes devotees' embodied acts, meaning any type of performance (doing and sharing doing) including all forms of *zikir* (such as serving rituals, whirling rituals, singing liturgical songs and other actions and interactions devotees perform with God in mind) as objects to examine post-tariqa Sufism in Turkey. As in Schechner's broad definition of performance, I examine devotees' spiritual "world as performance" and discuss how their "performances mark identities, bend time, reshape and adorn the body, and tell stories."[11] When analysing Sufi performance, one thing needs to be very clear. When I engage with the word "performance" in relation to Sufi practice, I do not mean theatre arts, performing arts, artistic events or any type of entertainment. This book engages with the idea of performance due to its capacity to improve any scholar's ability to imagine and create research that takes the human body as a source to question devotional and cultural processes. Performance perspectives inspire scholars to think outside of the box and to create multifaceted research that focuses on embodied knowledge.

It was Diana Taylor's seminal book *The Archive and the Repertoire: Performing Cultural Memory in the Americas* that encouraged me to carry my focus to embodied *Mevlevi* and *Rifai* culture in order to investigate what is not available in the archives about Sufism in Turkey. Taylor explains:

> By shifting the focus from written to embodied culture, from the discursive to the performatic, we need to shift our methodologies. Instead of focusing on patterns of cultural expression in terms of texts and narratives, we might think about them as 'scenarios' that do not reduce gestures and embodied practices to narrative description. This shift necessarily alters what academic disciplines regard as appropriate canons, and might extend the traditional disciplinary boundaries to include practices previously outside their purview.[12]

Such performance perspective opens a lens through which this book analyses how specific post-tariqa *Mevlevi* and *Rifai* devotional life and spaces are created anew in the process of each devotee's embodied actions. This book is about Sufi practitioners, who seek to unite with God by way of performance-oriented Sufi practices that overshadow the doctrinal and logocentric authority of conservative Islam.

In order to achieve this, I employ performance studies perspectives about human behaviour to examine post-tariqa Sufi devotional life by asking performance questions such as how does a devotee pray, look, walk, speak, cook, serve, dance or sing? How does the devotee behave, and how and why do certain behaviours change over time? What effects do certain behaviours have on the person performing (doing) the action or on the participants or observers present? How do devotees choose to display their actions? As Schechner highlights, anything can be studied "as" performance as long as analytical tools of performance studies have the potential to bring out new layers about the culture performing specific embodied acts. To analyse Sufi performance, I take Schechner's idea of performance as "doing" and "showing doing" and change the latter with "sharing doing" to show how devotees do not practice their performances to show their beliefs and values.[13] Rather, they perceive their performances as acts of sharing, teaching and transmitting. Although almost all of Sufi devotional performance is primarily doing, as some devotees express some of their performances include some level of "transmitting" when performed in the presence of an audience.[14] However, as discussed earlier, Sufi devotees' act of showing is not about presenting a theatre play, dance show or any type of artistic entertainment. Also, I cannot stress enough that Sufi performance is definitely not about showing off. Sufi performance is an act of seeking wisdom. Sufi performance is remembrance of God.

In such multidisciplinary performance research, it is necessary to be aware that although "From the vantage of performance theory, every action is a performance," "from the vantage of cultural practice, some actions will be deemed performances and others not; and this will vary from culture to culture, historical period to historical period."[15] For instance, "By the fourteenth century the popular entertainments and religious observances joined to form the basis for the great cycle plays celebrating and enacting the history of the world from Creation through the Crucifixion and Resurrection to the Last Judgment."[16] Although, scholars would call these enactments theatre today, "they were not named that at the time. The anti-theatrical prejudice of the Church disallowed any such designation."[17] Similar is true for the Sufi culture. Since the formation of tariqas in the eleventh century, Islamic orthodoxy has been disapproving of rituals and ceremonies such as *Sema* and certain forms of *zikir* due to their music and dance aspects. Although the Quranic texts do not include negative or condemning views about the practice of music and dancing, during the Ottoman Empire, orthodox *ulema* persistently rejected *Sema* and *zikir* rituals of Sufi orders. As discussed earlier, in my analysis of *Mevlevis'* and *Rifais'* actions and interactions, I examine both the rituals and everyday actions and interactions as devotional acts rather than acts of mere entertainment. Both fixed performances (such as the whirling rituals performed in the *semahane* of a *Mevlevi* lodge—where the performance and the audience space is clearly separated) and less-defined performances (such as a devotee's presentation of self in everyday life) discussed in this book are not performing artworks or entertainment. The idea of performance and theatricality discussed in this book illuminates how "not all theatrical performance is conventionally artistic, but it is always social, and often inventively so."[18] Whether devotees perform their rituals (such as whirling) in private or in public, they always describe them as sacred acts rather than artistic works.

I also take into consideration part of McAuley's principles about what can be studied as performance. She points out that "for an activity to be regarded as performance, it must involve the live presence of the performers and those witnessing it."[19] She also discusses further that

> there must be some intentionality on the part of the performer or witness or both, and that these conditions in turn necessitate analysis of the place and temporality which enable both parties to be present to each other, as well as what can be described as the performance contract between them, whether explicit or implicit.[20]

By examining how devotees perform a set of acts with their witnesses in mind (their spiritual teachers and friends that they share a sacred space with), I show how and why they choose to be present for each other. In addition, I follow devotees' cultural position regarding how they perceive themselves as spiritual practitioners acting and interacting in the presence of God. Devotees present themselves in everyday life by focusing on the idea that human beings, even when alone, performing ordinary tasks, are always in the presence of God. In such cases, God is their audience. Also, devotees explain how aside from performing for God, they also perform for their own consciousness (which as they explain is the spiritual self, the level of *nefs*[21] that is connected to God). In such cases, their consciousness (the spiritual self) becomes the audience of their actions and behaviours. Devotees seek to act with such high levels of awareness. Therefore, they constantly observe their own thoughts, words and actions. Although, once again, devotees do not use the word "performance" to express such devotional practices, they believe that they train self in the presence of God and others that witness their actions and interactions. They seek to perceive the world as a sacred site designed for human beings who observe, embody and express certain acts and behaviours in order to unite with God.

In the post-tariqa everyday life, devotees' acts of remembrance tend to be very expressive or performative (effective doings that can change each other's social reality).[22] Through the idea of performative, I depict how devotees' rituals have the potential to transform oneself and others witnessing. The idea of performative also informs my evaluation of how devotees practice and mobilise Sufism. Theorists such as John Langshaw Austin, Jacques Derrida, Judith Butler, Andrew Parker, Eve Kosofsky Sedgwick, Richard Schechner and Diana Taylor have employed the idea of the "performative" to mean different things.[23] In order to reclaim the term for her analysis of performing cultural memory, Taylor borrows the word "performatico" from contemporary Spanish to indicate performance analysis that is not related to specific modes of discourse.[24] Taylor finds this important to signal the expressive acts that are both involved with and separate from "Western logocentricism."[25] Borrowing Taylor's term, I take actions embodied by devotees and their production of Sufi space as "performatic."[26] This idea enables me to look at the intersections between spaces and embodied actions, as well as the discursive and the non-discursive realms of the *Mevlevi* and *Rifai* way of living.

Taylor's analysis of "performatic shift and doubling" is also valuable for the analysis of Sufi rituals as regeneration and mobilisation of Sufi way of living.[27] This book employs Joseph Roach's and Taylor's analysis of cultural continuity to explore how devotees generate their beliefs and values.[28] Taylor gives examples from cultures in the colonial history of the Americas, such as "colonisers and evangelists" holding on to their belief of "successful substitutions."[29] What Taylor identifies as "performatic shift and doubling" occurs when cultures preserve rather than erase their antecedents. Just like in Taylor's analysis of how a pagan deity might continue to exist within a Catholic image, this book discusses how Sufi teachings continue to exist in folk and touristic adaptations of the whirling ritual and that devotees experience and transmit their Sufi cultural beliefs and values within such shifts and doublings. Using Taylor's and Roach's theories, this book discusses devotees' practice of the whirling ritual performed simultaneously as worship and folk performance.

Also, I evaluate some of the ritual performances, such as the *burhan* (inserting skewers into dervish's body parts) ritual, as theatrical (effective doings that create powerful focus) to present how devotees practice their rituals to empower their perception of unity.[30] Engaging with the idea of theatricality, I do not intend to show how Sufi practices are like theatre in the sense that they are forms of entertainment. I use the theory of "theatricality" to discuss how devotees create powerful focus points that improve their relationship with God.[31] As Marvin Carlson suggests, with the concept of performance, "the metaphor of theatricality has moved out of the arts into almost every aspect of modern attempts to understand our condition and activities, into every branch of the human sciences."[32] Using theatricality as a tool, teachers teach, minorities transmit and preserve values, foreigners produce space, Yoruba people seek wisdom, immigrants hope to assimilate and many others attempt to participate in particular social processes. Once again, I cannot stress enough that while using the idea of theatricality as enhanced performatives that create powerful focus points, it is not my intention to disrespect the sacredness and religious meaning of Sufi practice. On the contrary, through the lens of the theory of performativity and theatricality open, I intend to discuss how Sufi-embodied practices are intense performances that improve a dervish's comprehension of God's unity.

Performativity (as effective doing) and theatricality (as enhanced performativity that reveals perception) are different ways of embodying and acting social roles that make up the society we live in. Theatrical acts create a sense of distance, focus and occasion, thus making performative acts more visible and accessible. As Conquergood explains: "Turner shifted thinking about performance from mimesis to poises,"[33] and "now the current thinking about performance constitutes a shift from poiesis to kinesis."[34] Focusing "on the productive capacities of performance set the stage for a more poststructuralist and political emphasis on performance as kinesis, as movement, motion, fluidity, fluctuation, all those restless energies that transgress boundaries and trouble closure."[35] Emphasising the dynamic qualities of performance, "postcolonial critic Homi K. Bhabha deployed the term 'performative' to refer to action that incessantly insinuates, interrupts, interrogates, antagonises, and decenters powerful master discourses, which he dubbed 'pedagogical.'"[36] The theatrical perspective would highlight these actions creating both direct appearance and reflective distance.[37] Conquergood illuminates the need to comprehend the movement between "Turner's emphatic view of performance as making not faking" and "Bhabha's politically urgent view of performance as breaking and remaking."[38] These ideas about performance also inform how devotees are theatrical in the sense that with their performances they constantly recreate Sufism according to the needs of the devotees.

Also, as Andreea Micu illuminates "human beings perform for a range of reasons, such as to communicate, entertain, reaffirm a sense of belonging, negotiate identity, transform conflict."[39] Performance "lies at the very core of who we are as a species, some social scientists have argued that homo sapiens is, in fact, homo performans."[40] Human beings learn how to act by witnessing each other's actions. We repeat and transform each other's performances. As Mica discusses, "we repeat and we create."[41] This sense of creative imitation or representation is a significant part of the post-tariqa Sufi devotional life due to devotees' need to adapt to changing social and political conditions in today's Turkey.

Examining embodied acts of Yoruba performers, Margaret Thompson Drewal also becomes aware of how "representation as mimesis (the exteriority or visualisation of an inner idea or feeling)" is different from "representation as kinesis (temporal, unfolding in the situated flow of human interactions)."[42] Drewal, in her study of Yoruba rituals, discovers that the practice of representation "embodies creativity, for representation itself is a form of creativity."[43] Along with Drewal's idea of representation as transformation, I follow Schechner's analysis that for traditions, including rituals, "to remain meaningful they must adjust to new circumstances and realities."[44] In Drewal's study on ritual, "Whenever improvisation is a performative strategy in ritual, it places ritual squarely within the domain of play."[45] In my work with the *Mevlevis* and *Rifais*, it was devotees' inclination to improvise, that drew them into the training. Devotees repeat and restore certain behaviours (roles) to build their relationships, thereby generating and questioning their actions and goals. With the idea of representation as transformation, theatricality and performativity becomes a powerful tool in the post-tariqa Sufi training through which devotees seek self-reflection and growth. Drewal also encourages her readers to understand ritual as a transformational process rather than a process of reproduction in which ritual is perceived as fixed, copy of an established system and/or duplication of the past with gradual change. I examine how the action of discovering the physical sensations happening in the body during *zikir* ceremonies is about seeking self-transformation. The way devotees practice *remembrance* is not fixed. Some practice devotion by serving (cooking, cleaning) one another; some continuously live and train under the same roof; some meditate in private; some teach Sufi music; some organise visits to orphanages and nursing homes; some organise seminars that focus on Sufism's relationship to current social movements; some organise tourist attractions; some teach whirling; some practice extreme forms of renunciation (such as eating and sleeping little) and many more.

In performance studies, another seminal research area, the embodied acts of individuals in everyday life help illuminate how I perceive devotees' everyday actions as performance. Erving Goffman has created the idea that performance exists in the quotidian, in spaces that are not designated as a site for theatre and/or any other performance.[46] This theory informs how devotees embody an aspect of their own selves and portray their own Sufi identities as they interact with one another and how such interactions shape post-tariqa Sufi practice. Examining *Mevlevi* and *Rifai* everyday life, I assess how devotees, without any or some intentional focus on creating theatricality or performativity, use role-playing as a medium to affect social processes and as a natural tool to know self and others. Also, I find it necessary to discuss once again the fact that when I use the word "role-playing" in relation to devotees repeating and recreating (mimesis) their spiritual teacher's behaviours, my depiction of role-playing is not about faking or tricking. It is about internalising and embodying certain behaviours of a devotee whose wisdom is respected, trusted and admired. Devotees accept their spiritual teachers as embodiments of God's unity. It is my intention to examine how role-playing is one of the basic attitudes of any human being's ordinary life, and it informs the restoration, mobilisation and transformation of post-tariqa Sufism in Turkey. Devotees use role-playing to learn, teach and inspire. Although some of them were not ready to use the word "performance" or role-playing while talking about their practices, I also choose to use the word "performance" to show how most of the devotees' devotional practices are beyond "the theatrical prejudice" that continue to exist in conservative Islamic circles. It is also important to point out that even devotees who avoided the word "performance," were interested in using words such as "embodiment," "representation," "imitation" and "enactment" while defining their devotional practices. It was encouraging to witness how most valued the idea and power of creating embodied knowledge.

This book claims performance is at the core of post-tariqa *Mevlevi* and *Rifai* devotional life. Devotees learn and transmit Sufi beliefs and values through a variety of embodied acts, including rituals and performances of everyday life (behaviours, actions and interactions). As Taylor further states, "Embodied performances have always played a central role in conserving memory and consolidating identities in literate, semiliterate, and digital societies. Not everyone comes to 'culture' or modernity through writing."[47] She further explains that it is imperative to reexamine the relationships between performance and the generation of knowledge because "we learn and transmit knowledge through embodied action, through cultural agency, and by making choices."[48] Taylor's idea influences my examination of how devotees seek to embody Sufi teachings and divine meaning in their rituals and prayers and carry the sensations they experience in the rituals to their practice of everyday life. Devotees remember, learn and communicate their teachings through embodied actions and, with their embodied acts, create temporary and permanent sacred spaces.

Coperformative Witnessing: Performing With the Devotees

Examining *Mevlevi* and *Rifai* cases of post-tariqa Sufi practice in Turkey, this book also takes performance ethnography as a methodology and follows Dwight Conquergood's idea that interpreting lives is radically different from analysing books.[49] Performing the rituals, participating poetry readings, singing liturgical songs, listening and sharing my ideas when the devotees gathered for *sohbets* (talks), and serving food and cleaning rooms with the devotees each day was my way of researching post-tariqa *Mevlevi* and *Rifai* space production in Turkey. Performance ethnography focuses on the movement of the body, the actions and interactions devotees' bodies convey in their ordinary lives as well as, out-of-the-ordinary events such as jinn possession.

12 Introduction

During extensive fieldwork, I followed Conquergood's three significant ideas of using coperformative witnessing as a method for field research.[50] The first guiding point is that "the art of fieldwork is performance;" the second, the people with whom I meet and perform everyday life during fieldwork "are not fools;" and the third is that I need to imagine Sufi culture as a "matrix of boundaries, borders, intersections, turning points, and thresholds."[51] As Peña explains,

> this mode of research is a deeply politicised way of seeing and being in the field" and that the point of departure needs to be twofold. It is crucial to remember how "the ethnographer and the 'subject' are always, and have always been, despite the insistence of more traditional ethnographic methods, engaged as interlocutors.[52]

Another crucial idea was that the

> coperformative witnessing does not rely solely on texts housed in archives, oral histories, maps, or statistics but also foregrounds sensual communication—the rich subtext and often deeply coded moments of bodied exchange—that produce knowledge, ideas, opinions, mores, and traditions.[53]

Consistent with Conquergood's methodology, Victor Turner states "if anthropologists are going to take ethnodramatics seriously . . . we will have to become performers ourselves."[54] Without these methodological ideas, it would not have been possible to examine the multilayered processes of post-tariqa Sufism and what some devotees describe as "versatile Sufism."[55]

Pnina Werbner's ethnographic research on Sufi cults, investigating the processes of Pakistani migration, has become a model with its emphasis on multiple voices showing how a Sufi group operates within the tribal area of Pakistan and expands into the secular space of Great Britain.[56] Werbner inspired me as a researcher to interact with devotees in Turkey and think critically about the multifaceted beliefs and values that generate present-day Sufism in Turkey. As a researcher, most days I attended classes, rituals, dinners, *sohbets* (talks) and other prayer/community meetings from morning to night in an apartment building and a wooden house converted into Sufi lodges, which gave me the opportunity to co-perform everyday life with the devotees. Building on the idea of a Sufi way of living, I show how religious Sufi practice is not just a result of a set of strict doctrinal rules. I examine the Sufi way of living as emotional, physically constituted and beyond normative rules and choices.

In order to witness how Sufi devotees live in contemporary Turkey, I also joined different Sufi communities primarily in Istanbul between 2010 and 2019 and met devotees who were lawyers, teachers, bank workers and artists, for whom Sufi worship/community gatherings were a significant part of their simultaneously religious and secular daily life. My encounters over the years showed me that although Sufi groups share knowledge and practice of primary Islamic sources such as the Quran, each needed to create its own unique path (way of worship) in order to survive the socio-political pressures of practising Sufism in Turkey. Despite their ability to adapt, post-tariqa *Mevlevis*' and *Rifais*' positions have always been complicated due to their close relationship with two opposing value systems in Turkey, secularism and religiousness. Post-tariqa *Mevlevi* and *Rifai* groups were aware that it was impossible for them to gain the support of either the secular majority or the religious-based groups in Turkey. Most were either too religious for the seculars or too heterodox for the conservatives. The perception of Sufism was no less complex in Turkey than in the rest of the world.

Comprehending Post-Tariqa *Mevlevi* and *Rifai* Sufism in Turkey

As in modern scholarly usage, the term Sufism relates to a wide range of social, cultural, political and religious phenomena causing controversy in different stratum of Turkish society. Due to the global war on terror and Saudi-inspired Wahhabism (a puritanical form of Sunni Islam not open to interpretation and adaptation), people recognise Islam as a source of violence, hatred and destruction, not only in the world but in Turkey.[57] Along with this identification, Sufism, recognised as the mystical dimension of Islam, has been the target of many state institutions (both secular and religious) and Islamic reformers in and out of Turkey. In the last two centuries, state institutions attacked Sufi tariqas perceiving them as a threat to their authority and to their modernisation plan. Both modernist Islamic reformers and Wahhabi Islamic organisations condemned Sufism. Most Sufi devotees received labels regarding their unreliability due to their departure from usual and accepted standards of Islamic law. Such arguments caused a paradigm shift with "twentieth-century social sciences" diagnosing "a crisis of Sufism, as popular religious practices were doomed to disappear in favour of 'modern' movements."[58] It is this book's focus to show how certain minority *Mevlevi* (known in the West as whirling dervishes)[59] and *Rifai* (recognised as howling dervishes in the West)[60] groups that have used a variety of performances (poetry classes, rituals, workshops, celebrations, etc.) as tools for making post-tariqa sacred space in Turkey, have managed to outlive such crisis.

Looking back, Sufism had a long and active role effecting every stratum of society during the Ottoman Empire. Some of the main Sufi orders dating back as far as the eleventh and twelfth centuries "played significant social and political roles, ranging from artistic, educational, and architectural influences to offering healing spaces and social networks of support for the poor."[61] However, this popular existence of Sufi orders has changed with the formation of the Turkish Republic. In 1925, Mustafa Kemal Atatürk, the founder of the Turkish Republic, at the beginning of the Republican Era of Turkey, passed a series of decrees that prohibited the production and maintenance of Sufi lodges in Turkey and the practices of Sufi sheikhs and dervishes. This legal act was part of Atatürk's social reforms (also referred to as "Kemalism") that were designed to convert the newly formed Republic of Turkey into a secular, modern nation-state. Atatürk believed that Sufi dervish lodges should be closed immediately in order to transform the long-existing religious Ottoman culture into a rapidly evolving intellectual culture educated through secular knowledge. According to Law 677, made effective on December 13, 1925, all the dervish lodges (tekkes and *zaviyes*) were closed.[62] Anyone attempting to open the closed dervish lodges (including the tombs) or to produce new Sufi worship spaces or to use any of the Sufi titles would be charged with at least three months in prison.[63]

As a result of the legal restrictions imposed in 1925, in the years following, devotees moved underground and practised their rituals, music and poetry in their private homes. However, while Eric Jan Zürcher points out that in the eighty-nine years following, Sufi gatherings in Turkey have been clandestine,[64] held in less populated urban neighbourhoods for fear of drawing attention, that was not the case for some Sufi groups that, with government's request, organised visible practices such as the folk performances of Sufi rituals and music starting in the 1950s such as *Sema* ceremony (*Mevlevi* whirling dervish ritual). The middle of the 1900s was the time when *Mevlevi* dervishes were starting to look for ways to mobilise their beliefs and values through performance of the *Mevlevi* whirling ritual.

In the 1950s, the government supported the organisation of Sufi activities by providing space for the practice of rituals, music and poetry as folk performances, tourist attractions and educational events (as long as the devotees did not act openly as sheikhs, *dedes* or dervishes). A set of social and political changes including the multi-party competition[65] starting in the 1950s encouraging political leaders to become responsive to the public's religious demands,[66] commodification and secularisation of Sufi rituals as folk performances and tourist attractions starting in the 1950s to improve the Turkish economy, the 1983 constitutional changes[67] easing the restrictions on religious practice, and the designation of Sufi cultural beliefs and values as part of World Intangible Cultural Heritage by UNESCO (in collaboration with the government) in 1973, 2005 and 2007 have shaped the life of Sufi devotees in Turkey. Also, as Ümit Cizre Sakallıoğlu writes, "Both military and political leaders after 1980 believed Islam could help create a socially disciplined and politically stable society ready to undergo the structural dislocations caused by the transition to popular capitalism and global patterns of lifestyles."[68] As a result, new or renewed Sufi groups emerged, who have had the ability to manage the social disruptions in the country.

Francesco Piraino and Mark Sedgwick also examine how the "crisis of Sufism" has started to shift becoming "a matter of transformation and renewal" with the emergence of new Sufi tariqas or transformation of existing ones.[69] Many scholars shed light on the fact that during the late twentieth and early twenty-first centuries, Sufi devotees migrated to Europe and North

America,[70] where they created fruitful encounters with New Age culture and Western academia, making the mobilisation of moderate Sufism possible.[71] In the second half of the twentieth century, with Turkish devotees travelling abroad to perform *Mevlevi Sema*, such encounters inspired Turkish Sufi groups, encouraging more and more followers to renew their systems.[72] Similar to the cases discussed in the Western context, this book documents the trajectories of specific minority post-tariqa *Mevlevi* and *Rifai* groups and individuals that are open to renewal and change.

Hermansen discusses "the expression 'post-tariqa' Sufism" and illuminates how "traditional forms confirming affiliation to a particular Sufi order through formal initiation by an authorised sheikh has in some cases been replaced by more diffuse forms of association and affinity."[73] Some of the post-tariqa cases in Turkey show how while formal initiation by an authorised sheikh is still a possibility (as in the case of the *Rifai* group), it is an optional, less-rigid association allowing the devotees the space and the freedom to contemplate their position as members of the modern Turkish society. The *Mevlevi* groups I will discuss in Part One have been practising *Mevlevi* teachings and rituals without any sort of initiation because *Mevlevi* teachers that lead these specific groups are not authorised sheikhs. They introduce themselves simply as *dedes* (a word used for male senior dervishes). In the *Rifai* group, on the other hand, it is devotees' choice to perform initiation or not. However, even in the case of a formal initiation, the practice is more voluntary regarding how a novice would design his/her training with the teacher. Considering the meaning of tariqa (way) as following the orders of the teacher and his teachings, post-tariqa practice may be more of a negotiation between the teacher and the novice. The post-tariqa practice in the *Mevlevi* and *Rifai* groups is open to changes and adaptations regarding the givens of each novice's diverse cultural backgrounds and social needs.

The desire to embody divine unity as "multiplicity" is at the core of these post-tariqa Sufi practices of piety.[74] Their spiritual teachers have strong faith in diversity. Considering all the negative connotations of tariqa in Turkey, more and more groups embrace new ways of practising Sufism.[75] As Francesco Piraino and Mark Sedgwick examine Sufi devotion transforms with "the emergence of new Sufi masters and public figures, often with interdisciplinary training and able to engage different audiences."[76] While "Sufi public figures" embodied "the mainstream religious authority of the alim," they also chose to become "intellectuals, journalists, politicians, and artists."[77] It is this book's focus to examine how specific *Rifai* and *Mevlevi* followers in Turkey embody a multilayered Sufi devotional living that engages with different cultural and aesthetic visions. These post-tariqa groups constitute great number of individuals who speak a variety of Western languages, study human and natural sciences and desire to question religious and scientific values. Interested in theatre, dance, poetry, these devotees mobilise their beliefs and values by creating a variety of performances, poetry, music and arts in a variety of public or clandestine spaces. Devotees' remaking of Sufi devotional

16 *Introduction*

life, as I will analyse in each chapter, are not in opposition to their beliefs and values; on the contrary, devotees design these practices to strengthen their idea of piousness.

The Challenge: Researching Non-mainstream Sufism in Turkey

Considering the plurality and diversity of ideas and practices among Sufi orders throughout the Muslim world,[78] it is not possible to claim to bring such a complicated and multifaceted subject, with all its dimensions, to clarity within the limits of a single manuscript. Sufism's history is full of moments, ideas and individuals that reveal its multi-dimensional nature. The origin history, the concept of unity, and *nefs* training show how varied and adaptable Sufism has been and continues to be today. Sufism's adaptability and its appropriation by different cultures all around the world make its belief system more difficult to define. Sufism's multi-dimensionality resists definition and lies in the diversity of its devotees' experiences globally. This book, based on extensive fieldwork, seeks to move beyond general definitions of Sufism and aims to bring out how specific groups and individuals choose to practice Sufi devotional life in the Turkish post-tariqa context.

Some basic definitions that inform this book discusses Sufism as "a distinctive voice within Islam's polyphony of faith and practice,"[79] and a tradition "that rises, grows, and undergoes change as it progresses through time and space."[80] Sufism's evolution has been studied extensively by Ahmet Karamustafa, Ahmet Yaşar Ocak, Margaret Smith, Christopher Melchert, Bernd Radtke, Nile Green, Alexander Knysh, and Bryan Turner. In these studies, it is possible to see how each conceptualisation of Sufism differs from one another, "reflecting the optics adopted by different observers in different times and under different circumstances" whom "by imagining and reimagining Sufism over and over again . . . display no less creativity and inventiveness than the Sufis themselves."[81] According to Knysh,

> the phenomenon called 'Sufism,' which has been so painstakingly and elegantly designed by the human imagination, or rather, by a long series of individual imaginations, is real in the sense that it has long-ranging and tangible sociopolitical, practical, cultural and institutional (material) implications.[82]

With this complexity in mind, this book focuses on the practices (rituals and everyday life performances) of specific *Mevlevi* and *Mevlevi*-inspired devotional groups and individuals and a clandestine *Rifai* group (who prefer to live and train in private spaces).

These are minority post-tariqa groups that struggle to maintain sacred spaces, make great effort to preserve their beliefs and values and work hard to adapt to current social and economic circumstances. They experience opposition from both the conservative Muslim communities and radical secular groups in Turkey. As in most Muslim countries, these devotees experience the separation between Sufism and the more orthodox forms of Islam in the Turkish Republic. This separation is due to the conservative idea that Sufism is an unofficial form of Islam or, according to a more exclusionary perception, a heterodox form of Islam. Sufism and its teachings, for many conservative Muslims, are esoteric interpretations of the Quran and the Hadith. The Religious Affairs Directorate (RAD) in Turkey is only in support of Sufi groups that are in perfect alliance with conservative Sunni Hanafi[83] Islamic doctrines, such as certain Nakshibendi movements. Therefore, there is limited space for an understanding of Sufism in Turkey that embraces renewal and transformation.

These post-tariqa groups also experience the criticism of radical seculars who fear religious symbols and believe that faith-related matters should have no place in the public space. Denunciation of any form of religious acts, including practices such as yoga, mindfulness, or listening to religious hymns, is still part of Turkish everyday life. This book focuses on groups that have survived radical secularist criticisms and found ways to maintain Sufi devotional life.

When researching Sufi devotional life in Turkey, what becomes clear along the way is the fact that although the media reflects some Sufi orders such as the *Mevlevi* and the *Rifai* order as part of Turkish cultural life, there is a lack of information about how Sufi followers struggle to preserve their worship practices and sacred spaces. Some struggle to organise ritual gatherings without access to the *semahanes*, ritual halls designed for the practice of *sema* ceremony (in the case of the *Mevlevi* groups discussed in Part One, devotees do not have regular access to the *semahanes* located in the *Mevlevi* lodges converted into museums). Others struggle with maintaining *tekkes* (Sufi lodges that are necessary for a variety of devotional practices such as communal living and training) without financial support from the government (in the case of the *Rifai* group discussed in Part Two). To examine the struggles of these Sufi groups, through historical and ethnographic data, this book analyses the commodified *Mevlevi* and not commodified (or more specifically non-commodifiable due to the devotees' rejection of performing their rituals as tourist attraction) *Rifai* devotional practices. In addition, due to unprecedented access to the living spaces of a clandestine *Rifai* group that converted two private homes to Sufi sacred houses, this book makes a major contribution to the study of Sufi devotional life by focusing on secret gatherings that have never been studied or written about before.

Today, *Mevlevi* and *Rifai* followers continue to face opposition from three different dominant groups/organisations in Turkey: secular elites, the Religious Affairs Directorate (RAD) and conservative Sunni religious groups. Most secular Turks believe that there are Sufi leaders and followers who have used Islamic and Sufi teachings as a political force to manipulate young minds, which is still the case in certain religious groups that use Sufi teachings as part of their religious practice. The RAD, on the other hand, does not recognise most of the teachings and rituals of minority Sufi groups, believing that some Sufi groups and individuals are a threat to the Islamic way of living in the sense that Sufism has mystical teachings that conflict with the doctrines of mainstream or strict Sunni Islam (following a belief system that is solely about certain Sunni religious dogma as imposed by the RAD). No matter what some *Mevlevi* and *Rifai* followers do, their groups and individuals lack a sense of belonging to any dominant group in Turkey.

There is no research available about minority post-tariqa Sufi groups that seek to practice their ritual performances despite legal restrictions and/or governmental support.[84] Although *Mevlevis* appear to be a dominant Sufi group in Turkey (due to their relationship with the government regarding the organisation of touristic and folk performances), that is not the case. In 2005, UNESCO proclaimed the Sufi ritual of *Mevlevi Sema* (known in the West through the whirling of dervishes on stages across the world) part of the World Intangible Cultural Heritage and two years later, in honour of poet Rumi's eight-hundredth birthday, UNESCO also declared 2007 the Year of Mevlana Celaleddin-i Rumi and Tolerance. That designation of the ceremony as cultural heritage increased the visibility of *Mevlevi* culture in Turkey, Europe and the United States. Yet *Mevlevi* followers have only been allowed to perform the whirling dervish rituals as folk performances at the lodges converted to museums and culture centres once a week for tourists. However, what is presented as tourist attraction does not express the complex and precarious position of *Mevlevis* in Turkey. *Mevlevis* seem to accept the current circumstances; however, some of them are aware that they live in diasporic sacred locations (removed from their homes), desiring to return. Their longing gives them the energy and the courage to search for ways to preserve their rituals, cultural beliefs and values.

Also, despite the range of research topics about contemporary Sufism, academic research on non-mainstream religiosity has been scarce. In Turkey, religious and cultural activities that are beyond strict boundaries—between the secular and the religious and/or the East and the West—continue to lack attention from researchers. Since 2005, although limited, scholars have produced valuable research on contemporary Sufism and the idea of Sufism as a moderate alternative to mainstream Islam. Meena Sharify-Funk, Merin Shobhana Xavier, Martin Van Bruinessen, Julia Day Howell, Elizabeth Sirriyeh, Jamal Malik, Saeed Zarrabi-Zadeh, Meena Sharify-Funk, William Rory Dickson, Shireen Hunter, Brian Silverstein, and Merin Shobhana Xavier have all investigated how a variety of Sufi groups embrace modernity. Most of this research on contemporary Sufism focuses on Sufi groups outside of Turkey or revolves around more political, dominant and mainstream (supported by Islamist political institutions) Sufi groups and their activities within Turkey.[85] It would be misleading to say that "Sufis are apolitical"; however, it is necessary to point out that there are Sufi groups that are not concerned with political power.[86] Regarding Turkey, I would like to point out that when I refer to dominant groups, I refer to those that have certain rights due to their interest in politicisation and alliance with the Islamists currently in power in Turkey. With minority post-tariqa groups, I refer to the formations that are in opposition to political Islam. The case studies focused in this book are post-tariqa Sufi groups and individuals that seek to practice a secular piousness that resists any attachment to politics.

As mentioned earlier, while there have been Sufi orders whose spiritual leaders devoted extensive time to political activities in Turkey, there have also been Sufi groups and individuals that devoted equally as extensive time to practising a sense of isolation from political individuals and groups. For instance, while there are groups (such as *Nakşibendis* and *Nurcus*) that have been directly involved with events that improve the ideas and practices of Turkish political Islam such as composing the deep structure of Turkish religious power in the governmental structures, there are also groups that focus more on seeking ways to preserve their cultural beliefs and values through ritual and sacred art practices. While Sufi groups that have held political power—such as *Nakşibendis*, *Süleymancıs*, and *Nurcus*—differ from one another in terms of how they have been involved in political activities, research shows that inspired by Arab and Kurdish traditions, the Naqshbandi-Halidi groups (mostly defined by their activities within a system called religious congregation) have formed the core of Turkish political Islam.[87] Although there is research available on such Sufi groups that are dominant political forces in Turkey, there is lack of research about how minority *Mevlevis* and *Rifais* without governmental support have been able to preserve their beliefs and values throughout the second half of the twentieth century until today.

In today's Turkey, there are *Mevlevis* and *Rifais* that seek to embrace an adaptable version of Islam. While some Sufi groups relate to conventional, doctrine-oriented Islam, others relate to what orthodox rulers have labelled as heterodox Islam (Islam that is open to adaptability and cultural diversity).[88] This book is about *Mevlevis* and *Rifais*, who, with their embodied acts, produce sacred spaces to create a post-tariqa piety that is free of doctrinal restrictions. Instead, these devotees seek to stay in harmony with the secular values of the Turkish society.[89] This merged version inspires a multicultural Sufi vision for a Muslim-dominant country that has struggled to preserve its secular values since its beginning.

Performance and Sacred Space Production: Mobilisation of a Multi-cultural Sufi Vision

Due to legal restrictions and lack of support for the production of official Sufi lodges in Turkey, the focus of this book also revolves around the idea of "making sacred space."[90] Michel de Certeau's claim that "space is a practiced place" provides the key idea through which this book examines the embodied dynamics supporting Sufi sacred space production. Here, I adapt de Certeau's idea to examine how the development of Sufi spaces is contingent on the embodied acts of Sufi followers, who with their prayers, classes, workshops and rituals change and make sense of the spaces they occupy. Due to the clandestine and private nature of some Sufi practitioners' devotional living, devotees' homes serve as places where Sufi knowledge is produced and Sufism mobilised. Devotees with whom I had the chance to practice everyday life during my fieldwork were open to living together with people from different religious and cultural backgrounds. In these groups, there were Sufi devotees who were Muslims, atheists, Christians and Jewish, practising simultaneously the teachings of a variety of religions and philosophies. No dogma or political gain was above the desire to experience training together. Devotees were aware of the fact that the performance of rituals is the core of the Sufi spiritual path. Through performance, devotees revive, reformulate, expand and mobilise Sufism as a way of living that is a synthesis of secular and religious values of the Turkish State. This research is groundbreaking in the sense that it provides both what is visible (the commodified performances of Sufi rituals) and what is not visible (the non-commodifiable, clandestine, private and underground Sufi everyday life).

Production of urban Sufi space plays a significant role in the generation of post-tariqa Sufism in Turkey. The urban Sufi devotion investigated in this book refers to a style of living and social organisation, rather than a particular density or size of settlement. Rachida Chih's argument shows how Sufi groups (or brotherhoods as in her statement) embraced urban living. She states:

> The emergence of an educated urban middle class that embraced ideas of progress, individualism and democracy appeared to leave little space for the old fashioned brotherhoods [Sufi orders], which were believed to attract only marginalised segments of society with little education, low social status or ongoing rural connections.[91]

Sufi groups discussed in this book include a high number of devotees from different religious, ethnic and national backgrounds, who are academics, doctors, lawyers and students who seek to escape from their materialistic urban everyday life. Emphasising the urban professionals' need for escape, John Voll, referring to Celia Genn's discussion on the development of modern Western Sufism, points out that "For many urban middle class professionals as well as those seeking alternative lifestyles, a major part of the appeal of Western Sufism is the provision of resources for spiritualist escape from materialist society."[92] In line with Voll's point, in the urban landscapes of modern Turkey, individuals come to post-tariqa Sufi gatherings for a variety of reasons, needs, questions and help. Most common among these are monotony in their daily lives, loneliness, mental and physical health issues, family problems, education and, as many devotees explained in the shrine, the main reason is discontent with the circumstances of the material world. They come to converse with people like themselves who value diversity. They blend their urban-middle- or upper-middle-class professional identities with their aim to move closer to God in a diverse environment.

There are groups whose devotees are reflective of the social, cultural, religious and economic diversities of urban Turkish society. In the *Rifai* group, there is a middle-class artist, who is an agnostic studying Sufism; a middle-class academic, who is a Buddhist practising the teachings of Rumi; middle-class Christians, who are teachers and dancers taking part in *zikir* rituals without practising Islam; an upper-middle-class Jewish musician becoming a *dervish* practising both Judaism and Islam; a middle-aged secular academic non-practising Muslim and a Muslim, who is a practising *imam* (Muslim leader who leads prayers in a mosque). In the *Mevlevi* groups, there were Christian dancers studying *Mevlevi* rituals, a secular pop singer studying Sufi music, an agnostic theatre-maker studying Sufi poetry, and many others. Devotees bring together new seekers from different cultural and religious backgrounds to mobilise the Sufi idea of living with each participant's social identities, education, capabilities and hobbies embodied in urban life, who then become volunteers to help shape the socioeconomic lives of others in the group. Today, with the mobilisation of Sufism in urban life, Sufi devotees invite new members to their ritual/community gatherings. When a member of the group meets someone interested in learning about the Sufi devotion, he or she invites the non-Sufi individual to participate in and network with devotees by sharing their individual urban identities, life experiences, capabilities, hobbies and education, helping shape the attitudes and values of others in the group.

Drawing on Henri Lefebvre's conceptualisation of space, I also examine devotees' creative processes and how they make space for their religious practices through "forces of production," such as "labor and the organisation of labor" in Sufi devotional living. As he states, "Any 'social existence' aspiring or claiming to be 'real,' but failing to produce its own space, would be a strange entity. . . . It would fall to the level of folklore and sooner or later disappear altogether."[93] Devotees preserve their beliefs, values and practices by producing a variety of spaces. Carrying their devotional acts to spaces such as hotels and culture centres, followers of Sufi teachings and practices attract and encourage more individuals from different backgrounds to learn about Sufism and become part of a spiritual community that has the potential to guide their life's journey.

I also follow Voll's idea about the provision of resources in order to point out that by creating various urban Sufi spaces, devotees offer ways for experiencing, studying, practising, sharing and teaching Sufism. In order to fight the difficulties experienced with busy work schedules, there is a significant commitment to Sufi sacred space production in cities such as Istanbul, Izmir and Ankara. Ethel Sara Wolper, in her book *Cities and Saints: Sufism and the Transformation of Urban Space in Medieval Anatolia,* discusses the life of Sufi dervishes and their lodges in the late thirteenth century and the late fourteenth century. Her discussion of how the Sufi spaces functioned as places for social activities identifies a viewpoint that is applicable to urban Sufi spaces in Turkey today. Wolper states that Sufi buildings, including hospices, tombs and houses, shared important characteristics: "each housed dervishes and provided a centre for communal activities, including prayer, study, discussion, conversation with visitors, accommodation of travellers, feeding the poor and sometimes the performance of *sama* or *dhikr*."[94] Similar to communal and social roles played by Sufi buildings in medieval Anatolia, today there are spaces created for temporary or permanent Sufi practice that followers attend to read, study, dance, sing and share ideas. Embodied acts of followers in these spaces—their "devotional labor"[95]—transform private homes and buildings to function as schools, community centres and Sufi lodges in which devotees guide each other about social and economic matters, such as finding a job, medical care, education or financial advice. Secular spaces such as cultural centres and hotels become sacred spaces only through devotees' "embodied performances—their voices raised in ecstasy, their praying and dancing bodies in motion, the labor and care they offer to maintain the shrine."[96] Devotees today continue to practice their religious rites in urban public sites that are considered secular by the Turkish government and transform these spaces with the gatherings and rituals they organise and perform on a daily or weekly basis.

The urban spaces consist of public and private spaces such as city apartment buildings and houses owned by a spiritual teacher, cultural centres, hotels converted into Sufi lodges and historical Sufi buildings converted into museums or foundation centres. The specific spaces I examine in Istanbul are a private house renovated by a group of devotees to function as a post-tariqa *tekke;* an apartment building converted into a residential sacred space; a historical house of a Sufi *dede* (senior dervish) converted into a culture centre; Yenikapi *Mevlevi* lodge, a historical Sufi site converted into a museum and a university; and the private flat of a Sufi *dede* that is used by the *dede* for his organisation of religious *sohbets* and classes. In Konya, there is also a hotel converted into a temporary sacred ritual and lodging space, Mevlana Celaleddin-i Rumi's shrine, the *Şems-i Tebrizi Türbesi ve Câmisi* (Shams of Tabriz Mosque) and other shrines visited during the *Rifai* order's pilgrimages. Sufi communities in these spaces may be viewed as microcosms of the Sufi devotees' different ways of living in modern Turkey and a way to engage the topics of secularism and modernity in relation to Sufism in Turkey, as well as social issues such as freedom of Sufi religious practice.

The ideas of modernity and secularism are central to the discussion of Sufi space production and generation of what some devotees express versatile, multi-cultural or all-embracing Sufism in Turkey due to rapid social, economic and political reforms enforced after the formation of the Turkish Republic in 1923. Building on Brian Silverstein's idea that "Turks tend to locate the modality of their modernity in what they call secularism *[laiklik]*,"[97] I examine how devotees while embodying modernity move beyond locating their values in a Turkish secularism perceived as the opposite of religiousness. However, to discuss secularism in relation to Sufi devotees, first, it is necessary to examine how some scholars have been critical of the universal claims concerning the issue of secularism and *laicite*.[98]

Esra Özyürek notes that "The particular form of governance called secularism, Asad urges us to study, takes such radically different forms in different contexts that it is difficult to come up with a single working definition for it."[99] Scholars often depicted Turkish "as authoritarian derivative of French laicite, measured in terms of its gaps, inconsistencies, and deficiencies with regard to the ideal model of French secularism."[100] It is true that Turkish secularism (*laiklik*) was similar to French *laicite*; however, it had transformed when applied to Turkish culture and government. Göle uses Seyla Benhabib's analysis of Jacques Derrida's notion of iteration to highlight the need to go beyond reductionism. Göle employs the idea that "In the process of repeating a term or a concept, we never produce a replica of the original usage; every iteration transforms the original meaning and adds new meaning to it."[101] As such, Göle states that "the French notion of laicite becomes laiklik in Turkish" and that the idea of secularism has key modifications in different countries and societies and is practised differently by different individuals and groups in Turkey. Likewise, as Özyürek notes in her analysis of Joan Scott's idea of secularism, "the difference between the two models [French *laicite* and Anglo-Saxon secularism] is simple but has serious social and political consequences."[102] Scott puts forward that "In France, the state protects individuals from religion; in America, religions are protected from the state and state from religion."[103] Similar to France, Atatürk had sought to protect individuals from religion and had to disregard the protection of certain Islamic institutions to decree the excessive authority these groups (especially tariqas) had gained during the Ottoman Empire. However, disrespecting any religious belief had not been part of Atatürk's vision. He accepted the presence of religion as long as it did not interfere with his state politics.

Although "Turkish secularism is inspired by the French 'laicite,' or the separation of church and state, religious affairs [including the practices in the mosques] in Turkey are regulated by the state."[104] According to Göle, it was "only on the issue of taking religion out of the public sphere that French and Turkish secularisms [were] similar."[105] As Özyürek notes that "Just like in France, in Turkey as well, the state sees its role in protecting its citizens from religious influences, while comparing to France, Turkish State takes an active role in educating citizens according to a particular understanding of Islam [Sunni Islam]."[106] This occurs even more in today's Turkey with government employing the RAD to mobilise Islam in and out of the mosques and other religious spaces converted to museums. All are controlled by a government that prioritises an Islamic agenda. However, in Turkey today, there are different Islamic individuals and groups that create their own idea and practice of secularism that is free of the particular (Sunni) understanding of Islam forced by the RAD in Turkey.

To examine the *Mevlevi* and *Rifai* cases of post-tariqa devotion, I had to move beyond depicting secularism as one dimensional. Secularism cannot be confined to Turkish *laiklik*. I seek to take Göle's question, "How does a Muslim experience of secularity transform and question our understanding of the secular age?"[107] further by asking how different Sufi individuals experience secular values in Turkey and modify the one-dimensional understanding of Turkish *laicite* according to their devotional living. Moreover, Göle encourages scholars to bring "into the picture those voices, practices and experiences that are classified as particularistic, religious, traditional, that are not in conformity with the universal norms of secular modernity."[108] This project seeks to follow Göle's multi-dimensional vision of the analysis of secularism as constantly evolving. This is vital to investigate how secular values are open to adaptation for each religious individual's and group's needs and how different devotees embody modernity and secularism while generating their devotional living.

Henri Meschonnic defines modernity as "inventions of thinking, of feeling, of seeing, and of meaning, the invention of forms of life."[109] What is common about devotees (in the case studies) discussed in this book is that they perceive modernity as moving forward, inventing new ideas, ways of life, technologies and art with the idea that all changes and circumstances are God's offer. To understand modernity in relation to post-tariqa Sufism in urban landscapes of present-day Turkey, similar to Göle's discussion of secularism, it is necessary to go against "acultural analysis of modernity."[110] Taylor, in his article "Two Theories of Modernity," encourages his readers to call to mind "the plurality of human cultures, each of which has a language and a set of practices that define specific understandings of personhood, social relations, states of mind/soul, goods and bads, virtues and vices, and the like."[111] Although modernity in Turkey is identified with Kemalism, Atatürk's six principles (republicanism, secularism, nationalism, populism, statism, and revolutionism or reformism),[112] as in Diana Taylor's analysis of "performatic shift and doubling," I discuss the devotional lives of devotees who preserved the Sufi beliefs and values that flourished in the Ottoman Empire while embodying the modern values of the Turkish State. This is their post-tariqa vision. For this reason, they tend to describe their practices as versatile, multi-cultural and all-embracing. And it is this all-embracing vision that allows many of them to focus on and restore their performatic practices as the core of their devotional living. They comprehend their practices as magical tools to restore their practice of remembrance of God (*zikir*) and produce post-tariqa sacred space.

Development of post-tariqa Sufi space depends on the multiple layers of the social and economic history of the Turkish government, shifting political situations and the living Sufi bodies who give meaning to the space. Even after the government forced religious organisations "into the private sphere of people's lives," Islamic beliefs and values "continued to have a vital and dynamic role" in Turkish society.[113] Peña's study of Guadalupan sacred space production encouraged me to analyse how minority Sufi groups create urban spaces through devotional labour. She extends Pierre Bourdieu's idea of "symbolic capital"[114] and argues that Guadalupan devotees, with their embodied acts or "devotional labor," produce a symbolic "devotional capital" in terms of the "regenerative effects of the ineffable."[115] In the cases of *Mevlevi* and *Rifai* devotees, as in Peña's analysis, it is the sacred beliefs and acts themselves that serve as mediums of devotees' social and economic development, through which "adherents communicate ways of remembering, knowing, interpreting, and coping . . . that affect not only the quality of life for these religious communities but also the legacies they leave behind."[116] *Mevlevi* and *Rifai* devotees produce their devotional capital by embodying and mobilising post-tariqa Sufism in a variety of commodified and clandestine spaces.

Therefore, this book only focuses on Sufi groups and individuals who one way or another use performance as a medium: to restore Sufi devotional life in Turkey (Part One), to transmit post-tariqa *Mevlevi* beliefs and values in a variety of public sites (Part Two), to transform consciousness by sacralising the body (Part Three), and to inscribe Sufi beliefs and values onto any site they occupy (Part Four). Each of these parts is related to one another in a sense that the nature of any ritual or everyday action performed by the *Mevlevi* and *Rifai* devotees carries some level of restoring, transmitting, transforming and inscribing. However, with the organisation of the book and each part under a performance-centred idea, I hope to provide a thorough analysis of how *Mevlevis* and *Rifais* generate post-tariqa devotional life and make sacred space. In Part One, I seek to show how *Mevlevis* and *Rifais* choose to restore Sufi devotional life in present-day Turkey despite the challenges posed by secular and Islamist groups and institutions. In Part Two, it is my hope that I show how and why *Mevlevis* use their rituals to transmit their idea of versatile Sufism and Rumi as a spiritual master, whose Islamic teachings are perceived in alliance with the secular Turks' vision (the desire to find a space to practice Islam without having to obey any doctrinal rules posed by conservative Sufi groups). With Part Three, focusing on *Rifai* devotees' idea of transforming oneself, I seek to create a vivid picture of how *Rifai* devotees seek to preserve some of their traditional rituals (*zikir*, *burhan* and renunciation) to train *nefs*. For *Rifais*, sacralisation of the body is a path to the realisation of the world as sacred. For this reason, in Part Four, I discuss in great detail the *Rifai* pilgrimage and how they inscribe their simultaneously religious and secular values onto a variety of private and public sites.

Note on Language

A book on Sufism requires a consistent system of transliteration due to the diversity of languages used in the books and articles and by the Sufi devotees who discuss Sufism. These are Arabic, Persian, Ottoman Turkish, Modern Turkish and Urdu, among others. Since this is an ethnographic project, I tried to use exactly the way devotees pronounce words, names and geographical locations that relate to Sufism in their original language, which is Turkish. Examples of these are *zikir*, *sema*, *meşk* and *zuhd*. However, for clarity,

26 *Introduction*

I used English versions of the words for Quran, Hadith, shariah, Sunni, sheikh and dervish. If there is a notable difference in this usage, I made a note to the reader in the footnotes. One last point to note is that following Turkish phonetic specificities, I have preferred to avoid the Arabic "al," prefaced before names.

Notes

1 A person who practices Sufism, as the mystical dimension of Islam. However, devotees of Sufism do not use the word Sufi to define themselves because Sufi also means one who have experienced all the levels of the Sufi spiritual training and has attained the goal of uniting with God. Devotees of a Sufi order prefer to express their position as they are always on the path of training to experience God's unity. Living as a Sufi requires the devotee to be aware of the fact that to reach to the level of *kamil insan* (mature human being) requires one to stay a student, ready to learn even when it is time to lead others.
2 *Mevlevi* is a word derived from *Mevlana* (meaning master), the title given to the thirteenth-century Islamic scholar, Sufi mystic and Persian poet Celaleddin Rumi (Jalaluddin Muhammad Balkhi Rumi) and used to define his followers. The *Mevlevi tarikat* (order or tariqa) is a Sufi order originated in Konya (a city located in Turkey) after Rumi's passing. Based on Rumi's teachings, the order was founded by the followers of Rumi's teachings.
3 "Tekke ve zâviyelerle türbelerin seddine ve türbedarlıklarıyla birtakım ünvânların men' ve ilgâsına dâir kânun" (The law relating to the closure of dervish lodges and tombs, and the abolishment of various titles.) (Law no. 677/1925).
4 Mostly the ones that seem to support the Justice and Development Party's conservative Islamic vision.
5 Erving Goffman, *The Presentation of Self in Everyday Life* (Edinburgh: University of Edinburgh, 1956).
6 Private conversation with a devotee, October, 2010.
7 I use the term "post-tariqa" to refer to contemporary Sufi groups (that function as foundations and associations due to 1925 legal restrictions prohibiting the existence of Sufi orders) and their ideals to move beyond the rigid rules of the Ottoman Sufi *tarikat* (translated as tariqa or order) system (way of life). The word "tariqa" (specifically meaning path and translated as order) refers to a system of practice, in which a group of devotees follow the path (the teachings and rituals) of a deceased Sufi mystic, whose name or title becomes the name the order. In the *Mevlevi* order, the order takes its name from the well-known Sufi mystic Mevlana Celaleddin Rumi. In the tariqa system, a senior dervish, who is considered a living descendant of the deceased Sufi mystic, is the one to lead the group of devotees, who choose to follow him. He is also the one who can give permission to his own senior dervishes to lead their own order. This new teacher receives the permission to teach the deceased mystic's words and deeds to others, who also choose to follow him. In this system, it is believed that each new group, led by a new teacher, who practices and teaches the ways of the deceased teacher, instructs the devotees on how to journey on the spiritual path of the deceased mystic and unite with God. The followers of post-tariqa orders usually follow the teachings of mystics such as Mevlana Celaleddin Rumi, considering his words and deeds contemporary in the sense that they are adaptable to the modern-day socio-political environment of Turkey. Most post-tariqa groups I have encountered during my fieldwork seem to move beyond the rules and regulations of the Sufi *boyar* kültürü (meaning the culture of complete

submissiveness to a spiritual leader). The devotees seem to prefer some sense of liberty in questioning and analysing certain ideas of the Islamic faith such as praying five times a day or memorising the Quran. The Sufi devotees that I analyse in this book are either Sufi teachers, dervishes or students of Sufism, who desire to perceive post-tariqa Sufism as a path to journey God by learning how to love and experience compassion to all of God's creation. For them, this desire is beyond all religious rules and restrictions. For this desire, they use their bodies to find what they call divine meaning. They dance. They sing. They constantly seek to perform different forms of *zikir* to embody and experience God's unity. This is the core practice of their post-tariqa Sufi life.

8 Richard Schechner, *Performance Studies: An Introduction* (London: Routledge, 2020), 4.
9 W. Michael Ashcraft, *A Historical Introduction to the Study of New Religious Movements* (London: Routledge, 2018).
10 Private conversations with devotees, December, 2012.
11 Schechner, *Performance Studies: An Introduction*, 12.
12 Diana Taylor, *Archive and the Repertoire: Performing Cultural Memory in the Americas* (Durham, NC: Duke University Press, 2003), xviii.
13 Schechner, *Performance Studies: An Introduction*, 4.
14 Schechner, *Performance Studies: An Introduction*, 4.
15 Schechner, *Performance Studies: An Introduction*, 12.
16 Schechner, *Performance Studies: An Introduction*, 13.
17 Schechner, *Performance Studies: An Introduction*, 13.
18 Joseph Roach, "Performance Studies," in *Critical Theory and Performance*, ed. Janelle G. Reinelt and Joseph R. Roach (Ann Arbor: University of Michigan Press, 2007), 457–458.
19 Gay Mcauley, "Interdisciplinary Field or Emerging Discipline? Performance Studies at the University of Sydney," in *Contesting Performance: Global Sites of Research*, ed. Jon McKenzie, Heike Roms, and C.J.W.L. Wee (Basingstoke: Palgrave Macmillan, 2010), 45, 37–50.
20 Mcauley, "Interdisciplinary Field or Emerging Discipline? Performance Studies at the University of Sydney," 45.
21 Although *nefs* has been translated as soul, ego, or self, devotees choose to express it as self or mind.
22 Teemu Paavolainen, *Theatricality and Performativity: Writing on Texture from Plato's Cave to Urban Activism* (Cham: Palgrave Macmillan, 2018), 103, https://doi.org/10.1007/978-3-319-73226-8.
23 John Langshaw Austin, *How to Do Things with Words* (Cambridge: Harvard University Press, 1962), 6; Taylor, *Archive and the Repertoire*, xviii; Claire Marie Chambers, Simon W. Du Toit, and Joshua Edelman, ed., "Introduction," in *Performing Religion in Public* (New York: Palgrave Macmillan, 2013), 13; Jacques Derrida, "Signature Event Context," in *Margins of Philosophy*, trans. Alans Bass (Chicago: University of Chicago Press, 1982), 326; Richard Schechner, "Performativity," in *Performance Studies: An Introduction* (London: Routledge, 2006), 125; Judith Butler, "Performativity Acts and Gender Constitution: An Essay in Phenomenology and Feminist Criticism," *Theatre Journal* 40, no. 4 (1988): 526; Andrew Parker and Eve Kosofsky Sedgwick, "Introduction: Performativity and Performance," in *Performativity and Performance* (London: Routledge, 1995), 2.
24 Esra Cizmeci, "World as Sacred Stage for Sufi Ritual: Performance, Mobilisation and Making Space with the Act of Whirling," *Dance, Movement & Spiritualities* 3, no. 3 (2016): 203, https://doi.org/10.1386/dmas.3.3.199_1.
25 Taylor, *Archive and the Repertoire*, 6. Here, Taylor uses the concept of logocentricism, which "entered the vocabulary of cultural studies courtesy of Derrida,

28 Introduction

who critiques its pre-eminence within Western philosophy. By logocentricism Derrida means the reliance on fixed a priori transcendental meanings. That is, universal meanings, concepts and forms of logic that exist within human reason before any other kinds of thinking can occur. This would include a universal conception of reason or beauty. The idea is closely tied to the notion of phonocentrism by which Derrida means the priority given to sounds and speech over writing in explaining the generation of meaning. This is so because it is in the directness of speech rather than in the metaphorical nature of writing that Western philosophy is said by Derrida to find transcendental meaning." Chris Barker, *The Sage Dictionary of Cultural Studies* (London: Sage Publication, 2004), 111.

26 Taylor, *Archive and the Repertoire*, 6.
27 The ideas of "performatic shift and doubling" according to Taylor, are "the proliferations of the signified," forms of multiplication and simultaneity rather than surrogation and absenting. Taylor, *Archive and the Repertoire*, 174.
28 Joseph R. Roach, *Cities of the Dead: Circum-Atlantic Performance* (New York: Columbia University Press, 1996), 2; Taylor, *Archive and the Repertoire*, 174–175.
29 Taylor, *Archive and the Repertoire*, 174–175.
30 Marvin Carlson, *Performance: A Critical Introduction* (New York: Routledge, 2018), 179–181. My comprehension of the idea of theatricality also evolved with many other sources: Austin, *How to Do Things with Words*; Taylor, *Archive and the Repertoire*; Erika Fischer-Lichte, *The Transformative Power of Performance*, trans. Saskya Iris Jain (London: Routledge, 2009). Paavolainen, *Theatricality and Performativity: Writing on Texture From Plato's Cave to Urban Activism*; Chambers, Du Toit, and Edelman, "Introduction"; Derrida, "Signature Event Context"; Schechner, "Performativity"; Butler, "Performativity Acts and Gender Constitution: An Essay in Phenomenology and Feminist Criticism"; Parker and Sedgwick, "Introduction: Performativity and Performance."
31 Carlson, *Performance*, 179–181.
32 Carlson, *Performance*, 3.
33 Dwight Conquergood, "Of Caravans and Carnivals: Performance Studies in Motion," *The Drama Review* 39, no. 4 (1995): 138.
34 Conquergood, "Of Caravans and Carnivals: Performance Studies in Motion," 138.
35 Conquergood, "Of Caravans and Carnivals: Performance Studies in Motion," 138.
36 Homi K. Bhabha, *The Location of Culture* (New York: Routledge, 1994), 146–149.
37 Paavolainen, *Theatricality and Performativity: Writing on Texture from Plato's Cave to Urban Activism*, 103.
38 Conquergood, "Of Caravans and Carnivals: Performance Studies in Motion," 138.
39 Andreea S. Micu, *Performance Studies: The Basics* (New York: Routledge, 2022), 1–2.
40 Micu, *Performance Studies: The Basics*, 1–2.
41 Micu, *Performance Studies: The Basics*, 2.
42 Margaret Thompson Drewal, "The State of Research on Performance in Africa." *African Studies Review* 34, no. 3 (1991): 2, 3, 19.
43 Margaret Thompson Drewal, *Yoruba Ritual: Performers, Play, Agency* (Bloomington: Indiana University Press, 1992), 3.
44 Drewal, *Yoruba Ritual: Performers, Play, Agency*, 3.
45 Drewal, *Yoruba Ritual: Performers, Play, Agency*, 7.
46 Erving Goffman, *The Presentation of Self in Everyday Life* (London: Penguin Group, 1959).

47 Taylor, *Archive and the Repertoire*, xviii.
48 Taylor, *Archive and the Repertoire*, xvi.
49 Conquergood, "Performing as a Moral Act: Ethical Dimensions of the Ethnography of Performance," 1–13.
50 Dwight Conquergood, "Performing as a Moral Act: Ethical Dimensions of the Ethnography of Performance," *Literature in Performance* 5, no. 2 (1985): 1–13; Dwight Conquergood, "Health Theatre in a Hmong Refugee Camp," *TDR: The Drama Review* 32 (1988): 174–208; Dwight Conquergood, "Performance Studies: Interventions and Radical Research," *TDR: The Drama Review* 46 (2002): 145–156; and Dwight Conquergood, "Rethinking Ethnography: Towards a Critical Cultural Politics," in *The Sage Handbook of Performance Studies*, ed. D.S. Madison and J. Hamera (Thousand Oaks, CA: Sage, 2006), 351–365. See also E. Patrick Johnson, *Sweet Tea: Black Gay Men of the South* (Chapel Hill: University of North Carolina Press, 2008); Drewal, "The State of Research on Performance in Africa," 1–64; and D. Soyini Madison, "Co-performative Witnessing," *Cultural Studies* 21, no. 6 (2007): 826–831.
51 Elaine A. Peña, *Performing Piety: Making Space Sacred with the Virgin of Guadalupe* (Berkeley: University of California Press, 2011), 3; Conquergood, "Performing as a Moral Act: Ethical Dimensions of the Ethnography of Performance," 1–13.
52 Peña, *Performing Piety*, 3.
53 Peña, *Performing Piety*, 3.
54 Victor Turner, *From Ritual to Theatre: The Human Seriousness of Play* (New York: PAJ Publications, 1982), 101. Victor Turner and Edith Turner point out that "We also hold that in studies of human culture and behaviour, the tension between motivation and scientific objectivity can sometimes prove fruitful. When the deeper levels of the self, deeply tinctured by culture, are reflexively engaged, the knowledge brought back from the encounter between self as subject and self as object may be just as valid as knowledge acquired by 'neutral' observation of others." Victor Turner and Edith Turner, *Image and Pilgrimage in Christian Culture: Anthropological Perspectives* (New York: Columbia University Press, 1978), xxv. The Turners, in this analysis, while challenging their position as researchers to remember to stay objective while focusing on a personally cherished Christian pilgrimage, also allow us to see that as interpreters of the rituals, we should be aware of our active role in the process.
55 Personal conversations with the devotees between 2011 and 2015.
56 Pnina Werbner, *Pilgrims of Love: The Anthropology of a Global Sufi Cult* (Bloomington: Indiana University Press, 2003).
57 Meena Sharify-Funk, William Rory Dickson, and Merin Shobhana Xavier, *Contemporary Sufism: Piety, Politics, and Popular Culture* (New York: Routledge, 2018).
58 Francesco Piraino and Mark Sedgwick, "Introduction," in *Global Sufism*, ed. Francesco Piraino and Mark Sedgwick (London: Hurst & Company, 2019), 3.
59 *Mevlevi* order is a Sufi order founded by the followers of the scholar and mystic Mevlana Celaleddin-i Rumi in the thirteenth century.
60 *Rifai* order is a Sufi order founded in the twelfth century by the followers of the Sufi mystic Ahmed Er-Rifai.
61 Sadeq Rahimi, "Intimate Exteriority: Sufi Space as Sanctuary for Injured Subjectivities in Turkey," *Journal of Religion and Health* 46, no. 3 (September 2007): 410, http://www.jstor.org/stable/27513026.
62 Shems Friedlander translated the Law 677 that prohibits the production and maintenance of Sufi spaces in Turkey as "Clause 1. All the *tekkes* (dervish lodges) and *zaviyes* (central dervish lodges) in the Turkish Republic, either in the form of *wakf* (religious foundations) or under the personal property right of its sheikh

30 *Introduction*

or established in any other way, are closed. The right of property or possession of their owners continues. Those used as mosques and *mescits* (small mosques) may be retained as such. All of the orders using descriptions as sheikh, dervish, disciple, *dedelik* (a kind of sheikh of an order) [or senior dervishes who train dervishes], *chelebilik* (title of the leader of the *Mevlevi* order), *seyyitlik* (a descendant of the Prophet Muhammad), *babalık* (elder of a religious order, a kind of sheikh [meaning father, referring to a *şeyh*]), *emirlik* (descendant of the Prophet Muhammad), *nakiplik* (warden of a religious order), *halifelik* (deputy sheikh), *faldjilik* (fortune teller), *buyudjuluk* (witch-craft), *ufurukchuluk* (a person who claims to cure by means of breath), divining, and giving written charms in order to make someone reach their desire: service to these titles, and the wearing of dervish costume, are prohibited. The tombs of sultans, the tombs of dervish orders are closed, and the profession of tomb-keeping is abolished. Those who open the closed *tekkes* (dervish lodges) or *zaviyes* (central dervish lodges), or the tombs, and those who re-establish them or those who give temporary places to the orders or people who are called by any of the mystical names mentioned earlier or those who serve them, will be sentenced to at least three months in prison and will be fined at least fifty Turkish liras." Shems Friedlander, *Rumi and the Whirling Dervishes* (New York: Parabola Books, 2003), 123.

63 Friedlander, *Rumi and the Whirling Dervishes*, 123.
64 Eric Jan Zürcher, *Turkey: A Modern History* (London: I.B. Tauris, 2004), 191–192; Bernard Lewis, *The Emergence of Modern Turkey* (Oxford: Oxford University Press, 1968), 410–411.
65 Multi-party competition is defined as such: "Turkey's shift to a multi-party political system in 1946 when the Democratic Party was founded constituted a turning point in Turkey's political history, including the role of Islam in the Turkish State. By this time, Islam was under the control of the state but remained an effective social and moral force in Turkey. The Democratic Party criticised the RPP's [Republican People's Party's] total control over Islam. In order to pacify the DP, the Prime Minister began to soften policies on Islam, including the addition of courses on Islam to the educational curriculum. When the DP party was elected to office in 1950, it maintained a similar approach to secularism even though it allowed a return to Arabic for the call to prayer, removed obstacles prohibiting religious practice and teaching and built new mosques." Helen Rose Fuchs Ebaugh, *The Gülen Movement: A Sociological Analysis of a Civic Movement Rooted in Moderate Islam* (London: Springer, 2010), 17. "During the transition from one-party politics to multi-party politics, the RPP based its strategy on struggling to hold on to power by adopting the policies the DP advocated . . . aware of the growing importance of religious cleavage and its contribution to the increasing popularity of the DP, the RPP tried to adopt a pro-Islam attitude." Huri Türsan, *Democratisation in Turkey: The Role of Political Parties* (Bruxelles: PIE–Peter Lang, 2004), 49.
66 Şerif Mardin examines the public's religious demands by stating that "Islam had an aspect which addressed itself to man's being in this world, to his basic ontological insecurity, which enabled it to fasten itself on to psychological drives. Islam has become stronger in Turkey because social mobilisation had not decreased but on the contrary increased the insecurity of the mean who have been projected out of their traditional setting." Şerif Mardin, "Religion and Secularism in Turkey," in *Atatürk: Founder of a Modern State*, ed. Ali Kazancıgil and Ergün Özbudun (London: Archon Books, 1991), 218.
67 According to the Turkish Constitution, Article 24, "Everyone has the right to freedom of conscience, religious belief and conviction. Acts of worship, religious services and ceremonies shall be conducted freely, provided that they do not violate the provisions of Article 14. No one shall be compelled to worship or

to participate in religious ceremonies and rites, to reveal religious beliefs and convictions or be blamed or accused because of his religious beliefs and convictions. Education and instruction in religion and ethics shall be conducted under State supervision and control. Instruction in religious culture and moral education shall be compulsory in the curricula of primary and secondary schools. Other religious education and instruction shall be subject to the individual's own desire, and in the case of minors, to the request of their legal representatives. No one shall be allowed to exploit or abuse religion or religious feelings or things held sacred by religion, in any manner whatsoever, for the purpose of personal or political influence, or for even partially basing the fundamental, social, economic, political and legal order of the State on religious tenets." "The Constitution of the Republic of Turkey," http://www.hri.org/docs/turkey/con2b.html.
68 Ümit Cizre Sakallıoğlu, "Rethinking the Connections Between Turkey's 'Western' Identity Versus Islam," *Critique* 13, no. 3 (1998): 18.
69 Piraino and Sedgwick, "Introduction," 3.
70 Ron Geaves, Markus Dressler, and Gritt Maria Klinkhammer, eds., *Sufis in Western Society: Global Networking and Locality* (London and New York: Routledge, 2009); Ron Geaves and Theodore P.C. Gabriel, eds., *Sufism in Britain* (New York: Bloomsbury Academic, 2013); Jamal Malik and Saeed Zarrabi-Zadeh, eds., *Sufism East and West: Mystical Islam and Cross-Cultural Exchange in the Modern World* (Leiden and Boston: Brill, 2019), 3–4; Francesco Piraino, "Between Real and Virtual Communities: Sufism in Western Societies and the Naqshbandi Haqqani Case," *Social Compass* 63, no. 1 (2016): 93–108; Catharina Raudvere and Leif Stenberg, eds., *Sufism Today: Heritage and Tradition in the Global Community* (London and New York: IB Tauris, 2009); Werbner, *Pilgrims of Love: The Anthropology of a Global Sufi Cult*; David Westerlund, *Sufism in Europe and North America* (London and New York: Routledge and Curzon Press, 2004).
71 Olav Hammer, "Sufism for Westerners," in *Sufism in Europe and North America*, ed. David Westerlund (London: Routledge and Curzon Press, 2004), 127–143; Marcia Hermansen, "What's American about American Sufi Movements?" in *Sufism in Europe and North America*, ed. David Westerlund (London and New York: Routledge and Curzon Press, 2004), 40–63; Mark Sedgwick, "The Reception of Sufi and Neo-Sufi Literature," in *Sufis in Western Society: Global Networking and Locality*, ed. Ron Geaves, Markus Dressler, and Gritt Maria Klinkhammer (London: Routledge, 2009), 180–197.
72 Charlotte A. Quinn and Frederick Quinn, *Pride, Faith, and Fear: Islam in Sub-Saharan Africa* (Oxford and New York: Oxford University Press, 2003); Rachida Chih, "What is a Sufi Order? Revisiting the Concept through a Case Study of the Khalwatiyya in Contemporary Egypt," in *Sufism and the "Modern" in Islam*, ed. Martin Van Bruinessen and Julia Day Howell (London: I.B. Tauris, 2007), 21–38; Martin Van Bruinessen and Julia Day Howell, eds, *Sufism and the "Modern" in Islam* (London and New York: I.B. Tauris, 2007); Marta Dominguez-Diaz, *Women in Sufism: Female Religiosities in a Transnational Order* (London and New York: Routledge, 2014).
73 Marcia Hermansen, *Varieties of American Sufism: Islam, Sufi Orders, and Authority in a Time of Transition* (New York: State University of New York, 2020), xii.
74 William C. Chittick, *The Sufi Path of Knowledge: Ibn al-'Arabi's Metaphysics of Imagination* (Albany: State University of New York Press, 1989), 24–25.
75 Piraino and Sedgwick, "Introduction," 3.
76 Piraino and Sedgwick, "Introduction," 3.
77 Piraino and Sedgwick, "Introduction," 3.
78 Brian Silverstein, "Sufism and Modernity in Turkey: From the Authenticity of Experience to the Practice of Discipline," in *Sufism and the "Modern" in*

Islam, ed. Martin Van Bruinessen and Julie Day Howell (London: I.B. Tauris, 2007); Kim Shively, "Sufism in Modern Turkey," in *Routledge Handbook on Sufism* (London: Routledge, 2020), 435; Zürcher, *Turkey: A Modern History*; Catharina Raudvere, *The Book and the Roses: Sufi Women, Visibility, and Zikir in Contemporary Istanbul* (Lund, Sweden: Bjarnums Tryckeri, 2002); M. Saffet Sarıkaya, "Cumhuriyet Dönemi Türkiye'sinde Dini Tarikat ve Cemaatlerin Toplumdaki Yeri [Sufi Orders During Turkey's Republican Period]," *SDÜ Fen-Edebiyat Fakültesi Sosyal Bilimler Dergisi* 3 (1998): 93–102; Béatrice Hendrich, "Contemporary Sufism and the Quest for Spirituality Transgressing Borders, Transgressing Categories," *European Journal of Turkish Studies Social Sciences on Contemporary Turkey* (2011), https://doi.org/10.4000/ejts.4523.

79 Alexander Knysh, *Sufism: A New History of Islamic Mysticism* (Princeton: Princeton University Press, 2017), 71; Marshall Hodgson, *The Venture of Islam 1: Conscience and History in a World Civilization*, 3 vols. (Chicago: University of Chicago Press, 1974), 79–83. Talad Asad also examined the idea of Islam as a "polyphonic" formation. Asad states, "A theoretical consequence of this is that traditions should not be regarded as essentially homogenous, that heterogeneity in Muslim practices is not necessarily an indication of the absence of an Islamic tradition." Talad Asad, "The Idea of an Anthropology of Islam," *Qui Parle* 17, no. 2 (2009): 1–30.

80 Knysh, *Sufism*, 66.

81 Knysh, *Sufism*, 66.

82 Knysh, *Sufism*, 74.

83 The Hanafi school is one of the four major Sunni schools of Islamic law (or *fiqh* meaning jurisprudence).

84 Sufism in Turkey, as well as its rituals, poetry, arts and literature, has been studied by scholars such as Franklin D. Lewis, Ö. Tuğrul İnançer, Anders Hammarlund, Annemarie Schimmel, Metin And, Talat Sait Halman and many others in the fields of history, religion and anthropology. However, the existing scholarship mainly focuses on historical, structural or textual analysis of Sufi practice as a process of regularisation rather than the embodied acts of devotees' everyday life and rituals changing in relation to the social and political life, which this project seeks to do. Two ethnographic studies produced by Catharina Raudvere and Fulya Atacan moved beyond discussing Sufism as regularisation and focused on Sufism as a lived practice in Turkey, with both of them studying the Cerrahi Sufi order, a group that legalised their religious activities as a research foundation. While Atacan focuses more on the organisation of the Sufi order and the group dynamics, Raudvere focuses on how a group of female devotees, aside from their participation in their sheikh's ritual gatherings in a historical Sufi lodge in Istanbul, also organise religious activities for women in a private apartment to come together and practice Sufi rites as well as interact with and support each other in other worldly matters. However, both of these projects also give emphasis to the idea that Sufism is a religious practice tied to doctrines and a set of rites rather than a multifaceted, embodied way of everyday living that is open to changes and adaptations according to each devotees' cultural background and socioeconomic needs.

85 Florian Volm, "The Making of Sufism: The Gülen Movement and Its Efforts to Create a New Image," in *Global Sufism*, ed. Francesco Piraino and Mark Sedgwick (London: Hurst & Company, 2019), 177–192. Silverstein, "Sufism and Modernity in Turkey"; Shively, "Sufism in Modern Turkey."

86 Fait Muedini, *Sponsoring Sufism: How Governments Promote Mystical Islam in their Domestic and Foreign Policies* (Palgrave Macmillan US, 2015), 32, https://doi.org/10.1057/9781137521071.

Introduction 33

87 Şerif Mardin, "The Nakşibendi Order in Turkish History," in *Islam in Modern Turkey: Religion, Politics and Literature in a Secular State*, ed. Richard Tapper (London and New York: I.B. Tauris, 1991); Ozan Çepni, "Güneydoğu Nurculara Kaldı [Southeast is in the Hands of Nurcus]," *Cumhuriyet*, February 13, 2018, http://www.cumhuriyet.com.tr/haber/egitim/925998/; Elisabeth Özdalga, "Transformation of Sufi Based Communities in Modern Turkey: The Nakşibendis, Nurcus, and the Gülen Community," in *Turkey's Engagement with Modernity*, ed. Celia J. Kerslake, Kerem Öktem, and Philip Robins (New York: Palgrave Macmillan, 2010), 69–91; Hakan Yavuz, *Nostalgia for the Empire: The Politics of Neo-Ottomanism* (Oxford: Oxford University Press, 2020). Yavuz states that "In Istanbul, five main Nakşibendi branches emerged, the economically wealthiest and most influential of which is the İskender Paşa, led by Nureddin Coşan. Presently the most powerful branch is the Erenköy Cemaati. The third and most conservative of the neo-Nakşibendi are the Süleymancıs." Yavuz, *Nostalgia for the Empire*, 133.
88 Şerif Mardin, *Din ve İdeoloji [Religion and Ideology]* (İstanbul: İletişim Publishing House, 1995), 94.
89 M. Kaplan, *Türk Edebiyatı Üzerinde Araştırmalar: Tip Tahlilleri [Research on Turkish Literature]* (İstanbul: Dergah Publications, 1985).
90 Peña, *Performing Piety*.
91 Chih, "What is a Sufi Order? Revisiting the Concept Through a Case Study of the Khalwatiyya in Contemporary Egypt," 21.
92 See John Voll, "Contemporary Sufism and Social Theory," in *Sufism and the "Modern" in Islam*, ed. Martin Van Bruinessen and Julie Day Howell (London: I.B. Tauris, 2013), 297; Celia A. Genn, "The Development of a Modern Western Sufism," in *Sufism and the "Modern" in Islam*, ed. Martin Van Bruinessen and Julie Day Howell (London: I.B. Tauris, 2013), 257–278.
93 Henri Lefebvre, *The Production of Space* (Oxford: Blackwell Publishing, 2011), 53.
94 Ethel Sara Wolper, *Cities and Saints: Sufism and the Transformation of Urban Space in Medieval Anatolia* (University Park: The Pennsylvania State University Press, 2003), 5.
95 Peña, *Performing Piety*, 10.
96 Peña, *Performing Piety*, 737.
97 Brian Silverstein, "Islam and Modernity in Turkey: Power, Tradition, and Historicity in the European Provinces," *Anthropological Quarterly* 76, no. 3 (2003): 511.
98 Nilüfer Göle, "Civilisational, Spatial, and Sexual Powers," in *Varieties of Secularism in a Secular Age*, ed. Michael Warner, Jonathan Van Antwerpen, and Craig J. Calhoun (Cambridge: Harvard University Press, 2010), 245–247; Charles Taylor, *Seküler Çağ [A Secular Age]* (Istanbul: Türkiye İş Bankası Kültür Yayınları, 2009); Talad Asad, *Formations of the Secular: Christianity, Islam, Modernity* (Stanford: Stanford University Press, 2003); Esra Özyürek, "Christian and Turkish: Secularist Fears of a Converted Nation," in *Secular State and Religious Society: Two Forces in Play in Turkey*, ed. Berna Turam (New York: Palgrave Macmillan), 99.
99 Özyürek, "Christian and Turkish: Secularist Fears of a Converted Nation," 99; Joan Wallach Scott, *Politics of the Veil* (Princeton, New Jersey: Princeton University Press, 2008), 91–92.
100 Göle, "Civilisational, Spatial, and Sexual Powers," 245–247.
101 Göle, "Civilisational, Spatial, and Sexual Powers," 245–247.
102 Özyürek, "Christian and Turkish: Secularist Fears of a Converted Nation," 99.
103 Scott, *Politics of the Veil*, 91–92.

Introduction

104 Nilüfer Göle, "Secularism and Islamism in Turkey: The Making of Elites and Counter-Elites," *Middle East Journal* 51, no. 1 (1997): 48.
105 Göle, "Secularism and Islamism in Turkey: The Making of Elites and Counter-Elites," 49.
106 Özyürek, "Christian and Turkish: Secularist Fears of a Converted Nation," 99.
107 Göle, "Civilisational, Spatial, and Sexual Powers," 245–247.
108 Göle, "Civilisational, Spatial, and Sexual Powers," 245–247.
109 Henri Meschonnic, Gabriella Bedetti, and Alice Ottis, "Modernity Modernity," *New Literary History* 23, no. 2 (1992): 404.
110 Charles Taylor, "Two Theories of Modernity," *The Hastings Centre Report* 25, no. 2 (1995): 24–33.
111 Taylor, "Two Theories of Modernity," 24–33.
112 All were formulated to separate the new state of Turkey from its Islamic Ottoman past, so that citizens would swiftly learn Westernised ways of living.
113 Sena Karasipahi, "Comparing Islamic Resurgence Movements in Turkey and Iran," *Middle East Journal* 63, no. 1 (2009): 94.
114 "Symbolic capital" in Pierre Bourdieu's analysis' "is one for which economism has no name" and is "less easily measured." Pierre Bourdieu, *The Logic of Practice*, trans. Richard Nice (Redwood City: Stanford University Press, 1980), 120–121. Also, as Nilüfer Gole explains, Bourdieu talks about "different forms of capital that give strength, power and profit to their owner" and these, as Göle explains, are "economic capital" (convertible into money), "cultural capital" (conferred by edicational credentials and institutions), "social capital" (achieved social connections and group membership) and "symbolic capital" (legitimated capital, source of prestige)." Göle, "Secularism and Islamism in Turkey: The Making of Elites and Counter-Elites," 46.
115 Peña, *Performing Piety*, 9–11.
116 Peña, *Performing Piety*, 11.

Part One
Restoring

1 Historical Perspectives
Post-Tariqa *Mevlevi* Devotion

I am waiting at the entrance of one the largest *Mevlevi* lodges in Istanbul. Built in 1597 on land donated by *Malkoç* Mehmet *Efendi* (the Chief Caliph of Janissary), Yenikapı lodge remained in use for 328 years until the collapse of the Ottoman Empire.[1] With eighteen dervish cells, the lodge at the time was considered one of the centres of *Mevlevi* training. Other than the dervish cells, it had a mausoleum, *semahane* (the ritual hall), a library, a fountain, a *muvakkithane* (the place where a dervish deals with the task of adjusting the prayer times according to the movements of the sun), harem, *misafirhane* (room for guests), cistern, bath, bakery, kitchen and cellar. Due to three big fires that occurred in 1903, 1961 and 1997, everything in the lodge was destroyed. Since then, the lodge went under construction and every section was rebuilt. Training in fine arts and music in the lodge was very common, and the devotees hosted many artists in their facility. Among those were Hamamizade İsmail Dede Efendi (1778–1846), a famous Turkish composer, and Sheikh Galip (1757–1798), a Turkish poet. As I sit and write at a bench near the lodge, I am imagining the dervishes meditating in their cells for a moment forgetting the fact that the lodge was open only for government-sponsored cultural events. I wait. I wait. I wait. I wait for someone to get some information, but no one seems to be in this quiet space reclassified as a museum. The lodge feels deserted. Once again, I look back at the security cabin and search for a gatekeeper to ask questions. But, no one seems to be there.

This tended to be the case when I first began to research *Mevlevis* in Turkey in 2009. Many reclassified lodges were under renovation to open as museums. Since then, the transformation or reclassification of worship sites has been a controversial and multifaceted issue in Turkey. For instance, the JDP government approved the classification of the largest *Mevlevi* lodge in İstanbul, Yenikapı *Mevlevi* Lodge, as the campus of university space in 2011 (Fatih Sultan Mehmet *Vakıf* University, Alliance of Civilisations Institute). In July 2020, the historic Hagia Sophia was reclassified from a museum back to a mosque. These two acts of conversion, both occurring under the leadership of Recep Tayyip Erdoğan, actually reveal how while some religious sites such as Hagia Sophia play a significant social and religious role (conveying

DOI: 10.4324/9781003118589-3

diversity) when converted to a museum, others such as Yenikapı *Mevlevi* Lodge lose its role and essence as a site for devotion when converted to a university (known to be controlled by the Islamists). As performative sites, both require the presence of specific performers in order to fulfil their roles.

Just to clarify the problem with such reclassifications in Turkey, I would like to talk about the role of Hagia Sophia. Many secular devotees conveyed widespread criticism when President Erdoğan announced the decision to reconsecrate Hagia Sophia on July 10, 2020. Hagia Sophia, referred to as *Ayasofya* in Turkey, means divine wisdom. Built in 537 during the reign of the Byzantine Emperor Justine, it was the largest Christian church of the Eastern Roman Empire. After the Ottoman conquest of Constantinople in 1453, Sultan Mehmet II converted it into an imperial mosque, adding four minarets around the building's grand central dome. Mustafa Kemal Atatürk, the founder of the Turkish Republic, turned the Hagia Sophia into a museum in 1934 in a symbolic break from its past as a place of worship. In 2020, a Turkish court reversed Atatürk's decision with Erdoğan signing a "presidential order turning the site back into a mosque almost immediately."[2] Today, Hagia Sophia has become a space in which *imams* recite from the Quran. Mosaics and frescoes that depict Jesus and Mary are not visible (draped with curtains). Hagia Sophia, built as an Orthodox Christian cathedral, first converted into a mosque after the Ottoman conquest, had been functioning as a museum, a multi-cultural space that had inspired people from different social, ethnic, religious and national backgrounds. It was a space encouraging unity and diversity. Today, the Hagia Sophia is in the control of the Religious Affairs Directorate (RAD). For many journalists, this was a political act that disappointed millions of people, most importantly Christians and secular Turkish people, who want the Turkish government to understand the vitality of Hagia Sophia and its role in representing and mobilising universal values of the secular Turkish society.

Nicholas Danforth, a scholar focusing on Turkey and the Middle East, explained, "As a museum, the Hagia Sophia symbolised the idea of there being common artistic and cultural values that transcended religion to unite humanity."[3] I had the chance to converse with tourist guides who express how for years, people from all around the world had visited Hagia Sophia without having to follow the regulations necessary to enter a mosque, such as taking off shoes or using of veils or hijabs. More importantly, Muslims and Christians were able to experience God side by side in Hagia Sophia. Today, many secular Turks often express "this is an act of polarisation" and an "act of undermining the multicultural values of world cultural heritage."[4] Before its final reclassification as a mosque, Hagia Sophia was simultaneously a secular and a sacred space in which people from all around the world embodied diversity.

Another reclassification undermining universal values was the conversion of the Yenikapı *Mevlevi* lodge to the Fatih Sultan Mehmet Vakıf University.[5] With these reclassifications, the government controlled the access of religious groups that opposed the JDP's Islamist vision. Although *Mevlevis*' concerns regarding the *Mevlevi* lodges have been slightly different from Hagia Sophia, it is an example of how certain reclassifications have undermined the cultural beliefs and values that flourish in such sites such as all-embracing beliefs and values of Rumi. While Hagia Sophia lost its universal and multilayered meaning due to its conversion to a mosque, Yenikapı *Mevlevi* lodge, reclassified as a university, lost its essence due to the absence of *Mevlevis*' performatic rituals. Between 2010 and 2020, I attended many ritual gatherings in the *Mevlevi* lodges in which visitors from all around the world expressed their disappointment regarding how the buildings in the Galata *Mevlevi* and Yenikapı *Mevlevi* lodges seemed extinct. Visitors longed to see the living, breathing *Mevlevis* organising and using the lodges for cultural activities. To them, what was important was how *semazens* embody unity and otherworldliness in the ritual gatherings. Without the embodied acts of the *Mevlevis*, whirling, singing and sharing poetry, the lodges become relics of the past. *Mevlevis* believe that the only instances that the Ministry of Culture and Tourism gives temporary access to the lodges are when there are events that serve the promotion and recognition of the government.

Due to such a lack of acknowledgements of *Mevlevi* culture in Turkey, there has been tension regarding how, why and where the whirling ritual can and should exist. However, it is also this tension that has inspired *Mevlevis* to constantly search for ways to restore their practices and to reorganise their living and working spaces to use the whirling ritual as one of the most powerful tools in practising remembrance. This idea of restoration allowed them to adapt to social and political conditions in Turkey. To examine *Mevlevis*' process of restoration, the next section will discuss how, in the first half of the twentieth century (including in the years of Turkish revolution), most of the Sufi groups including *Mevlevis* were silent practitioners that were organising private gatherings in their homes in order to make Sufi music and read Sufi poetry. To comprehend *Mevlevi's* and other Sufi devotees' position and post-tariqa vision, the following section will examine how most Sufi groups perceived the revolution and preserved their beliefs and values. Then, in the following section, I will discuss how, in the second half of the twentieth century, after the events leading to the commodification of *Sema* ceremony, *Mevlevis* started to take every opportunity to perform their rituals simultaneously as folk performance and religious ritual enacted for tourists. I will also examine minority Sufi groups' position in relation to the Islamists and discuss how devotees like Saygın *dede* and Narin *dede* (I will analyse in Chapter 3) refused to participate in the politicisation of Islam. In the last two sections, I will discuss a case study, Saygın *dede*'s group, to show how and why his group practice the whirling ritual simultaneously as tourist attraction and worship to restore their practice of remembrance and give the reclassified *Mevlevi* lodges the sacred meaning they have deserved.

Saygın *dede*'s case shows one of the many efforts to restore *Mevlevi* beliefs and values in Turkey, an atmosphere, in which *Mevlevi* identity is questioned by a variety of political Islamists, conservative Sufi and Sufi-esque religious groups (and their members), tourist agencies and the Ministry of Tourism and Culture. For this reason, devotees wanted to make sure that the ways they practised Sufi whirling ritual and their teachings were no threat to the authorities (the JDP government, the RAD and other Islamist groups) of today's Turkey. However, many *Mevlevis*, like Saygın *dede,* experienced a lack of belonging to any space. Because Sufi devotees had to give up some of their tariqa traditions (such as living and worshipping together under the same roof) when they lost their lodges. Also, Turkish media have been recognising these post-tariqa whirling dervish groups simply as non-*Mevlevi* folk dancers. Post-tariqa groups in Turkey tended to be formations that managed to preserve some of their beliefs, values and practices by adapting to the secular values of modern Turkey after the banning of the tariqas in the 1920s. Most tourist agencies have been employing them as non-*Mevlevi* dancers. Conservative religious groups and organisations have been criticising their legitimacy by disapproving their ways of ritual practice (such as dancing). Despite such preconceived ideas, most of these performers defined themselves as practising *Mevlevi* students, who have chosen to restore *Mevlevi* arts and rituals simultaneously as tourist attraction and worship. For instance, a *Mevlevi*, Narin *dede* explained his vision for Sufi devotion as restoring *Mevlevi* practices by generating a post-tariqa *Mevlevi* arts group. Before I move on to discuss how these devotees have used performance (most specifically the whirling ritual, which is a form of *zikir*) to make sacred space, it might be helpful to examine some of the key historical processes that continue to shape their restoration processes today. To understand how *Mevlevis* have sought to restore their practices in Turkey despite legal restrictions, it is vital to discuss how during the revolution, some Sufi groups, including *Mevlevis*, chose to stay in agreement with Atatürk's ideals and refused to unite with major political Sufi and "Sufi-esque"[6] formations such as the popular *Nakşibendis*, *Nurcus* and *Fethullahçıs*. Post-tariqa *Mevlevi* stories of renewal illuminate how some whirling dervishes have first dealt with the setbacks of the Turkish revolution and then the Turkish Islamisation by using performance as a medium to generate a modern Sufi vision that is in line with Atatürk's vision for the Republic.

Key Historical Events: The Revolution and Sufism

In order to understand the restoration of *Mevlevi* practice in today's Turkey, one needs to look into the links between the commodified performances of Sufi rituals (performed simultaneously as tourist attraction and worship), Sufi devotees' everyday life and interactions and the organisation of post-tariqa Sufi sacred spaces. Post-tariqa Sufi activities began in the early twentieth century, when the government prohibited the tariqas during the revolution. In the 1920s, there were Sufi opponents, who wanted to resist the closure of their sacred lodges. Some of the devotees engaged in silent opposition. Others were open, public and at times aggressive in their opposition. There were also devotees who fled Turkey to continue their Sufi practices abroad. However, there were also Sufi devotees who stayed and supported the closure of Sufi lodges.

Hülya Küçük, a Turkish scholar of Sufism, discusses such cases of opposition in detail, while also presenting accounts of Sufi sheikhs and dervishes who supported Atatürk's reforms and found ways to direct their energy to socially productive activities such as teaching.[7] Among the supporters, the Halveti sheikh Mehmed Şemseddin *efendi* (master) expressed his views that people did not need a *tekke* to practice the *zikir* ritual. Another sheikh, Kenan *Rifai*, whose legacy about the modernity of Islam continues to this day, believed in the vitality of the Kemalist reforms. To present his approval of the closure of the *tekkes* (Sufi lodges) to the press, he stated that, "out of the 300 or so in Istanbul, only a few were 'in the service of knowledge': furthermore, their part in history was over."[8] He conveyed that the tariqas had fulfilled their mission in this world. He examined Sufi devotees' position, explaining: "We are now, what we were earlier. Earlier we were in visible *tekkes*, now in an inner, heart, *tekke*. Allah wished so, and made it so. Everything from him is fine."[9] Many *Mevlevis* shared Kenan *Rifai's* vision and continued to direct their energy to socially productive activities such as teaching and creating *Mevlevi* arts in a variety of private and public spaces. Through teaching and practising arts, devotees sought to restore their practice of remembrance.

Unfortunately, studies about Sufi life and the activities of Sufi devotees (including *Mevlevis*) in Turkey are far from clear and remain limited, especially in Western languages. As Sencer Ayata notes, a sociological account of their underground history has yet to be attempted.[10] However, what is clear today is that Sufism, as Cemal Kafadar argues, "has always been much more than the sum of the fortunes of various orders," for the limits of its reach are defined by neither location nor organisation.[11] As a cultural tradition, it "continues to run as a deep current in modern, including secular, Turkish life."[12] During my fieldwork, I chose to focus on both visible and underground post-tariqa *Mevlevi* and *Rifai* groups, who instead of resenting Atatürk's act of closing the Sufi lodges, in the religious sense, chose to believe that the closing of the *tekkes* was necessary for the progress of Sufi culture. The groups and individuals I studied were adamant about generating a post-tariqa Sufi practice that is in harmony with the secular vision of Atatürk. These were individuals who believed that through education and arts, one could create a devotional life rich with both the mysticism of Islam and the ever-changing modern values inspiring the study of scientific knowledge.

Elderly devotees often discussed stories they heard from their grandparents and parents, who had to close their lodges during the 1920s' revolution. A *Mevlevi* and *Rifai*,[13] Melih *dede* explained to me how his father supported Atatürk's revolution and fought for the War of Independence. His family held no grudge against the fact that Atatürk closed the Sufi lodges because they trusted that one way or another, they would restore *Mevlevi* beliefs and values. Along with Atatürk, many devotees and their deceased family members believed that only through learning and growth could Turkey become a country free of false piousness, violence and outside domination.[14] In 1925, to express his views of tariqa, Atatürk said,

> The aim of the revolution which we have been and are now accomplishing is to bring the people of the Turkish Republic into a state of society entirely modern and completely civilised in spirit and form. This is the central pillar of our Revolution, and it is necessary utterly to defeat those mentalities incapable of accepting this truth.[15]

Sufi groups that supported Atatürk's modernisation plan moved underground and practised their rituals, music and poetry in less populated neighbourhoods and in their private homes.[16] Contrary to Sufi groups with an Islamist agenda, many *Mevlevis* have continued to support Atatürk's idea of modernisation.

In one speech, Atatürk articulated his fear of anti-regime groups that mobilised religious Turkish people through the politicisation of Islamic values.[17] According to Atatürk, ambitious politicians or religious figures could challenge the republican project of modernity through the use of Islamic beliefs and the religious practices of the public.[18] Islam had been the forerunner of the Ottoman order, and the rise against the old order required a complete estrangement from the past.[19] During the 1920s and 1930s, the Turkish government had to deal with rebellions against its authority that combined religious and ethnic elements. In particular, the Sheikh Said Rebellion of 1925 intensified Atatürk's and his supporters' fear that oppositional forces would appeal to religious sentiments.[20] This fear was one of the reasons for the state's restrictive strategies towards Sufi groups.

Due to such fears, the "preamble of the Turkish Constitution defines the purpose of the Republic as 'reaching the status of modern civilisations and the application of Atatürk's principles and revolutions.'"[21] The preamble also states that sacred religious beliefs are absolutely excluded from state affairs and politics by reason of the laicism (non-clerical or secular) principle and that sovereignty belongs to the Turkish people. This process also involved the banishment of religion in education, the legal system and public ceremonies—the destruction of independent religious organisations. The Caliphate was abolished in March 1924. Islam was given only a peripheral role in the new educational system. In 1928, the laicism principle was added to the Turkish Constitution as one of the fundamental characteristics of the regime. Meanwhile, the legal system of the country was completely secularised during the 1920s and 1930s. In these years, the Turkish government was unwavering about assuring political loyalty in relation to secularisation of the Turkish Republic.[22]

Devotees who supported Atatürk's vision believed that there were various related social and political causes for Atatürk's radical reforms. On one level, between 1923 and 1932, right after the Turkish War of Independence, the Turkish State was still under the threat of opposing forces, such as different ethnic, religious and national groups' social, political and economic demands. For this reason, Atatürk believed that the Turkish nation, despite its ethnic, religious and national differences, needed to unite as a modern nation that could engage in the processes of renewal in order to compete with Europe's social, political and economic development. Although the nation was experiencing a rapid break from its Ottoman past with cultural, educational, religious, political and economic reforms, including the change of the alphabet, clothing and women's rights, Atatürk believed that he had to realise his plan in an extremely short period of time, persuading the nation to strictly dedicate itself to carrying out his modern design for the Turkish Republic.

Atatürk was also aware of the well-known hospitality of Sufi orders and the socially active and influential aspects of their spaces. Schimmel also highlights the fact that Sufi order's "adaptability made the orders ideal vehicles for the spread of Islamic teachings."[23] For this reason, Atatürk believed that he had to take radical action to stop any Sufi group from influencing Turkish people to oppose the government's modernisation plans. The state sought full control of religious groups and their activities; therefore, when the Caliphate was abolished in 1924, the parliament passed a law to create the Religious Affairs Directory (RAD), which was responsible for assigning *imams* (Muslim religious leaders) to mosques and regulating all public expressions of religion.[24] RAD was created so that the state could regulate religious and social values of the nation and state elites.

This leads the discussion to the strict control of spaces and religious activities until the 1950s and individuals' and groups' determination in organising sacred gatherings. In the Republic of Turkey General Directorate of State Archives in Ankara, there have been a great number of correspondences between government representatives who investigated, enquired and started legal proceedings against sheikhs and other devotees who continued their religious activities in private and public settings.[25] I have come across correspondences evaluating the actions of religious Turkish citizens, including *imams* praying in Arabic in mosques, which was strictly prohibited at the time. Also, there are letters investigating the activities of *mürits* (devotees of specific sheikhs) who visited their sheikhs regularly in their private homes or about individuals who were investigated due to wearing religious garments. While one letter discusses how a sheikh's activities and home were investigated to control possible tariqa activities, another letter states how sheikhs and *mürits* were caught and delivered to courthouses for legal action. In these letters, such activities are considered as opposed to the secular regime of the Turkish Republic. It is clear from the letters in the archives that such rigid control lasted until the 1950s (until the end of the rule of the Republican People's Party). The letters I have come across after those years focus on replies written by government officers about their attendance at the celebration of

Mevlana's *urs* (literally meaning wedding, a word used for the death anniversary of *Mevlana*, the title used for Rumi in Turkey).

In his book, *Journeys of a Sufi Musician*, Kudsi Ergüner tells about his experience as a five-year-old boy attending secret religious ceremonies, where the minority Sufi community took precautions not to be disturbed by the police. He mentions that one of the Sufi lodges in Edirnekapi housed religious Sufi gatherings. Ergüner states, during the meetings, members "stood at each end of the street as lookouts to give warning of any police intervention."[26] However, it seems from the letters in the government archives and from oral historical accounts that despite the problems with the government and the police, devotees were nonetheless able to meet in private spaces to organise community/religious gatherings.

As an elderly *Mevlevi* sheikh, who grew up in a private home used as a sacred space for Sufi gatherings, explains, the strict control of ceremonial activities until the 1950s forced Sufi groups and individuals to continue their religious practices through the study and performance of Sufi texts. Journalist and scholar Hakan Yavuz's discussion also points to the importance of text-centric devotional living and states: "Government oppression during the 1920s and 1930s forced the Sufi orders to shift from a *tekke*-centric to a text-centric understanding of Islam."[27] Devotees could not live and train together as they used to do in Ottoman Sufi lodges but found ways to convert their private homes to temporary study spaces for discussing and analysing Sufi texts. However, this private text-centric devotion transformed once again when the Turkish government managed to control religion's dominance in the Turkish Republic. The secular government realised its agenda to resurrect *Mevlevi Sema* ceremony as a commodification of Turkish culture (a touristic folk performance) to promote its democratic character. For *Mevlevis*, this was another opportunity for renewal. This time they were going to shift from "text-centric" practice to performance-centric practice.

Commodification of *Sema:* Performance-Centred Restoration

Articulation of moderate Islam became more and more popular with the Turkish government's commodification of *Sema* ceremony as a tourist attraction. In the middle of the twentieth century, *Mevlevi* devotees found the need to come out of hiding when circumstances started to change, encouraging some groups to organise visible practices such as the commodified performances of Sufi rituals such as *Sema* ceremony (known as whirling dervish rituals in the West). As discussed earlier, a set of social and political changes, including the multiparty competition; commodification and secularisation of Sufi rituals as folk performances and tourist attraction starting in the 1950s; the 1983 constitutional changes[28] easing the restrictions on religious practice; and the designation of Sufi cultural beliefs and values as part of World Intangible Cultural Heritage by UNESCO have shaped the life of *Mevlevis* in Turkey. Paradoxically, the Turkish government's decision to promote *Sema* ceremony as a tourist attraction (starting in the 1950s) encouraged devotees to move to the public sphere to practise and share the true form of their rituals simultaneously as worship and tourist attraction.

Mevlevi cultural beliefs and values became visible in 1953 when ambassadors from the United States visited Konya (the Turkish city known as the birthplace of the *Mevlevi* order) as part of the European Recovery Program. The mayor of Konya contacted Sufi musicians and asked them to organise a performance of *Sema* ceremony. Following the first performance in 1954, the mayor initiated a festival, known today as Şeb-i Aruz (Rumi's *urs*), to commemorate Rumi's passing. The mayor invited the members of the former *Mevlevi* order, who were known to continue their practices in their private homes, including sheikhs and dervishes, to perform their *Sema* ceremony in the purely secular environment of a sports hall. Ergüner, who was a member of the *Mevlevi* order, reported, "The governor of the province told them that the festival was not meant to be anything more than a folklore performance. The governor warned them that they could get into serious trouble."[29] At the time, some government officials were still ignoring the fact that *Sema* ceremony was nonetheless an act of worship for *Mevlevi* devotees.

For the government, the religious whirling ritual was folklore, which Barbara Kirshenblatt-Gimblett explains as "survivals in a civilised society of behaviours that had their origins in earlier stages of cultural evolution."[30] She states that "The process of negating cultural practices reverses itself once it has succeeded in archaising the 'errors'; indeed through a process of archaising, which is a mode of cultural production, the repudiated is transvalued as heritage."[31] In the case of the *Mevlevis*, the repudiated was the Ottoman Sufi tradition. Kirshenblatt-Gimblett further asserts that "The very term 'folklore' marks a transformation of errors into archaisms and their transvaluation once they are safe for collection, preservation, exhibition, study, and even nostalgia and revival."[32] The Turkish government perceived Sufi rituals as relics of the past that are safe for collection and organised *Sema* ceremony as folklore. That this organisation lacked respect for *Sema* as a religious ceremony was so disturbing for some *Mevlevi* devotees that at one of the performances in 1961, a *Mevlevi* teacher, reacting to the use of the ceremony for political speeches, chased the television cameramen documenting political speeches out of the space, causing the government to ban the devotees of the *Mevlevi* community of Istanbul from the touristic festival in Konya. As an alternative, the following year non-devotee performers were trained to enact the ceremony.[33] However, this act could not stop the restoration of *Mevlevi sema*. Most of the performers designated as non-devotees in the traditional sense were either considered themselves students of Sufism or later had become students of Sufism, seeking to learn *Mevlevi* whirling, poetry and music.[34] Therefore, just the attempt to bring back *Mevlevi* whirling ritual as folk performance was performatic enough, inspiring more people to learn about *Mevlevi* devotional life. According to many *Mevlevis*, the government overlooked that the performance that they believed to be safe for collection was a *zikir* ritual. All the actions of the ritual, especially the singing and dancing, had a tremendous meditative quality arousing curiosity about *Mevlevi* beliefs and values. It was not possible for government to control devotees' intentions to remember God while performing the ceremony.

In 1973, *Mevlevi Sema* has become the agent advertising Turkey as a tourist destination with spectacles to see when the Turkish government in collaboration with UNESCO observed the seven-hundredth anniversary of Rumi's passing, formally recognised as the Year of Rumi. With this designation, the Turkish government permitted devotees to travel to London, Paris and across the United States to share Rumi's Islamic teachings and *Mevlevi* rituals. For the government, the designation by UNESCO and visibility of Islamic rituals outside Turkey were the perfect opportunity to announce the strength of its democracy and the moderate position of Islam in Turkey. In 2005, with another UNESCO proclamation of *Mevlevi Sema* Ceremony as Oral and Intangible Heritage of Humanity in collaboration with the Turkish government, the ceremony was used once again to promote Turkey.[35] Two years later, in honour of Rumi's eight-hundredth birthday, UNESCO also declared 2007 the Year of *Mevlana* Celaleddin-i Rumi and Tolerance. The designation of *Sema* as cultural heritage and the popularity of Rumi increased the visibility of Sufism and Sufi rituals as commodities of secular Turkish culture once again, while the Turkish government and its support of moderate Islam gained more recognition. This commodification act has also been an opportunity for *Mevlevi* and other Sufi devotees to restore their beliefs and values by practising and teaching the whirling ritual. A variety of *Mevlevis* managed to come together to practice *Sema* and share Rumi's teachings with persons and groups from different religious and national backgrounds. *Semazens* travelled abroad, organised workshops and taught Rumi's poetry with emphasis to moderate Islam. To do this, as many *Mevlevi dedes* explained, they had to be open to adapting the length and at times the content of the whirling ritual. At times, they had to reconstruct the ritual without letting of its devotional quality, which was to experience God's unity. Adaptation of the length or the content of the ceremony did not affect the fact that the *semazens* were whirling to meditate on God's unity.

During this period, with some *Mevlevis*' ability to adapt the *Mevlevi* ritual, *Sema* became a symbol of liberation for some devotees who, while practising Sufism, desired to stay in harmony with the secular values of the Turkish State. This was a way to share their idea of a piety that is in harmony with Islam and secularism. Today, these devotees and their younger generations believe that, in order for people to embrace a genuine *Mevlevi* practice, the state has to be secular. Özge, an elderly *Mevlevi* devotee, once discussed (in her Rumi poetry reading classes) the idea that "the only way to be a pious person is by free choice."[36] For her, that is the rule of Islam. Therefore, the government should always be secular, offering its citizens the freedom to choose how to live and what religion, idea or teaching to practice.

Threats to Secularism: Staying Away From Political Sufi and Sufi-esque Groups

While the democratisation process of the 1950s was a resurgence for the *Mevlevis*, it was also a comeback for the supporters of an Islamic government. Some devotees like Saygın *dede* believed that secular *Mevlevis* desired to stay away from political Sufi and Sufi-esque groups by only focusing on practising *Mevlevi* arts, including music, poetry, whirling and calligraphy. Saygın *dede* still remembers how his *Mevlevi* elders were experiencing tremendous lack of trust for the political Sufi groups in 1960s Turkey. They did not want to become part of any political group or ideology that was a threat to Atatürk's secular vision. The state had to stay secular. However, most were also aware of the fact that Turkish people were frustrated with the works of secular parties and were starting to seek welfare in the false promises of the Islamists.[37] Most of the conservative Sufi orders, who opposed Atatürk's vision, had not been visible until the leadership of the JDP government, who, according to Zana Çıtak, not only has been turning a blind eye to their public appearances but encouraging collaborations between the RAD and the brotherhoods.[38]

Due to people's concerns about secular parties, the introduction of multi-party competition in 1950 forced some politicians to reconsider their efforts to secularise society. In order to gain votes, political parties running for office and elected governments professed religious affiliation and became more empathetic to the public's religious demands.[39] Sena Karasipahi illuminates the fact that given historical reasons, Islam continued to be part of Turkish culture even after religion became secondary to the state. Turkish people, according to Karasipahi, became frustrated with and mistrusted their state's secularist policies. Moreover, in Turkey, revolution for people of the Turkish Republic was also problematic because the government prevented individuals from freely practising their Ottoman cultural beliefs and values.[40] The government expected complete estrangement from the remainder of Ottoman life, including organised religion. However, as Güneş Murat Tezcür identifies, "revolutionary regimes desperately seek sacredness that is bestowed by transcendental norms and goals for purposes of political stability."[41] Hakan Yavuz gives attention to the fact that Islam was more effective in attracting and uniting people than "constructed ethnic nationalism or socialism."[42] Moderate Islam continued to serve as a common language for expressing popular frustration, as well as an alternative way of solving people's problems.[43] However, most of the dominant political groups' acts of moderation were temporary, making sure that they look like they design an Islamic vision that would welcome all kinds of believers and non-believers. Saygın *dede* explained that his "elders were aware that Islamists were not all-embracing."[44] Also, Saygın *dede*'s grandfather believed that "it was unfaithful to use faith for political gain and devotional life could not be mixed with political life."[45] He said that his family had nothing to do with political organisations.

In the first half of the twentieth century, with the government developing awareness of the public's need for religion and tolerance for religious individuals and groups, Islamic activists started to work hard to accomplish their goals of mobilising Islam as a social force. This mobilisation, according to Metin Heper, is explained as "the modern politicisation of Islam."[46] Sevinç Bermek explains:

> When the DP [Democratic Party] came into power in 1950, all of the groups that had been suppressed under the single-party regime and during the Second World War supported it, including liberal and right-wing voters. But religious groups *Nakşibendi* and *Nurcu*—were its most numerous constituencies.[47]

Şerif Mardin says that in the 1990s, the *Nakşibendi* order was "an extraordinarily resilient revivalist movement, in which all of the successful elements of modern Turkish Islamic politics have originated."[48] More specifically, he discusses how the *Nakşibendi* order supported the creation of the first Islamist party, the National Order Party (*Milli Nizam Partisi*—founded by Necmettin Erbakan in 1970 and banned in the wake of the military coup in 1971). The party, reestablished under the name of the National Salvation Party (*Milli Selamet Partisi*)—or NSP—in 1972, signified the first major occurrence of the institutionalisation and politicisation of provincial Islam.[49]

In the second half of the 1990s, the leaders of a variety of political religious groups and well-known Muslim intellectuals became active in the Turkish State, and there was an agreement between dominant Sufi and Sufi-esque groups, such as the *Nakşibendis, Nurcus* and secularist political parties. Later, Islamist leaders gradually took on a more activist role by acting as lobbies for the economic ventures established by other Islamist groups in such sectors as textiles, construction and banking.[50] As Nilüfer Göle states, "democratisation and the liberal environment fostered the emergence of a more pluralistic and open society, which paved the way for the spreading of civil society and non-governmental organisations."[51] Various individuals, including artists and businessmen, sociocultural Islamic organisations and trade unions, thrived and began to affect and manipulate the political and economic life of the country.[52] Necip Fazıl Kısakürek, a Turkish Muslim thinker and famous poet, strongly denounced radical secularism and emphasised the importance of indigenous cultural, religious and national values. In his struggle, he gave great importance to the younger generation, trying to mobilise them around his ideal,[53] and has been very influential to the young Islamists who were raised with his ideas.[54] Nilüfer Göle's analysis of Islamist movements and their access to modern life, especially secular education, also shows how during the appearance of contemporary Islamist movements in Turkey (emerging after the 1950s and growing during the post-1980 period), "peripheral groups were moving to urban centres and gaining access to secular education and to the opportunity of upward social mobility."[55] Many Sufi elders were aware that Islamists were taking control of the country, and this was no good for the secular *Mevlevis*, who desired to restore their beliefs and values in harmony with Atatürk's vision.

Dominant Sufi groups such as *Nakşibendis* continued to increase their influence and secure their place in Turkey by considering the needs of the secular governments and secular citizens. Popular groups such as the *Nakşibendis* sought to influence centre-right political parties, such as the Justice Party (*Adalet Partisi*). They supported centre-right political parties' view of secularism and stopped supporting the religiously oriented political parties, showing the public that they believed that such parties endangered the establishment of democratic values in Turkey.

It was clear that religiously oriented parties' opposition to Atatürk's ideologies could disrupt the social order and peace, provoking a military coup. The success of political Islam in Turkey was achieved by the Islamist Welfare Party (WP), which obtained 21.3 per cent of the total vote and 158 seats in the 550-seat Parliament in 1996. The WP presented its ideas as Just Order (*Adil Düzen*), seeking social and economic equity, honesty, the elimination of corruption, and the reestablishment of cultural authenticity and traditional religious beliefs. With WP politicians' development of Just Order discourse and WP workers' administrative capability, the political party attracted primarily the conservative and culturally alienated middle and upper-middle classes, as well as the economically disadvantaged lower classes.[56]

While simultaneously preaching peace and stability in society, Said Nursi, the leader of the *Nurcus*, made it his goal to save young individuals studying at secular schools from atheism and the students attending religious schools from fanaticism.[57] *Nurcus* presented themselves with a different analysis of Islam,[58] perceiving the idea of science above faith, and were open to secularism.[59] Nursi's commentaries on the Quran, collected in his work *Risale-i Nur* (Epistle of Light), provided a further understanding of Islam and its relationship to modern scientific knowledge. Nursi "developed the teachings of the Quran on the truths of belief that incorporates the traditional Islamic sciences and modern scientific knowledge."[60] Although he did not present himself as a follower of Sufism,

> Nursi retained much more from Sufism than he was ready to admit. Indeed, the *Risale* can be seen as a work of synthesis through which he aimed at simplifying the complex meanings of the Quran and the Sufi cosmology for the ordinary Muslim.[61]

Devotees affiliated with the Nur movement distinguished themselves for upholding a view of religious education that should integrate the teaching of modern secular subjects and especially science. In these years, a variety of Sufi groups and organisations formed, who supported Nursi's vision and believed that they may regain the power they had during the Ottoman Empire.

Nursi's teachings reached and influenced wide swaths of the population with the increase of mass media and improvements in technology. Like works of younger generations, his ideas influenced the creation of a significant Islamic social movement known as the *Nur* movement. The most recognised *Nurcu* group has been the *Fethullahçıs*.[62] Its leader, Fethullah Gülen, a former civil servant, prayer leader and preacher, expressed liberal views in a newspaper interview in 1995, explaining that he urged the individuals who came to pray in his mosque to vote in elections and encouraged them to be understanding of both practising and non-practising Muslims.[63] The movement (which came into being during the late 1960s) first became a nationwide and then a transnational Islamic movement through the establishment of a wide network of media, educational institutions and business organisations both inside and outside of Turkey.[64] Islamists have expanded and have been enriched; the Gülen movement in particular became the main ally and collaborator of the AKP [JDP] government, until their eventual falling-out, which began with the 17–25 December 2013 corruption charges and ended with the 15 July 2016 coup attempt.[65] However, although such religious leaders had articulated certain liberal views and attracted many people with their Sufi-based teachings, most secular elites have had strong ideas about the fact that when a religious leader and/or a religious group is often related to politics, that connection eventually turns into a threat to Turkish democracy and secularism as in the case of Gülen.[66] Most of the minority groups such as the *Mevlevis* and *Rifais* also had such concerns. While dominant groups such as *Nakşibendis*, *Nurcus* and *Fethullahçıs* were working for the mobilisation of political Islam, some minority Sufi groups did not believe in the Islamist vision. As Saygın *dede* expressed, devotees who had faith in the necessity of a secular government were not happy with the use of Islam in state politics.

However, as discussed by Karasipahi and Heper, political Islam gained power in Turkey due to people's dissatisfaction with the performance of the parties in power. The nationalist development project and social democratic parties did not satisfy the needs of the impoverished and marginalised classes. Economic imbalances, increasing unemployment, and corruption were some of the main reasons for the success of the Islamic parties. Karasipahi argues that Islamic revivalism "accelerated and entered a new phase after the 1980s as the Islamic groups began to take advantage of the benefits of modernity and contribute to further politicisation and institutionalisation of Islam."[67] People's demands for a larger political and economic share in the system also played a large role in the success of the Islamist parties.[68] Like the former WP, the insistence of JDP (Justice and Development Party) on social welfare reform together with its Islamic past appealed to a large portion of the population.[69]

Justice and Development Party, Turkish Adalet ve Kalkınma Partisi (AKP), also called AK Party or Turkish AK Parti, came to power in Turkey in the general elections of 2002. JDP, drawing support from non-secular Turks, has been in power since 2002. The party, supported by the conservative Turks, has won six consecutive parliamentary elections and continued to face objections from secular segments of Turkish society due to its tactics for hiding its Islamist agenda. Today, due to JDP's conservative policies, many secular Turks feel unheard and left out in Turkey, while conservative religious groups receive the kind of support that they haven't had since the 1920's revolution. *Nakşibendis* have become more and more rigid and critical about how Islam should be practised in the last twenty years, especially with the strengthening of the JDP and their political Islamic discourse. Although, at first, RAD was created to serve Atatürk's modernisation plan, later, it has lost its sole purpose and has begun to serve Islamist's political agenda.[70] While through the use of RAD, the public expressions of Islam were restricted during the revolution, under JDP's rule, it has been used to promote a state-favoured conservative understanding of Islam.[71] Since then, the practice of Islam in the mosques has been confined to RAD's values, as if every Muslim shared the same Islamic path or as if every Muslim had to think, feel, speak and live the same way.

Mevlevi and *Rifai* devotees (discussed in this book) disagree with "the one sided and strictly doctrinal" values of the RAD.[72] They disagree with RAD's act of entitlement about how people should live in Turkey. It bothers them that *imams* receive the contents of their speech from a government organisation (the RAD), which seems to manipulate many young Turks with ideas about how any Muslim is responsible with the knowledge of specific Sunni doctrines. Such acts of Islamisation started to grow in 2010, when the RAD has risen in prominence with JDP's financial and moral support. The RAD's budget has grown tremendously under the JDP. Quran courses have drastically increased for students of all ages. The RAD, originally created during the revolution to only oversee religious affairs in the state, is now firmly under the control of President Erdoğan, issuing fatwas, wading into political issues and backing up the Islamist agenda. Today, the RAD is a super-sized organisation that is responsible for the promotion of Sunni Islam.[73] Although many Sufi groups in Turkey had adopted the Sunni doctrine, they did not agree with RAD's one-sided and fundamentalist perception of Sunni teachings. Although the majority of Sufi organisations had been adherents of Sunni Islam, there are differences of opinions about interpreting the Quran and the hadiths.

Tezcür's discussion highlights RAD's position further: "Turkish secularism is not only characterised by the marginalisation of religion's role in public life, but also the complete control of religious organisations by the state [Religious Affairs Directorate]."[74] Since then, RAD has controlled the mosques and *imams* by imposing specific Sunni Islamic values as the only way of Islam so that "Alevi minorities began to publicly criticise state policies for promoting Sunni Islam as the official state religion, under the guise of secularism."[75] As a result of RAD, not only Alevis but many religious groups such as post-tariqa *Mevlevi* and *Rifai* groups that are not aligned with RAD's Islamist vision despised RAD's messages as non-Islamic.

Melih, another *Mevlevi dede*, stated "my worries were not in vain."[76] He explained how he never wanted to be a part of any Sufi or Sufi-esque groups' Islamist agenda. For this reason, for Melih *dede*, it was a better choice to work in harmony with the government's commodification project. According to Melih *dede*, *Mevlevi* teachings (including rituals and poetry) play a significant role in the generation of a moderate Islamic vision in Turkey's future. It is also for this reason, *Mevlevis* like Melih *dede* and Narin *dede* wanted to take every opportunity to share Rumi's vision by accepting, embracing and embodying the commodification of their sacred whirling ritual. Despite their financial needs for ritual space and lodging, many minority post-tariqa groups have centred their devotion on the practice of sacred arts and refused to participate in political gatherings. For Narin *dede*, Sufi political groups' intentions have always been clear regarding Islamisation of the Turkish government. He added, "me and my friends never trusted politicisation of *Mevlevi* or any Sufi ritual. Commodification was better that politicisation."[77] Although, there was hope about Islamist parties' act of moderating "their discourse" and that even some of the most radical groups, as Soner Çağatay examines, would choose to "recognise that Turkey will remain somehow secular,"[78] many devotees believed that "Sufism and politics should not be in the same heart."[79] As explained by several elderly *Mevlevi* devotees I have encountered throughout my fieldwork, Islamists that tried to embody a moderate Islamic vision were not as transparent in their future endeavours as many had hoped.

In his original work, *Islam and the Secular State*, Abdullahi Ahmed An-Na'im argues for the need of a secular government, explaining, "In order to be a Muslim by conviction and free choice, which is the only way one can be a Muslim, I need a secular state."[80] Only a secular state can be impartial to all religious doctrine to embrace the idea that "compliance with Sharia cannot be coerced by fear of state institutions or faked to appease their officials."[81] Only a secular state can inspire the idea of religious piety out of "honest conviction."[82] In line with this view, some *Mevlevi* post-tariqa practices depict how devotees perceive any form of strict demand on following religious beliefs as false piousness and deceit. Aside from what is visible in the media about political Sufi groups taking stands against modern and secular values of the Turkish State, there have also been minority post-tariqa groups that have moved beyond the confines of discriminatory religious dogmas and created temporary spaces that support the idea of Sufism as what Narin *dede* explains as "a versatile tradition," constantly changing according to the devotees' needs.

As I will examine in detail in Chapter 3, Narin *dede* "have moved beyond such limitations and have used their ritual performances as a medium to create temporary sacred spaces."[83] In one of our private conversations, he explained:

> This to me was much more agreeable with my beliefs and values. I just wanted to practice *Mevlevi* sacred arts. Making sacred songs is my

devotion. My sacred art is not acceptable for the eyes and ears of conservative groups, who define themselves through the master [Rumi], limiting him to their discriminatory ideals. Such groups have gained their wealth and position by accepting the conditions of the Religious Affairs Directorate in Turkey. To them, Islam had nothing to do with whirling and singing. To me whirling, music and poetry is the core of Islam.

When I talk about post-tariqa Sufism in this book, as I discussed earlier, I refer to groups and individuals that design a performance-centred devotion and believe that focusing on performing Sufi music, whirling and poetry as sacred art forms has the potential to lead them to God's unity.

Despite their visibility, it was difficult to connect with *Mevlevis* who would be willing to talk about their post-tariqa worship and plans for mobilisation. Later, I found out that most were tired of the threatening comments of conservative Muslims and impolite questions and ideas of secular elites and only wanted to communicate their beliefs and values through whirling. For a long time, I attended a variety of commodified classes and workshops. Without asking questions, I watched their performances over and over again. It took me a while to realise how most of the staff working in the venues that housed whirling ritual performances recognised the *semazens* solely as dancers.

I have notes about the staff working in tourist agencies or performance organisations warning me that I would have to look for the *Mevlevis* elsewhere, "probably outside of Turkey," because to them "these performers [were] not *Mevlevis*, they [were] just dancers acting as whirling dervishes."[84] This felt like an act of ignorance to many *Mevlevis*. As Melih *dede* jokingly said: "Since our sacred spaces were reclassified as museums and our sema ceremony was advertised as folk performance or tourist attraction, it was not surprising that our *semazens* [were] called dancers."[85] I knew from one of the events he organised in the Galata *Mevlevi* lodge that he was not against the rumour that he was called a dancer. He was against the fact that being a dancer meant that he was not a *Mevlevi*. At that time, there were many quarrels between conservative Sufi groups and as some devotees emphasised, versatile Sufi groups that Islamists perceived as radical due to their inclination to restore or renew Sufi practice. Between 2008 and 2013, some of the devotees took initiatives to convince the Ministry of Culture to issue a formal notice to prevent the practice of *sema* as a dance show. On the one hand, acceptance of *Mevlevi sema* as a religious ritual rather than merely folk performance was a promising development for many *Mevlevis*. More importantly, both the conservative and versatile groups agreed that the ceremony was not only a folk performance. They also agreed that it was not an entertainment as many event agencies deemed and used in weddings or other social events. However, as more open-minded devotees highlighted, this was also an act of limiting *Mevlevi* beliefs and values to the conservative visions of the Islamists. Many political Islamist Sufi groups (or conservative devotees) knew that there were many female *semazens* or male *semazens* (that they deemed to be non-devotees) performing the ritual in a variety of public spaces. They were also aware that there were more and more people who considered themselves *Mevlevi* students and promoted the all-embracing and less doctrinal Islamic vision with their *Mevlevi* gatherings and ritual performances. Although I will discuss this conflict in more detail in Chapter 3, in the next section I will examine Saygın *dede*'s group, which is known for their desire to stay in harmony both with Atatürk's secular vision and with the Islamists.

Yenikapı *Mevlevi* Lodge

The day I entered the Yenikapı *Mevlevi* lodge for the first time in October 2010, my mind was full of imaginings about the everyday life of the *Mevlevi* dervishes when the lodge was built in 1597. This time it was open. I stopped at the gate and waited for the gatekeeper to finish his conversation with his co-worker. Then, I informed him that I was invited for *sema* lessons, which were also organised as part of Istanbul-European Capital of Culture 2010 organised events, another threshold leading me as a researcher into the *Mevlevi* culture. He welcomed me inside and directed me to a large building in the complex. Once again, the courtyard seemed extremely quiet. I remember feeling a bit uncomfortable. As I entered the building where the classes are held, I heard ladies talking in a room, walked by the entrance and peeked my head in to ask for the classes. As soon as they saw me, I was welcomed with a Sufi greeting gesture and, without talking, as if rehearsed, they placed their right hands on their hearts and nodded their heads forward. Their humble gesture was enough for me to take off my shoes, enter the room and take a seat near them.

Listening to their intimate conversations about family and health, watching them sitting in comfort and peace in the room, I thought how these devotees belonged to this space, embodying and transmitting the beliefs and values that flourished in the rooms of the historical lodge. I sat in the room with the devotees for fifteen minutes before the class. Two were reading *Mesnevi*; one was meditating (performing *zikir* quietly—repeating God's names) as she moved the beads on her *tesbih*; one was bringing in pastries and water while another was serving tea. One devotee walked into the class and began to serve water to everyone in the room. When she approached me with a tray full of glasses, first she lowered her body down to serve and smiled. She seemed very content with serving her friends. Younger devotees were conveying a sense of precision, care and love as they walked around the room, preparing food and serving the devotees sitting on the cushions on the floor. This act of *hizmet* (service) was a ritual that was practised in many Ottoman Sufi lodges. For *Mevlevis*, it was also a ritual performed as part of the *çile* (trial) training, a way to test a student's ability to stay in peace with her/his duties. In the Ottoman *Mevlevi* tariqas, devotees used to live together and perform certain tasks reminding themselves all was done for God and with God in mind. This gathering was also an opportunity for restoring *hizmet*.

It was clear that the government was allowing *Mevlevi* gatherings organised as part of *Tourism and Promotion Projects of Istanbul 2010 European Capital of Culture Program*. This was a project titled as Introduction of the Mawlawi [*Mevlevi*] Culture and Sema Ceremony. As part of the project, devotees were going to organise a total of fifty-nine *sema* ceremonies in 2010. There were also exhibitions that included photographs, illustrations and other artworks related to the *Mevlevi* culture. Also, there were roundtables attended by local and foreign speakers and classical Turkish music and Sufi music concerts on a monthly basis.[86] Around the same time, a journalist, James Bedding, presented a guide for sights and attractions organised for Istanbul-European Capital of Culture 2010 and pointed out: "A good place to learn about Sufi culture is at the *Introduction to Mevlevi Culture*, to be held every Sunday throughout the year at the Yenikapi *Mevlevi* Lodge."[87] During the events organised for Istanbul-European Capital of Culture of 2010, I met with Saygın *dede*, who at the time was teaching Rumi's *Mesnevi* and whirling ritual to a group of devotees, as well as organising the ceremonies performed simultaneously as worship and tourist attraction. Having met with Saygın *dede*, I found out that the government supported the participation of *Mevlevi* devotees under a secular organisation created by the *dede*. The designation of *sema* ceremony as part of World Intangible Cultural Heritage by UNESCO encouraged the Turkish government in 2009 to support projects that would include the direct participation of dervishes to enact the complete form of *sema* ceremony for tourists. It was clear once again that a lot had changed since the first ceremony performed as a folk performance in the 1950s.

For Saygın *dede*, it was his duty to restore *Mevlevi* beliefs and values in the Yenikapı *Mevlevi* Lodge, one of the most sacred spaces in Turkey (due to the presence of tombs of *Mevlevi* sheikhs in the lodge). Although Saygın *dede* expressed his contentment with taking part in the events, his voice was very emotional when he talked about the Yenikapı *Mevlevi* Lodge as a space of divine love. He liked to talk about the *dedes*, who lived and trained in the dervish rooms of the lodge during the Ottoman Empire. Saygın *dede* believed that one way to restore their beliefs and values was by using their Ottoman dervish lodges for their ritual meetings. For Saygın *dede*, *semahanes* (in the case of the *Mevlevi* lodges, large halls designed and organised for the performance of *Sema* ceremony) were crucial for the performance of the *Mevlevi* ceremony since these halls (due to the circular shape of the hall and the presence of the tombs) were designed specifically for the whirling rituals.

Saygın *dede* believed that a *semahane*, as a designated ritual space designed specifically for each devotional act, was necessary to perform the ceremony organised by Sultan Veled's son Pir Adel Çelebi. This was probably why the complete version of *Mevlevi sema* was only available at the *semahanes* of the historical *Mevlevi* lodges and the Mevlana Cultural Centre, a space constructed for the *Şeb-i Arus* (the day mystic Mevlana Celaleddin Rumi passed away) ceremonies that take place every year in Konya. The *Mevlevi sema* ceremony has been a lengthy ritual with sections including meditative walks, Quranic prayers and recitations from the Mesnevi. As I will discuss in the next section, when *sema* was enacted at the *semahane* of the Yenikapı *Mevlevi* lodge, Saygın *dede* and his devotees followed the full structure of the ceremony as organised by Sultan Veled's son Pir Adel Çelebi. The full ceremony, also called *Ayin-i Şerif*, was loaded with specific cultural and spiritual meaning.

Whirling Ritual: *Mevlevi* Practice of Remembrance

Not leaving any performative devotional moment out, Saygın *dede*'s ceremony started with the members of the orchestra taking their places quietly. Then, a *semazen* walked in to bring the red-dyed sheepskin mat called the *post*, where the leader of the order sits,[88] slowly and gently placing it on the floor. His actions were performative conveying a sense of ownership as he walked through the *semahane* holding the *post* that represents the seat passed to the spiritual leader (in this case, Saygın dede) by his spiritual guide.[89] Then, the *semazens* in their white *tennures* started to enter the *semahane* one by one, also walking slowly and gently. First, they took a bow in the direction of the red *post* and then walked to their sheepskins that were placed on the floor before the ritual, one next to the other. As Turkish historian Metin And explains, devotees believe that there is an imaginary line called *hatt-i istiva* (the equator) that divides the floor space into two symmetrical sections, starting from the *post* and extending to the entrance.[90] Throughout the ceremony, *semazens* carefully stepped over this line as they walked, due to its signification as the shortest path to reality and unity with God. Then, Saygın *dede* entered and very slowly walked to his *post*, conveying a sense of solemness. After he took his place standing in front of the red *post*, *semazens* took another bow altogether and followed the *dede*'s lead to sit down on their sheepskins and kissed the floor of the *semahane*. Every moment of the ritual was filled with devotional sounds and gestures.

In the first part of the ceremony, *Naathan* (the person who sings *Naat-ı Serif*, one of Mevlana's eulogies praising Prophet Muhammed) sang *Naat-Serif* (lines that praise Prophet Muhammed recited as a hymn without rhythm).[91] In this section, *semazens* remained calm and quiet in a sitting meditation. Staying in this state of meditation, *semazens*' concentration and discipline conveyed a sense of care, loyalty and commitment. There was complete silence in the *semahane*, and most of the *semazens* kept their eyes closed. After the *Naat-i Sharif*, the second part of the ceremony began with the chief double-drum player playing four notes as a sign. This, as Çelebi explains, symbolises Allah's message to His creation: "Be."[92] Then, in the third part, the reed flautist played a *taksim*, a kind of improvised piece, which was followed by another instrumental piece (*peşrev*, meaning prelude).[93] In the fourth part, called "Devr-i Veled," devotees' movements were supported by a musical part. Led by Saygın *dede*, as the spiritual leader, all the *semazens* stood in line and started walking after each other. They saluted each other in front of the *post* to slowly and deliberately started encircling the hall three times. Before the encircling, the *semazen* who arrived in front of the *dede*'s post positioned himself on the other side of the *hatt-i istiva* to come face to face, bow and greet the *semazen* following him. In this part, the *semazens* circumambulated the hall three times very slowly conveying their presence. As they walked, their bodies also reflected their sense of obedience and loyalty to the *dede* and the tombs present in the ritual space. After the third rotation, the *dede* took his place on the *post*. Saygın *dede* turned to the hall and greeted by bending his neck slightly.[94] In the fifth part, while the *peşrev* was being played, the *semazens* placed their black *hırkas* (cloaks) on the floor, carefully folded them three times, with the belief that each fold has a specific meaning: love, beauty and unity. As Nirgül Kılınç notes: "The whirling dervishes' black clothes symbolise their tomb, and their caps called *sikke* symbolises their tombstone."[95] At this moment, the space was vibrating with the crying sound of the *ney* (reed flute), communicating a sense of loss, longing and yearning.[96] The use of the ritual props and gestural interactions between devotees were establishing a sense of occupation or becoming one with the space.

When the Four *Selams* (greetings) started, the chief *semazen* walked towards the *dede*, kissed his hand with a sense of respect and care and the *dede* in turn kissed his *sikke*. This action performed by the *dede* indicated the authorisation and blessing given to the *semazenbaşı* (chief *semazen*) to begin the *sema* ceremony. The *semazens*, one by one, walked to the *dede* to receive his blessing and started to whirl, bending their heads slightly towards one shoulder, reflecting a sense of innocence and trust towards *Saygın dede* as their spiritual guide. As the speed of their turning increased, they kept their arms with the right palm turned to the sky (receiving divine light), and the left lowered with the palm turned downward (giving the divine energy to the earth through the thumb of the left hand), continuously whirling to the left towards their heart. *Semazens'* left feet also never left the ground throughout the whirling, fixing their body and the energy received into the earth. It was as if with each high-speed whirling, *semazens'* bodies, with *tennures'* and *sikkes'* colours mixing with the light colours of the walls and floors of the *semahane*, were becoming one with the space.

Nirgül Kılınç, Metin And, Cemalnur Sargut and many more scholars who have researched *Sema* discuss the "whirling of the body around itself" as "*çark.*"[97] Kılınç points out to the analysis of Cemalnur Sargut (a well-known female *Rifai* dervish and scholar) to discuss how

> dervishes turn around the ritual hall while whirling around themselves from right to left . . . *Mevlevi*s relate this movement to the turning of the electrons around atom . . . everything in the universe is always on action and on the move like whirling dervishes do.[98]

58 *Restoring*

This section, also called, Four *Selams*, included a final section, in which the *dede* himself slowly whirled to the centre, of both the equator and the hall performing what *Mevlevis* call *post sema'i* (the place of *Mevlana* and his followers by succession). As And says, "In this section with the yearning sound of the *ney*, the sound of the feet of the dancers and the rustle coming from their skirts make a unique harmony."[99] The solo sound of the *ney* transformed the room into a quieter and calmer environment, allowing the audience to hear the subtle footsteps of the *semazens* moving across the floor. In these last whirling moments, *semazens* turned slower, conveying a sense of peace. The strength of the mind of the *semazens*, their physical and mental presence and the discipline that they revealed inspired affection, kindness and openness. When Saygın *dede* turned back to the post, the *ney*'s improvisation and the whole *sema* stopped abruptly. Then, one of the singers recited from the Quran, reminding everyone once again that *semazens* whirled for devotion. In this sixth part, *semazens* sat and stayed bent after they kissed the floor of their ritual hall. There, they listened to the verses of the Quran in a state of meditation. In the final (seventh) part, the *semazens* returned to their *posts*, put on their outer garments and moved into a state of meditation with the chief *semazen*'s recitation of a prayer called *Dua-gu duası*, which was performed for their *pir* (Mevlana Celalleddin-i Rumi) and all the Sufi saints.[100] The performance ended with this final prayer. The sense of worship served as a form of communicable effect, arising from the way the devotees saluted each other and walked around the space in silence, their eyes loosely focused on their actions. Each gesture, according to Saygın *dede*, was specific in restoring their desire to overcome the egotism of the self. Saygın *dede* and the whirling dervishes left the space quietly and no one clapped, following the requests of the devotees who welcomed the audience at the door before the ceremony and as a result of the sensations conveyed by the devotees.

The ritual gathering at the Yenikapı *Mevlevi* lodge was reflective of both the conservative religious and secular values of contemporary Turkey. To stay in harmony with the values and beliefs of conservative religious vision of the RAD and other organisations, throughout the ceremony, only male dervishes whirled. This choice did not specifically reflect Saygın *dede*'s post-tariqa vision since he was more flexible in his whirling classes. The reflection of secular values was also clear with male and female devotees sitting side by side in the *semahane*. Also, hijab was not obligatory as in the mosques. On the contrary, there were many female devotees attending in their shorts. As Micu identifies, "we might choose to change the way we perform a certain ritual to make a point about the status quo that the ritual upholds or represents."[101] In this case, Saygın *dede* was making a point about the existing state of Islamic politics that regulated women's position in public. Although he respected the values of the conservative Sufi circles and did not allow mixed-gender performances, he was at least managing to change the way the ritual was received. Ultimately, it was his goal to create a gender-neutral whirling ritual performance. When I asked Deniz (one of the female devotees) about mixed seating, she explained that *Saygın dede* thinks it is necessary to move beyond certain religious rules to embody the secular values of Turkish society. *Saygın dede* was a secular devotee who believed that Islamic rules and principles should change according to modern values. Later, having watched female devotees' practice of whirling with *Saygın dede*, I asked Deniz, a female devotee, why only male dervishes performed in public ritual gatherings. She explained that there were some principles that Saygın *dede* preserved in public to avoid any conflict with the RAD and conservative Sufi groups. While some of the groups, like Saygın *dede* and his devotees, wanted to avoid conflict with the conservative groups and institutions and limited their practice of post-tariqa *Mevlevi* vision in government-sponsored events, there were also *Mevlevi* devotees, who were adamant about showing their all-embracing and gender-neutral post-tariqa vision in a variety of public sites (as I will discuss in detail in Chapter 3). These groups often articulated how *Mevlevi* practice of whirling was not an organised ceremony in Rumi's time. Today, there are many individuals and groups who share this idea and disregard any rule to practice the full version of the *Mevlevi* ceremony in the historical lodges. Saygın *dede* articulated that both groups were necessary to restore and mobilise *Mevlevi* tradition as a versatile post-tariqa practice in Turkey.[102] His main concern was his longing for a more permanent practice in the historical lodges in the presence of *Mevlevi* tombs.

Having visited various religious spaces such as *Mevlevi* lodges and Syrian monasteries in Turkish cities located in the Aegean, Marmara, Black Sea, Central Anatolia and Southeastern Anatolia regions of Turkey to converse with religious leaders, staff and others, I have come to understand the significance of sacred space production and maintenance for any religious group to live and train with people who share common beliefs and values. In 2014, when I visited Syriac Orthodox Monasteries in Southeastern Anatolia, I witnessed how and why devotees kept their sacred spaces active as lodgings in the sense that religious leaders and devotees regularly lived and practised their devotional living and considered their spaces as the source of their spiritual wealth and peace. When a devotee in the Deyrul Zafaran Monastery showed me the rooms in which they worshipped, he emphasised more than once the religious meaning and significance of their monastery in their religious practice. He said that they regularly trained there as they interacted with each other, shared ideas, worshipped and educated young devotees. This was very similar to the *Mevlevi çile* (trial) training that was once practised in the Yenikapı *Mevlevi* lodge.

What I did not know back then was that, as Pena states, "individual acts combined with collective efforts such as singing and praying make space sacred."[103] As Merin Shobhana Xavier examines:

> In Sufi traditions, spaces are often centralised around the authority of a shaykh. It is the spiritual and charismatic authority of the shaykh that

enables him or her to transmit *baraka*, or blessings, both in life and more so in death.[104]

Also as Pnina Werbner and Helena Basu discuss how Sufi masters, with their prayers "shape and reshape a sacred landscape."[105] Despite the reduced authority of the spiritual leader and a lack of formal alliance in post-tariqa groups, this sense of spiritual presence (*baraka*) conveyed by a Sufi teacher is still present. It was Saygın *dede*'s calm and comforting presence that made the historical space a temporary sacred home for his students. However, more importantly, aside from his charisma, what shaped sacred space, as Pena examines, was the embodied acts of the devotees. It was clear that aside from the presence of the tombs, it was Saygın *dede*'s and his devotees embodied acts that sacralised the Yenikapı *Mevlevi* Lodge.

Here, as Pena describes further, "A performance optic helps refocus our attention towards the places and times where power wordlessly changes hands—interactions that often define a community."[106] *Semazens*' whirling with their heads slightly bent and their arms raised and open, suggestive of their naïveté, represented what Metin And describes as "an act and drama of faith."[107] Although the event was not a theatre performance, devotees' act of worship was performative and theatrical in the sense that it created extremely powerful focus and put some audience members in a state of meditation. Some cried. Some placed their hands on their beating hearts. Some watched without any movement going into a deep state of meditation. Some said they felt ecstatic. The presence that devotees achieved seemed to be contagious.

The experience of commitment and joy conveyed in the Yenikapı *Mevlevi* Lodge did not occur only during the whirling ritual but also in the aftermath, when the audience extended the sensations experienced while witnessing the ceremony by sharing their feelings and observations. Some audience members were chatting about Sufi retreat centres. A group of elderly audience members, who were a British family, shared their knowledge of Rumi's teachings about divine love while others observed the lodge itself, staring at the windows and doors searching for signs of the dervishes' everyday lives. Some audience members were also conveying their perception of the space as a sacred Sufi lodge. One of the tourists asked me whether or not the dervishes lived in the lodge, and I replied that the space was no longer an active sacred lodge and that the dervishes only used the lodge during the daytime for Sufi classes and ritual performances.

There were also audience members waiting to chat with male and female devotees, who were standing by the entrance of the *semahane* planning their next meetings and gatherings. A Turkish audience member, a female graduate student, who knew one of the devotees, continued to wait to speak to Saygın *dede*. Selen, one of the devotees, introduced her to Saygın *dede*, who invited her to his Thursday night class. For this audience member, the historical Sufi lodge was a sacred space and the event was more than an introduction to *Mevlevi* culture. It was an act of remembering divine meaning. She was occupying the space as a seeker waiting to speak to Saygın *dede*, to witness the devotees' devotional acts and to ask his permission to attend his upcoming classes and gatherings.

What altered the meaning and feeling in the Yenikapı *Mevlevi* lodge was the embodied acts of the followers. As de Certeau suggests, space is always in the process of transformation.[108] As in Peña's analysis of the Second Tepeyac in relation to de Certeau's theory, the development of sacred space "is contingent on the multiple layers of institutional and popular history, shifting political and economic climates, and the living, breathing bodies that give meaning and make sense of the space."[109] Peña describes further how when left alone, "the shrine would remain a superficial structure invoking but never realising the vibrancy and legitimacy of its counterpart."[110] As in the case of the Second Tepeyac, the renovated lodge becomes a sacred space with devotees' movements and words shaping the halls and rooms of the lodge. The sacred space production meant restoring Sufi practice as well as the space. Pena's analysis of Gaudalupan performatic processes informs how devotees' "voices raised in ecstasy, their praying and dancing bodies in motion, the labor and care they offer to maintain the shrine—inscribe their histories, beliefs, and aspirations on the environment."[111] Before and after the ceremony, *semazens* greeted other devotees from their group using physical gestures specific to *Mevlevis*. They held and kissed each other's right hands and saluted with their right hands on their hearts. The sense of simplicity and peace in their actions created an intimate atmosphere for an audience consisting of a group of tourists (having seen the event advertised in the brochure of *Istanbul 2010 European Capital of Culture Program*), guests (people who either attended Saygın *dede*'s classes or devotees' friends) and devotees of the group. Devotees were also very respectful and loving to each other and behaved the same way to all audience members. They were enthusiastic, energetic and affectionate as they conversed with one another and their guests. As one of the devotees explained, he perceived the lodge as a temporary home of divine love and sharing, while another devotee pointed out that the audience members were their guests and she wanted to make sure that they were comfortable and peaceful during their time in the lodge.

These were acts of restoration. Before the *Sema* ceremony, when we (as the audience members) started to take our shoes off to enter the *semahane*, the devotees welcomed us at the door. They seemed to enjoy communicating with the guests very much as they entered the *semahane* one by one, with a calm voice, smiling and answering quick questions in Turkish and English. Everyone received a booklet that provided a brief historical overview of Rumi as the *pir* of the *Mevlevi* order, his work and *Mevlevi* culture. The information in the booklet stated that *sema* was a religious *zikir* ceremony where the dervishes used whirling to achieve a union with God. We were also asked to be respectful and stay quiet during the ritual. Clapping during or after the ceremony, leaving our seats or taking flash photographs was not allowed. In these cultural events at the lodge, the application of rules to peacefully perform the ritual was the affirmation of the respect granted to the devotees. However, more than the information in the booklet, it was devotees' kind and humble words and gestures that won the respect and admiration of the audience.

As these devotees explained, if they presented their gatherings as cultural events, they managed to receive permission to use the sacred lodges, but most of the time, they needed some sort of reference to manage such affairs. *Saygın dede* and his devotees received access to use the space only for one year as part of the events organised for Istanbul-European Capital of Culture 2010. When the event ended, the devotees' emotions were twofold. They were happy to have had the chance to worship and share their beliefs and values in the lodge, but they were sad that they had to leave. As Deniz explained, she felt overjoyed coming to the lodge in the morning and yet felt heartbroken that she had to leave at the closing time of the museum. She said it was not only that she had to leave the space but also that she had to return to spaces that require another set of actions and interactions that had nothing to do with her devotional living. Since then, not much has changed, devotees have been using the lodge by applying for permission from the government to create cultural events. Performing rituals daily in the sacred lodges has been out of the question.

Unlike orthodox Syriac monasteries in the southeast of Turkey, such as the Deyrulzafaran Monastery in Mardin, in which monks lived, worshipped and trained together, *Mevlevi* devotees lacked such privilege. Since certain qualities of monastic life are vital to Sufi devotional living—such as renouncing worldly life, seeking a life separated from society, seeking reclusion for meditation and exhausting the body through hard physical labour—they long for such a privilege in contemporary Turkey. Due to a lack of communal living and training spaces, some devotees moved to Europe and the United States and managed to raise funds to build *Mevlevi* lodges to preserve their customs. Others, who stayed in Turkey, had to take every opportunity to use the lodges as museum sites. In our conversations, although Saygın *dede* several times expressed his gratitude for the opportunity to worship in the historical *semahane* with his devotees and share the experience with non-devotees, he admitted his longing for the old days, the times before the closure of Sufi lodges when all the dervishes lived and trained together. He said if he were a dervish living with his teacher in this lodge, he would spend most of the day awake, serving, walking in the courtyard, meditating in his cell (meaning the small room for dervishes), writing religious poetry and composing music. He said although he did not resist the social and political changes (including the closure of Sufi lodges) that have affected Sufi devotees' lives, he longed for a devotional living experience in a permanent *Mevlevi* space, where he could be surrounded by other *dedes* and dervishes.

Saygın *dede* referred to the importance of living together in a *Mevlevi* lodge in order to fulfil the needs of the *nefs* training that used to exist in the *Mevlevi* tariqas during the Ottoman Empire. As I spent more time with the

Mevlevis in the lodge, I have come to understand the isolation experienced by the devotees due to their inability to use the lodges for communal activities and their commitment to consecrating the places they occupy temporarily. As Saygın *dede* explained, *Mevlevis* experienced *çile* training by looking for ways to mobilise their devotional practice in alternative ways and spaces. This was a training because they had to stay at peace when dealing with such hardships. Working hard to organise as many ritual performances as possible (especially the ones organised in the sacred Sufi sites) has been his devotees' devotional labour. As I participated in Quran, *Mesnevi* and *sema* lessons with Saygın *dede*'s devotees, I witnessed how they used their time effectively and struggled with the fact that they could use the space only for the duration of the cultural event.

Despite all the hardships, Saygın *dede* believed that it was his and other *Mevlevi* teacher's duty to show that *Mevlevi* lodges were not abandoned and only the presence of *Mevlevi semazens* could bring out the meaning these sacred spaces deserved. Saygın *dede* was adamant about restoring *Mevlevi* devotional life and carrying out his post-tariqa vision by organising *sema* classes in the historical lodges. He performed and taught whirling. This was his way of restoring his practice of remembrance (*zikir*). He believed that the desire to learn about Rumi's whirling brought individuals together and guided the process of restoring post-tariqa *Mevlevi* devotional life. This idea of restoration (as staying open to change) allowed him to adapt to social and political conditions in Turkey. Although he did not explain how, he also said maybe one day he may find a way to produce a permanent space for devotees to train together night and day, maintaining accessibility for individuals from different cultural and religious backgrounds. This was his and his students' ultimate hope. The next chapter will be about a post-tariqa *Rifai* group (whose master and teacher is simultaneously a *Mevlevi* and *Rifai*), which has realised this vision. Also, as I will discuss in detail, this has been a *Rifai* group that has managed to restore *Mevlevi çile* (trial) training (that required collective living and training) in two permanent training sites.

Notes

1 Honouring the restoration of Yenikapı Mevlevihanesi, the Republic of Turkey Ministry Directorate General of Foundation published a book about the *Mevlevi* Lodge, which has been very helpful, considering the lack of information about its history and cultural life. The book can be obtained from the *Mevlevihane*. Nezih Üzel, *Aşıklarin Dünyası: Yenikapı Mevlevihanesi [World of Lovers: Yenikapı Mevlevi Lodge]* (Ankara: Republic of Turkey Ministry Directorate General of Foundation, 2010).
2 Bethan McKernan, "Erdoğan Leads First Prayers at Hagia Sophia Museum Reverted to Mosque," *The Guardian*, July 4, 2020, https://www.theguardian.com/world/2020/jul/24/erdogan-prayers-hagia-sophia-museum-turned-mosque.
3 Amberin Zaman, "Erdogan's Order Making Hagia Sophia Mosque Brings Cheers, Mourning," *Al-Monitor*, July 10, 2020, https://www.al-monitor.com/pulse/originals/2020/07/turkey-hagia-sophia-church-mosque-erdogan-divide-pompeo.

64 Restoring

html#ixzz6est3NNwC. Also cited in Ishaan Tharoor, "The Trouble with Making Hagia Sophia a Mosque Again," *The Washington Post*, July 13, 2020, https://www.washingtonpost.com/world/2020/07/13/hagia-sofia-mosque-erdogan/.

4 Personal communication, August 5, 2020, July 11, 2020.

5 Fatih Sultan Mehmet Vakıf University is founded in 2010 by a group of foundations that carried out Islamist worldviews. This was a time in which JDP government made some of the significant government sites available for the use of religious foundations that support their political vision.

6 Volm, "The Making of Sufism: The Gülen Movement and Its Efforts to Create a New Image," In *Global Sufism*, ed. Francesco Piraino and Mark Sedgwick (London: Hurst & Company, 2019) 190. Volm discusses "it would be an exaggeration to speak of the Gülen Movement as a Sufi movement. There neither exist traditional *zikir* ceremonies, identifiably Sufi styles of clothing, nor elements typical of other Sufi movements. Therefore, the Gülen Movement is Sufiesque but not truly Sufi, which is why internal texts written before the coup attempt to speak of Fethullah Gülen as a 'Sufi in his own way', a 'contemporary Sufi' (Çağdaş bir Sufi) or a 'Post-Sufi'. In any case, the movement can also be described as a representative of a post-tarikat-Sufism." More on the terms used to define the Gülen movement can be found in the following sources: Zeki Sarıtoprak, "Fethullah Gülen: A Sufi in His Own Way," in *Turkish Islam and the Secular State: The Gülen Movement*, ed. M. Hakan Yavuz and John L. Esposito (New York: Syracuse University Press, 2003), 164; M. Enes Ergene, Geleneğin Modern Çağa Tanıklığı: *Gülen Hareketinin Analizi [Tradition Witnessing to the Modern Age: Analysis of the Gülen Movement]* (İstanbul: Yeni Akademi Yayınları, 2005), 357; Doğan Koç, *Strategic Defamation of Fethullah Gülen: English vs. Turkish* (Lanham: University Press of America, 2012), 7.

7 Hülya Küçük, "Sufi Reactions After Turkey's National Struggle," in *The State and The Subaltern: Modernisation, Society and the State in Turkey and Iran*, ed. Touraj Atabaki (London: I.B. Tauris, 2007), 123–143.

8 Küçük, "Sufi Reactions After Turkey's National Struggle," 139.

9 Semiha Ayverdi, Ken'an *Rifai* ve Yirminci Asrın Işığında Müslümanlık *[Ken'an Rifai and Islam in the Light of the Twentieth Century]* (İstanbul: Hülbe, 1983), 17–100.

10 Sencer Ayata, "Patronage, Party, and the State: The Politicisation of Islam in Turkey," *Middle East Journal* 50, no. 1 (1996): 40–56, accessed October 29, 2020, http://www.jstor.org/stable/4328895.

11 Cemal Kafadar, "The New Visibility of Sufism in Turkish Studies and Cultural Life," in *The Dervish Lodge: Architecture, Art and Sufism in Ottoman Turkey*, ed. Raymond Lifchez (Berkeley: University of California Press, 1992), 307–322.

12 Kafadar, *The New Visibility of Sufism*, 313; Suha Tabi-Farouki, *Beshara and Ibn Arabi: A Movement of Sufi Spirituality in the Modern World* (Oxford: Anqa Publishing, 2007), 71.

13 Melih *dede* considers himself both as a *Mevlevi* and a *Rifai* because his spiritual teacher, who passed away, had trained first in a *Mevlevi*, then in a *Rifai* order in India. Melid *dede*'s Sufi teacher (shaikh) had been an initiated dervish in a *Mevlevi* order, who has received his right to teach the *Mevlevi* way and lead a *Mevlevi* order. However, then he had chosen to continue his devotional practices with a *Rifai* sheikh and also had received permission to teach the *Rifai* way and lead a *Rifai* order.

14 Personal communications with *Mevlevi* and *Rifai* devotees.

15 Lewis, *The Emergence of Modern Turkey*, 410–411.

16 Zürcher, *Turkey: A Modern History*, 191–192; Lewis, *The Emergence of Modern Turkey*, 410–411.

17 Mustafa Kemal Atatürk, *Nutuk [Oration]* (Ankara: Türk Tarih Kurumu Yayınları, 1981 [1999]), 943.
18 Zafer Tarık Tunaya, *Turkiye'de Siyasal Gelişmeler [1876–1938] [Political Developments in Turkey (1876–1938)]* (Istanbul: Bilgi Üniversitesi Yayınları, 2002), 141–145.
19 Atatürk, *Nutuk [Oration]*, 21–23.
20 The leader of the rebels was "*Sheikh* Said of Palu, the hereditary chief of the Nakşbendi order," and they were also identified as a Kurdish rebellion led by sheikhs, "who had urged their followers to overthrow the godless Republic and restore the Caliph." Lewis, *The Emergence of Modern Turkey*, 266; and Güneş Murat Tezcür, "Constitutionalism, Judiciary, and Democracy in Islamic Societies," *Palgrave Macmillan Journals* 39, no. 4 (2007): 489.
21 Tezcür, "Constitutionalism, Judiciary, and Democracy in Islamic Societies," 483.
22 Tezcür, "Constitutionalism, Judiciary, and Democracy in Islamic Societies," 488.
23 Annemarie Schimmel, *Mystical Dimensions of Islam* (Chapel Hill: University of North Carolina Press, 1975), 240.
24 Tezcür, "Constitutionalism, Judiciary, and Democracy in Islamic Societies," 488.
25 *Başbakanlık Cumhuriyet Arşivi (BCA)* The Republic of Turkey General Directorate of State Archives, 1935, 49; 1936, 12, 14; 1938, 11, 13; 1950, 41. In the archives, there are also letters about certain *tarikat*-related books' sales prohibition.
26 Kudsi Ergüner, *Journeys of a Sufi Musician* (London: Saqi, 2005), 22.
27 Hakan Yavuz, *Islamic Political Identity in Turkey* (Oxford: Oxford University Press, 2005), 218.
28 "The Constitution of the Republic of Turkey," http://www.hri.org/docs/turkey/con2b.html.
29 Ergüner, *Journeys of a Sufi Musician*, 47.
30 Barbara Kirshenblatt-Gimblett, *Destination Culture: Tourism, Museums, and Heritage* (Berkeley: University of California Press, 1998), 304.
31 Kirshenblatt-Gimblett, *Destination Culture*, 161.
32 Kirshenblatt-Gimblett, *Destination Culture*, 161.
33 Ergüner, *Journeys of a Sufi Musician*, 47.
34 Personal communications with *Mevlevi* and *Rifai* devotees.
35 According to UNESCO, intangible cultural heritage is "Traditional, contemporary and living at the same time: intangible cultural heritage does not only represent inherited traditions from the past but also contemporary rural and urban practices in which diverse cultural groups take part." Intangible heritage is "inclusive: we may share expressions of intangible cultural heritage that are similar to those practiced by others. Whether they are from the neighbouring village, from a city on the opposite side of the world, or have been adapted by peoples who have migrated and settled in a different region, they all are intangible cultural heritage: they have been passed from one generation to another, have evolved in response to their environments and they contribute to give us a sense of identity and continuity, providing a link from our past, through the present, and into our future. Intangible cultural heritage does not give rise to questions of whether or not certain practices are specific to a culture. It contributes to social cohesion, encouraging a sense of identity and responsibility which helps individuals to feel part of one or different communities and to feel part of society at large." It is also "representative: Intangible cultural heritage is not merely valued as a cultural good, on a comparative basis, for its exclusivity or its exceptional value. It thrives on its basis in communities and depends on those whose knowledge of traditions, skills, and customs are passed on to the rest of

the community, from generation to generation, or to other communities." And it is "community-based: intangible cultural heritage can only be heritage when it is recognised as such by the communities, groups or individuals that create, maintain and transmit it—without their recognition, nobody else can decide for them that a given expression or practice is their heritage." UNESCO, "Intangible Cultural Heritage: What is Intangible Cultural Heritage?" accessed July 19, 2011, http://www.unesco.org/culture/ich/?pg=00003.

36 Personal conversation with Özge, a *Mevlevi* devotee, August, 2012.
37 Personal conversation with Özge, a *Mevlevi* devotee, August, 2012.
38 Zana Çıtak, "The Transformation of the State-Religion Relationship Under the AKP: The Case of the Diyanet," in *Turkey's New State in the Making: Transformations in Legality, Economy and Coercion*, ed. Pınar Bedirhanoğlu, Çağlar Dölek, Funda Hülagü, and Özlem Kaygusuz (London: Zed Books, 2020), 180, 167–188.
39 Ali Fuat Başgil, *Din ve Laiklik [Religion and Secularism]* (Istanbul: Kubbealti Negriyati, 1954 [1998]).
40 Karasipahi, "Comparing Islamic Resurgence Movement in Turkey and Iran," 94.
41 Tezcür, "Constitutionalism, Judiciary, and Democracy in Islamic Societies," 479–501.
42 Yavuz, *Islamic Political Identity in Turkey*, 55.
43 Şerif Mardin states, "Islam had an aspect which addressed itself to man's being in this World, to his basic ontological insecurity, which enabled it to fasten itself on to psychological drives. Islam has become stronger in Turkey because social mobilisation had not decreased but on the contrary increased the insecurity of the men who have been projected out of their traditional setting." See Mardin, "Religion and Secularism in Turkey," 218.
44 Personal conversation with Saygın *dede*, December, 2011.
45 Personal conversation with Saygın *dede*, December, 2011.
46 Metin Heper, "Islam and Democracy in Turkey: Toward a Reconciliation," *Middle East Journal* 51, no. 1 (1997): 32–45.
47 Sevinç Bermek, *The Rise of Hybrid Political Islam in Turkey: Origins and Consolidation of the JDP* (London: Palgrave Macmillan), 34, https://doi.org/10.1007/978-3-030-14203-2.
48 Şerif Mardin, "Turkish Islamic Exceptionalism Yesterday and Today: Continuity, Rupture and Reconstruction in Operational Codes," *Turkish Studies* 6, no. 2 (2005): 152; Şerif Mardin, *Türkiye, İslam, ve Sekülarizm: Makaleler 5 [Turkey, Islam and Secularism: Articles 5]* (İstanbul: İletişim, 2011), 183–185.
49 Karasipahi, "Comparing Islamic Resurgence Movement in Turkey and Iran," 96.
50 Ayata, "Patronage, Party, and the State: The Politicisation of Islam in Turkey," 45.
51 Göle, "Secularism & Islamism in Turkey: The Making of Elites and Counter-Elites," 47.
52 Ümit Cizre Sakallıoğlu, "Parameters and Strategies of Islam-State Interaction in Republican Turkey," *International Journal of Middle East Studies* 28 (2006): 244.
53 Necip Fazıl Kısakürek, *Konuşmalar [Conversations]* (Istanbul: Büyük Doğu Yayınları, 1999), 95.
54 Karasipahi, "Comparing Islamic Resurgence Movement in Turkey and Iran," 104–105.
55 Göle, "Secularism & Islamism in Turkey: The Making of Elites and Counter-Elites," 52–53.
56 Göle, "Secularism & Islamism in Turkey: The Making of Elites and Counter-Elites," 96.

Historical Perspectives 67

57 Heper, "Islam and Democracy in Turkey: Toward a Reconciliation," 39.
58 Şerif Mardin, *Religion and Social Change in Modern Turkey: The Case of Bediuzzaman Saidi Nursi* (Albany: State University of New York Press, 1989), 228–229.
59 Heper, "Islam and Democracy in Turkey: Toward a Reconciliation," 39.
60 Ibrahim Abu Rabi, *Islam at the Crossroads* (Albany: State University of New York Press, 2003), 1. Also, see the evaluation of Karasipahi, "Comparing Islamic Resurgence Movement in Turkey and Iran," 104.
61 Vicini, *Reading Islam*, 103.
62 For a detailed analysis of Gülen, refer to Yavuz Çobanoğlu, "Altın Nesil," in *Peşinde: Fethullah Gülen'de Toplum, Devlet, Ahlak, Otorite [Behind the Golden Age: Society, Sate and Authority for Fethullah Gülen]* (Istanbul: İletişim, 2012).
63 Heper, "Islam and Democracy in Turkey: Toward a Reconciliation," 32–45.
64 Ahmet T. Kuru, "Globalisation and Diversification of Islamic Movements: Three Turkish Cases," *Political Science Quarterly* 120, no. 2 (2005): 261.
65 Çıtak, "The Transformation of the State–Religion Relationship Under the Akp: The Case of the Diyanet in Turkey's New State in the Making," 168.
66 Personal communications with secular Turkish lawyers, scholars, journalists, and tourist guides, between 2010 and 2020.
67 The Welfare Party (WP–*Refah Partisi*) was reestablished in 1983 under the leadership of Necmettin Erbakan and was followed, after its closure by the Constitutional Court in 1998, with the Virtue Party (*Fazilet Partisi*, 1997–2001); the Felicity Party (*Saadet Partisi*, 2001-present); and the Justice and Development Party (AKP–*Adalet ve Kalkınma Partisi*, 2001-present). Karasipahi, "Comparing Islamic Resurgence Movement in Turkey and Iran," 97.
68 Karasipahi, "Comparing Islamic Resurgence Movement in Turkey and Iran," 96–97.
69 Karasipahi, "Comparing Islamic Resurgence Movement in Turkey and Iran," 97.
70 Ioannis N. Grigoriadis, "Islam and Democratisation in Turkey: Secularism and Trust in a Divided Society," in *Religion and Democratisations*, ed. Jeffrey Haynes (London: Routledge, 2011), 163.
71 For a detailed scholarship on the history of RAD, see İştar B. Tarhanlı, *Müslüman Toplum "Laik" Devlet: Türkiye'de Diyanet İşleri Başkanlığı [Muslim Society "Laic" State: Religious Affairs Directory in Turkey]* (Istanbul: AFA Yayınları, 1993).
72 Personal communications with *Mevlevi* and *Rifai dedes* (senior dervishes).
73 Svante Cornell, "The Rise of Diyanet: The Politicisation of Turkey's Directorate of Religious Affairs," *The Turkey Analyst*, October 9, 2015.
74 Tezcür, "Constitutionalism, Judiciary, and Democracy in Islamic Societies," 488.
75 Ayşe Öncü, "Becoming 'Secular Muslims': Yaşar Nuri Öztürk as a super-subject on Turkish Television," in *Religion, Media, and the Public Sphere*, ed. Birgit Meyer and Annelies Moors (Bloomington: Indiana University Press, 2006), 230.
76 Personal communication with Melih *dede*.
77 Personal conversation with Narin *dede*, May 5, 2015.
78 Soner Cağaptay, *The Rise of Turkey: The Twenty-First Century's First Muslim Power* (Lincoln: University of Nebraska Press, 2014), 33.
79 Personal conversation with Narin *dede*, May 5, 2015.
80 Abdullahi Ahmed An-Na'im, *Islam and the Secular State: Negotiating the Future of Shari'a* (Cambridge: Harvard University Press, 2008), 1.
81 An-Na'im, *Islam and the Secular State*, 1.
82 An-Na'im, *Islam and the Secular State*, 1.
83 Personal conversation with Narin *dede*, May 5, 2015.
84 Personal communications with managers, tourist guides, and other staff that are involved in the organisation of the ritual performances.
85 Personal communication with a devotee, May 4, 2013.

68 Restoring

86 "Istanbul 2010 European Capital of Culture Program," accessed November 14, 2011, http://www.logictours.com/logicozel/2010.pdf.
87 James Bedding, "Istanbul, European Capital of Culture 2010: City Highlights," accessed January 9, 2010, http://www.telegraph.co.uk/travel/festivalsandevents/6946035/Istanbul-European-Capital-of-Culture-2010-city-highlights.html.
88 The color of red, as And explains, is the color of union and ceremony. Metin And, "The *Mevlana* Ceremony," *The Drama Review* 21, no. 3 (1977): 86–87.
89 And, "The *Mevlana* Ceremony," 86.
90 And, "The *Mevlana* Ceremony," 86.
91 And, "The *Mevlana* Ceremony," 88.
92 Celaleddin Bakır Çelebi, "Hz Mevlanaya Göre Sema [Sema According to Mevlana]," *Analiz Aylık Sektörel, Kültürel ve Siyasal Dergi* 1 (2008): 24–25.
93 And, "The *Mevlana* Ceremony," 88.
94 Abdülbaki Gölpınarlı, *Mevlana'dan Sonra Mevlevilik /Mevlevism After Mevlana/* (İstanbul: İnkilap Kitabevi, 1953), 375.
95 Nirgül Kılınç, "*Mevlevi* Sema Ritual Outfits and Their Mystical Meanings," *New World Sciences Academy* 6, no. 4 (2011): 814.
96 When I asked *Saygın dede* about the reed flute, he showed me Rumi's lines from the *Mesnevi* and explained that the reed flute captures the meaning of the ceremony, the sense of divine meaning or longing experienced by the *semazens*: "Listen to the story told by the reed, of being separated. Since I was cut from the reedbed, I have made this crying sound. Anyone apart from someone he loves/understands what I say. Anyone pulled from a source longs to go back. At any gathering I am there, mingling in the laughing and grieving, a friend to each, but few will hear the secrets hidden within the notes." Coleman Barks, *Rumi: The Big Red Book* (New York: Harper Collins, 1995), 65–67.
97 Kılınç, "*Mevlevi* Sema Ritual Outfits and Their Mystical Meanings," 814; And, "The *Mevlana* Ceremony," 86–87; Personal conversation with Saygın *dede*, November 2, 2022.
98 Kılınç, "*Mevlevi* Sema Ritual Outfits and Their Mystical Meanings," 816.
99 And, "The *Mevlana* Ceremony," 86–87.
100 As explained by one of the *semazens*, Mevlevis believe that the first whirling is enacted as the dervish's birth to truth; the second is the witnessing of the magnificence of creation; the third is the transformation of joy into love and, by this means, the sacrifice of mind to love; and the fourth whirling is performed to return to their mission in everyday life. During these sections, they gradually achieved a rhythmic whirling that was accomplished through physical and mental release, and when they complete the sequence and return back to their mats, they believe that they become impartial to worldly passions and desires. For more information on the spiritual journey that dervishes experience in *sema* ceremony, see Ö. Tuğrul İnançer's chapter "Rituals and Main Principles of Sufism During the Ottoman Empire," in *Sufism and Sufis in Ottoman Society: Sources, Doctrine, Rituals, Turuq, Architecture, Literature and Fine Arts*, ed. Ahmet Yaşar Ocak (Ankara: Atatürk Supreme Council for Culture, Language and History, 2005), 144, 123–182.
101 Micu, *Performance Studies: The Basics*, 10.
102 Personal conversation with Saygın *dede*, October 5, 2010.
103 Peña, *Performing Piety*, 46–47.
104 Merin Shobhana Xavier, *Sacred Spaces and Transnational Networks in American Sufism: Bawa Muhaiyaddeen and Contemporary Shrine Cultures* (London: Bloomsberry Publishing, 2018), 10.
105 Pnina Werbner and Helen Basu, "The Embodiment of Charisma," in *Embodying Charisma: Modernity, Locality and the Performance of Emotion in Sufi Cults*, ed. Pnina Werbner and Helen Basu (London: Routledge, 1998), 3.

106 Peña, *Performing Piety*, 147.
107 Talat S. Halman and Metin And, *Mevlana Celaleddin-i Rumi and the Whirling Dervishes* (İstanbul: Cem Ofset Matbaacilik San, 1983), 34.
108 Michel De Certeau, *The Practice of Everyday Life* (Berkeley: University of California Press, 1984), 117.
109 Peña, *Performing Piety*, 43.
110 Peña, *Performing Piety*, 43.
111 Peña, *Performing Piety*, 43.

2 Designing a Post-Tariqa Communal Sufi Training

By the end of a very productive year filled with ethnographic research, having spent extensive time with a variety of *Mevlevi* groups in a variety of *Mevlevi* lodges and houses, I was feeling more and more curious about how Saygın *dede*'s students' devotional practices would be like if they had permanent spaces in which they could train together as in the Ottoman *Mevlevi* lodges. My mind was busy with a variety of questions that may never be answered, but there was one stubborn question that was gnawing away at my mind. How would a post-tariqa Sufi group create communal life in today's Turkey? As this question continued to occupy my mind, I decided to search for groups that organised private ritual gatherings hoping that they may have somehow created communal living and training spaces. Although I was asking the right question, it took me several months before I had a chance to meet Veli *efendi*, a *Rifai* teacher, who welcomed me to his private spaces, an old wooden house and a residential building that students maintain for regular communal worship. Years later, checking my notes and descriptions about where the wooden house was located, the look of the street and the look of its wooden architecture, I remember every minute of witnessing Veli *efendi's* and his students' restoration of their *zikir* practices in this small, sandalwood smelling ritual space. As discussed in Chapter 1, *Mevlevis*' process of restoring their practice of *zikir* was more about bringing back, recovering and reforming *Sema* ceremony in a site (Yenikapı *Mevlevi* lodge) that is available for temporary use. With their embodied acts, *Mevlevis* restored their practice of *zikir* and the historical lodge as a temporary sacred space. In the case of the *Rifai* dervishes (known in the West as howling dervishes due to their loud *zikir* ceremonies), the process of restoration was about their goal to improve and adapt the *Mevlevi* çile training (also as a form of *zikir*) in a permanent space. In this case, the act of restoration was about how devotees recovered the spiritual training to its divine purpose in the hectic everyday life conditions of modern Istanbul and maintained their wooden house as a permanent sacred site designed for communal rituals.

On a summer evening, having arrived for the first time at the wooden house, I saw the yellow light reflecting from the small window on the second floor and the white lace curtains swaying regularly to inform the late arrivers about the level of activity taking place in one of the rooms. This window seemed like one of the two (the one on the third floor, also small) connections of the house with the street. I remember thinking how they probably preferred to block up other window openings for more privacy. Throughout the initial months of my fieldwork, I used to imagine a secluded Sufi space in Istanbul in which female and male students interested in science and progress lived and trained together. My hope, as I will explain further in the next section, was due to a phone call I received a year ago. I was hoping that I could find a space in which devotees lived with a spiritual teacher whose way of devotional living undermined generalisations about Sufism as a fanatical religious practice (as many secular Turks perceived due to the growing number of conservative Sufi groups). It was easy to contact the members of political Sufi groups, who were visible, in good financial condition and open to students who wanted to research their Islamist worldview. However, minority and underground Sufi groups, who have valued Atatürk's secular vision as much as their moderate Islamic beliefs and values, were somehow invisible.

It was in July 2011, a publicist I met through my father's business partner, offered to introduce me to a businessman, whom she believed could help me get in touch with the students of Sufi orders whose activities were not as accessible or open to the public. When I explained that I had attended a number of gatherings looking to meet with a Sufi master who is devoted to universal Sufi concepts, dedicated to human rights and in support of both religious and secular education, he said I should meet Veli *efendi* (master Veli). When I met Veli *efendi*, his students have been consistently living and training together in an old apartment building converted into a sacred Sufi space, regularly participating in devotion while performing work-related activities in their everyday life. Although they were not completely secretive, these devotees, similar to Saygın *dede*'s group, chose not to reveal their names, places of worship or their ways of living and training to their co-workers and, in certain cases, to their family members and friends.

It is also important to make clear once again that the RAD (Religious Affairs Directorate) was aware of the devotional spaces of such secluded groups but did not interfere with their activities as long as they did not challenge the government's political agenda. At least, this was the case until the coup d'état attempt that occurred in July 2016. After that, most of the minority groups have closed their sacred sites to become even more secretive and their leaders have left Turkey. Although, at that time, between 2009 and 2010, I came across newspaper articles and TV programs about a variety of Sufi groups and congregations in Turkey such as the Halveti Cerrahi order (whose sheikh has become a public figure due to his extremist views about gender segregation), I had not come across any articles about Veli *efendi*, his secluded order, their spaces or their ritual practices. Although the government was aware of the perpetuation of Sufi religious practices and even though the devotees legalised their community as a civil society organisation, the legal code was not different; thus, there was still pressure on Sufi groups, whose practices did not follow the RAD's teachings. As discussed earlier, after the revolution, all Sufi groups stayed underground not to threaten the government's secular ideals, with the strengthening of the JDP since 2002, only groups whose vision was different from RAD preferred seclusion. As discussed earlier, during my fieldwork (before the coup d'état attempt) Veli *efendi* and his students preferred not to announce their place of worship (their wooden house and residential building converted into a Sufi lodge).[1] Most of the students specifically chose not to inform their parents, co-workers or friends that they were affiliated with a Sufi group. To respect their privacy, I do not share the locations of the houses and the names of the devotees.

Also, despite this secluded group's rejection of involvement in commodified activities such as tourist attractions as in the case of Saygın *dede*'s group, Veli *efendi* was also aware of his ritual performances' performatic power to effect social processes. Although he would not call the empowering qualities of *Rifai* rituals such as *zikir* ceremony and *burhan* as performatic, as I will discuss in detail in Chapters 4 and 5, he and his devotees were aware of their rituals' ability to transform the minds of any participant present in the ritual hall. His comments about learning to "act with *edep*" or "God in mind" through "imitation of senior dervishes" in everyday life were much more obvious in relation to my analysis of "presentation of self in everyday life" as performance. He used expressions such as "bir davranışın ya da hareketi tekrar ederek onu içselleştirmek [internalizing a behavior or movement by repeating it]," "bir fikrin veya öğretinin bir öğrencide vücut bulması [an idea or teaching embodied in a student]," and "Allah'ın birliğinin bir dervişte tecessüm etmesi [God's unity embodied in a dervish]" rather than the word "performance" to express how he perceived devotees' desire to act and interact with God in mind as an embodied practice. To him and almost all the devotees, the word "performance" was evocative of an entertainment rather than a worship practice. He was also aware that some of his younger or less-experienced students were interested in making their behaviours visible to earn the respect of their teacher (Veli *efendi*) and senior dervishes. However, their comprehension of showing was also an act of remembrance. It was not a pretence or showing off. Devotees actions and behaviours shifted when they were physically in the presence of Veli *efendi*. They wanted to act like him or be like him by staying in peace with everyone around them. It was clear that they wanted "to be worthy of their teacher's generosity and compassion by trying to behave like him."[2] They were trying to learn to act with *edep* by imitating Veli *efendi* or the senior dervishes.

What was unique about Veli *efendi*'s performative practices of *zikir* was that he sought to restore a training that used to be one of the core devotional practices in Ottoman *Mevlevi* orders. This was a training that *Mevlevis* called *çile*, a trial that devotees practised to train their *nefs* (translated and explained as consciousness, self, mind or ego during Veli *efendi*'s talks with English-speaking guests). Similar to *Mevlevi* students, *Rifais* also used the body as a primary tool to restore and transmit Sufi meaning. While *Mevlevis* restored their *zikir* practices by commodifying and performing their whirling rituals (as a form of *zikir*) simultaneously as worship and tourist attraction, Veli *efendi* (having received a formal Sufi training in both *Mevlevi* and *Rifai* tariqas outside of Turkey) combined his *Mevlevi*, *Rifai* and secularist vision to restore *Mevlevi çile*. Veli *efendi*'s training was a practice in which devotees shared a communal space to execute a variety of duties (*hizmet*) with God in mind (performing *zikir*). While performing *hizmet*, devotees' expressive acts served as a medium for knowing oneself and teaching others. Through this training, devotees were constantly restoring their behaviours and inspiring others to restore their own. Devotees perceived *Rifai* devotional life as a journey to train their body and mind. They defined themselves as a student, seeker and traveller. These devotees avoided identifying themselves as Sufis due to the nature of their beliefs and practices that highlight a devotee as a person travelling, training, studying and practising towards becoming a Sufi—one who embodies God's unity. While emphasising the quality of *Rifai* training as a journey, it is important to point out that the Arabic word *Sufi* "refers only to one who has attained the goal."[3] There are various opinions regarding the etymological sources of the word "Sufi," and all the definitions emphasise attributes of the expected spiritual state instead of the journey which devotees claim to be experiencing.[4] Instead, devotees used terms such as *mürit*, student, initiate, *fakir* and dervish (implying a devotee waiting at the threshold, seeking transformation)[5]—all terms implying that the seeker was in the process of training the mind and body to unite with God. In *Rifai* practice, corporeality was the medium through which the devotees discovered their connection to divinity. As a devotee explained, the journey of "*nefs* training is a very long and challenging process."[6] Therefore, in conflict with the self, the dervish's body longs for a performatic intervention in order to search for a new manifestation of his or her human soul and the physical world. The seekers performed the *seyr-i süluk* (mystical journey) to learn to be free from their worldly veils in order to seek to become part of the divine personality by training the inner self. Devotees perceived Sufi practice as a search, path, quest and journey. Training of the soul required intense mental and physical preparation and exercise, experiencing internal conflict and sleepless nights. Devotees explained that they face their fears, anxieties and resentments during the training process.

In the initial months of my field research with *Rifais*, I remember filling pages and pages of thick descriptions in my notebook to share with my thesis advisor, whom I used to meet in London regularly each month. In my notes, there are descriptions of so many different performatic acts as I watched and participated in students' activities such as serving dishes, cleaning, talking about books, praying, performing *zikir* ceremony and *burhan* ritual (as I will analyse in Chapters 4 and 5). All these activities were different forms of *zikir*, embodied to act with God in mind. This idea of acting, interacting and behaving with God in mind, as Veli *efendi* explained, was a common practice for all Sufi orders. However, each Sufi master executed his own way or path for designing a practice. While whirling, making music, writing poetry and *sohbet* were the most prominent *zikir* rituals for Saygın *dede*, for Veli *efendi*, *devran zikri*, service, *çile* and *burhan* were primary. Although ceremonies such as *devran zikri* and *burhan* were powerful forms of ceremonial *zikir* for experiencing God's unity, many were also aware of the idea that their acts of worship such as *hizmet* were also performatic acts that inspired devotees to train their minds. The way they executed their everyday actions were tools for witnessing and learning from each other's embodied acts. With or without awareness, all of them were constantly performing and watching one another as they talked, walked, served and cleaned. As one of the dervishes described, these acts were practices of self, a training that they experienced in the presence of God. Veli *efendi* and his students believed that they were always in the presence of God. They just needed to train at all times to be aware of this unity. Also, as Veli *efendi* restored this post-tariqa training based on a variety of performatic acts, with their embodied acts, their labour, devotees were also creating and maintaining two permanent sacred spaces, which I refer to as the wooden house and the residential building.

Not a Coincidence But *Kısmet*: My Participation as a Co-performer

I would like to give a brief account of the events that led me to meeting with Veli *efendi* that I shared with his students, who perceived my story as similar to theirs and welcomed me in their more intimate conversations. Due to this sharing, my field research with Veli *efendi*'s group had become a great example of Conquergood's theory of co-performance, allowing me to become a student as well as a researcher trying to make sense of post-tariqa *Rifai* practice.

A year ago, when I was teaching in New York, my friend Selin, who was a historian in Turkey, contacted me to inform me that someone she met at a Sufi music concert took her to a Sufi house, where she witnessed a performance of a *zikir* ceremony. Selin explained to me that the female and male dervishes lived in the same home with their spiritual master. When Selin told me that she met dervishes who resided together with their master, I was excited to return to Turkey for more field research. However, as discussed earlier it took months before I had the opportunity to meet the master because Selin lost the contact details of the student she met at the concert and had no recollection of the location of the space. Later, a co-worker of my father's offered to introduce me to a businessman she knew well who had contacts with various Sufi groups in Turkey.[7] In the meetings with the businessman, after articulating names of spiritual teachers I had already met, the businessman decided to introduce me to a master (known to be a *Rifai* and a *Mevlevi*) recognised for his embodiment of the Sufi idea of unity, gender equality, application of *nefs* training and devotional *zikir* gatherings in his private home.

In the evening of the day I met with Veli *efendi* and had a two-hour discussion on Sufism, Turkey and my research, I also met with my historian friend, Selin, who coincidentally called to invite me to dinner. I told her that

I finally had the chance to meet with a spiritual master who informed me that his students live with him in his lodge. After Selin and I exchanged information about the master she met months ago and the master I met that day, we realised that it was the same person. When I finished telling this story to the students, Nur said this was not a *rastlantı* (coincidence) but *kısmet* (fortune) coming directly from God. Nur informed me that the idea of unity meant that all comes from God. According to students, they came together to maintain sacred spaces under the guidance of the same master because this was God's giving. After this sharing, a sense of bonding occurred between me and the students who listened to my journey. As a result, they started sharing their stories of meeting Veli *efendi*. They started chatting with me more often and introduced me to their family members as their friends. I was no more an outsider coming to observe their customs. They knew I was a PhD student researching their rituals to write a thesis. But for them, I was also a student seeking to learn about Veli *efendi's* teachings. I was thankful for their welcome and was ready to learn how one becomes a student of Sufism.

My participation as what Conquergood defines as an interlocutor allowed me to become part of devotees Sufi journey. This meant that at times I was awkward. I couldn't express myself clearly. I stumbled. The confusion was ok since I was taking performance as both an object and a method of study. However, following Conquergood's commitment to performance as a tool of knowledge production, I have become a "co-performer" that experienced everyday life side by side with them.[8] This meant that I was going to attend all the activities and serve the community regularly on certain weekdays for a year. My engagements with the students were very precious and valuable since the *efendi* welcomed me as a student (without any further recognition, promise of alliance or initiation) studying post-tariqa Sufi practice in Turkey. For Veli *efendi*, it wasn't unusual that I sought to be in his presence as a student, seeking to learn about Sufism, while also as a researcher investigating how he designs post-tariqa communal training as a religious and secular social practice in the modern everyday life of Turkey.

In the first months, while attending gatherings with the students in the houses, I needed to decide the level of participation I was comfortable with. As Margaret Thompson Drewal states, some researchers find it difficult to perform the actions and behaviours that come with the ceremony and "That would be true of highly formalised practices that require apprenticeships with years of training in order to master the techniques of drumming or carving."[9] However, as she also points out, "Because most performance in Africa is participatory, there are many diverse kinds of roles researchers can take in addition to more technical kinds of performance."[10] This was also true in regard to Veli *efendi's* devotional practice. Activities performed in the houses were participatory. As a researcher seeking to examine students' daily lives and a student of the *efendi*, I first served in the kitchen, helping students clean up after meals. Aside from washing dishes, I was comfortable with participating *devran zikri* and poetry readings and since those were part of my training as an actor; thus, I participated in *meşk* (classes in which students practice and recite Sufi hymns). While acknowledging that general descriptions and theoretical analysis of Sufi rituals in Turkey have tremendous value in creating this project, my coperformative witnessing provided a multifaceted look into Veli *efendi*'s process of designing a post-tariqa *çile* training. Without Conquergood's method, I could never learn how and why they volunteered to maintain their permanent sacred spaces as a safe haven for training their minds. Before moving onto examining devotees' actions and behaviours in more detail, I would like to present Veli *efendi*'s role in the *Rifai* practice.

A Poet, Composer and Father: Organising *Rifai* Sites

Veli *efendi* was the spiritual leader and *mürşit* (teacher) of the group. His background played an important role in restoring his *Rifai* practice. Veli *efendi*, raised in a Sufi family that valued and practised poetry and music, pursued his education at a liberal arts college in Turkey. As a young student, he studied Western and Eastern scientific knowledge and philosophy as part of his education. After completing his degree, he travelled to Egypt, Iran and India to receive Sufi education. Training in a variety of Sufi tariqas and receiving his spiritual teacher's permission to teach, he began to teach Sufi poetry in his private home in Turkey. In the 1990s, Veli *efendi* and his initial group of friends started to organise *sohbet*, *meşk* and *zikir* gatherings. His students founded an official Sufi society that believed in practising Sufism as what he terms as versatile tradition. Devotees of the *Rifai* group follow the guidance of Veli *efendi* as their teacher by training with him and organising a variety of religious/community gatherings (such as *sohbets*, *meşks*, *zikir* gatherings and courses on Sufi religious teachings and other religious texts).

Veli *efendi*'s students believed that their teacher had gone through *nefs* training and reached the level of *kamil* insan (the mature or perfect person who is equipped with divine qualities). Devotees studied with *efendi* as their teacher believing that he had divine qualities and that he was constantly observing them whether he was physically there or not. Some students had spiritual beliefs such as that their teacher was aware of how the rituals were performed inside and outside the house. Devotees tended to perform what was offered by their teacher as God offers it. Veli *efendi* asked his students to follow certain rules such as avoiding any form of arguments, pursuing generosity, practising compassion, exercising satisfaction with whatever God provided, staying patient at all times, concealing the wrongdoings of others and refusing any attachment to worldly desires.

Ian Richard Netton describes that

> while the truly humble Sufi Shaykh . . . would never, under any circumstances, compare himself to the Deity, nonetheless his presence in the Order or house is a sign of a greater Authority. Obedience to the shaykh [sheikh] or Master is obedience to God.[11]

He states that "because of the difficulties and temptations of the Sufi path, a master is absolutely essential for the Sufi."[12] In line with this analysis, devotees accepted Veli *efendi*'s authority perceiving his physical and spiritual presence as the main component of Sufi devotion. Most of them were not connected to Veli *efendi* through a promise of alliance as in the Ottoman tariqas; however, they respected his authority and admired his wisdom. They loved him. More importantly, they trusted him. In the daily life, the students knew that their teacher was always there to guide them through the understanding and awareness of their *nefs*.

Students also perceived *efendi* as a spiritual father in the sense that he tended to guide them in their personal health, work and at times family matters. If a student was sick, Veli *efendi* made sure that he or she got the necessary treatment and informed other students to take care of their spiritual siblings by finding a doctor, cooking for him or her or keeping tabs on his or her well-being. If a student needed a job or wanted to go on to study in graduate school, Veli *efendi* was there to encourage the student to work and make sure that he or she got the necessary guidance from another student who had connections with applicable businesses or had already completed his or her education. Because of the wisdom, depth and the impact of *efendi*'s words and actions, students submitted their hearts to him as their spiritual *baba* (father) as well as their teacher. His kindness and generosity seemed to be his way of restoring the Ottoman Sufi tradition that considers a spiritual master's presence in Sufi devotional life as vital in Sufi spiritual training. Some of his students were not connected to him by way of an initiation but due to their love, respect and admiration for his character.

Veli *efendi* was also a poet and composer because he wrote music and religious poetry to share his spiritual journey with his students. He also guided his students to study liturgical songs that were created by various Sufi mystics. As in the *Mevlevi* devotional life, these songs were perceived as divinely inspired, informing the students about various mystics' ideas and experiences about practising remembrance. Veli *efendi* believed that studying religious poetry and music was vital to enhancing divine meaning; therefore, students studied the *efendi*'s compositions, along with other Sufi masters' work.

Becoming Veli *efendi*'s Student: A Path to Modern *Dervişlik*

Only people who have references from friends, family members and colleagues come to the wooden *house* to meet with Veli *efendi*. However, there was a productive communication between more public *Mevlevi* and *Rifai* groups. People who have spent extensive time in the *Mevlevi* groups were more likely to meet the right person who would introduce them to one of Veli *efendi*'s students. The individuals interested in coming to meet with Veli *efendi* tended to be people with close ties to one of *his* students. Similar to my journey, most had attended the gatherings of a variety of popular Sufi groups as well as accessible *Mevlevi* groups before being referred to the secluded gatherings of Veli *efendi*. Students chose to participate in the *Rifai* practice after articulating to Veli *efendi* their desire to study *tasavvuf* (Sufism) and asking for permission to attend his gatherings. If *efendi* deemed it appropriate, they started to attend gatherings as a student in the houses. These students participated in the *Rifai* training by attending gatherings every Thursday and by taking a variety of responsibilities such as helping in the service such as teaching, cooking, cleaning or assisting guests (coming from other countries). Some students received additional recognition when they received a *tespih* (rosary or prayer bead) that they believed to be sanctified with *efendi's* prayers. Veli *efendi* gave *tespihs* to the students he thought were ready to start to follow a schedule for meditation on God by performing silent *zikir* regularly—repeating God's names as they counted the beads on their rosaries (referred to as *tespih çekmek*). Therefore, *tespih çekmek* was a significant part of a *Rifai* student's life through which she or he practised individual meditation on God's names.

The members consisted of a large number of students who were searching for their spiritual path. Each practitioner had a different reason or motive for what they called "submitting their heart to the *efendi*."[13] Some students arrived in need of love, togetherness, guidance about family problems or to learn Sufi poetry and music, but the most common drives were to find answers to ontological questions, to become aware of who they were and simply to become a peaceful and happy person. Dervish Nur said students came with one or two motives and stayed because they discovered a higher purpose. In her thirties, she explained she learned more from her teacher and spiritual siblings about human interaction than she learned in school (referring to her entire schooling experience including two bachelor degrees she received in her twenties). Some students also explained they were more active in regard to arts, reading, travelling, dancing and singing that they used to be in their school years. They said they learned to respect each individual's ideas and needs and create healthier relationships with their family, friends and co-workers.

The students arrived in the world of Veli *efendi's* training from the individualistic lifestyles of modern social life. Because *teslimiyet* (submission) to a teacher was a challenging practice, the students believed that one was able to continue the path by only truly believing in a spiritual teacher's sincere devoutness to God. It was common for well-educated practitioners of Sufism to visit different orders and attend a number of meetings, classes and workshops before finding a teacher to whom they would dedicate themselves. They all believed in *kader* (fate) or God's fortune and did not commit to a teacher's path until they found one that they admired, trusted and could follow with ultimate dedication.

The practice of an informal submission for these students was a voluntary process, in which they chose to discuss their everyday life problems and concerns with their teacher. Since conversations between Veli *efendi* and the students tended to be private, I was only able to witness some of the experiences of students (with whom I spent extensive time). Most of them were taking Veli *efendi*'s teachings as a guide, a reference point before they were making final decisions about their lives. Veli *efendi* was interested in designing a system in which he would be there for his students when they needed guidance but would not guide them by telling them what to do. Instead, he would share a Sufi story from Rumi's *Mesnevi* or a sacred poem to guide a student dealing with specific problems. He would also often joke about his position as a teacher reminding his students that the answers they sought were not with him but in their own minds and hearts. He could only try to guide them on how to use their minds and hearts more effectively.

Most of his students, who decided to continue their spiritual training with him, also received agency by obtaining texts to study individually and to discuss with their teacher. Then some of them, upon the completion of their theoretical and practical training, received initiation through a promise of alliance, in which the *efendi* bonded the student to his spiritual training. As Veli *efendi* explained, mostly students who had been training with him for a long time (at least six to twelve months) went through such initiation. All this process was carried out entirely for students who desired and asked for such an alliance and who were committed to continuing their lives as a dervish.

With this initiation promising their submission to Sufi path, students received permission to practice the path more in the traditional sense of an Ottoman dervish. Devotees recognised these individuals as dervishes in the sense that they either lived with or devoted their non-work time to their practice of *zikir*.[14] I refer to such students as dervishes since they were distinguishable not only through their intimate relationship with the teacher and senior dervishes but also from the traditional dervish *hırkas* (cloaks) and the necklaces they wore (as offered by the *efendi*) and more importantly through their actions and interactions inside and outside the *house*. Dervishes often expressed their position as taking responsibility for acting with compassion at all times.

As in Ottoman Sufi orders, for *Rifais*, the word "dervish" meant one who waited in the doorway or on the threshold of something, ready to move on and transform himself or herself in every moment of his or her daily life. In the *Rifai sohbets* I attended about dervishness, I learned that the role carried heavy responsibilities. In my notes, there were explanations about how dervishes were obliged to act with awareness of self (their mind or thoughts). Dervishes were the ones who had to act selfless. Dervishes' consciousness had to be awake at all times. Dervishes avoided the word "I." Instead, they called themselves *fakir* (poor), ones who seek to live void of any identity other than their spiritual presence (the knowledge that they are united with God). The burdens of dervishes were heavy if they acted selfishly. Their consciousness did not rest in such situations. Because they had learned to be self-aware and selfless. Arrogance and anger did not suit them. They had to be aware of their own feelings. They were responsible for the well-being of others. They were obliged to look out for others. They were the ones responsible with constantly meditating and learning more about their mind's habits. They had to act "remembering Allah, his unity and that every living and non-living being will one day return to Him. Dervish desired to be one with God."[15] In the group, dervishes sought to learn from Veli *efendi* that every moment, every action and every interaction was an opportunity to move on and to experience God. Dervish Şale once said, although "most of the theoretical ideas about dervishness may alter when one is in real life training," especially "in midsts of severe family and health problems," keeping in mind the idea that a dervish is the one who aims "to seek self-transformation to move closer to God," it is "possible to experience true dervishness."[16] Dervishes were expected to convey great devotion to God and were seeking to be respectful of every living and non-living creature they interacted with in their daily life. Although some had responsibilities that seem to contradict their renunciatory nature such as overseeing lavish events, travel plans and other material matters in contrast to the living conditions in the *house*, their compassion for everyone and everything was visible in their humble attitudes.

Maintaining Sites

What made Veli *efendi*'s process of restoring *çile* training possible was all the students' hard work in maintaining two sacred sites. These spaces, as discussed earlier, were the wooden house and the residential building (or *Rifai* home). The space students gathered for regular classes and gatherings was the *Rifai* home. This was a home that Veli *efendi*, *dedes*, dervishes and students used for communal lodging. In the *Rifai* home, students performed *hizmet* as part of their training; interacted with each other from morning to night; performed rituals; made music; read religious poetry; arranged community gatherings to advise each other on religious and societal issues (taking the role of both a performer and an audience); organised *sohbets* to discuss Sufi teachings and, as mentioned earlier, held classes to help each other on everyday topics, such as using the computer and playing musical instruments. This residence was a post-tariqa Sufi lodge in which every member of the group was continuously learning from each other.

In the building, there were different flats occupied by the students. The devotional and material activities took place simultaneously in one room. While one student was reading the Quran, another student could be dealing with searching for a job online. Also, there were times when students meditated. Veli *efendi* wanted to create a way of living that is a synthesis of religious and secular values, in which students could use the *Rifai* home as a family home. In his vision, this had to be a space, in which they could study and practice their material life responsibilities in addition to the time they prayed and meditated.

Despite economic differences, Veli *efendi* wanted to create an egalitarian environment by making sure that each student served one another when necessary. Whether a student was a highly educated upper-middle-class businessmen who owned factories or a low-income clerk who only made as little as 800 Turkish liras a month, both were responsible for a variety of tasks, such as serving tea or carrying chairs in their gatherings. While regarding each student as a unique character affected by different personal, cultural, social, religious and economic backgrounds, as a teacher Veli *efendi* was also determined to remind each student about the idea of unity as manyness of one reality, meaning that each human being was different, yet united in God.

His respect for differences was visible since his students came from many religions, sects, groups (including Sunnis, Shiis, Alevis, Jews and Christians) and national and cultural backgrounds (including Turkish, British, Italian, Arab, American and Bulgarian). Veli *efendi* once said that each person was very different and added: "Here we experience the manyness of one reality [God]. Our interactions with each other in the *Rifai* spaces are part of the training we pursue to respect each other's differences in life."[17] The *efendi* wanted to guide his students to perceive the *Rifai* home also as their life school in which they trained, experienced divine meaning and prepared for the challenges of living in the material world (meaning students' responsibilities outside of the sacred spaces such as work). As in Peña study of Guadalupan devotion, devotees' behaviours combined with their practice of Sufi poetry, music and *zikir* made the spaces sacred[18] Their spaces, as Veli *efendi* explained, were the life schools as well as sacred houses and community centres in which students trained to embody the divine. These post-tariqa spaces, while providing the students with some seclusion to study with their spiritual siblings, also prepared their minds and bodies for the actions and interactions in the secular social life of Turkey.

Due to legal restrictions and the absence of financial support from the government, students developed ways of living, walking, serving, praying, studying, organising gatherings and performing rituals in their small spaces. Veli *efendi* organised the use of the rooms according to the needs of his students. If a student were to stay in the residential building, he or she would reside in a room shared with other students. Certain rooms were designed to accommodate three to six students, while other rooms were designed to accommodate only one student; however, none of these arrangements were designed to be permanent. There was constant adjustment. They had to restore how they used the spaces for the needs of the devotees. According to the spiritual training of each student, the conditions of everyday living could change. Some continued to stay in multiple-bed dormitories, while others lived in a room with a single bed. The living conditions could change for the needs of the students' social roles and spiritual practice. A student could have a private room when Veli *efendi* asked a student to perform meditation retreats, when a student was writing his or her thesis or when a student from other cities and countries came to stay as a guest in the residential *house*. There was constant transformation in the living spaces to meet students' and guests' needs. This was their way of restoring communal living and training that existed in the Ottoman Sufi *tekkes* while also adjusting to the pace of modern everyday life in Turkey.

82 *Restoring*

The building and the house were "practiced places" open to transformation.[19] They constantly transformed their spaces to live and train together. Devotees perceived the home and the wooden house (although both lack the architectural design and the religious symbols of the historical Sufi *house* buildings) as sacred as Muslims, Jews and Christians perceive their mosques, synagogues and churches. Devotees' commitment to produce permanent sacred spaces showed how they perceived their "practised" places vital to continuing to live and train together.

Michel de Lefebvre's critical views about the vitality of the sacred space illuminate my analysis of *Rifai* practice by providing the necessary enquiries about the relationship between space as the material and the sacred beliefs and values as spiritual. He asks:

> What is an ideology without a space to which it refers, a space which it describes, whose vocabulary and links it makes use of, and whose code it embodies? What would remain of a religious ideology—the Judeo-Christian one, say—if it were not based on places and their names: church, confessional, altar, sanctuary, tabernacle?[20]

Just like Christians relate to their churches and Muslims to their mosques to make their beliefs and values tangible, students regarded their *Rifai* home and the wooden houses as places where they were able to embody their beliefs and values. The act of maintaining sacred sites was also the act of practising *zikir*. As they restored their sacred sites, they also restored their spiritual practice. The labour given to make the *Rifai* home was also the performatic labour that make up the *çile* training. These sacred sites were also necessary for devotees who preferred to simultaneously experience the privileges of monastic life such as interacting and learning from one another on a regular basis and the privileges of non-monastic life such as studying, working, starting a business or developing a specific career path.

Performatic Everyday Life: Restoring Self (*Nefs*)

With *Rifai* students' embodied acts, Sufi practice constantly shifted as they performed their daily rituals and as they blended their actions in the sacred spaces with their actions outside (at work and other spaces they visited throughout the day). Goffman's examination of "presentation of self in everyday life" illuminates how students as ordinary individuals, without some or no intentions, use performance as a tool for shaping their lives.[21] Goffman explains how the practices of everyday life "are not 'acted' or 'put on' in the sense that the performer knows in advance just what he is going to do, and does this solely because of the effect it is likely to have."[22] However,

> the incapacity of the ordinary individual to formulate in advance the movements of his eyes and body does not mean that he will not express

himself through these devices.... In short, we act better than we know how.[23]

Interacting in the houses, most of the *Rifai* students, especially the dervishes, were mindful performers who sought to be aware of their actions and their effects at all times. To achieve this, they constantly "restored" their "behaviours" to act as they "learned" from the senior dervishes and Veli *efendi*.[24] Also, students' everyday performances revealed the complex relationships that existed between the Sufi body, Sufi sacred space and Turkish society. These students' everyday performances revealed how they restored their *nefs* and maintained their sacred sites. The restoration processes of themselves and their spaces conveyed how *Rifais* generated post-tariqa Sufism in contemporary Turkey.

As discussed earlier, Veli *efendi* modified the *çile* (trial) tradition of the Ottoman *Mevlevi* tariqa as a form of *nefs* training. In the *Mevlevi* order, *çile* was formulated for devotees as an everyday training in the *dergah* so that devotees could learn their *nefs* through devotional labour. In the Ottoman *Mevlevi* orders, this training had to last for one thousand and one days, through which a dervish trained his *nefs* and comprehended his unity of existence. To experience the training, it was believed that, first, the seeker would search for a Sufi teacher with whose path he or she could unite mentally and spiritually. The mental and spiritual connection to the sheikh was perceived as central to the *nefs* training due to the idea and practice of *biat* (an oath of alliance) to the sheikh as a spiritual father and teacher. A seeker, then, could only start training if such a connection is experienced. The training would start by performing service in the kitchen of the sheikh's *dergah*. Service in the *Mevlevi* order required that the devotee sat for three days in a state of meditation and watched the tasks performed in the kitchen.[25] At the end of the three-day meditation, the sheikh would give the seeker the opportunity to leave the *dergah*. But as Shakina Reinhertz explains, staying and choosing the life of a *mürit* would mean that the student would be brought before "*kazanci dede* (the master of service), who would send him or her into the kitchen to begin their training through service."[26] As she explains:

> This newly-accepted *mürit* [pupil] would stay in a small room with several other initiates and all would be given such menial tasks as sweeping the floors, washing dishes, and mending the dervishes' shoes. During the first eighteen days, if at any time the *mürit* failed to live up to the standards of the *dergah*, their shoes would be placed facing the door and they would know this was a sign to leave at first light without protest, never to return again.[27]

After the completion of the eighteen days, the *mürit* would perform all tasks articulating the word *Alhamdullillah*—all thanks be to God. Reinhetz's analysis shows that *hizmet* was designed to be rigorous in order to test the student's ability to stay open to direction and at peace with their orders. The training also included meditations in dervish cells, long retreats, service and performance of rituals before the devotee fully becomes a dervish through a full ceremony. It is believed that through the *çile*, the *mürits* seek to release what Rumi calls the veils and pursue the inner journey (self-transformation) to become aware of their unity with God.

An adaptation of *çile* was used by Veli *efendi* to teach the students the idea of selflessness, unity, love, generosity and compassion as they interacted in the *Rifai* spaces. With this training, students practised recognising their thoughts, feelings and behaviours. Through this training, Veli *efendi* expected the students to learn how to carry the awareness that they gained during the *çile* to their actions and interactions outside of the *Rifai* spaces. The students perceived *çile* as what the *efendi* called a preparation class (*hazırlık dersi*) to train their *nefs*. In the preparation class, students served and attended classes, *sohbets* and ceremonies regularly. Similar to a *mürit* in an Ottoman Mevlevi tariqa, students also performed meditation and worked in the kitchen.[28] However, students were also free in organising the time and effort they devoted to such practices. Therefore, compared to what was required in an Ottoman tariqa, the schedules and commitment were more flexible since most of the students had work obligations or lived in their private homes. Veli *efendi* believed today's *çile* to include devotees' work obligations. Today's *çile* was the ability to be able to go back and forth between the life of worship and the hectic everyday life of modern Turkey. According to their work schedules and other family responsibilities, some students chose to only perform tasks such as sweeping floors and washing dishes once a week, while others devoted more time to such activities. Some chose to serve the community as drivers, teachers, cooks and/or tour guides for guests visiting from other cities or countries. The amount of work tended to be rigorous for students who sought to devote all their labour to the needs of the group. These students wanted to test their abilities regarding how to stay open to direction and at peace with their actions and interactions in times of exhaustion. The practice of post-tariqa *çile*, according to a senior dervish, was even more challenging in present-day Turkey because modern everyday life was more hectic. They sometimes worked and performed *hizmet* (service) in the *house* all night long—cleaning, cooking, teaching and taking classes, organising gatherings, assisting guests and performing collective rituals. They worked at banks, hospitals, schools, pharmacies and markets, as well as studied for their exams. Since the Turkish government did not support or provide income for their worship activities, students, while providing income for their sacred sites, also maintained their spaces themselves by working on their water and gas systems, electricity and sewage, doing other construction, and repairing their furniture—all as part of their *çile*, preparation for training the *nefs*.

Rifais believes that *nefs* can be developed and refined if a devotee pursues a journey by going through the seven stages. The first is the lower stage known as *nefs-i ammara*, explained as the commanding self or the unruly animal self; the second stage is *nefs-i lavvama*, the blaming self, the self of awakening conscience that takes its first step to return to God; the third stage is *nefs-i mulhima*, which is described as the inspired self that is aware of the difference between doing right or doing wrong; the fourth stage is *nefs-i mutmainna* and in that stage the self is secured and enjoys a relationship with the Divine; the fifth stage is *nefs-i raddiya*, the stage of the content self, in which the soul is in harmony with reality; the sixth stage is *nefs-i mardiyya*, the gratified self, who is in total submission and pleasing to God; and the final stage, the seventh stage, is *nefs-i safiyya* or *nefs-i kamiliye*, the purified self or the mature self. People who attain this final stage are also called *kamil insan* (mature or perfect human being).

Practising service, students sought to become aware of their *nefs-i ammara*—their self or soul "in its fallen state, or in its ordinary everyday reality far from its primordial nature"[29]—as they interact with each other in the sacred home. They observed their teacher's and spiritual siblings' actions and behaviours. Through a performatic experience, students became aware of who they were and how they acted and behaved first in the *Rifai* home, in the physical presence of their teacher and spiritual siblings, then in their daily life in a variety of settings outside of the home. Through witnessing the actions of their teacher and their interactions with their spiritual siblings, students sought to become aware of their *nefs-i lavvamah*, which is the soul that alerts itself to its own shortcomings.[30]

According to *Rifai* cultural beliefs and values, when a student was initiated in the path as a dervish, his or her daily actions and behaviours inspired admiration and spiritual feelings in other students (who spend most of their time with them) and non-students (who interact with dervishes inside and outside the houses without knowing that they are dervishes).[31] Senior dervishes' actions and behaviours transmitted certain beliefs and values such as love, peace, kindness and generosity. A dervish like Esen continued her spiritual journey through the end of the path to reach the level of *nefs-i mutma'innah*, which is the soul at peace,[32] and prayed to stay in this final path to live as a mature human being.

To experience that state, there was a constant desire to move from one *hizmet* to another. However, it was important to remind oneself to not perform the task for the sake of appearing responsible and good but for the sake of love of God. Even when the students were in the kitchen washing dishes, as Ece once explained, it was necessary to be aware at all times that as students, they performed service for God by serving our *efendi* and siblings, not to gain favour. In the performance of washing dishes, the task was divided among three students. One performed the task of washing dirty dishes in a *leğen* (large pan), while a second student rinsed and handed the clean dish to the third student for drying. The act of washing dishes was performed in the same order and students switched places with each other by touching each other's shoulder and asking for permission to perform *hizmet* (service) to God.

The students did not perceive the actions performed in the house as obligatory. As one of the students (Nur) explained, once a guest curious about Sufi practice came to meet with Veli *efendi* and asked questions about Sufi devotion. Nur pointed out that the guest asked Veli *efendi* why all the students had to serve and obey a spiritual master. The *efendi* answered politely that they don't have to serve or obey. He said it was not a matter of obligation. If it was a matter of obligation, then there would be no path. It had to be a matter of free choice. It was their desire to learn from one another.

Turner's scientific study of human action suggests that performance "cannot escape reflection and reflexivity."[33] As human beings every day, we try to make sense of our needs and desires. Our relationships with one another change, and the play of preparing a meal, reading to our child or presenting an idea transform as we recognise and identify ourselves and others in action. In everyday life, we are tightly connected to the people around us. We live collectively, watch and observe each other in action. One is performing, the other is watching. This sense of "reflection and reflexivity" allows us to restore our behaviours, play different roles, discover new ways of interacting and at times choose to be more expressive in our interactions.

Students usually learned by imitating (not copying but repeating and restoring) each other's behaviours such as humbleness, calmness and patience. Veli *efendi* explained, "It is ok to repeat each other's actions because through imitation one makes it her/his own."[34] Schechner's theory of "restored behaviour" and Drewal's idea of "repetition with critical difference" inform my analysis of how devotees watch, repeat and recreate each other actions and behaviours.

The practice of *edep* (Sufi manners that emphasise the embodiment of unity, love, compassion and peace) was a teaching devotees embodied as they moved around their sacred spaces. *Edep* is "a consequence and application of faith and may be described as orientation, right comportment and proper attitude; it is faith concretised in day-to-day activities, strictly religious or otherwise."[35] If a student acted with *edep*, that meant s/he was aware of all the behaviours s/he embodied. As one of the senior dervishes (Esen) explained, "her *efendi* is polite, generous and loving" with his students as well as the guests visiting his house.[36] Esen believed she was responsible for learning to act with such *edep* and the way to learning was through watching his *efendi*, recognising oneself to become aware of her mind's habits and repeating her *efendi*'s behaviours. In her case, repetition meant embodying the way her *efendi* talked, walked and interacted with his students. However, this repetition was not about copying her *efendi*'s actions. On the contrary, it was about repeating, thinking and restoring his words and movements to make them her own. Drewal theorised such repetitive actions as "repetition with critical difference" emphasising each repetition's originality. Schechner, on the other hand, explained such repetitions as restored behaviours, analysing how each action repeated is new, never a copy of the one before. As Esen was feeling responsible for acting as polite and generous as her *efendi*, she was not trying to create an exact copy. She was trying to invent her own ways to act polite and generous. What she witnessed in Veli *efendi* speech and movement, she was trying to find in her own voice and her own body.

In the *house*, certain gatherings tended to be very busy and challenging for students. They worked for five to ten hours on such evenings. In such demanding gatherings, dervishes focused on their affection for the *efendi*, articulating their love for his devotion, purity and dedication. They would often say that their master or father was always available to guide them. The *efendi* slept very little and spent most of his time praying. Remembering and articulating his devoutness, kindness and generosity, dervishes were the ones who sought to act and behave like their *efendi* in every moment of their everyday life. There was tremendous support within the community. More and more students, as soon as they fulfilled their work and family duties, arrived at the sacred spaces and joined the service to help Esen and other senior dervishes who lived in the *Rifai* homes. Following each other's actions and directions, students (students and dervishes) prepared the dining areas with love and care.

During these busy days, students would try to stay alert and work with efficiency. They would watch and listen to one another's requests as they work. They would respond to each other with interest and respect. They would rush around the space, making sure everything is in order. The service in the *Rifai* spaces, especially for dervishes who lived with the *efendi*, resulted in complete exhaustion through which the student had no time to think about their material needs and desires. Devotees meditated through focusing on various tasks. Their bodies would feel overcome with exhaustion that they would discuss how they would feel free of undesirable thoughts and emotions.

Ziya, a beginning student, explained that in performing service in the wooden *house*, he was mindful of Esen's (a senior dervish) pace and the tone of her voice—and he sensed how her body moved. Performing service in the presence of his *efendi* and dervishes, Ziya said he learned to be alert. He sought to be mindful of his spiritual siblings who worked around him. Ziya said he had a memory of how he moved along with his fellow students in the wooden *house* and remembered his bodily experience when he was at home helping his wife serve dinner or at the university teaching his students. Ziya said training in the *Rifai* spaces, he learned how to act and liberate his mind from any thought other than his spiritual practice. Arriving at the wooden house tired and then serving for hours, then performing rituals, although exhausting, was also a fulfilling experience, especially at the Thursday night ceremonial *zikir* gatherings, with students starting to arrive around five in the evening with the night ending at one or two in the morning. As I will discuss further in Part Four, at these evenings, devotees would serve, sing, dance and pray all night long.

At the time, Esen, a senior female dervish in her late thirties, had been living in the *Rifai* home for almost nine years. Aspiring students like Esen, who underwent a period of intense training in self-discipline, would learn to control their instincts and desires, guided by Veli *efendi*. When a student gained a higher level of awareness of humanity as a senior dervish, he or she would be more responsible for his or her actions and interactions than a non-dervish student, who has not sought the full knowledge of the Sufi spiritual path.

Veli *efendi* said Esen passed the preparation class and got initiated into the *efendi*'s path as a dervish after two years of training. Her submission to the *efendi* was visible in her embodied actions. She slept and ate very little, rarely sat and was always in the process of cooking, cleaning, making religious music and serving her spiritual siblings. She smiled most of the time, she was content with her role as a senior dervish. She was content with living by her teacher. There is not one day that Esen was absent from the *Rifai* home or the wooden house, except for those times when a family member was sick or in need of her help. With the aim to serve God through serving the sacred sites, Esen said she believed that the service she performed is a vehicle for experiencing and sharing her spiritual self.[37] She worked as a music teacher during the day. She left the *Rifai* home every morning to work in a middle school and returned to the home to spend time with her siblings. There were six other female and ten male dervishes like Esen who chose to devote their lives to their group. Some of them never married or had children. Instead, as Esen explained, they perceived the *Rifais* as their family.

A priest of the Yoruba people, Kolawole Ositola, in his article on ritual performance, states that through ritual, people "gain the sense of thought and reflection."[38] Through the practice of *hizmet* and *edep*, participants sought thought and reflection while also restoring their actions and behaviours as well as their spaces. Many devotees also expressed in various ways that their ability to act with *edep* when experiencing hardships and conflict affected their appearance and character outside of the *Rifai* spaces. As dervish Ceren once explained, since she started to study with her spiritual siblings, she slept better and woke up with a clear purpose. For Ceren, who was a journalist, all the things she had to do regarding her work were part of her responsibilities in life. She was aware that she needed to produce meaningful work, but she also knew that her work and other material responsibilities of her daily life were not her main means to be happy. She believed that it was the awareness of divine meaning that she gained in her *Rifai* training that allowed her to distance herself from the stress caused by her reliance on material matters. She said she trusted that she could do her best.

Veli *efendi* would also appoint some of the dervishes as his *halifes*, which meant authorising his disciples as successors to teach others. There were both female and male students who devoted extensive amount of time to such piousness. *Halifes* had many responsibilities in other cities and countries, such as organising gatherings like classes and workshops about *Rifai* teachings, creating alternative Sufi associations and foundations to help people in need and producing alternative urban spaces such as Sufi coffee houses and bookstores that welcome people interested in Sufi teachings. For Veli *efendi*, *halifes* were the most humble ones fully devoted to the divine journey and ready to work away from the relative comforts of the home. However, such devotion required some level of sacrifice. The students needed to give up some of their personal needs.

One day, I arrived at the *Rifai* home. It was a crowded evening with many female students arriving and taking their places on the floor of the room located in a flat used for female lodging (like female dormitories). As students were preparing for the class, Hatice informed us that she would soon be chatting on Skype with Ebru, who was a young *halife* that Veli *efendi* entrusted to teach Sufism in a small village in India. Since most of us knew and missed Ebru very much, we all gathered around Hatice's computer. The moment the connection started, Ebru had a gloomy smile on her face. As soon as she saw all of us trying to show our faces on the computer screen to say how much we missed her, her face froze for a second and the next moment, when she raised her hand to say hello, she burst into tears. It became clear that she did not only miss us but also that her living conditions weren't easy. She had been away from home for nine months. That evening, Ayşe, a close friend of Ebru (they were roommates when Ebru lived in the *house*), shared her thoughts with me about how Ebru was there to fulfil her dream. Although she was there to be of service to young people, who are in need of spiritual support, according to Ayşe, she was also there because she was training her own mind. Ayşe said this was not an easy task. At the time, Ebru was visiting another Sufi space in India teaching children to read and write in a class focusing on Sufi poetry. Ebru was one of the youngest *halifes* who was committed to the Sufi path. She was in her mid-twenties and having completed her undergraduate and graduate education in Turkey had devoted her life to people in need. I knew she was not expecting or even prepared when she received this assignment from her teacher, Veli *efendi*. She knew she would need to leave Turkey all by herself to live and serve in India. However, she did not know how long she would need to stay there by the time she left Turkey but I knew and remembered that it was her life's mission to help people. Ebru's case was only one of the many that taught me how challenging yet fruitful post-tariqa *Rifai* practice can be for a dervish. Ebru had a choice not to go, but she knew she was up for the challenge.

Choosing to take such responsibilities was part of some female students. Female *Rifais* tended to be as active as the male dervishes regarding taking responsibilities such as teaching or producing sacred houses abroad. Although their teacher, the leader of the group, was a male, the students believed that Veli *efendi*'s vision required that there were as many highly educated female *halifes* who were active members of the group regarding taking some level of managerial roles in the *Rifai* sites outside of Turkey. There were female *halifes* fluent in other languages, including English and French and who worked as pharmacists, teachers, academics, artists, etc., in a variety of public institutions in Turkey. Some were single; some were married, but their role as a dervish was at times more important than their social roles as wives, daughters or mothers. At times, some would be ready to quit their jobs if such responsibilities were offered by their teacher.

Veli *efendi's* idea of producing and experiencing the sacred sites as life schools allowed female students to practise Sufism as a versatile tradition that is open to change and interpretation. While most of the female students were not veiled, there were a small number of veiled female students as well. Although most of them studied the Quran, most of them focused on the inner dimension of Islam. Non-veiled and veiled female students lived side by side and discussed their ideas about the rules and principles of Islam. It was an act of *edep* not to judge one other. The idea of the sacred sites as schools encouraged female students to study, read and do research about their beliefs and values. Also, there were a great number of female students, who were either graduate students or PhDs, spending time in the Sufi hospices to share their knowledge with less-educated female and male students by tutoring them on various subjects such as foreign languages, grammar, history, music and poetry. Female students experienced the Sufi hospice as a space where they can practice Sufi teachings and rituals freely without having to confront male oppression.

One night, Deniz, a young beginner student, had tea with me at one o'clock in the morning after all the dishes were done. She said that at the *house* in the presence of her *efendi*, she felt peaceful and that she released her mind of her material ambitions and desires. She worked at her bookstore during the day and arrived at the lodge in the evening not only to attend *sohbets* but also to experience an environment where she was with people who also sought to embody Veli *efendi's* idea of *edep*. At work, Deniz said, she encountered people whose main goal in life was power, success and money in the material world. She said although she had a peaceful workspace, she had to interact with a variety of people during the day when shopping in the market, mailing a letter at the post office or even when walking on the street. In the *house*, she said she was with people who acted with *edep*, who sought to stay compassionate with one another. She explained how her practice of *edep* in the house taught her to be in harmony with people at work.

As anthropologist Erving Goffman states, "interaction (that is face-to-face interaction) may be roughly defined as the reciprocal influence of individuals upon one another's actions when in one another's immediate physical presence."[39] While the *efendi* with his continuous presence influenced his students' actions, students influenced one another's actions when they were in one another's immediate presence. Their spatial practice ensured "the continuity and some degree of cohesion"[40] regarding their practice of remembrance. Devotees' regular training in the sacred sites "implies a guaranteed level of competence and a specific level of performance"[41] that inspired students to embody Sufi ideas of love, unity, compassion and peace. By embodying Sufi teachings and practices consistently in the houses, students trained their *nefs* and witnessed their *efendi's* interactions (who is regarded as *kamil insan*, meaning a spiritually mature person who has journeyed through the levels of his *nefs*) and actions of senior dervishes who conveyed a sense of unity, love, compassion and peace in their interactions with their *efendi* and spiritual siblings. The sense of continuity and cohesion in practising Sufism inspired students to experience God's unity. This sense of restoring self and spaces with their embodied acts will become more clear in the following chapters, especially when I discuss the group's Konya pilgrimage in Chapter 5.

Although due to legal restrictions and secular bias students did not reveal their affiliations with the *Rifai* order as students of the *efendi* or title as a dervish in public, their embodied actions conveyed their spiritual state. Devotees explained that they recognised one another in non-Sufi settings from each other's embodiment of love and compassion. As a beginner student, Elif, who had been participating in another Sufi group's meetings for a month, said she learned about *efendi*'s group after meeting with Rüya, one of *efendi*'s dervishes, who was a pharmacist, during visits to her store. Relating how they met, Rüya joked Elif was keeping her busy, distracting her from her work. It was clear that Rüya was a bit perturbed by Elif's curiosity, who was visiting the pharmacy often, asking many questions and keeping Rüya from her duties, sometimes bringing pastries she cooked and staying over thirty minutes, preventing Rüya from serving her customers. According to Elif, Rüya's calm and peaceful presence inspired her to converse with her each time she visited. As they were sharing the story, Elif teased Rüya, saying that her pharmacy felt more like a place where she wanted to purchase spiritual guidance. After a stressful day, Elif said she would feel like she was visiting a childhood friend. In Rüya's pharmacy, she would feel at home. Elif said she found comfort in Rüya's presence. She said she liked her calm voice and the serene look in her eyes. Rüya's embodiment of divine meaning was inspiring her to act and behave with a memory of how she acted in the presence of her *efendi*. Rüya's transportation (sense of generosity achieved through the silent performance of *zikir*) inspired Elif to learn about Sufism. They conversed on news, politics, religion and meditation and one day Rüya invited Elif to meet with Veli *efendi*. At the time, Elif was practising Sufi teachings, and she was shaping Sufi practice through her efforts in teaching English to students on weekends. Her efforts enabled a young student to pass the English exam to continue her graduate education. As Veli *efendi* explained, the presence of the permanent sacred spaces allowed devotees to spend lots of time for making and shaping themselves and their spaces. As they performed their activities and rituals, students explored their *Rifai* spaces as sacred life schools where they could search for answers to their spiritual needs and ontological problems.

Salemink states that the "ritual form of identification is especially effective because of the partly nonverbal, practical, and performative character of ritual events."[42] In the group, through the embodiment of Sufi religious teachings in daily life and performance of individual and collective rituals, each student experienced, transformed and defined their identity. The feeling and sensations that students experienced and repeated regularly in the *Rifai* spaces inspired them to be mindful in their everyday lives. Training together, students sought to learn how to transform any space they occupied with Sufi idea of unity.

As a Sufi group that continued to adapt to the *çile* training, *Rifais* were also keen on going beyond the scholarship that deemed Sufism an old-fashioned and orthodox Islamic practice only suitable for rural life yet unsuitable for educated urban individuals who embody ideas such as free will, critical thinking and rational choice.[43] Another aspect of their devotional spaces was that students moved beyond the conservative idea that female students could only practice rituals in private spaces organised for women. Although the *Rifais* practised some level of gender segregation in the wooden house out of respect for less-educated conservative guests (as a way to fulfil some of their needs), they also sought ways and maintained spaces to have male and female students worship together in the same room in the residential building. Similar to Saygın *dede*, Veli *efendi* tried to adapt to the needs of both conservative and open-minded students. However, by encouraging more and more mixed gender participation, it was his desire to teach the significance of renewal and change in the *Rifai* practice.

The secluded spaces were used and transformed to develop, express and live a new identity through a distinct spatial practice. As Victor Turner states, it is true that the "inversion of prescribed everyday social roles is made possible by the out-of-the-ordinary ritual time/space" characterised by the notion of *communitas* or "anti-structure."[44] In a metropolis such as Istanbul, we are now confronted with *Rifai* actors who were creating and occupying their own spiritual spaces within secular urban spaces. As Nur once explained, "people look for therapeutic ways to deal with the damaging rhythms of modern urban daily life, which threaten the physical, social and psychological endurance of human beings."[45] For the students, reconsideration of spiritual teachings and practices was among the solutions to overcome the sense of loneliness that came with living in the hectic urban environment of Istanbul. Some students chose to spend most of their free time in the *Rifai* houses and enjoyed learning from other students, who also chose to socialise in the residential building. As a devotee in his thirties (Anıl) also explained, "I live in a house full of people, who volunteer to teach me and help me practice music to experience divine meaning."[46]

It is necessary to point out once again that compared to more public *Mevlevi* performances, which I will continue to discuss in the next chapter, Veli *efendi*'s group chose to stay away from government-related occurrences, spaces and events to preserve his group's sense of isolation, which he deemed necessary for the *çile* training. He refused to perform tourist attractions in public spaces. He did not want his students to participate in commodified events. However, he did encourage his students to give free classes (English, Turkish, poetry, mathematics, etc) to people in need. Also, although his vision for seclusion was vital for his and his students' Sufi journey, he never criticised the commodified events. Veli *efendi* knew that the commodified

Mevlevi events were accessible to people who knew nothing about Sufism. He was also aware that making commodified *Mevlevi* events more accessible was important for the mobilisation of *Mevlevi* Sufism as moderate, modern and all-embracing Islam.

Notes

1 As I did in the previous chapters, in order to respect their privacy, I will not reveal the identities of the devotees while analysing their everyday lives. Instead, I will give alternative names for the members and even for the private locations where I gathered with them.
2 Personal conversation with a senior dervish, May 11, 2013.
3 William Stoddart and R.W.J. Austin, *Sufism: The Mystical Doctrines and Methods of Islam* (Wellingborough: Thorsons Publishers, 1976), 20–21.
4 Tanvir Arjum summarises them as the following: *safa* (purity), referring to the purity of their hearts; *saff* (rank), perceiving them as the first rank before God; *suffah* (the platform), due to Sufis' resemblance to those of the *ashab-ı suffa* (meaning People of the Platform, a group of Companions of the Prophet who had devoted their lives to worship and learning); *suf* (wool), as a consequence of their habit of wearing wool; and *safwah* (the chosen, the select), for their being the chosen ones. Tanvir Anjum, "Sufism in History and its Relationship with Power," *Islamic Studies* 45, no. 2 (2006): 224.
5 In Sufism, the word "dervish" (the title given to a devotee who is initiated in the path) means one who sits in the doorway or on the threshold of something, ready to move on and transform him/herself in every moment of his/her everyday life.
6 Personal communication, October 12, 2012.
7 This businessman grew up in a religious neighbourhood and attended private religious gatherings of a Sufi group with his father.
8 D. Soyini Madison, *Critical Ethnography: Methods, Ethics and Performance* (California: Sage Publications, 2011), 186; D. Soyini Madison, "Rethinking Ethnography: Towards a Critical Cultural Politics," in *The Sage Handbook of Performance Studies*, ed. D.S. Madison and J. Hamera (Thousand Oaks, CA: Sage, 2006), 351–365.
9 Drewal, "The State of Research on Performance in Africa," 33–34.
10 Drewal, "The State of Research on Performance in Africa," 33–34.
11 Ian Richard Netton, *Sufi Ritual: The Parallel Universe* (Richmond: Curzon Press, 2000), 11.
12 Netton, *Sufi Ritual: The Parallel Universe*, 11.
13 Personal communication, August 4, 2012.
14 Unless I talk about a person specifically as a dervish, a senior dervish, or student, I generally refer to individuals as devotees or students.
15 Conversation with two senior dervishes, March 8, 2012.
16 Conversation with a senior dervish, March 8, 2012.
17 Personal communication, November 5, 2012.
18 Peña, *Performing Piety*, 46–47.
19 De Certeau, *The Practice of Everyday Life*, 117.
20 Henri Lefebvre, *The Production of Space*, trans. Donald Nicholson-Smith (Oxford: Wiley-Blackwell Publishing, 1991), 44.
21 Goffman, *The Presentation of Self in Everyday Life*, 73–74.
22 Goffman, *The Presentation of Self in Everyday Life*, 73–74.
23 Goffman, *The Presentation of Self in Everyday Life*, 73–74.
24 Schechner, *Performance Studies: An Introduction*, 10.

94 Restoring

25 Shakina Reinhertz, *Women Called to the Path of Rumi: The Way of the Whirling Dervish* (Prescott: Hohm Press, 2001), 29–30.
26 Reinhertz, *Women Called to the Path of Rumi*, 29–30.
27 Reinhertz, *Women Called to the Path of Rumi*, 29–30.
28 Reinhertz, *Women Called to the Path of Rumi*, 29–30.
29 William C. Chittick, "The Perfect Man as the Prototype of the Self in the Sufism of Jami," *Studia Islamica* 49 (1979): 136.
30 Chittick, "The Perfect Man as the Prototype of the Self in the Sufism of Jami," 136.
31 Personal communication, November 5, 2012.
32 Chittick, "The Perfect Man as the Prototype of the Self in the Sufism of Jami," 135–136.
33 Turner, *From Ritual to Theatre: The Human Seriousness of Play*, 105.
34 Veli *efendi*'s *sohbet*.
35 Syed Rizwan Zamir, "'Tafsir al-Quran bi'l Quran': The Hermeneutics of Imitation and 'Adap' in Ibn-i Arabi's Interpretation of the Quran," *Islamic Studies* 50, no. 1 (2007): 16–17.
36 Personal communication, January 4, 2012.
37 Pnina Werbner, "Stamping the Earth with the Name of Allah and the Sacralising of Space Among British Muslims," *Cultural Anthropology* 11, no. 3 (1996): 320.
38 Ositola Kolawole, "On Ritual Performance: A Practitioner's View," *TDR: The Drama Review* 32, no. 2 (1981): 35.
39 Goffman, *The Presentation of Self in Everyday Life*, 26.
40 Lefebvre, *The Production of Space*, 33.
41 Lefebvre, *The Production of Space*, 33.
42 Oscar Salemink, "Embodying the Nation: Mediumship Ritual and the National Imagination," *Journal of Vietnamese Studies* 3, no. 3 (2008): 270.
43 See works of J.D. Howell, "Sufism and the Indonesian Islamic Revival," *The Journal of Asian Studies*, no. 60 (2001): 701–729; Tayfun Atay, *Batı'da Bir Nakşi Cemaati: Nazım Kıbrısı Örneği [A Nakşi Congregation in the West: Nazım Kıbrısı Case]* (İstanbul: İletişim Yayınları, 1996).
44 Victor Turner, "Introduction," in *Celebration: Studies in Festivity and Ritual*, ed. Victor Turner (Washington, DC: Smithsonian Institution Press, 1982), 29; Victor Turner, *The Anthropology of Performance* (New York: PAJ Publications, 1987), 44–45; Salemink, "Embodying the Nation: Mediumship Ritual and the National Imagination," 270.
45 Personal communication, November 28, 2012.
46 Personal communication, November 28, 2012.

Part Two
Transmitting

3 Whirling "Anytime and AnyPlace"*

One rainy evening, I arrived at the Fatih district of Istanbul, an area recognised for its conservative Turkish Muslim residents. Having arrived at a historical Sufi lodge, I was invited into a large, crowded room filled with male devotees sitting on the carpet covering the floor of the entire space. It was as if everyone knew one another. On the other side of the room, I saw Tuğrul İnançer, a conservative scholar and teacher of Sufism, known for his discriminating comments about women's role in public.[1] For the devotees, it was clearly his presence that sacralised this space, which was a recognised historical Sufi *tekke* called the Nurettin Cerrahi *tekke* (a historical non-*Mevlevi* Sufi lodge built in 1710–1720—located in the Fatih district of Istanbul). To me, the space gained multilayered meanings with the embodied acts of the devotees and tourists: at times, a touristic bazaar, a living history museum or a period movie set (with props and costumes).

This was a space used by the devotees of a Cerrahi Sufi group (which used to be a Sufi order founded by Nurettin Muhammed El-Cerrahi, whose tomb is placed in the courtyard of the historical *tekke*). By this time, I had visited all the historical *Mevlevi* sites, conversed with many *semazens* and attended most of the whirling ritual gatherings in and around Istanbul, Izmir and Konya. Having heard about the Sufi music and *zikir* ritual performances at the Nurrettin Cerrahi *tekke*, despite my reservations about their spiritual teacher or leader Tuğrul İnançer, I decided to take this opportunity presented by a friend, who seemed to know enough important people in the group to get permission for my participation as a guest. He said, "you should see this gathering. It is a mixture of what is modern and anti-modern in Turkey."[2] I comprehended what he meant as soon as I arrived at the *tekke*. At first sight, it felt like a Sufi space out of this time or more clearly a period movie set or living history museum such as effectively interpreted historical villages. It was a male-dominated space as in many Ottoman *tekkes*. Most of the women were veiled. Despite the law, there were many men wearing dervish garments in the courtyard. Although this would not be confusing and out of time in today's Turkey, where it has been possible to see many Sufi figures in public, or even on media, back then it was still early to feel this as Turkey's new ordinary. With JDP turning a blind eye to Sufi organisations that

DOI: 10.4324/9781003118589-6

embody Ottoman tariqa traditions in more than ten years, there have been more and more Sufi or Sufi-esque groups that carry out RAD's conservative and political Islamist vision.

I remember a sign at the entrance saying *Foundation for the Research and Sustenance of Turkish Sufi Music and Folklore*. Although this sign was probably a reminder for all the visitors that this was a space assigned to a foundation, not a tariqa, anything else other than the sign was conveying otherwise. Here, it is necessary to give attention to Raymond Lifchez's discussion about different Ottoman Sufi lodges to talk about the meaning of this space for Sufi devotees. He states, the lodges "are referred to by a variety of names: *tekke, hanekah, asitane, zaviye, dergah*."[3] *Tekke* (or *hanekah*) is the generic term used for any dervish facility, *asitane* (grand lodge) is the main *tarikat* facility, *zaviye* is a dervish hostel or residence belonging to no particular order and *dergah* is the *tekke* with a tomb attached to it.[4] *Dergahs* had a critical importance in the Sufi devotional practice, since the saints' tombs acted "as a permanent focus for devotion towards the spiritual manifestation of the saints (and to their visualisation after death), a devotion parallel to the respect and homage paid them during their lifetime."[5] Therefore, Sufi *dergahs*, although converted into museums or universities, have been the most valuable sites for Sufi devotion. Although I will discuss the significance of *Rifai* pilgrimage and role of Sufi shrines in Sufi practice in Chapter 5, here I would like to reflect on their meaning for the Cerrahi devotees further to examine the use of the historical space as a *tekke* further.

Before entering the Nurrettin Cerrahi *tekke*, most of the devotees were first stopping and praying in front of the salutation window of a tomb located in the garden of the space. As Baha Tanman identifies, this is a ritualised act in which the pilgrim performs "a number of reverential acts, pausing at set intervals as he crossed the floor to take up an attitude of supplication (*niyaz*), feet pressed together, toes crossed, head bowed" and "after completing devotions there, the pilgrim would retreat from this window with the same motions of respect."[6] In the presence of the tomb, devotees were praying with a sense of focus, conveying obedience and submission to the deceased spiritual teacher. Most of the devotees seemed to perform devotion by locating themselves at the foot section of the tomb (believing that it was considered disrespectful to stand at the head). Tanman discusses further:

> A dervish would arrive at the threshold of the tomb and adopt there an attitude of humility, taking care not to step on the threshold, which he regarded with great reverence as the point of transition between the manifest and esoteric worlds.[7]

Before entering the tomb, devotees seemed to convey their respect at the threshold, lowering their body according to the entrance, bowing and then kissing the door lintel to the right of the entrance. During these gestures, devotees would be expected to recite "the *besmele* [basmala] or [exclaim]

'*Destur* [permission],' requesting permission from the deceased to enter the tomb."[8] Devotees would also be expected to deliver their greetings to the saints: "'*Esselamu aleykum ya veliyullah*!' ('Hail to you, oh friend of God!')."[9] From their bows and kisses, it was clear that these devotees were feeling affection and praying because they believed that *evliyas*' (saints') spirits would continue to guide them in their spiritual journey. Devotees' actions were also conveying the significance of their visitation. Historically, although, the lodges and mausoleums were locked up for a long time in the Republican period, their spiritual significance continued to grow with pilgrims' coming to pray in such Sufi sites. The quality of devotees' bodily movements were confirming this historical knowledge.

As the devotees performed their devotion at the *tekke*, tourists were observing their acts of praying and kissing the frame of the window as a sign of love for the saints. Devotees' embodied acts were conveying the sense of sacredness in the space. The tourists were audience members who were waiting to be invited into the *semahane* to watch the ritual performance. Cengiz (a devotee friend that defines himself a *Mevlevi* by heart) also informed me later that there were members of the group who made arrangements with tourist agencies to invite tourist audiences. Side by side, devotees and tourists were creating a space where pious and secular acts seemed to occur simultaneously and in harmony. However, something was missing in this gathering. It seemed different from the simultaneously sacred and touristic gatherings of Saygın *dede* and the secluded gatherings of Veli *efendi*. I was not seeing the desire and joy that Saygın *dede*'s devotees conveyed at the Yenikapı *Mevlevi* lodge or Veli *efendi*'s devotees transmitted in their *Rifai* home. This was probably because no one seemed to interact with one another. I did not see anyone looking into each other's eyes or smiling other than a devotee answering tourists' questions. Everyone seemed to be either deep in thought or too careful as they performed their tasks or interacted (only when necessary). Bodily movements seemed more mechanic, planned, or too rehearsed.

Men and women were using separate entrances to enter the same large building at the back of the courtyard. I was able to see through a window of the building on the right side of the courtyard where male devotees were performing *namaz*. Then, as the male devotees completed their *namaz*, they came out and walked to the entrance of another building that, as Cengiz explained, was the ritual space. Female devotees, mostly veiled, were entering the same building from a different entrance with stairs going to the second floor of the ritual space. Then Cengiz directed me towards the door through which male devotees entered. A male devotee standing inside asked me to take off my shoes, welcomed us in and placed our shoes in a large closet. The greeting rituals were very similar to the gatherings in the *Rifai* home. We passed through a hall covered with carpets and rugs filled with male devotees selling dervish *mests* (ankle-high leather slippers that cover the feet), serving tea, answering another group of English-speaking guests' questions (as Cengiz explained, these were invited guests, from either other

Sufi groups abroad or individuals who had come to watch the whirling ritual) and helping others with their coats. Inside, there were male devotees, their children and devotee and non-devotee guests. While one devotee was sitting and meditating, conveying a sense of devotion and giving the space a sacred feeling, another devotee was selling dervish objects, giving the space a touristic feeling. Regarding the commerce of dervish objects and devotees' communication with the tourists, the duties performed in the Nurettin Cerrahi *tekke* were different from the duties performed at the Yenikapı *Mevlevi* lodge or the *Rifai* home. The sense of seclusion was somewhere between Yenikapı *Mevlevi* lodge and the wooden house. Also, the sense of devotion was strong, but probably because there were business transactions, it felt like a small touristic bazaar as well as a ritual space.

Just on the left side of the room, Cengiz stopped by the male devotee selling *mests* who greeted Cengiz. He offered to buy me a pair as a gift and knowing the Sufi custom that the offer should not be refused, I agreed. There was also a devotee selling *tesbihs*, who was talking to an English-speaking male tourist. The tourist asked the devotee his favourite colour of the *tesbih* and in a humble tone, the male devotee said, "it is the quality of the devotional act that counts," trying to explain to the guest that the colour of the *tesbih* did not matter. This conversation was specifically conveying how devotees were embodying mixed codes in the space, trying to share their religious values as they sold their worship items to the tourists.

As soon as I put my *mests* on, another devotee wearing dervish headgear and a *hırka* (a woollen shirt-like garment or cloak with long sleeves)[10] guided us into the ritual hall, the *semahane*, a large room filled with mystical objects and the smell of incense. This was a rectangle-shaped room with its floors covered with Islamic carpets and rugs, walls covered with framed Quranic passages (calligraphies) and *kandil* lights hanging from the ceiling. The devotee asked me kindly to sit behind a rope that was placed in the corner of the room to separate the audience from the worship space. As I sat behind the rope on the floor and began to wait for the ceremony, I realised that I was the only woman in the space (thinking that the female tourists were still outside the building waiting to be guided in) and that I was not going to be able to participate in the ritual or communicate with the devotees. Sitting by myself, I noticed Cengiz sitting on the floor by the door near a group of male devotees on the other side of the room. Male devotees were taking their places, with their backs to the rope. As I was watching the male devotees sitting and meditating by counting the beads on their *tesbihs*, I was witnessing the sense of concentration and calmness in their part of the room.

After a while, a male devotee brought in the group of tourists who were waiting in the courtyard. As the tourists walked down the hall, the devotee was guiding them towards their seats. His body was conveying a sense of devotion as he seated the tourists, greeting them with a slight bow, showing his respect. With the tourist audience members coming in and taking their places next to me, I was no longer the only female present in the male section

Whirling "Anytime and AnyPlace" 101

of the ritual space. However, like the mosques and in comparison to Saygın *dede*'s and Veli *dede*'s groups, the space was male dominated. There were ten other women behind the rope. Then, I noticed additional women upstairs in a dark space, sitting in the mezzanine and realised that the separate entrance with the stairs was female devotees' way to climb to the upper section of the ritual space. As audience members, the female tourists and I were able to share the men's ritual space, while female devotees were in a separate section, on the mezzanine facing the audience.

Women were visible behind the latticework wooden windows but not to male devotees, who were placed under the mezzanine. I finally saw some male devotees greet each other by placing their right hands on their hearts, slightly moving their heads forward and taking their seats on the floor. After a while, İnançer arrived and the ceremony began with extensive Quran readings, *Salavatı Şerifs* (chants that praise Prophet Muhammed) and then the *zikir* ceremony. İnançer's arrival seemed to create a sense of rigour or discipline in the room. Some devotees seemed to adjust their upper bodies straightening their backs and concentration increased even more. The *zikir* started with devotees seeking God's forgiveness and continued with devotees repeating *"la ilaha illallah"* ("there is no deity but God") in a rhythmic manner. Devotees performed *zikir* in a seated position. As they chanted, they regularly moved their heads down and to the left, directing their energy into their hearts and back, then vocalised the phrase again. The space was very crowded with around one hundred men, young and old, sitting on their knees, delivering the phrase *"la ilaha illallah."*

In a short while, the *semazens* entered in their ritual garments—the black cloaks, white *tennures* and *sikkes*[11]—and filled the empty rectangular space between the male devotees performing *zikir* and audience members sitting behind the rope. They did not seem like they had enough space to perform. It was clear that this space was not specifically arranged for the *Mevlevi* ceremony. I also was not expecting to witness a *Mevlevi sema* in the Nurettin Cerrahi *tekke* because as analysed by İnançer, *sema* ceremony was a specific form of *zikir* that was practised only in the *Mevlevi* order.[12] However, devotees were also performing *sema* ceremony. This, according to Catharina Raudvere, showed how *Mevlevi sema* "[was] the emblematic image of Sufi rituals."[13] When I asked a devotee from the Cerrahi order about the *sema* ceremony, he said they organised *sema* ceremony for the Thursday night gatherings. He explained, "this was for the tourist guests,"[14] confirming my experience of the *tekke* as a living history museum. However, I was not clear whether the whirling was a worship for the *semazens* as it was for Saygın *dede*'s group. But, before I go on analysing my personal conversation with the *semazens* to discuss this confusion, I would like to provide some more details about the execution of the whole event.

The spectatorial aspects of this gathering brought forth the notion of theatricality that is also visible in living history museums because Cerrahis unintentionally created a space that directed the focus of their tourist audiences to the *semazens*. This allowed them to create a distance between male devotees' worship experience and the tourist audience. The space arranged for the whirling ritual was in between where the male devotees were sitting and repeating God's names and where the tourist audience was sitting and watching behind the rope. When *semazens* started whirling in front of us, a tourist next to me said to her friend in a low tone that she was glad that the whirling dervishes were close to them, making it clear that she came to the lodge to witness the performance of *Mevlevi sema*. While the rope and the whirling ritual separated us completely from the male devotees sitting and repeating God's names on the other side of the room, some of the tourists like me changed their position to be able to see the male devotees. We were able to hear the deep and low voices of the male devotees, their repetitive chanting and images of their heads moving swiftly in between the whirling dervishes' white *tennures*. It was as if there were four different groups in the room: men sitting and repeating "*la ilaha illallah*" on one side, an audience watching behind a rope, women repeating "*la ilaha illallah*" upstairs and *semazens* performing the whirling ritual in the middle of the male devotees and the tourists. Sitting behind the rope, we were now able to watch the male devotees' rapturous movements as they performed *zikir*, the *semazens* whirling in a state of peace with their eyes closed and women moving their heads to the rhythm of the *zikir* behind the latticework windows in the upper room. Some tourists were looking up and observing the women's section, some were watching the feet of the *semazens*, while others were constantly changing their position to see the dervishes throw their heads side to side and chant. The whirling ritual performed as a tourist attraction in between male devotees chanting, and the audience members allowed male devotees a level of privacy as if they were actors performing behind an invisible fourth wall on a proscenium arch in a theatre. While one part of the room felt like a ritual hall, the other part felt like a living history museum.

Throughout the gathering, there was performatic shift and doubling occurring in every corner of the lodge, with devotees performing their touristic acts, fulfilling their position as a foundation to preserve the space for their devotional practices. With the sign presenting the space as a foundation for research at the entrance, devotees praying in front of the tomb, the devotee selling *mests* for tourists, devotees guiding guests, the audience sitting behind the rope and *semazens* blocking devotees sitting and performing *zikir*, devotees were embodying and transmitting their religious values, while also conveying their relationship to the commodified and touristic values of modern Turkey. It was clear that the devotees welcomed the female guests in the male section of the *zikir* hall and placed me and the female tourists next to male tourists, taking into consideration the modern values of the Turkish State. While female devotees did not have access to the male section of the *zikir* hall, which was clearly in line with the religious values of their conservative teacher, the female tourists were able to sit in the same room with male devotees, who chanted and whirled. Through the doubling of secular and religious acts, it was clear that the devotees created ways, such as the use of the rope and the performance of the whirling ritual, to stay in harmony with the demands of the Ministry of Culture and Tourism while also practising their strictly religious codes (in accord with the mainstream Islamic doctrine), such as the division of male and female worship spaces. The government and the Cerrahi group were clearly aware of the fact that Rumi's whirling was popular as the symbol of secularism and moderate Islam; therefore, it was necessary to give the *semazens* a place in between the tourists and the male devotees performing their own form of *zikir*.

The religious gathering at the Nurettin Cerrahi *tekke*, while providing the opportunity for tourists to witness the whirling ceremony, also allowed the tourists to witness the sense of devotion practised by male devotees performing Cerrahi *zikir*. As in Taylor's analysis, "the performative shift and doubling ... preserved rather than erased the antecedents."[15] Devotees, by doubling their performance of ritual gathering as a religious event and tourist attraction, managed to present the tourists a piece from Rumi's Islam. Devotees played the government's commodification game and took the performance of the whirling ritual as an opportunity to meet the demands of the ministry. They were practising devotion in a historical Sufi lodge, protecting their rights as a foundation and transmitting *Mevlevi* cultural beliefs and values. At the time, by having tourists attend their ceremony, they were managing to stay in harmony with the secular values of the Turkish State. However, I believe that was not much of a concern in recent years, at least since the JDP took control of all government agencies. I find it necessary to point out that today, many conservative groups do not seem to worry about the secular values articulated in the constitution. This is a difficult time for Sufi groups that challenge the JDP Islamist worldview with their mixed-gender gatherings.

Later, when I had a chance to converse with the *semazens* performing the ceremony, they helped me answer some of my questions about their performance of the whirling ritual as a touristic performance. Some of the *semazens* seemed to consider themselves both *Mevlevi* and Cerrahi (following certain teachings and rituals of both traditions). I realised that it did not matter to them whether they belonged to one or more groups. Some described themselves simply as students of Sufism. Only one of them seemed to be the dervishes of Tuğrul İnançer, who did not want to comment on their practice. The rest were students seeking to practice whirling "anytime and anyplace" as Rumi did in his time.[16] When my devotee friend, Cengiz, informed me that he would bring me to the Cerrahi group's gathering, I knew from Catharina Raudvere's and Fulya Atacan's studies that the group was a Sufi order that has continued their religious activities in the lodge since the 1980s.[17] Although Law 677 concerned the closure of Sufi spaces and use of Sufi titles, due to their historical and artistic importance, in the 1950s and again in the 1990s, the government allowed the opening of some Sufi shrines to the public.[18] Raudvere points out that "It appears to have been common knowledge during the whole Kemalistic era that Sufi gatherings took place, and many right-wing and/or nationalist politicians were (and still are) affiliated with *tarikats* [*tariqas*]."[19] At the time, "All this was tolerated as long as the orders did not act openly as religious organisations [religious orders]."[20] However, as I mentioned in Chapter 1, with the strengthening of the Islamist groups in Turkey and the JDP's support for the restoration of Ottoman values and traditions, Sufi groups' desire to emphasise their religious values in public was no more a problem. Lately, political parties (such as Cumhuriyet Halk Partisi [Republican People's Party]) trying to protect the secular values of the Turkish State have not been able to interfere much with how Islamists organised and held their events. As I discussed earlier, the problem was no longer emphasising Islamic values but how they were emphasised due to JDP's conservative vision. According to the RAD and conservative Sufi groups that support the RAD's vision, devotees should not mobilise Sufism in a way that threatens conservative Islamic values. Therefore, Islamists were promoting the religiousness of Rumi's poetry whenever and wherever possible. It was clear that the group did not necessarily organise the whirling performance for his devotees but for the tourists visiting this historical space. This was important because while some of the *semazens* performing the ritual that night whirled for devotion, some whirled to fulfil their teacher's agenda to create a touristic performance. While *sema* was a worship for Saygın *dede*'s group, it was a touristic performance for some Cerrahis. Regarding the case of the *semazens* performing for devotion at the Nurrettin Cerrahi *tekke*, their performance showed the level of homelessness and confusion experienced by the *Mevlevis* in Turkey. Although, as I will discuss in the following sections, it was clear that most of the *Mevlevis*' open-mindedness was their guide to constantly adapt to new conditions, their desire to perform anytime and anyplace also showed their determined attitude for transmitting their version of Sufism and Rumi. Some elderly *semazens*, musicians and/or poets performed Sufi poetry and whirling anytime and anyplace as long as they saw an opportunity to share *Mevlevi* cultural beliefs and values. Many even changed how they defined their religious identities and called themselves Mevlana's students instead of devotees that follow the path of one living spiritual teacher.

"A *Mevlevi* By Heart"

Meeting with a variety of people who considered themselves students of Mevlana or *Mevlevi* has played an important role during the first months of my field research, when I knew very little about the multifaceted nature of *Mevlevi* culture in Turkey. As a member of the Sufi community, Cengiz took or directed me to several *Mevlevi* gatherings and he helped me get in touch with *semazens* who would be willing to speak with me. He was also the first devotee who informed me about how devotees were in constant need to seek and produce spaces for their collective practices, such as *sohbets* and performance of rituals. He considered himself "a *Mevlevi* by heart," meaning a practitioner of *Mevlevi* teachings without any connection to a specific *Mevlevi* group.

Born and raised in Istanbul, he was known to be sociable and knew many people from different cultural, religious and economic backgrounds. Upon calling him and hearing his way of speaking, I realised how he was including Allah's name in every sentence as if talking was *zikretmek* (remembering God in each moment). Also, when I thanked him at the end of our phone call, he said to me that he only acts in the service of Allah. Although for me thanking a person was a usual way of delivering my gratitude in social life, I later found out that for Cengiz it was a lack of acknowledging God's unity and that Cengiz was seeking to remind himself of his devotion to God in every moment of his day-to-day interactions. This was his way of practising remembrance at all times.

The next day, I woke up and travelled to Cengiz's office as planned. I dressed as I always do but made sure it was modest and with minimal skin exposed. And I did remember to put a shawl to use as a headscarf in my bag, just in case I arrived at a place full of veiled women. A friend drove me to the address. Kindly, two men at the entrance welcomed me in. I informed one of the gentlemen that I had an appointment with Cengiz, and he accompanied me to the sixth floor. I arrived at an office that looked like a combination of a *Mevlevi dergah* room, library and museum. It was clear from the objects and books in the office that Rumi was an important part of Cengiz Bey's life. The secretary informed me that Cengiz Bey was performing his *namaz* (*salat* or Muslim prayer)[21] and offered me a seat at a comfortable chair by a collection of *Mevlevi* books placed on six large, white, clean and organised bookcases. He had about five hundred colourful books about Islam, Sufism and Rumi, all organised by subject. Then, I looked around, observing the necklaces, rings, dervish and *semazen* statuettes and sculptures and Sufi marble artworks placed in glass cases on his desk, in cabinets and on the coffee table. The walls of the office were also filled with framed Quranic texts.

After a while, a door opened right behind his desk and Cengiz walked in wearing khaki pants and a polo shirt and approached me to shake my hand. I later found out that the room he walked out of was a private space in his office to perform *namaz* or meditate with the *zikir* ritual. Meeting Cengiz in his office, I understood how he sought to act and behave with God in mind and as a result consecrated the places he occupied throughout the day as sites of his spiritual training. Cengiz defined himself as a member of the Sufi community in Istanbul and as a businessman who attended religious/community gatherings of various Sufi groups, whose heart was in Rumi's *Mesnevi* (Masnavi or Mathnavi). Although he never articulated this, it was clear from his conversations with other devotees in meetings we attended together that he formed social and economic networks as well as spiritual bonds with devotees of various Sufi orders. For Cengiz, there were different kinds of Sufi groups and individuals in Turkey. Some of them were functioning as Sufi orders, continuing the rules and principles embodied in Ottoman

Sufi tariqas, such as regularly training with a spiritual leader. Some were only gathering to study Sufi texts, music and rituals. Cengiz explained to me in detail how he had been studying Rumi's teachings for ten years. He was interested in consecrating his private spaces to remember God (perform *zikir*) as he worked in his office and spent time at his home, therefore he has been transforming his living spaces with Sufi books, objects, religious hymns and prayers hung on the walls.

I learned from him that in Turkey, there were students who practised only specific aspects of *Mevlevi* devotion. These people had different ways of identifying their and their associates' practice of Rumi's teachings. Some of these identified themselves as devotees, *Mevlevis*, students, Sufi artists, Sufi dancers and *semazens*. Although they all had different ways of studying and practising *Mevlevi* teachings and rituals, some were not associated with a specific spiritual teacher as required in the traditional *Mevlevi* circles (*Mevlevi* tariqas in Europe and the United States continue this tradition and some secluded groups in Turkey as in the case of Veli *efendi's* group). The common thread among them was their desire to practise Rumi's teachings and rituals, create temporary spaces for their devotional gatherings and share *Mevlevi* beliefs and values with the secular public.

Mevlana's (or Rumi's) Students Versus Conservative "Tarikatçiler"

Secular *Mevlevis* called themselves Mevlana's students and desired to avoid any contact with conservative groups that secular people tend to refer to as "*tarikatçiler*."[22] These were individuals who practised Rumi's teachings and his whirling ritual anytime and anyplace without following any rules regarding the symbols, length or the space of the ceremony. All they seemed to care about was the intention of their performance. They performed in a variety of commodified spaces with a desire to transmit Rumi's vision and encouraged people to move beyond conservative and reductionist views about Sufism. Also, many of them emphasised the fact that they have adopted a more modern (post-tariqa) and secular approach to studying and practising Sufism. They were aware of the strictly doctrinal ideas of some conservative Sufi groups and desired to show their difference as secular and democratic Sufi practitioners embracing the process. Most believed that Rumi's vision of Islam was beyond the negative ideas that secular elites continued to hold about Islamic faith (due to how dominant and political Sufi groups present Sufism as one-sided and strictly doctrinal practice). For them, Rumi's Islam is moderate, all-embracing and adaptable.

It was in the first years of my fieldwork in Turkey that I witnessed how each moment was an opportunity to interact with secular elites, who are judgmental about the appearance of Sufism in public. These were individuals who had guided my critical thinking about *Mevlevis* and Rumi's image in the secular Turkish society. Even lengthy family gatherings on the Aegean Coast of Turkey proved to be invaluable in developing my understanding of how and why some *Mevlevis* chose to introduce themselves as students rather than *Mevlevis*. As discussed earlier (in the Introduction), the Aegean Coast, especially Izmir (where I was born and raised), housed families who followed Atatürk's ideas devotedly and perceived Ottoman religious life as the opposite of progress, modernity and civilisation. Secular Turks (who consider themselves followers of Atatürk) still feel uncomfortable with the appearance of Islamic symbols and acts in public. In the summer of 2010, during my first visit back to Turkey as a research student, having breakfast with my aunt and her friends in a beautifully flowered garden of a beach house in Çeşme, I was perusing an article in *Aktüel* (a Turkish magazine) about whirling dervishes in Turkey. An elderly friend of my aunt (Aslı), having heard from my grandmother that I was researching Sufism, said, "how interesting it is that you are attempting to study such a 'different' topic."[23] I immediately knew what she meant by "different." As a passionate follower of Atatürk's secular ideas against religion, she was expressing her surprise at my desire to research such an Islamic topic. Aslı asked: "What are you studying exactly?" I answered, "I am researching *Mevlevi*' performances and religious/community spaces in contemporary Turkey."[24] Taking pride in her attachment to Atatürk's secular ideas, she said, "I thought dervishes did not exist anymore?" When I explained how I am focusing on post-tariqa groups' performances such as the whirling ritual, Ayşen, a doctor, shared her enchantment with the idea of peace and compassion in Rumi's religious poetry. Then, Elif shared a recognised Sufi proverb attributed to Rumi: "Come whoever you are, wanderer, worshipper, lover of leaving (it doesn't matter). Ours is not a caravan of despair. Come, come even if you have broken your vows a thousand times. Come, come yet again, come."[25] An older lady friend of my aunt wanting to continue the conversation said, "I know very little about Rumi's teachings but I read Shams Tabrizi's ideas [a wandering dervish, whom Rumi perceived as a master and friend] in Elif Şafak's novel."[26] In writing *The Forty Rules of Love*, Şafak was criticised by some scholars and critics for demeaning Sufi teachings by taking them out of their Islamic context. Yet secular Turks took interest in Şafak's interpretation. As I was sipping my tea, listening in delight to their fascination with Şafak's novel, one of them cautioned me explaining how Sufi sheikhs deceive people in Turkey.[27] After saying that, she made a grimace and told me once again to be careful. To comfort her, I said that I would. That night, writing about this conversation in my journal, I thought of how due to generalisations created by the media, people in Turkey knew very little about post-tariqa Sufism in Turkey. To them, Sufism was either extinct or extremist.

Many *Mevlevi* devotees as secular members of Turkish society seemed to share similar concerns and took every opportunity to discuss Rumi's idea of diversity. According to Rumi, the interpretation of a sacred text is true if it "makes you ardent and hopeful and active and reverent."[28] *Mevlevis* expressed that there were a great number of secular elites who searched for a spiritual direction through Rumi's poetry and whirling. For this reason, these devotees wanted to teach their version of Rumi's life and poetry to individuals who are curious about how Rumi embraced spirituality. Many devotees talked about Rumi's father in order to emphasise how Rumi was simultaneously a man of Islamic doctrine and spiritual meaning. As Franklin Lewis evaluates, Rumi's father "Bahâ al-Din's preoccupation with the presence of God and with divine intimations and promptings cannot escape the notice of even a casual reader of the Macaref [also known as Ma'arif, often translated as Gnosis]."[29] His father had a

> predisposition to mystical visions of an almost surreal, synaesthetic or even psychedelic quality. He describes visions in which he hovers in the air, predicts the life span of individuals, sees colours, fluids and matter flowing within and without himself and other objects, and sometimes talks with God as one would with a friend.[30]

Although

> hagiographers would have us believe, Rumi did not know of his father's mystical proclivities until Borhân al-Din introduced them to him . . . [g]iven his near obsession with purity of heart, the divine presence and his frequent visions, it seems extremely implausible that Rumi knew nothing of his father's mysticism.[31]

Mevlevis also respected the fact that Rumi's works are in great connection with the Quran and the words of Prophet Muhammed. However, they also sought to transmit the idea that his teachings showed that his connection to a spirituality beyond doctrinal practice was also full of revelations. Many students believed that Rumi was able to see the unity in Islam. The problem for many of them was witnessing how conservative Muslims distorted or avoided some of Rumi's spiritual ideas and therefore they thought it was their responsibility to cherish and transmit the multilayered quality of his teachings.[32] Rumi's commitment to diversity also encouraged the students to adapt to socio-political circumstances in present-day Turkey. Today, in the post-tariqa *Mevlevi* circles, it is possible to meet a great number of *Mevlevis* who take specific actions to practice Sufi ritual in public to share what they believe to be the true form of Rumi's teachings. Most of them legalise their presence in the country as civil society organisations (some as foundations [*vakıfs*] and some as associations [*derneks*]).[33] They use and if necessary commodify their religious rituals as cultural, educational and/or touristic activities to get permission to use public spaces, such as cultural centres and museums (controlled by different government agencies, including the Ministry of Culture and Tourism, the Education Department and the Directorate General of Foundations) to generate *Mevlevi* practice. They trusted that transformation and adaption of *Mevlevi* cultural beliefs and values were necessary for the dissemination of Rumi's teachings as long as they preserved its spiritual meaning. Along with these ideas, these students believed that transmitting Rumi's vision in a variety of spaces was the key to the mobilisation of the all-embracing aspect of *Mevlevi* teachings. In this regard, it may be that there was some rivalry between conservative Muslims and secular *Mevlevis* to attract Mevlana's vision to their side.

One example of this dilemma was the conservative writer, former politician and member of a *Mevlevi* foundation Fatih Çıtlak's views about the exploitation of Rumi's views. In a newspaper article, the conservative writer and former politician Fatih Çıtlak said:

> Unfortunately, the concept of the *Mevlevi* order was desecrated. There have been people looking to gain financial benefits from the *Mevlevi* order and those who exploited the mystic's views and attempted to blend them with their own views for personal gains.[34]

This was part of an interview conducted with the Rumi's twenty-second-generation grandson, Faruk Hemdem Çelebi, and one of the leaders of the order, M. Fatih Çıtlak. When I read this article in 2014, having participated in Çıtlak's classes and gatherings, I was familiar with his concerns about male and female *semazens* whirling together and non-Muslims practising *Mevlevi* rituals. However, his desire to restrict Rumi's poetry and rituals to his conservative vision was not clear at the time. Rumi's words or whirling, according to a *Mevlevi*, Narin *dede*, did not need anyone's protection. As the head of the International Mevlana Foundation, Çelebi's concern was about the practice of *Sema* solely as entertainment. In the interview, Çelebi states: "Despite our foundation's efforts and despite designation by UNESCO with a preservation status, 'sema' [the whirling ritual of the order] is being performed irresponsibly everywhere."[35] Çelebi articulated a slightly different concern when speaking about his desire for the preservation of Rumi's legacy and the protection of the sacred values of the ceremony. Çelebi has been working to disseminate the secular and multi-cultural values in Rumi's teachings since 1996. Çelebi's concerns were equally important for all the *Mevlevis* since while UNESCO attempted to protect *Sema* ceremony and Rumi as inheritances of Sufi culture, the designation could not go beyond representing Sufism as an immobilised spiritual culture of Turkey. The information on the website failed to inform the reader that *Sema* was performed as a *zikir*, involving both vocal and instrumental compositions; readings from the Quran; recitation of verses from *Mesnevi* (the spiritual teachings of Rumi); singing of the "*Naat-ı Serif*" (the poem of Mevlana praising Muhammed); meditative walking and saluting positions; and whirling as an inspirational spiritual force.[36]

David Smith's discussion illuminates the idea that UNESCO's promotion of cultural knowledge lacked careful analysis and essential information. Smith argues UNESCO's aim to promote survival of "traditional folklore, knowledge, and artistic expressions throughout the world, including oral traditions and expressions, performing arts, social practices, rituals and festive events, knowledge and practices concerning nature and the universe and traditional craftsmanship," did not go far enough: "The problem lies, perhaps, in the ways in which we have attempted to understand and classify knowledge. The Western philosophical tradition has largely marginalised and discounted knowledge, which cannot be represented in propositional form (and, preferably, written down)."[37] Most *Mevlevis* agree that UNESCO's advertising of *Sema* through imprecisely written and recorded publicity, corresponding to the Turkish government's commodification of Sufism, was inadequate in terms of providing detailed information about the ceremony's role in Sufism. Çelebi, in a number of major newspapers, voiced his concerns about the use of *Mevlevi* beliefs and values by individuals, who distort Rumi's message and use *Sema* ceremony as folk performance, expressing his discomfort with corrupted individuals who present themselves as *Mevlevi* spiritual teachers.[38] Many *Mevlevi* devotees shared Çelebi's concerns about the use of *Sema* ceremony as folk performance; however, they were also aware that the performance of the whirling ritual in commodified spaces was also an opportunity to mobilise Rumi's multi-cultural Sufi vision.

However, for Çıtlak, the matter was beyond the preservation of *Mevlevi* cultural beliefs and values. As stated in the article, Çıtlak's concern was slightly different from Çelebi's. He said "There are people who claim to be *Mevlevi* but not Muslims. No one has the right to spoil the *Mevlevi* order under the guise of being its faithful members. They do not know what *Mevlevi* beliefs are really about."[39] This, for many *Mevlevi* devotees, who believe in the universality of Rumi's message, was an attack on the deeper meaning of Rumi's teachings. Although Çıtlak has been one of the well-known writers and teachers delivering Rumi's teachings, according to Cemal (a *Mevlevi* teacher) or Narin *dede*, his comments about *Mevlevi* culture and non-Muslims contradicted Rumi's ideas. In his discourses, Rumi shares a story about non-Muslim followers of his teachings. He states:

> I was speaking there one day when a party of unbelievers was present. In the middle of my talk they began to weep with emotion and show signs of ecstasy. Someone asked: "What can they understand? What do they know? Only one Muslim in a thousand understands this kind of talk. What could an unbeliever understand that would cause them to weep?" Rumi answered: It isn't necessary for them to understand the inner meaning of what we say. The vessel of this meaning is the words themselves, and this they do recognise. After all, everyone knows of the Oneness of God, Creator and Provider, the source of all life, where all things return. When anyone hears these words, which are a description and expression of God, a universal emotion and inner feeling stirs them, since out of these words comes a scent of their Beloved and their Quest. The ways may vary, but the goal is one. Don't you see that there are many roads to the Kaaba? For some the road is from Rum, for some

from Syria, others come from Persia or China or by sea from India and Yemen. So if you consider the roads, they are beyond counting, with infinite differences. But when you consider the goal they are all in accord with one desire.[40]

According to people who described themselves as Mevlana's students, Rumi was interested in universal emotions that each human being carried due to their connection to God. In one of his quatrains, he says: "Know this well that the lover of God cannot be a Muslim, in the sect of love there is neither faith nor unbelief."[41] He goes on:

> God has opened up His table not only to the Muslims, but also to non-Muslims and even to those who deny Him, and He feeds them all generously. He does not distinguish between them as believer or unbeliever, in terms of keeping them alive.[42]

In another poem, Rumi also describes how

> belief and unbelief are like the white and yellow of an egg. There is a membrane that separates them. Therefore, they do not mix with each other. With God's grace and favour, when the mother hen takes it under her wings, both belief and unbelief vanish and the chick of unity cracks the egg and emerges.[43]

For *Mevlevi* devotees, who embody a post-tariqa vision, it was disturbing to witness how some conservative scholars in Turkey, despite all the words and teachings that support the universal claims of Rumi, still discuss whether or not one can practice Sufism as a non-Muslim or not. This debate, according to one of the students (Cemal), was useless considering most of the *Mevlevi* groups around the world comprised people from different religions, who have been mobilising Sufism with the universal teachings of Rumi.[44]

Such crude reductionist views about *Mevlevi* culture was not new. Sufi history is also full of accounts in which Islamic orthodoxy has been disapproving of *Mevlevi* rituals that include dancing and music such as whirling.[45] Although the Quranic texts do not include negative or condemning views about such practices, during the Ottoman Empire, orthodox *ulema* persistently rejected *sema* and the *zikir* ceremonies of Sufi orders. However, considering the importance of Quranic names that are used to define God and the auditory aspect of the Quran, vocalisation of these names continues to have a critical importance for many Sufi practitioners. Embodiment of divine names and Quranic verses through vocalisations and movements of *zikir* rituals (including *Sema*) have been regarded as the central aspect of *Mevlevi* devotion to enhance divine meaning. *Mevlevi* religious poetry recited and sung in ritual gatherings, such as Quranic texts and divine names, has been perceived as divinely inspired since devotees do not perceive poems as a product of

112 *Transmitting*

human effort. Rituals were also influential in the sense that they attracted secular elites to learn about *Mevlevi* beliefs and values.

For this reason, practitioners of *Mevlevi* beliefs and values, whether they called themselves *Mevlevis* or Mevlana's students, continued to look for ways to learn and transmit Rumi's message through music and dance. Secular elites, who have a limited tolerance for the appearance of Islamic symbols in public, love and cherish the music and dance aspects of the *Mevlevi* culture. Many secular Turks seek to move beyond ideas that undermine Rumi's vision to a segregationist perspective about *Mevlevis*. What was common in Çelebi's, Çıtlak's and Narin *dede*'s concerns was the fact that whirling ritual performances have been powerful tools for transmitting Rumi's spiritual vision and his idea of multi-cultural and universal piety. It was this common idea that have inspired many *Mevlevis* to perform or teach whirling without limiting the experience of the ritual to any rigid idea, role or meaning.

A Secular *Mevlevi* Teacher: Narin *dede* and His Students

One late summer afternoon in the Old City of Istanbul (also known as the Historic Peninsula—the part of the city surrounded by the Golden Horn in the north, Bosphorus in the east and the Marmara Sea in the south), having walked by the sea of Marmara, I met Narin, an elderly *Mevlevi dede*.[46] The old city is a very popular tourist destination housing all the mysterious Roman, Byzantine and the Ottoman Empire historic sites and wonders, most still standing taking any person interested in human history back hundreds of years. Travelling in slow steps on the cobblestoned streets of the Cankurtaran neighbourhood, located right below the Hagia Sophia, it is possible to observe old Istanbul's colourful wooden houses. That day the *Dede Efendi* House (the renovated house of Hammamizade İsmail *dede*—a *Mevlevi* that lived between 1778 and 1846) immediately visible with its charming purple-brown colour and bay windows, was the place Narin *dede* arranged to gather with his devotee friends and students of *Mevlevi* arts and whirling. At the time (between 2012 and 2014), Narin *dede* was organising a variety of classes, workshops, and performance gatherings, taking every opportunity presented to him by the tourist agencies, the Ministry of Tourism and Culture and other cultural associations and/or foundations that generate touristic and cultural events. Since his gatherings were simultaneously educational, artistic, touristic and organised under a non-profit cultural organisation, he was able to get permission to use the *Dede Efendi* House.

The *Dede Efendi* House was one of the many historical Istanbul houses that have survived, thanks to the efforts of *Eski Evleri Koruma Derneği* (the Association for the Protection of Old Houses), which was founded in 1976 with the desire of Perihan Balcı, whose mission was to find ways of repairing the surviving old houses (built during the Ottoman Empire). Once a lodging place for many Sufi artists (during the Ottoman period), who gather to practice Sufi music, poetry, prayer and whirling gatherings, the surviving house seemed to be standing today to support contemporary *Mevlevi* artists and visitors coming together to practice *Mevlevi* beliefs and values. This gathering organised by Narin *dede* was one of the many attempts in which how post-tariqa *Mevlevi* groups were managing to receive permission to gather in a variety of historical Sufi spaces in Istanbul.

Narin *dede* was the grandson of a dervish who sought to continue *Mevlevi* devotional life by teaching and performing *sema* ceremony in public spaces. Like other devotees, he also created a secular organisation to legalise his activities and used the gatherings, classes and workshops as his association's income. For Narin *dede*, producing commodified performances and workshops of *sema* ceremony was a way to continue practising and sharing Sufi beliefs and values. Several times, he invited me to his private home office to introduce me to other students studying Sufi rituals and poetry. As he believed that art education was the most significant aspect of *Mevlevi* Sufism, he was interested in creating networks for people who study Sufi poetry.

His office was a small room that included two comfortable sofas and a large desk with an old computer placed on it. The walls were covered with Islamic writings and poems and marble artworks that Narin *dede* created. He also had a library, where he displayed and protected his Sufi books. His space was welcoming, and Narin *dede* and his wife were very hospitable and kind. One day, Narin *dede* organised a small gathering in his office to introduce me to another student researching Sufism to have us talk about our research plans, and he shared some of his religious music compositions to celebrate our efforts to preserve Sufi cultural beliefs and values. Narin *dede*'s wife served me and the other research student tea as we discussed Sufism and our projects. Every time I visited him and his wife at this sacred space, there would be another student also visiting to either organise events, schedule classes or share their artwork. His private home/office was simultaneously a sacred school in which people from different professions came together to practice *Mevlevi* devotional living and also a public relations workplace in which he organised his Sufi events and gatherings. He wanted to restore *Mevlevi* practice by sharing *Mevlevi* music, whirling and poetry as sacred art forms.

Narin *dede* believed that through performing and teaching *sema* ceremony, he created a space for himself and for beginner devotees to practise Sufism. When I visited *Narin dede* in his home, he explained to me that non-*Mevlevi* individuals created projects and applied for financial support from the Republic of Turkey's Ministry of Culture and Tourism for performances of whirling, Sufi music and poetry; however, Narin *dede*, in our conversations, more than once stated that it was important to him that devotees, who practised their rituals for divine meaning, organised the performances of *sema* for the public to open up space for their devotional acts and to share the true form of Rumi's beliefs and values. More specifically, he believed it was necessary to create public spaces for *Mevlevi* arts, rituals and teachings. He said,

> it is important to create such spaces for Sufi gatherings in which open-minded devotees train secular and religious people in Sufi teachings and practices and where students who are interested in *Mevlevi* spirituality can witness another dimension of religious experience that does not go against the secular values of Atatürk.[47]

Narin dede believed that due to the government's closure of Sufi lodges and the commodification of Sufi cultural beliefs and values, he had to organise Sufi events in cultural centres and museums to experience Sufi spirituality and mobilise Sufism as a religious practice in Turkey. In our meetings, Narin *dede* extensively voiced his opinions about how with the closing of Sufi lodges by Mustafa Kemal Atatürk in 1925, devotee artists, raised by devotee family members, practised Sufi teachings in private gatherings while growing up and then started to move to public spaces to share their Sufi cultural beliefs and values. With modernisation and the promotion of Sufi arts, music and rituals as folk performance by the Turkish government, some of these artists trained in the private Sufi gatherings and formed new Sufi identities with the desire to adapt to secular society. More specifically, Narin *dede* was carrying his practices to secular spaces and creating gatherings out of Sufi worship practices to make Sufism part of his and others' secular everyday life. He said to me once that his Sufi devotional life consisted of teaching his students at home, reading Rumi's poetry in his room, singing liturgical songs after breakfast with his wife, praying as part of a *sema* performance in a hotel conference room and creating *Ebru sanatı* (marbling art) with his students in the office. Narin *dede* explained, although he was getting old, he needed to learn how to use the computer and write emails in order to network with tourist agencies and officials in the Ministry of Culture and Tourism, forming good relationships with people working for such organisations to get their permission to use cultural centres and museums for the practice of *Mevlevi* devotional living. Narin *dede*, while using his private, domestic *Mevlevi* worship to restore *Mevlevi* practice in temporary public spaces, also sought to merge the interactions achieved in public spaces with his devotion in domestic spaces for a more regular practice.

Bringing together devotees, secular Turks and non-Muslims to practice *Mevlevi* rituals, Narin *dede* did not expect to understand everybody's beliefs and values. He also did not expect his students to understand his position as both a secular (in the sense that he believes that government institutions and their representatives should be separate from religious institutions) and religious Sufi *dede*. As Diana Taylor states:

> [T]he problem of untranslatability, as I see it, is actually a positive one, a necessary stumbling block that reminds us that 'we'—whether in our

[religious convictions or political affiliations]. . .—do not simply or problematically understand each other.[48]

When Narin *dede* invited me to meetings and introduced me to his students, comprised of individuals from different religions, I witnessed his aim as he sang, conversed with his wife and students and read poetry. Embodying Sufi beliefs and values, Narin *dede* was seeking to produce temporary Sufi sites in which there would be a welcoming and peaceful environment for people interested in learning about Rumi's life, poetry and whirling. Sharing the teachings of Rumi and his message about divine love and teaching Sufism through Sufi rituals, music, poetry and art, *Narin dede* continued to practice remembrance. He believed that he was restoring Sufi ideas of love and peace with his devotee students by creating a community in which he could continue practising *Mevlevi* arts. *Narin dede*'s focus was more pragmatic and aimed at restoring *Mevlevi* beliefs and values as an organic practice rather than a temporary reclamation under governmental auspices of the sites of the past.

For Narin *dede*, each moment in the gatherings—talking about the dervish objects, listening to liturgical songs, reading Rumi's poetry and discussing Rumi's life—was an act of worship. This act of sharing was similar to the *sohbet* (talk) ritual practised in the Ottoman Sufi orders, in which the spiritual teacher would talk about a Quranic verse or teachings of a Sufi mystic and would answer devotees' questions about how to apply Rumi's teachings to their everyday lives. Narin *dede* as a *Mevlevi* dervish was also adamant about restoring the *sohbet* ritual by teaching Rumi's spiritual journey. He liked to talk about the divine quality of Rumi's works. In one of the gatherings (organised for the performance of a whirling ritual and *sohbet*), I listened to him explaining to his students visiting from Europe how and why Turkish dervishes referred to Jalal ad-Din Muhammad Balkhi (also known as Jalal ad-Din Muhammad Rumi, or in the English-speaking world, as Rumi) as *Mevlana* (master), explaining Rumi's role as spiritual guide and leader. For Narin *dede*, it was also important to explain Rumi's relationship to Islamic knowledge. As Franklin Lewis highlights Rumi "did not come to his theology of tolerance and inclusive spirituality by turning away from traditional Islam;" instead, he produced his religious teachings "through an immersion in it [Islamic teachings]; his spiritual yearning stemmed from a radical desire to follow the example of the Prophet Muhammed and actualise his potential as a perfect Muslim (or *insan-ı kamil,* meaning perfect human)."[49] He discussed how Rumi created his beliefs and his religious poetry through his knowledge of the Quran, the *Hadith*, Islamic theology and the works of Sufi mystics.

In this *sohbet*, while providing facts about Rumi's life, Narin *dede* also expressed his idea of annihilation in a spiritual guide as a step towards the idea of annihilation in God. He talked about Rumi and Shems, the wandering dervish Rumi met in Konya.[50] Students familiar with the wandering dervish knew that studying with him was the turning point in Rumi's life and that Shems, according to Sufi sources, was recognised as eccentric and unorthodox, filled with intense devotion for God.[51] Narin *dede* explained how after studying with Shems, Rumi moved to a place beyond the doctrines and rules of religion. As Lewis illuminates in detail, Rumi experienced a spiritual transformation so that he "became more ecstatic in his worship, expressing his love for God not only in a careful attitude in self-renunciation and control, but also through the joy of poetry, music, and meditative dance."[52] In a workshop, he shared Rumi's words, saying "In my hand there was always the Koran—Now I seized the lute out of love! In my mouth there were always words of laud—Now it is poetry and quatrains, and songs {Divan 2351}."[53] For *Narin dede*, the *sohbets* were opportunities for him to experience and share Rumi's idea of divine love and unity.

Talking to Narin *dede*'s students, I became aware of the fact that some individuals who travelled to Turkey to train with Narin *dede* were dance students interested in exploring the meditative qualities of whirling. Similar to the dance teacher and mystic George Ivanovich Gurdjieff, who studied in various Sufi *tekkes* and trained his dance students, Narin *dede*'s students were interested in attending Sufi gatherings in Turkey and practising whirling to achieve what Gurdjieff identifies as "new states of sensation or perception."[54] One of them explained that she meditated as she whirled to Sufi liturgical songs.[55] Narin *dede* and his wife also introduced me to a young devotee (Mert), who was generous in expressing his experience with *Mevlevi* beliefs and values. When I asked him about his relationship to *Mevlevi* culture, he explained himself, saying, "I am not a dervish but I am a student of Sufism."[56] As discussed earlier, most of the *Mevlevis* were identifying themselves with the word "student" rather than "dervish" to stay in harmony with the law restricting the use of Sufi titles. Mert also did not want to confine his practice to any historical label. He was simply a student who was practising Sufism by attending *sohbets* and classes in different *Mevlevi* groups. He was content with being involved in the spiritual journey and valued his study of *Mevlevi* religious beliefs and values. Although he was not initiated in a specific Sufi order, as he later explained, he had been attending a variety of gatherings and studying with various religious teachers.

I have also met with Narin *dede*'s *semazens*, who were teachers and lawyers that made Sufi gatherings part of their modern urban living by performing and sharing *sema* ceremony. One of Narin *dede*'s *semazens* (Cenk) expressed that he "comes from a very Kemalist family, who regard Sufi tariqas as Islamic extremists. If it wasn't for studying Sufi music and whirling with Narin *dede*, I might have never learned about Sufism as an Islamic devotion."[57] Cenk explained that after studying *sema* with Narin *dede*, he started to look for Sufi groups that are in harmony with Atatürk's secular vision. He found a spiritual teacher who organised *sohbets* every week, in which devotees studied Sufi teachings at a designated private space. What was important to him was that Narin *dede* and his new spiritual teacher were not conservative. They did not intimidate him with rigid rules such as *namaz*. Cenk's case was a great example of how secular individuals were becoming links that informed one another about post-tariqa Sufi groups that believed in the necessity of a secular Turkey. Most of the students were interested in attending the ritual gatherings and classes of more than one spiritual teacher. As I attended some of these with them, I realised they were preferring to attend gatherings of post-tariqa groups because the ones that considered themselves tariqa required a promise of alliance.

Narin *dede* performed several roles to restore his practice of remembrance (*zikir*). At times, he was a *Mevlevi* artist, teaching Sufi arts. At other times, he was a spiritual teacher organising *sohbets* to deliver Rumi's vision and a *semazen* generating whirling workshops to inspire people to embody God's unity. Narin *dede* needed to make use of various secular spaces to create temporary sacred sites. He believed that the desire to learn about Rumi's poetry or whirling brought individuals together and guided the process of restoring post-tariqa *Mevlevi* devotional life. Through a process of renewal, Narin *dede* managed to bring back and make *zikir* (remembrance) a part of his and his students' lives. Narin *dede* found ways to restore his and students' practice of remembrance (*zikir*) by rearranging and reconstructing *Mevlevi sema*, poetry and liturgical songs in a variety of private and public spaces.[58] Narin *dede* was a Sufi devotee who recreated his idea of practising *zikir* in the secular environment of Turkey. Despite continuous tension present regarding how, why and where the whirling ritual can and should exist, Narin *dede* chose to search for ways to teach *Mevlevi* arts as one of the most powerful tools in practising remembrance. This idea of mobilising *Mevlevi* beliefs and values through whirling performance and *Mevlevi* arts influenced many of his students, who one way or another made it their mission to embody and transmit Rumi's vision of an all-embracing Sufism.

Ayşe's Performances: A Female Devotee Whirling in Public

One of these students was Ayşe, who, at the time, was a young female *semazen* whirling in public spaces. One day, I watched Ayşe whirl slowly and steadily in the middle of a large conference room at one of the most exclusive hotels in Istanbul. Her body was moving in front of a large window looking directly to the fishing boats floating on the Bosphorus. Her hair slightly visible from the *sikke* conveyed how post-tariqa whirling ritual belonged to all genders. Ayşe's body was conveying how she was free to whirl anywhere she desired in today's Turkey. Despite all the criticism of the conservative Muslims, who believed that a woman could only whirl in the privacy of her home, Ayşe, wearing the exact costume that male *semazens* have worn for centuries and whirling in front of a crowded group of tourists, overthrew all the one-sided segregationist ideas about Sufism and the practice of Islam in Turkey. Her performance was carrying out a vision that made the whirling ritual a multifaceted practice ready to transform according to any practitioner's need. With whirling, she transmitted her post-tariqa *Mevlevi* vision.

Ayşe was a professional *semazen* in her twenties. She was a *semazen* desiring to show how women could practice Rumi's whirling in public in contemporary Turkey. Ayşe was interested in showing how a woman could practice her devotion freely in a secular country and how Rumi's Islam was a religion beyond doctrinal limitations. Ayşe believed she performed whirling simultaneously as a worship and tourist attraction with male *semazens*, which according to many conservatives, such as Fatih Çıtlak, was a break from the *Mevlevi* tradition. Ayşe believed that Rumi's words and whirling exceeded the *Mevlevi* tradition.

Metin And states, in Rumi's time, whirling was not a structured and planned ceremony.[59] It was Rumi's grandson Sultan Veled who organised whirling as a religious ritual performed in public by the male dervishes. Rumi practised whirling individually on the streets and in private without any structure or form. *Mevlevi sema*, stylised by Rumi's son Sultan Veled, took its final form with the organisation of the ritual by Sultan Veled's grandson, *pir* Adel Chelebi. The whirling, during Rumi's time, according to Metin And, was performed "anytime and any place"[60] to connect the dervish's mind to the infinite, initiating an emotional relationship between human being and god.

Walter Feldman's analysis of *sema* also supports Ayşe's vision. Feldman states that during the Ottoman Empire, *sema* was performed in public spaces and "was conceived of both as a ritual which would benefit the participants and as a spiritual concert which would spread spiritual benefit among the audience as well."[61] Ayşe devises, organises and performs whirling performances in secular and religious spaces for the public. She is full of desire to mobilise and empower a modern urban *Mevlevi* way of living. The most important aspect of this mobilisation is the translation of religious values through performance for the secular and non-devotee public. Ayşe explained that some conservative people criticised her for getting involved in groups that distorted *Mevlevi* rituals. However, she wanted to trust that by performing with a variety of groups and in a variety of spaces, she was able to show her determination as a female *semazen*, who desired to practice *Mevlevi* ritual in public. Also, she explained, since there was no financial support or space for *Mevlevi* dervishes, she believed that it was every *semazen*'s right to generate commodified ritual performances that are simultaneously religious and touristic to make enough money to pay for the basic needs.

She also explained how her performances had the power to bring together secular and religious individuals who sought to learn about Rumi's universal message. As a female *semazen* performing in international business meetings and cultural events organised in the most popular Istanbul hotels, such as Four Seasons, Hilton, Sheraton and Çırağan Palace Hotel, she was in the midst of the secular and religious conflict in Turkey. At times, while conservatives were not happy with the gender-neutral performances of the *Mevlevi sema*, secular elites criticised the appearance of religious rituals and symbols in public. However, Ayşe believed that her performances created a balance between the rigid ideas of conservative Muslims and the biased ideas of secular elites. She perceived her performances as a proof of how the *Mevlevi* belief system (the true teachings of Rumi) has been the symbol of a faithfulness that is beyond any one-sided doctrine. Her performances were performatic acts that provoked people to question Sufism, Rumi, diversity and gender segregation in Islam.

Jürgen Habermas questions the appearance of religious acts in the public sphere due to their potential to weaken democratic values such as social egalitarianism. Although Habermas does not talk about the Turkish context, his ideas open a lens through which I examine how the Ayşe's performance relates to the secular public life in Turkey. Habermas later modified his early views, reconsidering the public articulation of a religious voice, stating that religious arguments must enter the public sphere "in translation."[62] By translation, he means that the public articulation and expression of religious beliefs and values should not be about imposing doctrinal beliefs and values on non-religious citizens or people from other religions. The idea of religion entering the public sphere in translation informs how and why Ayşe is determined to bring Sufi religious teachings and practices to the public in translation as an Islamic performance embodied by a female devotee. Ayşe's performance highlights Habermas' question about "how religions can constructively participate in political processes within democratic nation states."[63] According to Ayşe, "her whirling alters the strictly doctrinal and confrontational recognition of Sufi orders, fanatical Islam and women's role in Islam."[64] Considering the fear of religious groups limiting secular Turks' freedom of choice and speech in Turkey, Ayşe believed that female whirling rituals performed simultaneously as worship and tourist attraction made accessible the egalitarian aspects of Rumi's beliefs and values, such as his ideas of love, unity and peace. Ayşe said she could whirl "anytime and anyplace" simultaneously to worship and to share her love for Mevlana.

Saayan Chattopadhyay's presentation of religious traditions transforming to new forms also illuminates Ayşe's perspective. Chattopadhyay argues, "for religious traditions to continue through history, they must be translated or better transmediated—put in a new form."[65] Writing about the public performances of Purja in India, he states that

> the emergence of theme-based public worship . . . offers a new space in the making of modern social imaginaries, a space in which spectatorial, performative, and ambivalent spatial aspects erect a translucent facade over religion, devotion, faith, and spirituality.[66]

Although not specifically about whirling, Chattopadhyay's idea of public space and worship informs how Ayşe, through the organisation of her solo whirling performances, offered a new space for individuals to experience Sufism as a synthesis of the secular and religious values of Turkey.

As Taylor examines performed acts "generate, record, and transmit knowledge . . . they change over time . . . but their meaning might very well remain the same."[67] The religious meaning in Ayşe's performances was no different from Saygın *dede*'s or any other *Mevlevi* groups' practice of *Sema* ceremony. With Ayşe's performances, the spaces and the audiences were changing very often, but her desire to meditate and practice *zikir* was not changing one bit. Taylor's idea of performatic shift and doubling as well as Nancy Fraser's conceptualisation of "public spheres" as "arenas for the formation and enactment of social identities"[68] inform how Ayşe as a devotee altered and used *Mevlevi* embodied acts to generate what she called "versatile Sufism."[69] Ayşe was interested in mobilising the adaptability of *Mevlevi* cultural beliefs and values. She believed that many *Mevlevis* struggled with preserving the true form of Rumi's beliefs and values due to conservative Muslim's portrayal of *Mevlana* (meaning master, the title by which devotees use to refer to Rumi) as a conservative Islamic preacher. She said, "I do not have to practice *zikir* according to any authoritative rule. My devotion is between me, my spiritual teachers and God. There is no rule or no one in the middle."[70]

Instead of practising what Michael Brown calls "cultural closure," devotees like Ayşe felt like they should share their beliefs and values with non-devotees. *Mevlevi* devotees, due to the Turkish government's secularisation and commodification of *Sema* in the 1960s, could not prevent outsiders from witnessing and using certain aspects of their cultural practices, such as the whirling ritual.[71] What is visible in Ayşe's *Mevlevi* performances was that despite the absence of designated *Mevlevi* spaces, she managed to preserve and transmit her post-tariqa vision. Ayşe accepted the hardships of this transformation and could not find comfort in staying tied to any dogma or any traditional space. She was motivated to mobilise her vision of Rumi as love, peace and compassion to all of God's creation. Ayşe used performance as her dominant tool for devotion, for remembering God and for consecrating any space she whirled. Aside from engaging in whirling ritual as a devotional performance, Ayşe was mindful of the fact that performance also served her as a medium through which she met devotees who shared her vision. Her whirling was her devotion, her language and her job. She said, "I chose to live my life as a *semazen* and I trust my plan."[72] Her inclination to perform and share the whirling ritual in a variety of spaces made her whirling public and accessible. All she needed was her whirling to practice and preserve *Mevlevi* cultural beliefs and values.[73] It was her goal to generate events that promoted Rumi's Islam as a multifaceted faith system that was open to changes and adaptations. Rumi was the embodiment of what devotees such as Saygın *dede*, Narin *dede*, Ayşe and many others call all-embracing, versatile, universal and multi-cultural Sufism.[74] For this reason, all of these *Mevlevis* desired to embody Rumi's words in their everyday life. The ultimate desire was to transmit Rumi's all-embracing vision "anytime and anyplace."[75]

Notes

* Talad S. Halman and Metin And, *Mevlana Celaleddin-i Rumi and the Whirling Dervishes* (Istanbul: Dost Yayinlari, 2005), 34.
1 "Ömer Tuğrul İnançer'den komik savunma [Funny defense from Ömer Tuğrul İnançer]," December 23, 2014, https://www.sozcu.com.tr/2014/gundem/omer-tugrul-inancerden-komik-savunma-688069/.
2 Personal communication, October 18, 2011.
3 Raymond Lifchez, "The Lodges of Istanbul," in *The Dervish Lodge: Architecture, Art, and Sufism in Ottoman Turkey* (Berkeley: University of California Press, 1992), 73.
4 Lifchez, "The Lodges of Istanbul," 73.
5 Lifchez, "The Lodges of Istanbul," 73.
6 Baha M. Tanman, "Settings for the Veneration of Saints," in *The Dervish Lodge*, ed. Raymond Lifchez (Berkeley: University of California Press, 1992), 134.
7 Tanman, "Settings for the Veneration of Saints," 134.
8 Tanman, "Settings for the Veneration of Saints," 134.
9 Tanman, "Settings for the Veneration of Saints," 134.
10 The *hırka* and/or the headgear tend to be the signs that a devotee is a dervish. It is considered a diploma for the devotee and shows his/her standing. As Annemarie Schimmel points out, "For to bless someone by placing headgear on his head means to honor him, and . . . is a highly important occasion in the dervish orders." Annemarie Schimmel, *Deciphering the Signs of God: A Phenomenological Approach to Islam* (Albany: State University of New York Press, 1994), 39. Some of the Sufi mystics such as Yunus Emre criticised the use of these garments, pointing out the fact that some people wear them too early in their spiritual elevation. However, Cengiz informed me later that all the devotees assisting the guests are dervishes, the ones who are closest to the teacher.
11 The black cloak represents the tomb or worldly attachments; the white *tennure* represents the dervishes' shroud (the burial garment); and the *sikke* (long hat), the dervishes' gravestone, both signifying dervishes' seeking death in life. Costumes were designed to signify the dervish as a human being who has given up the desires of the material world.
12 İnançer, "Rituals and Main Principles of Sufism During The Ottoman Empire."
13 Catharina Raudvere, *The Book and the Roses: Sufi Women, Visibility and Zikr in Contemporary Istanbul* (London: I.B. Tauris, 2003), 15.
14 Personal conversation with a devotee, September, 2011.
15 Taylor, *The Archive and the Repertoire*, 46.
16 Talad S. Halman and Metin And, *Mevlana Celaleddin-i Rumi and the Whirling Dervishes* (Istanbul: Dost Yayinlari, 2005), 34.
17 Fulya Atacan, *Sosyal Değişme ve Tarikat: Cerrahiler [Social Change and Tarikats: Cerahhis]* (İstanbul: Hill Yayın, 1990), 43; Raudvere, *The Book and the Roses*, 15.
18 Hillary Summer Boyd and John Freeley, *Strolling Through Istanbul: The Classic Guide to the City* (London: I.B. Tauris, 2009), 257.
19 Raudvere, *The Book and the Roses*, 28.
20 Raudvere, *The Book and the Roses*, 28.
21 *Namaz* is the form of worship that is a five-times-daily obligation as one of the five pillars of Islam. Aside from the spiritual benefits, *Namaz*, with its repeated standing, bending, bowings, and preceding sitting or standing up positions, is regarded by Muslims as a healthy form of exercise.
22 "Tarikatçiler" can be translated as "people of tariqa," meaning sectarian devotees who promote the conservative tariqa system. Devotees and some secular Turks use this term either for "yobaz" (meaning fanatic fundamentalists or what they

also call "backward-looking" individuals) or what they label as "fake devotees" (people who use Sufi cultural beliefs and values as a tool to manipulate "immature minds" to gain some sort of power over people). As devotees I met along the way explain, some people fall into the traps of "yobaz" or "fake devotees" simply because they are illiterate or "in need of belonging to a community due to social and/or psychological problems." As Ceylin, an educated female devotee once explained she and her devotee friends meet many young women and children "who have not been aware of how yobaz or fake devotees manipulate them" and somehow managed to pull away from such "dangerous" groups and communities after witnessing "modern post-tariqa *Mevlevi* groups" seeking to mobilise Rumi's idea of love and unity (as diversity). Conversations with a variety of *Mevlevi* devotees who seek to teach the true form of Rumi's teachings.

23 Personal communication, July 14, 2009.
24 Personal communication, July 14, 2009.
25 Personal communication, July 14, 2009.
26 Personal communication, July 14, 2009.
27 Personal communication, July 14, 2009.
28 To see the full version of this section, refer to 3125 in *Mesnevi*, Volume V, available at "Full Text of Rumi's The Mathnawi, Vol. 5 and Vol. 6," in *Internet Archive*, trans. Reynold A. Nicholson, accessed November 30, 2020, https://archive.org/stream/RumiTheMathnawiVol5Vol6/Rumi_The-Mathnawi-Vol-5-Vol-6_djvu.txt.
29 Franklin D. Lewis, *Rumi, Past and Present, East and West: The Life, Teachings and Poetry of Jalal al-Din Rumi* (Oxford: Oneworld Publications, 2003), 82.
30 Lewis, *Rumi, Past and Present, East and West*, 82.
31 Lewis, *Rumi, Past and Present, East and West*, 82.
32 The most controversial of these scholars is a Turkish expert on Rumi studies, Mikhail Bayram, who lives in Konya and teaches at the Selçuk University in Turkey. He has written books and given interviews that challenge Rumi's teachings.
33 Gonca Bayraktar Durgun and Emrah Beriş note that "The civil society associations in Turkey operate mainly in two different legal statuses, accordingly to which they are called either 'associations' or 'foundations.' The state plays a significant role in regulating the proliferation of these organizations and the nature of their activities. To begin with, the groups must carry out certain obligatory legal procedures in order to earn official recognition. The state also has the authority to close down associations or foundations on the charge of operating illegally; this authority may give it the upper hand in its relations with civil society organizations, as in such cases the administrators can face legal punishment." Gonca Bayraktar Durgun and Emrah Beriş, "Civil Society and Perspectives on Turkish-American Relations," in *Turkish-US Relations: Perspectives from Ankara*, ed. Ralph Salmi and Gonca Bayraktar Durgun (Boca Raton, FL: Brown Walker Press, 2005), 32–33. As Daniella Kuzmanovic notes, "associations and foundations are prohibited from engaging directly in any kind of 'political activity'." Daniella Kuzmanovic, *Refractions of Civil Society in Turkey* (New York: Palgrave Macmillan, 2012), 8. The majority are associations "because it is easier to set up an association than a foundation. To establish an association only seven founding members are needed to complete the legal procedure to satisfy the legal requirements for official recognition by the Ministry of Internal Affairs. The conditions for becoming a foundation are more stringent, as they require the founding members to dedicate a certain amount of funds and property to the aims of the foundation. Thus, foundations require a greater amount of financial and social support." Durgun and Beriş, "Civil Society and Perspectives on Turkish-American Relations," 32–33.
34 "*Mevlevi* Leaders Move to Reclaim the Order," *Daily Sabah*, December 13, 2014, https://www.dailysabah.com/turkey/2014/12/13/mevlevi-leaders-move-to-reclaim-the-order.

35 "*Mevlevi* Leaders Move to Reclaim the Order."
36 More information on UNESCO's promotion of *Mevlevi Sema* can be found at the following webpage: UNESCO, "*Mevlevi Sema* Ceremony," accessed July 19, 2011, http://www.unesco.org/culture/intangible-heritage/39eur_uk.htm.
37 More on this discussion can be found in David Smith's online article, "Networking real-world knowledge," *AI & Society* 21 (2007): 421–428, https://doi.org/10.1007/s00146-007-0105-6.
38 Mert İnan, "Mevleviler 'Stajyer Postnişin'e Tepkili [*Mevlevis* React to 'Trainee Postnishin']," *Milliyet*, July 28, 2020, https://www.milliyet.com.tr/gundem/mevleviler-stajyer-postnisine-tepkili-6269897; "O Kişi Sahte *Mevlevi* Şeyhi [That Person is a False *Mevlevi* Sheikh]," *Vatan*, January 20, 2020, http://www.gazetevatan.com/-o-kisi-sahte-mevlevi-seyhi—1297534-yasam/.
39 "*Mevlevi* Leaders Move to Reclaim the Order."
40 Mevlana Celaleddin Rumi, *Fih-i Mafihi [Discourses of Rumi]*, trans. A.J. Arberry (Ames, IA: Omphaloskepsis), 175, accessed October 30, 2020, http://rumisite.com/Books/FiheMaFih.pdf.
41 Şefik Can, who is a Turkish *Mevlevi* spiritual leader respected for his teachings of *Mesnevi*, shares his examination of Rumi's ideas in *Fundamentals of Rumi's Thought: A Mevlevi Sufi Perspective*, ed. and trans. Zeki Sarıtoprak (New Jersey: The Light Inc, 2005), 169.
42 Can, *Fundamentals of Rumi's Thought*, 169.
43 Can, *Fundamentals of Rumi's Thought*, 169.
44 Personal communication, January 18, 2019.
45 Metin And, *A Pictorial History of Turkish Dancing: From Folk Dancing to Whirling Dervishes, Belly Dancing to Ballet* (Istanbul: Dost Yayınları, 1976), 32; Madeline C. Zilfi, *The Politics of Piety: The Ottoman Ulema in the Postclassical Age 1600–1800* (Minneapolis: Bibliotheca Islamica, 1988), 136; Mehrdad Kia, *The Ottoman Empire: A Historical Encyclopedia*, vol. 2 (Santa Barbara: ABC-CLIO, LLC, 2017), 18.
46 Narin *dede* was one of the controversial senior *Mevlevi* dervishes whose right to the *Mevlevi dede* (senior dervish) title is questioned by either conservative Sufi elders or Sufi individuals who tend to be critical of the use of Sufi titles in current day Turkey (due to legal restrictions of such titles). However, I have conversed with a variety of Sufi elders, who more than once explained how Sufi devotees continue to gain and receive such titles by an act of initiation performed in their private homes.
47 Personal conversation with Narin *dede*, May 5, 2015.
48 Taylor, *The Archive and the Repertoire*, 15.
49 Lewis, *Rumi Past and Present, East and West*, 10.
50 William C. Chittick, *Me & Rumi: The Autobiography of Shams-i Tabrizi* (Louisville: Fons Vitae, 2004), xi.
51 Chittick, *Me & Rumi*, xi.
52 Lewis, *Rumi Past and Present, East and West*, 274.
53 Lewis, *Rumi Past and Present, East and West*, 163.
54 G.I. Gurdjieff, *Views from the Real World* (New York: Dutton, 1973), 227–228.
55 Personal communication, August 4, 2012.
56 Personal communication, August 4, 2012.
57 Personal communication, June 5, 2011.
58 Richard Schechner, *Between Theatre and Anthropology* (Philadelphia: University of Pensylvania Press, 1985), 35.
59 Halman, *Mevlana Celaleddin-i Rumi and the Whirling Dervishes*, 34.
60 Halman, *Mevlana Celaleddin-i Rumi and the Whirling Dervishes*, 34.
61 Walter Fedman. "Structure and Evolution of the *Mevlevi* Ayin: The Case of the Third Selam," in *Sufism Music and Society: In Turkey and the Middle East*,

Part III: Structure and Evolution, Swedish Research Institute in Istanbul Transaction, ed. Andres Hammarlund, Tord Olsson, and Elisabeth Özdalga (London: Routledge and Curzon Press, 2001), 49–66.

62 It is possible to see Habermas' latter view in a variety of sources. For a detailed account of Jurgen Habermas' ideas in relation to performing religion in public, refer to: "Religion in the Public Sphere," *European Journal of Philosophy* 14, no. 1 (2006): 10; Jurgen Habermas, *An Awareness of What is Missing: Faith and Reason in a Post-Secular Age*, trans. Ciaran Cronin (Cambridge: Polity, 2010), 16; Jurgen Habermas, "'The Political': The Rational Meaning of a Questionable Inheritance of Political Theology," in *The Power of Religion in the Public Sphere*, ed. Eduardo Mendieta and Jonathan Van Antwerpen (New York: Columbia University Press, 2011), 25.

63 Josh Edelman, "Introduction," in *Performing Religion in Public*, 9. Refer to Austin Harrington, "Habermas' Theological Turn?" *Journal for the Theory of Social Behavior* 37, no. 1 (New York: Palgrave Macmillan, 2007): 45–61.

64 Personal conversation with Ayşe, March 2, 2013.

65 Saayan Chattopadhyay, "From Religion to Culture: The Performative Puja and Spectacular Religion in India," in *Performing Religion in Public*, ed. Claire Marie Chambers, Simon W. du Toit, and Joshua Edelman (New York: Palgrave Macmillan, 2013), 194. Also see Lawrence Babb and Susan Wadley, ed., *Media and the Transformation of Religion in South Asia* (Philadelphia: University of Pennsylvania Press, 1995).

66 Chattopadhyay, "From Religion to Culture," 206.

67 Taylor, *Archive and the Repertoire*, 20–21.

68 Nancy Fraser, "Rethinking the Public Sphere: A Contribution to the Critique of Actually Existing Democracy," in *Habermas and the Public Sphere*, ed. Craig J. Calhoun (Cambridge: MIT Press, 1992), 125.

69 Personal communications with *Mevlevis* between 2010 and 2019.

70 Personal conversation with Ayşe, June, 2017.

71 Brown gives an example of cultural closure, offering his discussion of native groups rejecting non-native employees from learning their local language. These groups, according to Brown, are trying to keep certain aspects of their culture unknown with an aim to prevent their beliefs and values from being appropriated. These behaviours, as Brown points out, are the opposite of UNESCO's policy of publicising heritage in order to save it. Michael F. Brown, "Heritage Trouble: Recent Work on the Protection of Intangible Cultural Property," *International Journal of Cultural Property* 12, no. 1 (2015): 40–61, https://doi.org/10.1017/S0940739105050010.

72 Personal conversation with Ayşe, June, 2017.

73 Halman, *Mevlana and the Whirling Dervishes*, 34.

74 Personal communications with *Mevlevis* between 2010 and 2021.

75 Halman, *Mevlana and the Whirling Dervishes*, 34.

Part Three
Transforming

4 Sacralisation of the Body and Mind

The *semahane* looks like it is shaking with devotees' jumps, breath, and sharp and strong voices. There is enormous desire and commitment to repeating "*la ilahe illallah.*" They sing and jump with such commitment and joy as they repeat, restore and embody God's unity. Inhaling and exhaling sharply and deeply, some of the devotees follow the lead of the *dede* feeding the line "*Hayy,*" one of Allah's names, meaning ever-living. I hear the drums, the flute and other dervishes singing an *ilahi* (liturgical song) along with the dervishes repeating "Hay." The *dede* feeds the lines using a unique vocal technique as if he is howling. It is a wailing sound that is hard to describe even with the word "howling" or compare with any other sound I have heard before. It is strong. It is a breath forced out with a sound coming from deep down in the body. It is a jumping chorus singing, howling and chanting, all at once. Words do not seem to be enough to describe the sounds, the movements, the level of commitment and the intensity of the energy in the room. What I witness is a passionate chorus filled with enormous joy, energy and desire. A chorus that is invested in each sound and movement. I hear sharp sounds that are reminiscent of a saw cutting through wood. This sound travels together with the lamenting sounds of a dervish vocalising a liturgical song. This time, it is as if the room vibrates with the dervishes' sounds. The bodies of the devotees standing tightly together seem to form a circular shape that looks like a ring. They keep their bodies close as they dance, not letting go of each other's hands and shoulders. They are standing in the circle and they are jumping as one body. It is as if their minds are one. Their bodies are one. It is clear that they value this sense of togetherness. They chant together creating more energy with each word. The sense of "communitas" is visible. The sense of togetherness in the first ring (the first circle of dervishes) seems to inspire more and more participants (who stand and participate outside of the first and the second rings) to chant and dance together with the devotees performing in the first ring. This seems to be their time to release all thoughts other than God's unity. Their movements seem to convey this message. Their voices and actions convey their commitment to the idea of manyness of one reality (God's unity).

This thick description is one of the many notes I took about *Rifai zikir* ceremonies. I have many descriptions similar to this one, but none of them seems to do justice to what I witnessed in the *semahane* of the wooden house on Thursday evenings. Therefore, instead of trying to describe what happened in the *Rifai* ritual hall, for now, I will try to examine how devotees' discussed their ceremony. Ceremonial *zikir* is one of the primary communal rituals that *Rifai* devotees gather to perform regularly throughout the year every Thursday evening and every evening during their four-day pilgrimage to the Rumi's *urs* in Konya. As discussed earlier, *Rifais* are recognised as howling dervishes in the West due to the intensity of the sounds and movements that make up their *zikir* ceremony.

In Veli *efendi*'s group, the ceremony had a very significant role in each devotee's worship practice that almost no one in the group missed the Thursday *zikir* gatherings. Participating in ceremonial *zikir* was also not obligatory; however, devotees believed that they longed for the gathering due to the sense of divine unity, love, energy and freedom experienced in the performance of *zikir* ceremonies; therefore, almost all of the devotees regularly participated in the ceremony to enhance divine meaning. These rituals even took precedence over work and family responsibilities. The wooden house located in a secluded neighbourhood, as discussed in Chapter 2, made the execution of this loud and passionate ceremony possible despite legal restrictions.

In *zikir* gatherings, Veli *efendi* got the chance to see and converse with all of the *dedes*, dervishes and students. Sometimes, Veli *efendi* led the collective *zikir* ceremony; at other times, one or two of the *dedes* led and the *efendi* made time for his devotees and guests who ask for spiritual guidance. The *efendi*'s room would become like a therapist's office in which individuals talked about their personal problems and asked for *efendi*'s opinions. Often, he would enjoy making jokes and telling stories about Sufi mystics such as Abdülkadir Geylani and Mevlana Celaleddin-i Rumi, whose words, according to many devotees, had a soothing effect on the students' hearts. At times, he would recite a liturgical song to pray for his devotees or a poem to answer a question offered by a guest. He would invite his male and female musician dervishes—Melek, Esma and Bora—to the room for Melek to play the reed flute, Esma to sing and Bora to play *qanun*. With or without intention Veli *efendi*'s *sohbets* tended to be performatic, inspiring his devotees to experience God's unity.

Performatic Wooden House

The wooden house was a space that Veli *efendi*'s family inherited from their elders. It was a small structure that put a roof over many devotees' (students and dervishes) heads. The house had very small rooms sized five to eleven square meters (the *semahane* and the *efendi*'s room being the only large rooms), covered with rugs and with every corner filled with students' religious property, such as Sufi music instruments, prayers written on framed papers and *tespihs* (rosaries or prayer beads) hanging on the walls. Also, the four-floor wooden house was renovated, designed and organised by the students according to the needs of the Thursday night *zikir* ceremonies to accommodate a large number of participants.

The first floor, the entrance (only large enough to accommodate three people) was where the students walked in and handed their shoes to a male student, a gatekeeper who welcomed the arriving devotees and placed the shoes in a small room equipped with shoe racks right by the front door. The second floor had two rooms and a very small kitchen with a window opening to the stairs. One of the doors, on the right side, opened to a small five-foot passageway that connected the kitchen to another small room in which female students ate meals, chatted and prayed. This small room also had two large windows one looking to the street (the one with the lace curtains that I could see when I arrived at the house), the other (larger window) connected to a larger room (*semahane*, the second room of the second floor). This larger room was the main area of the *semahane*, the space where *zikir* ceremonies were performed by the male devotees. This *semahane* had two entrances and two windows. The second window was near the ceiling and opened onto the stairs. This room was a small balcony located in the *semahane*, serving as an additional space for female ritual participation or observance. Some of the female devotees participated in the ceremony from the small room connecting to the *semahane* (the second room on the second floor), while other female devotees used the entresol (also located in the main space of the *semahane*, but with an entrance through the small kitchen area on the third floor). While the male and female students had separate sections for the practice of the ceremony in the wooden house, this usually was not the case in the residential building, where I have participated in mixed-gender *zikir* ceremonies and in the pilgrimage sites (as I will discuss in Chapter 5).

On the third floor, there was a four-square-meter hall. On the right side of the hall, there was a door opening to the room of Veli *efendi*, and on the left, another small kitchen-like space where male students served tea. This small tearoom connected the female students to the entresol located in the main area of the *semahane*. The fourth floor was a very small attic, in which male students sat, ate, chatted and prayed. Both the male and female students occupied each other's spaces when necessary, to serve or when there was *sohbet* or *meşk* after the ceremony. Performing service, students moved around the space carefully and with caution, especially when sitting, standing, moving their arms, walking and serving tea to avoid causing accidents in this small space. Although it took me a while to comprehend, some nights, the wooden house held around one hundred people, especially when Veli *efendi* had students and student's guests visiting from other Turkish cities or other countries.

The students gathered regularly every Thursday evening in the wooden house to participate in the *zikir* ceremony. Followers of the regular Thursday gatherings included all the followers, the senior dervishes, the students and sometimes invited guests. Thursday gatherings began with a group of students arriving at the wooden *house* to prepare the space for the evening.

This group included the *dede*'s wife, female and male dervishes and some of the students. These students prepared the wooden *house* by cleaning the space and preparing meals (usually soup, rice, potatoes with meat and *helva*), which were cooked in very large pans to make sure there was enough food for everyone, even the last-minute guests. At the end of the ceremony, senior dervishes made sure to distribute the leftovers to low-income devotees who were in need of assistance.

After the preparation of the food, they would begin to prepare the rooms for what they called *lokma yapma* (meaning having a meal) around 6:30 p.m. to make sure everyone was fed until 8:00 p.m. right before the ceremony starts. Due to the lack of public transportation in the neighbourhood where the wooden house was located and because the area tended to be quite deserted, students who owned cars would collect the ones who lived or worked near them to commute together to the wooden house. Also, students who lived or worked in the same area tended to come to the house as a group by taxi. Having travelled with various groups of devotees throughout my field research, I witnessed students' dedication to these gatherings, which was visible as they prepared for the gathering while travelling.

In the cars and taxis, they would make sure that they were appropriately dressed for the ceremony. Because most of them arrived directly from work, they would carry their long dervish coats and shawls in their bags and put them on over their regular clothes before arriving at the *house*. Walking down the narrow street of the wooden *house*, students would share their excitements, which was visible in their energetic walk. They would walk like a child jumping in joy as if they were going to a fun fair, festival or celebration. In quick steps, they would approach the door of the house. Female students would want to make sure that their clothes and hair looked tidy. Some students would explain how they could feel their heartbeat as they got ready to participate in the ceremony. They would often talk about how once they touched the door of the house, they would feel that they were where they belonged. Most students would also articulate how they felt as if the wooden house was the home of their spirit.

From the first moment students arrived, their actions reflected their commitment to the place. The first thing the students did when they arrived each week was to stand at the entrance, touch their foreheads to the threshold of the wooden door and kiss the door before entering. This was the act of love and respect that students offered to the house as their sacred space.[1] The devotees also believed in the value of the buildings and clothes they used and pointed out that every material property in the world, from the pillow we slept on to the clothes we wore, belonged to Allah. They tended to describe all the objects used and the places they occupied as united in God. Veli *efendi* explained this by saying just as we should take care of our material body as an offer from God, we should learn to take care of other material givings in the same manner, remembering His unity. With their idea of material space as God's giving, students would sacralise the wooden *house* as the house of

God. Senior dervish Metin explained, the doors, walls and floors of the house and the objects in it, including the utensils, chairs and tables, were sacred.

The students would enter the *house* and greet the male student (the gatekeeper) who opened the door to welcome them and take their shoes to place in the small shoe closet located at the entrance. The students would greet by placing their right hands on their hearts and bowing slightly forward, conveying a sense of respect for his labour. Then, they would walk up the stairs to greet other students who have already started serving the meal. Female students would enter the room on the second floor while male students would walk to the third and fourth floors to participate in the dinner ritual. Female students would prepare and distribute the meal from a window (located in the second-floor kitchen—opening to the stairs), where male students would receive and carry trays of food upstairs while female students would have their meal in the room located on the second floor. Although female and male students would have their meals in different spaces, they would interact with one another throughout the evening when (after the meal) the male students would finish their meals and move to the large room, the *semahane*, on the second floor to perform *namaz* before the *zikir* ceremony (as I will discuss in more detail in Chapter 4).

Performatic *Zikir*

Zikir ceremony gatherings were filled with performatic moments in which devotees embodied and expressed their longing for God. As different devotees explained, their *zikir* ceremony was recognised by their guests as joyous, loud, energetic, musical, powerful, intense and physically rigorous. Devotees chanted God's names; they sang hymns about God, the Prophet Muhammed, the founders of the order, other prophets and deceased Sufi masters; they moved to the rhythm or danced for hours without a break. By continually repeating the names of God, dervishes said that they experienced a dreamlike state in which they brought into their awareness God's loving and compassionate attributes. Devotees believed that as they experienced these states mentally and physically, their hearts were introduced to divine love. By embodying the same movements, words, chants and intentions that other devotees had done in the past, dervishes believed that they experienced the wooden house as a path to journey to a place outside of the material world. In this place, they believed that they connected to all the Sufi mystics and teachers, who have manifested their devotion with their embodiment of divine meaning. *Zikir*, as Veli *efendi* articulated, united brothers and sisters of all the Sufi *silsile* beginning with the Prophet Muhammed. *Zikir*, according to a senior dervish, opened a place in his heart for experiencing God's unity.

The collective *zikir* ceremony in the *semahane* of the wooden house would often begin with some of the male and female devotees performing ablution and/or *namaz*. After preparations such as ablution and *namaz*, devotees would start taking their places in the *zikir* circle. Either Veli *efendi* or one of the *dedes* would lead the ceremony. The leader would organise the participants' locations in the room, making sure that all the devotees got a place in the *zikir* circle. Then, the ceremony would start with the participants moving to a sitting position, either with legs crossed or with feet curled under the hips. After the *dede* recited Quranic passages and other Sufi texts, he would begin the ceremony with the phrase "*la ilahe illallah.*" Later, after repeating the first line over and over again, he would continue with the repetition of the Quranic names and attributes of God such as *Allah* (The Exalted), *Hayy* (Ever Living), *Ahad* (Unity) and *Kayyum* (The Sustaining), all repeated in different rhythms accompanied by percussive instruments. As the names and rhythm of the ceremony changed as guided by the leading dervish, devotees would also change their positions and movements.

In the first part of the repetition, they would accompany the recitation by moving their heads from the right to the left shoulder towards the heart. When the *dede* fed them new lines, devotees would move their heads forward and back in a rhythmic manner. Then when the *dede* fed them another line, devotees would stand up and move their shoulders with their heads. When the energy of the ceremony increased, devotees would continue their recitation as they bent their knees slightly and moved their upper body down and up as if they were bowing. While continuing the same movement, devotees would lock their arms and hold each other's hands as they continued chanting the names. As the names were recited, the rhythm and the volume would change with the *dede* feeding them lines and offering a different pitch and melody each time. Because most of the participants in the room were practising *zikir* for years, the group would manage to move and chant in unison. Unless the leader of the ritual would direct the *dedes* and dervishes in the first circle by slowing or quieting them down, the energy, pace and rapture would continue to grow.

Devotees also perceived *zikir* as a strenuous activity because the *dede* increased the volume and pace of the movements as devotees chanted, recited and moved. Such moments occurred two or three times throughout the ceremony, each lasting approximately fifteen minutes. However, although such moments required a lot of energy, as dervish Kerem said, without the experience of those moments, the embodiment of divine energy and joy would not be possible. *Rifai zikir* ceremony would be highly demanding, both mentally and physically. When I asked Kerem, who, at the time, was a professional athlete, how his experience and energy in athletic activities were different from the rigorous performance of the *zikir*, he said he felt more driven and energetic when he performed *zikir* because he performed to recall God's attributes and to create a bond with Him, His meaning. The sense of devotion inspired and motivated him to move faster and to chant louder for longer periods.[2]

As the volume and intensity of the ceremony increased, it was possible to hear male devotees reciting God's names aloud in every corner of the wooden house. Devotees participated in the *zikir* in the corridors and other rooms along with the devotees performing in the *semahane*, increasing the sense of devotion in the house. Sometimes, a group of female and male dervishes would ask *efendi*'s permission to perform *zikir* together silently, sitting in the *efendi*'s room. Every corner of the house—the rooms and the corridors—was filled with the devotees participating in the *zikir* ceremony. The staircases and walls would vibrate with the sounds of the ritual—devotees moving their feet and vocalising God's names. In such moments, as the students explained, the space transformed into a temple outside of time and space in which people celebrated their love for God.

By repeating God's Quranic names in unison, devotees sought to stay on the threshold and thus were remaining on the journey to God. As Werbner states, "In Sufism the human being is a model for the universe, a microcosm of the macrocosm, and the journey towards God is a journey within the person."[3] Devotees sought "self-purification," which could be

> perceived as a move toward the transformation of the self, the nafs [*nefs*], through a transcendence of bodily desires and needs. By totally denying the self, the nafs [*nefs*] is purified . . . with the saint, the Prophet and ultimately God.[4]

Performing *zikir*, devotees sought to deny their material selves and reminded themselves of their spiritual purpose. They remembered that they are on their journey to God. They remembered the sense of energy, joy and dedication they experienced in their performance of *zikir*.

Zikir is marked by its use of repetition. Drewal discusses in her essay "The State of Research on Performance in Africa" that there is a fundamental problem with the study of performance and of our understanding of the nature of repetition in performance. Repetition is generally seen as structurally restrictive. However, she argues, "our failure to reckon with the temporality of performance is in large part due to objectivist epistemology that turns temporally constituted, and constituting, subjects into static objects."[5] Analysing the idea of repetition, she pays close attention to the notion of "representation" and separates her idea of "representation as mimesis (the exteriority or visualisation of an inner idea or feeling)" from "representation as kinesis (temporal, unfolding in the situated flow of human interactions)."[6] Drewal, while analysing Yoruba ritual, comes to the conclusion that representation "embodies creativity, for representation itself is a form of creativity."[7] Although Yoruba people practice creativity in a different context when improvising certain dramatic acts, the idea of representation as a form of creativity exists in *Rifai* devotees' performances. Devotees believed that through repetition of same movements, they could create new physical sensations and improve their spiritual awareness. They sought to transform by sacralising their minds and bodies.

Joseph Roach employs the concept of "kinaesthetic imagination" to discuss the "idea of expressive movements as mnemonic reserves," including "patterned movements made by bodies," "residual movements retained implicitly in images or words," and "imaginary movements dreamed in minds."[8] Kinaesthetic imagination activates all these forms through which the performance of *zikir* creates a memory of divine experience in the body.[9] Thus, the sensations experienced while performing the expressive movements informed devotees' minds and bodies inspiring them to remember the peace, joy and energy they experienced in their ceremonies. Roach's analysis informs how devotees transformed their minds and bodies while jumping in ecstasy. This analysis shows there is a strong relationship between the performance of *zikir* (the physical sensations reserved in the bodily memory) and devotees' perception of themselves in their ordinary lives.

The process of learning that comes with devotees' practice of *çile* (Chapter 2) in everyday life continues and improves with their practice of *zikir* ceremonies. As Bruce Kapferer states, "ritual is an organisation of practice ... in which the participants confront the existential conditions of their existence."[10] The confrontation embodied during the *zikir* ceremony does not begin or end with the repetitive moments of the collective ceremony. The sensations affected the actions and behaviours of the devotees even after the ceremony was over. The sense of breathing, energy and joy experienced during the performance of the collective ceremony inspired the devotees to remember their experiences and apply such sensations to their everyday life. Therefore, it is necessary to analyse *zikir* not as a structurally restrictive ritual separate from daily social life. Instead, *zikir* ceremony is a performatic ritual that inspired a sense of liberation, creation, transformation, joy and energy. Performing *zikir*, devotees sought to become aware of their body as a sacred temple designed for the training of the *nefs*. On certain nights, singing and dancing for four hours without a break, Esen said moving and chanting God's names in exhaustion, she could sense her breath, her spirit in joy and her sense of freedom from any person, any idea, any desire and any fear apart from God. She said she laughed. She celebrated. She cried. She screamed.

Examining Sufi ritual as embodiment highlights the strong emotional identification made possible through devotees' practice. Devotees' repetitive movements moved beyond ritualisation. Their actions brought their focus to the experience of the sensations. The experience of the divine took over the meaning of the divine. Devotees' movements, sounds and energy affected each devotee's journey as they sought to move to a place where they were alone with God. Bringing together such interdisciplinary knowledges about the universe, religion, Sufism and science, devotees sought to find balance between their spiritual experiences and the material world. Seeking to remember the sensations discovered through the practice of *zikir*, devotees, when they were outside the lodge, taking care of duties at work or home, also reminded themselves of the experience of unity that came with the performance of collective *zikir*. A devotee explained:

> Especially when I am outside the lodge, I continuously remind myself to not let go of the sense of joy and freedom I experience performing the

zikir ceremony. And as I remember, I feel on the path as a devotee. Dervish means one who waits at the threshold to move to a place where the awareness of God overcomes material desires and attachments. When I remind myself that I am at the threshold seeking a way to move closer to God, my needs and desires about the material world become less indulging and I find myself at a place of peace. Performing *zikir*, I feel mental and physical freedom and joy.[11]

Devotees emphasised the fact that, through the practice of *zikir* ceremony, along with their everyday *zikir*, they healed their mind, body and soul.

Ritual inspires human beings to experience different ideas and identities and transform from one condition or role to another. Schechner examines rituals as "collective memories encoded into actions" that help people (and sometimes animals) deal with difficult transitions, ambivalent relationships, hierarchies, and desires that trouble, exceed, or violate the norms of daily life."[12] Through rituals, people discover and enter new realities. Rituals are tools with which people use to experience change, to become selves other than their usual selves. People temporarily become or enact another and tend to perform sets of actions that slightly differ from the ordinary moments of everyday life. Aside from the spiritual aspects, devotees also perceived *zikir* as a social practice through which they discovered a balance between their spiritual and egoic selves.

Oscar Salemink's analysis highlights how ritual can be a tool for knowing self. Salemink states "Ritual always refers to boundaries, categories, and groups and therefore is a social phenomenon that concerns questions of identity and identification—giving a partial answer to the question 'who are we?'"[13] For Veli *efendi*, *zikir ceremony* is an embodied practice that refers to the idea that human beings long to return to their true selves. That true self is connected to God. It is a parallel universe that devotees seek to discover. The universe is God's unity and as each living and non-living thing is part of that whole. Embodiment of this information inspires them to open their heart to comprehending this perception. They move. They chant. They remember. They unite.

Through performance of *zikir*, the *efendi* said that a devotee could activate their memory of God, remember their Sufi values and interact with others with such awareness. With the energy experienced in chanting and moving, devotees believed that they connected to a higher self that they could continue to remember in their everyday lives. Rüya, a senior dervish, described her experience performing silent *zikir* during work and says, "Performing *zikir*, I remember what I learned from training in the *house*. I experience the stillness. It is physical and mental. My muscles release, I breath deeper and I feel more sensitive, calm and compassionate towards myself and others."[14]

As Turner explains, "performances of ritual are distinctive phases in the social process, whereby groups and individuals adjust to internal changes and adapt to their external environment."[15] The experience of divine meaning as joy, energy and unity allows devotees to adapt to their urban environment. Rüya said she sought to carry the experience that she gained through the performance of *zikir* to her daily life to detach herself from her material attachments. Silently repeating God's names, she concentrated and remembered the warmth, joy and confidence she experienced while performing the ceremony.

As devotee Yasemin once explained, the movements, chants and feeling of energy inspired a sense of freedom, allowing her to release undesirable thoughts: "I am there with others. I hear them and I see them until I stop hearing and seeing them. At that moment, I only seek to experience the beloved."[16] For Yasemin, *zikir* connected her mind to her breath and she developed a deeper connection with the present moment. Through finding her connection with the breath, she believed she was transported to another realm or dimension. She explained this as consciousness transformation. She no longer lived in her thoughts. She was able to focus on her breath, embrace her thoughts and allow them to pass. She explained that she used to be a prisoner of her mind (or ego), but with remembrance of God's unity she was the master. This level of consciousness created a sense of peace through which she was able to stay in harmony with every being and object around her. She sensed the unity, that there were different people, animals, trees, flowers, fruits and objects, yet all were interrelated to serve the divine essence of God. She explained that she began to perceive everything as a different characteristic or manifestation of the same ultimate truth. With this experience, she explained, she was able to transcend what she perceived as self separate from everything in the universe. She was able to "identify with everything in the universe."[17] Along with Yasemin, the depth of the transcendent experience gained through the performance of *zikir* inspired a great number of devotees to study the correlations between science and religion as they discussed neurolinguistics and consciousness. They were aware of how their embodied acts were transforming their minds and bodies and they wanted to know more.

With practice of *zikir*, devotees also improved their notion of listening spiritually (*sema*) to the sounds of the universe. It was common practice in Sufism for devotees to regularly listen to repetitive tunes as support for meditation and as a means of access to the state of selflessness. For dervishes, music was the food of the soul tired of the regulations of the material world. In Sufism, *sema* symbolised the action of listening to Sufi hymns of various forms with heart and soul in a spiritual fashion. The meaning of the word *sema* suggested that it was the act of listening that was spiritual (as in the *Mevlevi sema* ceremony). Moreover, listening could refer to any sound, whether natural, artificial or artistic, as well as to the sounds of the cosmos.

The word *sema* is also synonymous with the word "understanding." For *Rifais*, that was an understanding and acceptance of the call from God, which could lead to rapture and the revelation of mysteries. The meanings contained within the Quran were "infinite and ever-new, because there is no repetition in the [divine] self-disclosure . . . of which the cosmos, the human and the Quran are three manifestations."[18] The receptiveness "to the infinitive of meanings is only possible when one opens oneself to divine mercy by learning the *edep* [manners] of listening."[19] The *edep* of listening guided devotees to pay full attention to the divine discourse, the words, thoughts and sounds. With such concentration, the students listened without getting distracted and thus were able to control the mind. The students often depicted their experiences referring to "how the mind became free of any images and thoughts other than the sacred sounds."[20]

Therefore, *sema* gives a clue to the understanding of the Sufi *zikir* ritual. Although the word *sema* is used in the West when referring to the *Mevlevi zikir* and *sema* ceremony of the whirling dervishes, the word has a deeper religious meaning for all kinds of Sufi *zikir* rituals. Muslim mystics' concern in creating and listening was to give the music true meaning. Sufi hymns, according to Yiğit *dede*, articulated the devotees' desire and need to submit to the beloved God. As Yiğit *dede* pointed out, Sufi music is the lively expression of the divine meaning, sacred harmonies and sounds from the cosmos. Certain Sufi teachers only make moderate use of music, whereas others are passionate about the act of *sema* together with the act of dancing (as in the case of the *Mevlevi* teachers). In Sufism, in the debates about music and dance and their legitimate status and proper use in Islam, the emphasis is always on the act of listening rather than on making the music and whirling. Throughout the centuries, Sufi mystics have written mystical poetry for devotional purposes and other mystics and musicians have composed music inspired by the poems of Sufi mystics. These compositions are regularly performed with percussion and harmonium. The *efendi* considered such activities as encouraging mystical feelings. To experience mystical feelings, dervishes regularly organised music classes on Sundays and Tuesdays. Female devotees gathered in the third-floor apartment of the residential *house* to study with Veli *efendi*'s students. Nazan, who held a PhD in Sufi music, and Esen, also a music teacher, whose primary focus was on Sufi musical instruments were the ones teaching the female devotees the liturgical songs. With guidance from the *efendi*, Nazan and Esen taught compositions created by Sufi mystics, including the compositions of their own master. Male devotees gathered on the fourth floor to study with Yiğit *dede*, who was a Sufi musician trained in a Sufi family. Although female and male devotees attended classes separately, both Nazan and Yiğit *dede* structured these classes in a similar fashion and brought the male and female students together in the worship room on the fifth floor to share their liturgical songs with one another in the presence of Veli *efendi*.

Liturgical songs practised in these gatherings were poems written and composed by different Sufi mystics. Vocalisation of these songs played a significant role in experiencing and transmitting divine meaning. The lyrics of the songs were about divine love, longing, the relationship with one's master, mystics' thoughts and feelings in pursuing the spiritual journey. Therefore, as discussed in Rumi's poetry, liturgical songs were studied as divine texts. The lyrics, as in the case of Rumi, were not considered products of human effort.

Rather, they conveyed divine essence. Thus, the classes were regarded as acts of worship and devotees studied these songs and recited them with a sense of devotion as if they were praying.

For the classes, devotees gathered in a small living room and sat in a circle—some on the floor, some on sofas. Due to the size of the room and the large number of devotees, chorus members would sit side by side, close to each other and, similar to the feeling in the wooden *house*, were aware of each other's movements and sounds even if they did not look at each other. Everyone was given a booklet comprised of all the liturgical songs to be studied until the yearly pilgrimage to Konya, where female devotees performed the liturgical songs as part of honouring the spirits of the deceased mystics. Throughout the year, students discovered how divine meaning was articulated and embodied by Sufi mystics. The students became both performers and audience in these classes. They performed for themselves and others present. They watched themselves and others present. Sitting in the circle, they would "witness each other's dedication," "absorb each other's voices" and "experience the emotional changes in each other's vocalisations."[21] It is important to point out that as explained by Nazan, some of the musical notes were put together to convey feelings of joy while others to inspire feelings of longing according to the experience discussed by the mystics. Nazan once said that music drives the devotees to relate to and feel the spiritual experiences of the mystics who wrote the poems and composed the music. They would relate to the sense of longing experienced by the mystic and identify their practices through the words of the mystics. Devotees also listened to the recordings of their *zikir* ceremony and their *ilahis* in their everyday lives.

Burhan: *Rifai* Body as a Sacred Performative Subject

It was in one of the *zikir* ceremonies at the wooden house, I saw a dervish walking through other devotees who continue performing *zikir*. He came with a vessel filled with skewers, bowed in the direction of the master (Veli *efendi*) and left the vessel on a clean sheet placed on the floor in the middle of the *zikir* circle. Then, the sound of the percussion started to grow, and a devotee handed a skewer to Veli *efendi*, who also continued to move to the rhythm, performing *zikir*. In that moment, devotees kept their eyes open as they moved and chanted. The *dede*, feeding a strong sound, transformed the *zikir* to a forceful but low-pitch tone through which devotees continued to repeat another Quranic name. Veli *efendi* took his time dancing moving his body up and down in the *zikir* circle. Then after a while, he looked into the eyes of a senior dervish, held the skin on his neck with one hand and inserted a skewer through his skin. At this moment, *zikir* started to become louder and faster again. Then, devotees started to move and repeated God's names so fast that as they jumped it was hard to see the others in the room. Nothing seemed planned. Every action happened spontaneously in the moment. It was as if with the actions performed, the devotees felt more emotional because their faces were wet with sweat and their eyes were full of tears. The devotees' bodies in motion conveyed a strong sense of commitment, passion and freedom. Dancing bodies and facial expressions demonstrated a sense of pride, respect and devotion to the proof conveyed by their teacher. The senior devotee showed no sign of pain when Veli *efendi* inserted the skewer, and he continued to move and perform *zikir* with the skewer inserted through his skin.

Burhan (showing proof) was another ritual that devotees practised to transform their minds and bodies. Devotees believed that *burhan* was a ritual based on an event about their *pir*, Ahmed Rıfâî. The story revealed that the pir of the *Rifai* order (Ahmet *Rifai*) did not die after a snake bit him. Veli *efendi* talked about the fact that they performed *burhan* to experience *keramet* (miracle), "not only to show" the proof to others "but to remind" themselves that God exists and that they are part of God's essence.[22] When I first witnessed the performance of *burhan* in 2011 during a pilgrimage to the tombs of Sufi saints in and near Konya, my mind was filled with questions: How does Veli *efendi* insert the skewers? Why does he insert the skewers? Was this something studied and mastered so that devotees do not get hurt? Was the skewer real? How does the *efendi* stop the blood? How do devotees continue to dance with those skewers inserted in their bodies? How are they so awake and full of joy? Upon my first witnessing, in the next years, on and off, I had the chance to participate in a countless number of *zikir* rituals that included performance of *burhan*.

According to *Rifais*, the physical self (the body) needed a performatic intervention in order to act with full spiritual awareness. Veli *efendi* believed that the practice of *burhan* also inspired his devotees to stay free of the demanding social, economic and political crisis that at times challenged their spiritual progress. In *Burhan*, the body was a sacred performatic subject that simultaneously experienced God's unity and also a vehicle that created an effect on the devotees witnessing the insertion. Witnessing the act, as Veli *efendi* explained, changed their perception of the world. For dervishes, the act of disfiguration paved the way for the beautification of the *nefs* (soul, self or mind)—a performance of the healing of the mind and body. For Veli *efendi*, performing *burhan* was also more than a devotional act. It was devotees' celebration of the journey. It was their confidence in the path, shaping who they are by inspiring them to believe in a spiritual self beyond this world. *Burhan* convinced devotees that everything in this world is transitory. Devotees witnessed God's proof, His unity and while witnessing the proof, devotees' idea of this universe and their idea of themselves changed.

As Elaine Peña examines, "Public or private, collective or individual, the devotional acts have regenerative effects that transcend the moment of execution."[23] Devotees performed this highly evocative and formalised action to transcend that every knowledge and reality is visible. As Veli *efendi* explained, the reality is flexible and multifaceted. In the *Rifai* group, *burhan* was performed during the *zikir* ceremony with Veli *efendi* inserting skewers into different parts of dervishes' bodies, who stood in the first two circles (comprised of male senior dervishes and dervishes) to prove that the natural laws of the world may sometimes not be valid. Devotees performed *burhan* when the music and chanting were strong and emotional, making the space ready for the devotees to experience the incontrovertible truth. Devotees were performing these extreme acts of physical disfiguration of dervishes 'body parts in order to embody God's unity.[24] Piercing a skewer through the cheeks, eyes, abdomen or throat was a common practice. For the devotees, the experience of divine meaning, the otherworldliness, was real.

What devotees experienced is also similar to Rouget's analysis of trance as "trancendence of one's normal self, as a liberation resulting from the intensification of a mental or physical disposition."[25] Performing *burhan*, dervishes experience a moment of clarification about God's power. Zeki *dede* explained, "his belief is justified and reformed."[26] During the insertions, devotees continued to move and perform *zikir*, keeping their eyes open to witness the rest of this miraculous process of experiencing proof. Even the devotees witnessing *burhan* experienced a sense of unity. Having performed *zikir* at high speed for hours, as Burcu later explained, it was as if every part of her body was dancing involuntarily. Burcu explained that this moment of witnessing has the potential to bring a sense of conviction and confidence to her actions.

In the three years in which I witnessed the ritual, Mehmet was the only dervish who shared his experience with *burhan* with me in detail. As Mehmet explained, in such rapturous moments, "[they] witness God's power and [their] master's relationship to the divine. It is not shocking. It is what [they] know, what [they] assert, and what [they] live for."[27] Mehmet promised me that it is not painful and encouraged me further to perceive it as delightful and rapturous. One night, I was in the kitchen washing dishes with two other dervishes and Mehmet walked in to nibble on cookies after the ritual ended. One senior dervish patted his shoulder and asked him jokingly how he was feeling after his first *burhan*. In reply, Mehmet said: "Ohhhh . . . I want it again."[28] Then sounding joyous with his first experience, he said that feeling the skewers in his body was miraculous. He only felt as if a mosquito had bitten him. He continued to move and speak with the skewers in his body. He said, "it is out of this world."[29] Then he said, "Now when I think about it, I say yes, of course, certainly. This is His power and I was very lucky."[30] Like Mehmet, other devotees felt the skewers in their skin looked content and happy as the *efendi* inserted the skewers. The skewers stayed in each devotee's body around five to ten minutes. When taking the skewers out, the *efendi*'s eyes also transmitted a sense of confidence. He looked serious, showing not one bit of concern in his eyes.

The insertion also contributed to forming new levels of the dervish's spiritual journey. Veli *efendi* also discussed *burhan* as a search for transformation through which the performer may gain a new spiritual awareness. This status affected the devotees' position both in terms of transcendent realm and in the social milieu of the order. The hierarchical position changed. According to Veli *efendi*, different parts of the body posed different levels of difficulty for the performer in terms of controlling pain. The most difficult sections such as around the belly button required more bodily control. Since these are considered dangerous zones, only senior dervishes performed them. This sense of witnessing how senior dervishes moved beyond the natural laws persuaded devotees to recognise the *efendi* and their senior dervishes (*dedes*) as their teachers along the path.

Devotees experienced what some called "the power of unity," and others "the power of connectedness," or "the power of togetherness."[31] The devotees and guests stood hand in hand, alert, keeping their eyes open, to witness *burhan* while repeating "*Kayyum*," another Quranic name of God. Repeating specifically this name, devotees were aware that God had power over the functions and qualities of objects and spaces, as well as human beings. As Veli *efendi* once discussed, if God wanted, the quality and function of each material would change.

Victor Turner states that when participants of a religious or secular event experience "liberation of their human capacities of cognition, affect, volition and creativity," they are able to experience spontaneous communitas—"we are all in this together."[32] This was visible when the group moved and recited together. More than half of the guests were already standing and performing with the devotees, but with the increase of energy during the performance of *burhan*, the vibrations grew so incredibly strong that after a while even the ones who initially resisted leaving their seats started to move with the devotees. With each repetition, it was as if the devotees were moving their head the first time, with more desire and commitment. Each repetition was new. Each repetition was transformative. As the devotees' bodily energy transformed with the act of skewering, the kinaesthetic sense in the space inspired guests to move and chant in the same rhythm with the devotees.

Analysing Turner's theory of communitas, Micu states, "The experience of togetherness momentarily abolishes the differences in status between the members of the community. Communitas has the temporary ability to bring people together as equals who share a common experience."[33] As devotees repeated the same chants and moved shoulder to shoulder, it was possible to see Turner's notion of communitas at work. No one seemed to care about their social principles. Devotees were performing the ritual as equals, interested only in the experience of God's unity. They did not seem to worry about each other's identities or statuses. They were hand in hand with people, who might have no connection to their way of life other than the common desire to comprehend God's unity. All was there seeking to know their true self.

Burhan ritual is a quest for a new self or mind. Devotees who are academics see some correlations between secular artistic and religious ritual performance as well as links between artists' and Sufi devotees' longing for a renewed self. Although the method of performing the insertion and the experience of injury, pain and blood are different for devotees, the goal is somewhat similar. Beginning in the 1960s and throughout the 1970s, artist Hermann Nitsch conducted a series of performances that frequently entailed dismemberment of animals and large quantities of blood. Art historian Roselee Goldberg describes Nitsch's performance in terms of ritual:

> Such activities sprang from Nitsch' belief that humankind's aggressive instincts had been repressed and muted through the media. . . . These ritualised acts were a means of releasing that repressed energy as well as an act of purification and redemption through suffering.[34]

Antonin Artaud also explains, "if the existing body is a machine, it is, according to Artaud, an automation that must be destroyed in order to be rebuilt as its true self."[35] Longing for a self or mind that is free of limitations, biases, generalisations and attachments, although coming from totally different places for each artist and devotee, is clearly the common need both in the practice of disfiguration in certain art forms and Sufi rituals. Also, artist Gina Pane "does art performances including self-inflicting cuts to her body," believing that ritualised pain had a purifying effect.[36] The goal was similar for the devotees seeking release from their dualities. Although it was a different kind of purification, the goal for both can be analysed as the transformation of self, imagining a mind set free of social pressures.

To explain his vision for uniting with God (in his *sohbets*), Veli *efendi* often illuminated how Mevlana Celaleddin-i Rumi provided a valuable discussion about *nefs*' duality by emphasising the fact that God also sought to remove dualities to achieve union with His creation:

> In His presence there is no room for two egos. You say "ego," and He "ego"? Either you die in His presence, or He will die in your presence, so that no duality may remain. Yet it is impossible that He should die, either in the universe or in the mind, for "He is the living, who does not die." He has grace in such measure that, were it possible, He would die for you to remove the duality. But since His death is impossible, you die so that He may become manifest in you and the duality be lifted.[37]

According to Veli *efendi*, Rumi emphasised the most significant aspect of Sufi devotional life by explaining the fact that it was a spiritual human need to be one with God.

As Morgan Clarke discusses in her analysis of *burhan*, "one can also learn to see the extraordinary [the miracle] in the seemingly ordinary."[38] Clarke examines how "Everyday miracles can include finding a banknote when one needs one, or even catching an unusually fast bus, if only one learns to recognise them."[39] The experience of the extraordinary "does not therefore lie beyond the social, rather, it is constituted within it."[40] This sense of embodying the extraordinary while performing the necessities of everyday life is also vital for *Rifai* devotees' practice of the universe as unity.

Performing *burhan*, devotees embodied God's power and accepted fully that there was an experience that was beyond the needs and desires of this world. As Ceylin said, she sensed the mortality of her body and immortality of her spiritual self. This, she explained, was causing excessive liberation from the idea of the world as a material space and allowed her to see the magic of the ordinary life.

Renunciation: Purifying the Body

Renunciation practices such as rejection of too much food and sleep also affected *Rifai* devotees' perception of ordinary life. One of the most cited Hadith sayings due to its message for a fight against one's own soul is "We have returned from the lesser jihad (warfare) to the greater jihad."[41] This is a difficult fight, as Hoffman identifies, because one needs "to purify the soul of all forms of evil and negligence."[42] According to Karabulut, "spirit's origin" is "divine, and by its very nature," it is longing "to return to it's heavenly home; but the soul [*nefs*] is of earthly origin, and pulls the spirit back to earth."[43] Such analyses make it clear that some dervishes trained to resist earthly desires through fasting and other forms of asceticism. In the past, Sufis "practiced almost incredible feats of self-denial, shunning all forms of luxury, eating the barest minimum necessary to keep alive, avoiding sleep (a mark of 'heedlessness'), and spending their nights in devotion and self-examination."[44] *Zuhd* in Veli *efendi*'s group was a common practice for dervishes who seek to let go of their attachment to excessive food or sleep.

Veli *efendi* and his devotees perceived the body as a medium to connect to and generate spiritual experiences, therefore, practised certain forms of renunciation, avoiding all forms of luxury, eating just enough to stay alive, sleeping very little (when impossible to stay awake) and spending their nights in meditation. These devotees sought to learn to direct their mind activities. Disciplining and regulating the body played a significant role in such devotees' Sufi practice.

There is research that illuminates how "Sufism grew out of . . . earlier ascetic tradition."[45] There are accounts of dervishes interested in "celibate poverty, subsisting off alms, and separating themselves from the general society, both by moving from place to place, and by their antinomian disregard for rules and conventions."[46] Aside from the term *zuhhad* used for the practitioners of *zuhd*, there were numerous other terminologies to describe renunciation in Sufi practice. These were "ascetics," "due to their austere lifestyles;" "reciters," due to their emphasis on the instruction of the Quran; "worshippers," due to their strict adherence to their devotions; "preachers," due to the delivery of emotive sermons; and "weepers . . . due to their shedding of tears when moved by eloquent speech, or the remembrance of death and the hereafter."[47] Within such ascetic lifestyles, some dervishes dressed differently and shaved off all the hair on their body, including their eyebrows. Some dervishes violated social and religious norms by refusing to wear clothes. Some practised bodily mortification such as self-mutilation.[48]

Although Veli *efendi*'s devotees were more modest regarding such choices, some of his dervishes believed that renunciation opened a lens through which devotees perceived proof, God's unity, His existence. Some qualities that shaped the *zuhd* mentality in the *Rifai* order was satisfaction with low income and living in less comfortable conditions (such as small spaces); isolation; opposing certain desires such as food, cigarette and alcohol; avoiding too much talking; giving up desires to have romantic relationships, to marry and to have children; and investing all spare time to meditation and service to the people. According to Zeki *dede*, although "the world that we see seems so real, it is only a mirage of God's essence."[49] As Veli *efendi* explained, some seekers expected to release worldly passions to discover what they called the deeper identity by answering all the heart's questions.

Veli *efendi* often discussed how human beings desired to return to their origin. He explained how human beings may feel uncomfortable, upset, feeling lonely, aggressive and powerless because they may not be aware of the fact that they live ignorant of their true nature. The analysis of the fourteenth-century Sufi Persian poet Hafız's words can illuminate Veli *efendi*'s depictions further: "the heart belongs to the spiritual world but has forgotten its origin, and its own nature."[50] To realise the spiritual potential of the heart, "Disciplining one's soul through sleeplessness, isolation and eating as little food as possible polishes the mirror of the heart so that the traveller can find union with the Divine."[51] Veli *efendi* believed that such self-discipline could open up the blocks in the hearts. Zeki *dede* referred to Sufi mystic Mevlana (Master) Celaleddin-i Rumi to explain his idea of how material needs, desires and possessions were veils of divine meaning. Rumi states in his Fih-i Mafih:

> All desires, affections, loves, and fondness people have for all sorts of things, such as fathers, mothers, friends, the heavens and the earth, gardens, pavilions, works, knowledge, food, and drink—one should realise that every desire is a desire for food, and such things are all veils. When one passes beyond this world and sees that King without these veils and coverings and that what they were seeking was in reality one thing. All problems will then be solved. All the heart's questions and difficulties will be answered, and everything will become clear. Allah's reply is not such that He must answer each and every problem individually. With one answer all problems are solved.[52]

Devotees cultivated their dependence on God to provide for their needs (*tevekkül*). Although they worked for a living and had the resources to satisfy their hunger, they preferred to stay hungry in order to keep the mind still and quiet.

Veli *efendi*'s vision was visible to me in the practices of three female devotees: Esen, Derya and Ebru. I knew that there were others in the group but due to Esen's and Ebru's openness to allow me to join them or sit with them as they practised their daily chores and meditation, I was able to witness their experiences and hardships. Often, I would see how Esen fell asleep for two to three hours in a room and woke up to either perform her chores or practice silent *zikir*. At the time, Esen was working part time as a music teacher, where she would need to travel to Taksim, a crowded neighbourhood in Istanbul, three times a week. Aside from this, she would go and visit her family once a week or when they needed her help. She had an old model mobile phone (definitely not a smart phone), through which she would contact her family. Apart from her work and family relations, she was very busy with her chores and rituals. Esen would speak and move in a very quiet manner. It was almost like her presence was unknown in the *Rifai* houses.

Derya and Ebru, having finished their graduate education, were also at the *Rifai* houses most of the time and had a variety of responsibilities such as cleaning and organising the residential spaces. Because they were bilingual, they would also attend gatherings with Veli *efendi*'s foreign guests and attend to matters regarding their travel and sightseeing plans. Although Esen and Ebru were very thin and looked weak, they weren't. I would only see them eat once or twice a day, usually some bread, cheese and olives for breakfast, and then a cup of soup and some bread for dinner. I knew they enjoyed eating but preferred hunger and sleeplessness to any form of excessive comfort.

Ebru once explained the difference between the two by discussing her mind activities. When she

> feeds herself more often and sleeps more than five hours a day, she starts to get busy with anxious thoughts. She worries about the health of her mother, worries about money, worries about what she is doing in this world.[53]

Having practised self-discipline for more than two years at the time, Ebru was confident with her choice to live with less. She was a peaceful person, content with what she had and in good relations with her friends in the group. Like Esen, she was very productive during the day, writing poetry, reading and taking care of her daily responsibilities. She was not concerned for her health. Ebru perceived her practice of renunciation as the most healthy way of living for her. She said:

> I know how hard it is to live in the capitalist system. I did that for eleven years after I graduated. I worked, tried to make more money, hoped to become a successful businesswoman, but once I achieved that, I understood. I felt the calling. Twice, I traveled to meditation centres in India . . . participated in yoga and meditation classes in Turkey. I knew what I was feeling . . . something beyond this world. . . . Then, I found Veli *efendi*. Here, I am happy and peaceful.[54]

146 *Transforming*

Ebru also believed that despite all her efforts to renounce this world, she still held some family connections. She believed it was her duty to support her family. She provided financial and emotional support, but they were no longer at the centre of her life. The centre of her life was not family, work, or any other attachment, it was her divine journey, any activity that inspired her perception of unity.

Derya, on the other hand, was feeling weak. She was very thin (too thin, looking unhealthy) and did not enjoy eating food. She would explain, "she had no other option."[55] Derya was a very social and talkative person. I would usually see her taking care of guests, friends or answering people's questions. She was interested in guiding everyone in the group and would know everyone's problems and needs. Despite her physical weakness, she needed to work to support her mother, who had health problems. I knew that she was in need of financial support not for herself but for her immediate family. When she could not find a job, the *efendi* sent her to live in a *Rifai* house in California. There, she started to make money to support her family. The last time I saw her, she was still very thin but feeling stronger. She said to me, "I finally understood why I do not want to eat."[56] With this sentence, she smiled and brought her hand to her heart, sharing her remembrance of God.

Some of the devotees also renounced certain social statuses and family ties. For instance, Esen lived a life of celibacy, preferring to stay single for the rest of her life. She desired to practice music and serve in the *Rifai* houses. Esen was happy with her choice to live side by side with her dervish friends. She believed that the more her body and mind were invested in the devotional activities, the more she felt connected to God's essence. With the practice of *zikir*, *burhan*, fasting and sleeping little, these devotees believed that they slowed down the constant journeying of their minds and achieved a sense of unity with the universe. This practice of sacralisation of the mind and body, as I will discuss further in the next chapter, paved the devotees' way to perceive and experience the world as the space of unity (as manyness of reality).

Notes

1 By liminality, I am referring to Arnold Van Gennep's idea of "right of passage" and Victor Turner's further treatment of the concept of "liminality" as the phase of uncertainty that transpires in the middle processual stage of a "rite of passage." In the Sufi case, a student moves ahead of the pre-ritual status (which is the earlier stages of the *nefs*, when a student is not aware of divine meaning) but has arrived the middle (liminal) phase, in which he or she has gained some understanding of God's unity and is training to reach the final stage (which is uniting with God). For more information, refer to Arnold Van Gennep, *The Rites of Passage* (Chicago: University of Chicago, 1960); Victor Turner, "Betwixt and Between: The Liminal Period in Rites de Passage," in *The Forest of Symbols* (Ithaca, NY: Cornell University Press, 1967); Victor Turner, *The Ritual Process: Structure and Antistructure* (Chicago: Aldine Publishing, 1969); Victor Turner, *Dramas, Fields, and Metaphors: Symbolic Action in Human Society* (Ithaca: Cornell University Press,

1974); Turner and Turner, *Image and Pilgrimage in Christian Culture Anthropological Perspectives.*

2 In sharing their experiences of performing *zikir*, devotees avoid the word "trance" because the *efendi* believes that even in the rapturous state, a devotee should seek to be aware of his/her actions and behaviours. The moment of rapture seems ecstatic because the devotees' heads start moving very fast, almost uncontrolled, and their eyes seem unaware of their motions and behaviours. However, even though that might be the case for some practitioners, trance is not advised by the *efendi* or the *dedes* (senior dervishes). Practitioners believe that a devotee needs to be awake and aware of God at all times, in all environments.

3 Werbner, "Stamping the Earth with the Name of Allah and the Sacralising of Space Among British Muslims," 321.

4 Werbner, "Stamping the Earth with the Name of Allah and the Sacralising of Space Among British Muslims," 321.

5 Drewal, "The State of Research on Performance in Africa," 1–64.

6 Drewal, "The State of Research on Performance in Africa," 38.

7 Drewal, "The State of Research on Performance in Africa," 1–64.

8 Roach, *Cities of the Dead: Circum-Atlantic Performance*, 26.

9 Roach, *Cities of the Dead: Circum-Atlantic Performance*, 26.

10 Bruce Kapferer, *A Celebration of Demons: Exorcism and the Aesthetics of Healing in Sri Lanka* (Bloomington: Indiana University Press, 1983), xi.

11 Personal communication, June 17, 2012.

12 Schechner, *Performance Studies: An Introduction*, 52.

13 Salemink, "Embodying the Nation: Mediumship Ritual and the National Imagination," 267.

14 Personal communication, March 25, 2011.

15 Victor Turner, "Body, Brain and Culture," *Performing Arts Journal* 10, no. 2 (1986): 26–34.

16 Personal communication, November 5, 2012.

17 Personal communication, November 5, 2012.

18 Zamir, "'Tafsir al-Quran bi'l Quran': The Hermeneutics of Imitation and 'Adap' in Ibn-i Arabi's Interpretation of the Quran," 14.

19 Zamir, "'Tafsir al-Quran bi'l Quran': The Hermeneutics of Imitation and 'Adap' in Ibn-i Arabi's Interpretation of the Quran," 14.

20 Personal communication, December 17, 2012.

21 Personal communications with the devotees, between December 12, 2012 and November 5, 2013.

22 Personal communication, June 11, 2013.

23 Peña, *Performing Piety*, 58.

24 Paulo Gabriel Hilu da Rocha Pinto, "Mystical Bodies/Unruly Bodies: Experience, Empowerment and Subjectification in Syrian Sufism," *Social Compass* 63, no. 2 (June 2016): 197–212, https://doi.org/10.1177/0037768616628791.

25 Gilbert Rouget, *Music and Trance: A Theory of the Relations Between Music and Possession* (Chicago: University of Chicago Press, 1985), 13–14.

26 Personal communication, November 18, 2012.

27 Personal communication, December 5, 2013.

28 Personal communication, December 5, 2013.

29 Personal communication, December 5, 2013.

30 Personal communication, December 5, 2013.

31 Personal communications, December 21, 2013.

32 Turner, *From Ritual to Theatre: Human Seriousness of Play*, 44.

33 Micu, *Performance Studies: The Basics*, 9.

34 Roselee Goldberg, *Performance Art from Futurism to the Present* (New York: H.N. Abrams, 1988), 164.
35 Ros Murray, *Antonin Artaud: The Scum of the Soul* (London: Palgrave Macmillan UK, 2014), 141.
36 Dawn Perlmutter, *Investigating Religious Terrorism and Ritualistic Crimes* (London: CRC Press, 2004), 161.
37 Lewis, *Rumi: Past and Present, East and West*, 418.
38 Morgan Clarke, "Cough Sweets and Angels: The Ordinary Ethics of the Extraordinary in Sufi Practice in Lebanon," *The Journal of the Royal Anthropological Institute* 20, no. 3 (2014), 407–425, http://www.jstor.org/stable/43907697.
39 Clarke, "Cough Sweets and Angels," 408; Michael Gilsenan, *Saints and Sufis in Modern Egypt: An Essay in the Sociology of Religion* (Oxford: Clarendon Press, 1973), 31; Michael Gilsenan, *Recognising Islam: An Anthropologist's Introduction* (London: Croom Helm, 1982), 80, 83.
40 Clarke, "Cough Sweets and Angels," 420.
41 Heather Selma Gregg, *The Path to Salvation: Religious Violence from the Crusades to Jihad* (Lincoln: Potomac Books, University of Nebraska Press, 2014), 94.
42 Valerie J. Hoffman, "Eating and Fasting for God in Sufi Tradition," *Journal of the American Academy of Religion* 63, no. 3 (1995): 465–484, http://www.jstor.org/stable/1465088.
43 Savaş Karabulut, "A Comparative Study on Asceticism in Buddhism and Islam," Master's thesis, Seoul National University, Seoul, South Korea, 2008, 89.
44 Karabulut, *A Comparative Study on Asceticism in Buddhism and Islam*, 89.
45 Christopher Melchert, "Origins and Early Sufism," in *Cambridge Companion to Sufism* (Cambridge: Cambridge University Press, 2014), 3; Louis Massignon, *Essay on the Origin of the Technical Language of Islamic Mysticism*, trans. Benjamin Clark (Notre Dame, Indiana: University of Notre Dame Press, 1997).
46 Mark Sedgwick, *Western Sufism: From the Abbasids to the New Age* (Oxford: Oxford University Press, 2016), 73.
47 Gavin N. Picken, "Al-Ḥārith Al-Muḥāsibī and Spiritual Purification Between Asceticism and Mysticism," in *Routledge Handbook on Sufism*, ed. Lloyd Ridgeon (London: Routledge, 2020), 19; Also see Massignon, *Essay*, 113–115; Knysh, *Sufism*, 6–7.
48 Sedgwick, *Western Sufism*, 73–74.
49 Personal communication, June 15, 2013.
50 Ali-Asghar Seyyed Gohrab, "Sufism in Classical Persian Poetry," in *Routledge Handbook on Sufism*, ed. Lloyd Ridgeon (New York: Routledge, 2020), 192.
51 Gohrab, "Sufism in Classical Persian Poetry," 192.
52 Margaret Smith, *Readings from the Mystics of Islam* (London: Luzac, 1950), 36.
53 Personal communication, June 12, 2013.
54 Personal communication, September 4, 2014.
55 Personal communication, November 19, 2013.
56 Personal communication, October 12, 2015.

5 World as Manyness of Reality

Rifai devotees' perception of self-transformation and space had become explicit with how they performed their Konya pilgrimage for five years between 2010 and 2015. *Rifais* organised a physically and mentally demanding four-day pilgrimage and with their embodied acts transformed the spaces they visited in Konya, including their hotel, buses, shrines and mosques. I participated in the pilgrimage with the *Rifais* after voicing my desire to Veli *efendi,* who in return welcomed me to travel with them every year between 2010 and 2015. As a graduate student conducting research, the *efendi* welcomed me to stay at what some devotees call the *tekke* hotel, a space that was a temporary combination of the residential building and the wooden house. Sharing a small room with six or seven female devotees, I was able to experience every moment of the pilgrimage. Moment-to-moment interactions travelling together for many hours in the buses, walking to the shrines, living in a small hotel room, sleeping, dining and worshipping together, we witnessed each other's sicknesses, discomforts, worries, exhaustion and injuries. Such co-performance of the pilgrimage side by side with Veli *efendi,* senior dervishes and other devotees allowed me to comprehend how devotees embody and inscribe their idea of post-tariqa Sufism as they performed their values in a variety of public spaces.

Experiencing Konya as a Tourist

One of the most religious and industrial cities in Turkey, Konya is the birthplace of the *Mevlevi* Sufi culture. The city has become a popular tourist destination since the Turkish government launched religious tourism initiatives beginning in the 1990s.[1] Coleman Barks, who translated, adapted and performed Rumi's religious poetry in 1997 with *The Illuminated Rumi,* also had a profound effect on Rumi's and Konya's name recognition for English-speaking people. In 2010, Kevin Gould from *The Guardian* wrote about Konya, calling readers' attention to Rumi as a poet and Sufi saint:

> Rumi is one of the world's most read poets. . . . Today's Rumi's tomb is Turkey's second most-visited tourist attraction. . . . Rumi was . . . a Sufi saint who loved all religions, and whose own religion was love.[2]

As Konya Museum Manager Yusuf Benli also said, many tourists from different countries visit the *Mevlana* Museum depending on the time of year.[3] *Hürriyet Daily News* reported in July 2013 that "The Mevlana Museum of Konya attracted 900,000 visitors during the first half of 2013."[4] More recently in 2019, *AA (Anadolu Agency)* reported that "Mevlana Rumi museum drew 3.4M visitors in 2019."[5] Historian Metin And also wrote about how the *Mevlana* annual festival (*Şeb-i Arus* or Rumi's *urs* festival) "attracts vast crowds of every race, colour and creed from all around the world."[6] Thousands of tourists come to Konya to see Rumi's lodge and the whirling ceremony every year.

Rumi's *tekke* dates back to Selçuk times (thirteenth century), but the mosque and the rooms surrounding the shrine were built by Ottoman sultans. Formerly used as lodgings, there are human-sized figures dressed in period costumes in the small rooms to depict the male *Mevlevi* dervishes. There are tombs in the shrine that belong to the family members of Rumi, as well as people who reached high ranks in the *Mevlevi* order. The shrine, established as a museum in 1927, also exhibits texts of Rumi (*Mesnevi* and *Divan-ı Kebir*) and many of Rumi's personal belongings as well as those of other *evliyas* (saints).

Visiting the museum as a tourist in 2010, I entered the gate of the shrine and remembered my first visit to the shrine with my family as a high school student in 1996. Back then, the unrenovated shrine was not functioning as a well-organised museum. There were no signs for tourists, security guards or displays of Rumi's books and objects. As a museum, it was a well-organised touristic site. Tourists spend time in the museum to observe the figures depicting male dervishes' lives during the Ottoman Empire, examine the rooms, relax at the museum's café, read and purchase literature about Rumi and *Mevlevi* culture in English, Spanish, French and other languages.

Despite the functioning of Rumi's lodge and shrine as a museum, security guards did not get in the way of female devotees who were dressed in their everyday non-religious outfits and recognisable through their embodied actions, most specifically through their silent performance of *zikir* and teary eyes. Many female devotees (who are members of different Sufi groups) wished to remain inside the shrine and perform devotion. Their presence and devotion were allowed in the public space as long as they performed *zikir* alone in silence. As I will analyse further in this chapter, only Veli *efendi* and his female and male devotees were able to receive permission to come together to perform *zikir* collectively in the courtyard of the shrine (standing in front of a large window facing Rumi's tomb) in an almost inaudible tone.

The tombs were organised in a way that allowed visitors to constantly move in a queue, ensuring that there was constant flow of visitors facing the tombs and praying. Entering the room with the tombs, visitors first walked shoulder to shoulder, facing the tombs of Rumi's family members in the North part of the room where Rumi's tomb was placed. The museum, not only with the presence of physical objects such as scriptures and *kandil* (oil) lamps but also with the devotee pilgrims' embodied actions, transformed into a sacred performative site in the sense that it was "constructed in the process of its expression."[7] It was a space in flux, in which every moment transformed with each devotee's actions. There were devotees who came to the shrine to worship in the presence of Rumi's tomb. They opened their hands to pray, kissed the silver-plated step beside Rumi's tomb and sat on the floor to meditate.[8] Their bodies conveyed devotion as they closed their eyes and moved their lips, repeating God's Quranic names. Some of them had earphones to listen to a recorded *zikir* ceremony, and they repeated God's names quietly with the sound of the recording.

In 2010, I met a young *Mevlevi* devotee, Jale, sitting on the floor and praying, with her back against the wall. Back then, there were not sections specifically designated for devotion. After she completed her prayer, she looked up and offered me a place next to her on the floor. There was a peaceful smile on Jale's face and her eyes were teary out of the joy of feeling what she later said was "Hazret's [a word used to refer to Sufi mystics as Holiness] spiritual presence."[9] As Jale said, she believed that in the presence of Sufi mystics' tombs, she could pray for a connection and bond with the masters' spirits, which may pass their divine meaning to her. In this way, she said that a devotee can mature and experience *ilham* (sensing and inspiration) from the masters' spirits. Many non-devotee visitors were watching devotees like Jale, who were in the museum to worship. Witnessing the embodied actions of devotees like Jale, tourists, while experiencing Mevlana's *tekke* as a museum, were observing its sacredness.

Konya residents also told mythical stories about Rumi's tomb to tourists. *Mevlana Türbesi* (the tomb of Rumi), his coffin covered with a large velvet cloth decorated in gold, was placed next to Rumi's father's, Baha al-Din Valed, whose coffin stood upright. Residents of Konya explained the elevation of the coffin through a supernatural story. I first heard the story when I visited Konya as a young girl, then again during my visit in 2010. Sufi devotees claimed that when Rumi died, "his father's tomb rose and bowed in respect and devotion."[10] This story, according to a devotee shopkeeper, symbolised the spiritual power of Rumi as a Sufi saint. Hearing the story from a shopkeeper in a gift shop near the museum, Ece, a traveller I met during my visit, came to the hotel lobby with a desire to share it. She expressed to me that although she did not believe the story to be more than a legend, she felt curious standing in front of the elevated coffin. Ece said, "There was a heavy energy in the room. The coffins. Whispering sounds of devotees. . . . Their lamentation."[11] Ece said she believed Konya to be a mystical place. Ece was not a devotee or a practising Muslim. She was simply a traveller who came to Konya to see the whirling dervish ceremonies. In Konya, Ece, hearing the story of the upright coffin from the devotee shopkeeper and witnessing devotees' embodied acts in Rumi's shrine, experienced the museum as a mystical place. While the modern-looking *Mevlevi* Museum offered a friendly,

152 *Transforming*

stress-free and leisurely experience for the tourists, it also provided a space for some devotees to perform silent *zikir*.

Sema ceremonies, due to high demand, took place in a large cultural centre designed specifically for the performance of the ritual simultaneously as tourist attraction and worship. I went to see the *Şeb-i Arus* ceremonies with Ece and her mother to have the chance to hear their opinions about the *Mevlana* Cultural Center and the *semazens*' performances. The Turkish government opened the *Mevlana* Cultural Center for the *Şeb-i Arus* in 2004 to meet the increasing demand of Turkish and foreign tourists. The cultural centre had a three-thousand-seat *semahane,* and during Rumi's *urs* festival (between December 7 and 17), the tickets to the evening performances of the ceremony would sell out weeks in advance.[12] Travel agencies provided tickets and also offered information for English-speaking tourists. Such agencies offered Turkish and foreign tourists a variety of tour options for different budgets. The travel websites designed for foreign tourists advertised the ceremony as *Rumi Commemoration Tours*[13] to make the festival more familiar to non-devotees who might not recognise the more formal name, *Şeb-i Arus*. Such a sales pitch emphasising Rumi's beliefs and values was common due to Rumi's recognition as a Sufi master. However, the *Turkey Travel Planner* website advertised Konya's *Mevlana* Cultural Center as "the world's grandest and most modern whirling dervish *tekke,*"[14] while the space was actually more like a sports arena than a dervish lodge. The colourful lighting used during the performance of the ceremony felt out of place, making it hard to focus on the devotional act of the ceremony and sacred purpose of the event. The arena, whose architecture lacked any connection to a Sufi dervish lodge, did not function as a residence or school for dervishes. The Mevlana Cultural Center was also a significant political arena for Turkish politicians and their speeches, further diminishing the sacred meaning of the space. Many politicians attended *Şeb-i Arus* ceremonies in order to make an appearance in the honouring of Rumi, who was recognised by the Turkish people as the believer of peace and unity.

Visiting Konya by myself as a tourist in 2010, I attended the ceremony for three nights, including the night of the union on December 17. The Konya Turkish Sufi Music Ensemble, a group created by the Turkish Ministry of Culture and Tourism in 1989, performed the whirling ceremony. The ensemble followed the original structure of the ceremony (as discussed in Chapter 3) and the whirling of the *semazens,* as well as their use of space, instruments and garments, conveyed discipline and dedication. One of the nights, a member of the audience attending the ceremony from Paris explained to Ece's mother that although she first was uncomfortable sitting in her chair, listening to the politicians and observing the detached and impersonal design of the cultural centre, later she concentrated on the *semazens*' whirling and forgot about her discomfort. Although Ece's mother was upset that the government did not allow the performance of the ceremony in the Mevlana museum in the presence of Rumi's tomb, she admitted that while watching the ceremony she forgot about the lack of intimacy in the large hall. However, the ceremony performed as a tourist attraction in this massive hall did not do justice to the multifaceted and rich history of the *Mevlevi* culture in Turkey. Unhappy with the commodification of Sufi cultural beliefs and values, most Sufi devotees did not attend the touristic ceremony in the cultural centre. Rather they gathered in private homes and hotels in Konya to perform their devotional rituals and visit the tombs of Rumi and other Sufi shrines that were located in and near Konya. Veli *efendi* and his devotees were one of these groups.

Konya is a city that also houses many more Sufi shrines that *Rifai* devotees visit and worship at every year. Pilgrimage to the tombs of old Sufi masters is a significant form of worship in many Sufi orders. Devotees of various Sufi orders regularly visit Sufi shrines in a number of Turkish cities, and every year in December travel to Konya to honour Rumi's *urs* (meaning wedding and used to refer to the death anniversary of a Sufi saint) or *Şeb-i Arus* (also meaning wedding night and referring to the night Rumi passed away and the whirling dervish performances organised for Rumi in the city of Konya). While tourists visit Konya to attend the *Şeb-i Arus* celebrations, many Sufi devotees travel to Konya to honour Rumi and other Sufi mystics, whose tombs are in and near Konya, sacralising the now-touristic city with their embodied acts.

As Kenneth Lymer argues:

> Orthodox forms of Islam are directly related to mosques and classrooms, but . . . this is not the only vehicle of expression of religious beliefs; spirituality can also be demonstrated through the practice of domestic rites and pilgrimages to saints' shrines.[15]

Moreover, Elaine Peña points out that "the sacred is a dynamic, organic and complex impression of one's spiritual world."[16] Peña's analysis highlights how the mental and physical transformations experienced during pilgrimage had a significant effect on devotees' perception of everyday life as part of their spiritual journey. During my journeys, I witnessed how devotees embodied Sufi spirituality (including the sense of rapture, unity, love, longing and freedom) as they prayed, walked, sang, whirled and interacted with each other, in their hotel, buses, as well as in a variety of mosques and shrines. The devotees' four-day journey reflected various modes of performance and spectatorship that were key to understanding the practice of Sufi pilgrimage in different urban spaces of Konya.

My first visit to Konya came out of a preliminary research plan to experience Konya and *Şeb-i Arus* ceremonies as a tourist; my second (2011), third (2012), and fourth (2014) journeys were with Veli *efendi* and his devotees. More recently, journeying to Konya under numerous circumstances, I had various encounters with Turkish and foreign tourists, non-devotee and devotee shop workers, *semazens*, scholars and students from different countries. Devotees of Veli *efendi*'s group travelled to Konya every year between 2011 and 2015, during the time of *Şeb-i Arus* ceremonies in December. Each year, they reserved the same hotel, converting it into a *tekke* for devotees' accommodation and performance of rituals. While my travelling to Konya as a tourist or guest researcher was not demanding since I was visiting the sites during the day and resting at my hotel in the evening, the trips to Konya with the *Rifais* were mentally and physically demanding as I performed rituals without a break for four days with the devotees, who during pilgrimage performed *zikir*, prayed, meditated, sang liturgical songs and attended the *efendi*'s *sohbets*. In the case of the *efendi*'s group, pilgrimage was more than travelling to a sacred space, such as the tomb of Rumi. For each devotee, it was a journey within oneself and the ability to transfer divine awareness and meaning to everyday life through the emotional, spiritual and physical effects experienced during pilgrimage.

Although, like the Hajj to Mecca, pilgrimage to Rumi's *urs* was a "remarkable synthesis of sacred and secular" that combined "extreme piety . . . with unadorned commercialism," perhaps "the greatest synthesis of all is the shared experience" of devotees—the mutual support and desire to perform collectively the physically demanding ritual acts.[17] Robert Bianchi points out that "The hajj works because of good sense and mutual support of the pilgrims, not because of the staggering resources their governments marshal to assist and control them,"[18] and pilgrims, as discussed by Razaq Raj, seek to experience "purification, repentance and spiritual renewal during the journey of hajj."[19] During their pilgrimage, *Rifai* devotees, through shared experience in their rituals, also seek to move beyond the idea of Konya as a touristic city and experience the places they reside in and visit as spaces of divinity.

Rifai Pilgrimage: Converting a City Hotel Into a Temporary *Tekke*

Preparations to travel to Konya started months before December. Devotees chartered buses depending on the number of participants to travel to Konya to visit Sufi shrines. With their *efendi*, devotees resided in a hotel located near Rumi's tomb, travelling in and out of the hotel to journey to other shrines in and near Konya. During the four-day pilgrimage, devotees worshipped day and night in the shrines, the buses and their hotel that was converted into a *tekke*. Most of the devotees did not share their pilgrimage plans with co-workers or family members. Due to legal restrictions and social enmity, devotees did not announce their involvement with a Sufi group and as a consequence experienced difficulties in organising their work schedules and family obligations. As a devotee, Tuba, who works at a bank, once said:

> We need to be creative in regard to finding ways to escape our ordinary lives. My husband knows that I am a devotee in a Sufi group. However, I never revealed my involvement with a Sufi group to my parents. Especially my mother, although religious, is very judgmental towards *tarikats*. She believes that *tarikats* are fanatic Islamic organisations.

However, my husband is very supportive of my Sufi living. He takes care of our son when I need to attend meetings and rituals in the *tekke* and he takes time off from work when I travel to Konya.[20]

Tuba's husband also had to plan his job and other duties (including parenting) according to Tuba's pilgrimage schedule. For the past two years, explained Tuba, "We come up with the same plan. We tell our bosses and families that we will visit our friends outside of the city. This is our way of keeping our family out of worry."[21]

The Konya pilgrimage brought together individuals who were devotees of *the efendi* and his guests, who were friends and family or who were devotees from other Sufi groups (mostly outside of Turkey). Although I will not reveal their geographical locations, I think it is necessary to point out that the *efendi* led and guided groups of devotees in different parts of Turkey and different parts of the world, including Eastern and Western Europe, the United States and India. During my fieldwork, Veli *efendi* travelled to other Turkish cities and abroad at least once a year and usually stayed around two weeks. I had the chance to meet with some of those senior devotees who visited the residential *tekke*, and others I got to meet and talk with during my first pilgrimage with the *Rifai* group to Konya. There were also guests (non-devotee guests coming to meet with the *efendi*) visiting from abroad and other places in Turkey. It was either the *efendi* or the devotees who invited these guests to participate in the pilgrimage.

During the final months of preparations, senior dervishes would make sure that there was one devotee assisting each guest before their arrival and during the journey. Devotees were responsible for their guest's transportation, accommodation, guidance about rituals and other needs throughout the journey. Devotees would pick their guests up at the airport, place them in a room with other guests as organised by a senior dervish, and travel with them throughout the journey, making sure that they receive necessary information, including basic theoretical guidance, such as the meaning of prayers, God's Quranic names and information on the teachings of Sufi mystics whose shrines devotees visit during their pilgrimage to Konya. Devotees also assisted their guests in more practical matters, such as medical needs when they got sick (which is very common due to the hectic schedule and cold weather), clothing and questions related to Turkish food.

Each year, the group travelled to the same hotel in Konya and converted the entire space into a *tekke*. There was also one other hotel that was booked every year to accommodate the large number of guests and the devotees assisting the guests. However, all the worship activities were performed in the main hotel (*tekke* hotel). Guests and devotees staying at the other hotel would leave the *tekke* hotel only at nighttime after the ceremony. The owner of the *tekke* hotel, raised in a Sufi family, had strong emotional connections to the Sufi culture through his family and supported the Sufi religious activities of Veli *efendi*'s group by welcoming the devotees to convert the hotel into a *tekke* for four days, including December 17, Rumi's *urs*.

Most of the devotees would stay in the *tekke* hotel with Veli *efendi* and would receive help from hotel workers in organising their rooms to accommodate up to seven devotees. Because there were only three or four beds in each room, hotel workers would provide mattresses to place in between regular beds and in the corridors of each floor. Hotel workers also helped devotees by carrying furniture around or out of the rooms so that when the hotel was out of mattresses, devotees could use sleeping bags.

The other aspect that made the hotel feel like a sacred home was that the hotel workers did not occupy devotees' spaces unless it was absolutely necessary. In the four days the devotees resided at the hotel, there were only five hotel workers on site, which allowed devotees to feel as if they were in their own home. These hotel workers tried to stay out of the way, keeping their presence, including serving and cleaning activities, limited. They were aware that devotees were responsible for serving tea and light food during ritual gatherings. Hotel workers were practically invisible with devotees rarely seeing them, except during breakfast hours. The only meal that devotees had in the hotel was breakfast because they converted the entire dining room of the worship hotel into a prayer hall in the evening. They prepared the prayer hall by taking out all the tables and most of the chairs, except for the ones placed in one section of the room for female chorus members. Devotees also covered the entire floor of the dining room with large cloths and filled the air with incense. In addition, devotees placed a variety of instruments (that were used during the *zikir* ritual gathering) in one section of the dining room.

Another performatic aspect that made the hotel feel like a *tekke* is the embodiment of *edep* (manners), the sense of morality and generosity conveyed by the devotees in sharing their spaces as if they were in the residential or wooden *tekke*. In sharing rooms, for instance, devotees constantly sought to be caring about each other's comfort. In organising living areas, considering that beds were warmer than floor mattresses, devotees drew lots to decide on sleeping conditions. Devotees numbered the beds and floor mattresses and wrote the numbers on small pieces of paper, putting them in a bag for each individual to randomly pick their beds and mattresses. Even then, devotees who drew beds offered the elderly devotees who drew floor mattresses turns to sleep on the beds. The performance of *edep* was significant in every moment of the pilgrimage when getting dressed, taking baths and talking in the rooms. Rooms were very small and crowded so devotees constantly observed one another's actions and interactions in order to respect each other's needs. Each person was careful about giving enough space to the other person, in using the bathroom or preparing his or her clothes. Each action was performatic in the sense that devotees were trying to provide comfort for one another. This was also their embodiment of Veli *efendi*'s idea of kindness and generosity.

In the 2013 pilgrimage, as mentioned earlier, we were seven people in the room with mattresses and bags occupying the entire floor. In every moment of the day, even after exhausting evening *zikir* gatherings, devotees sought to be aware of each other's spaces, trying not to step on each other's beds, bags and other belongings as they moved from one point of the room to another. To make sure that each person was comfortable, every morning devotees got up five minutes apart from each other so that each person could use the bathroom and have enough time to get ready while others stayed warm in their beds. Aside from their desire to make sure that each person was comfortable, what made devotees sensitive about their use of the *tekke* hotel was the presence of their *efendi* in the space. As Aylin explained,

> any space we occupy in the *tekke*, including our beds, is sacralized with the *efendi*'s prayers and our *zikir*. Since we are here in a hotel with our *efendi* praying and performing *zikir*, we should be aware that even the floor we step on is sacred.[22]

As in their residential building, although female and male devotees did not share rooms, they shared other living spaces and interacted with each other from morning to night. They served together, performed *zikir* together, travelled together in the buses and attended *sohbets* together. Also, it is important to note that although women did not perform *zikir* ceremonies shoulder to shoulder with male devotees (usually positioned at a separate section in the same room), that was only done so that there was no controversy with the more conservative guests, such as Sufi masters visiting the hotel from other countries to participate in the *Rifais' zikir*. As mentioned in the previous chapter, in his own ways, Veli *efendi* sought to create and preserve a gender-friendly environment. As in the residential home, both male and female devotees served tea, water and desserts to one another (including female devotees) throughout their journey. This especially was an important practice for Veli *efendi*, who was aware that only female devotees served in more conservative Sufi groups.

Every action devotees performed contributed to the sacralisation of the hotel. As if they were in their residential or wooden *tekke*, devotees organised eating, sleeping, bathing, praying, dancing, walking, chanting and *sohbet* times together. They observed each other's actions and behaviours. Their actions were guided through each moment of the pilgrimage experience. As Peña states,

> backstage and front stage ideological, symbolic, and material motives shape dimensions of the tradition; both 'formal' motives, which are 'structured around the clergy, the sacraments and the individual's relationship with God,' and 'popular' religious motives, which devotees hide from official surveillance, also inform the sacred performance.[23]

While Islamic doctrine inspired individuals to act within doctrinal codes of behaviour, according to certain sacraments, our interactions with each other and the actions and behaviours in between the performance of more structured communal rituals informed what devotees experience as divine meaning. During the four days of retreat, collective living and worshipping with devotees from different cultural, religious and socioeconomic backgrounds, devotees witnessed and guided each other's spiritual journeys as they travelled to and within the spaces.

Devotees had a hectic and strict schedule in the four days they visited Konya. Most only slept three to five hours each night, perceiving each moment as an opportunity to embody divine meaning. Although it was not obligatory, most of the devotees woke up with the morning *ezan* (call to prayer) around 5 a.m. and performed *abdest* (ritual washing or ablution) in the room, through which devotees prayed, cleansed and prepared their body and mind for the *namaz*. Even the devotees, who did not practice *namaz* and *abdest* in their ordinary lives executed the rituals believing that all day and night should be filled with acts of remembrance of God. After the *abdest*, they got dressed and walked to the tomb and mosque of Sufi mystic Şems-i Tebrizi to perform morning *namaz*. Then, devotees came back to the hotel for breakfast. After breakfast, devotees got ready to leave the hotel to either visit the shrines or participate in the *efendi*'s *sohbets* in the dining room. In the evenings, upon arrival at the hotel, female devotees rehearsed for the evening recitation of liturgical songs, while male devotees prepared the dining room for the evening *zikir* gathering. Devotees ate dinner at a small restaurant right next to the hotel reserved only for the group. Then they returned to their rooms to get dressed for the evening *zikir* gathering and perform liturgical songs, prayers, *zikir*, *sema* and *burhan* along with other rituals all night long. Most devotees stayed in the prayer hall after the *zikir* gathering to listen to *efendi*'s night *sohbets* and more liturgical songs vocalised by senior *dervishes*. Most of the devotees went to bed around 1 a.m. or 2 a.m. The entire day was filled with actions and interactions that inspired devotees to remember God's unity.

Şems-i Tebrizi's Mosque

As stated earlier, each day started with the devotees waking up around 5 a.m. to perform *namaz* and meditation in *Tebrizli Şems*' (Shems of Tebriz) mosque (that housed the Sufi master Shems' tomb in the main praying area). Shems was a wandering dervish recognised for his tremendous influence on Rumi's spiritual teachings and practice. Although the actual burial place of the master is unknown, the symbolic tomb has constituted a significant place in the hearts of the devotees. Almost all the devotees perceived praying in the Shems-i Tebrizi mosque as a highly emotional activity. Arriving in Shems' spiritual presence, the devotees said they felt as if they were surrounded by His energy, which allowed them to renew their connection to God. Devotion to a mystic's spirit has been perceived as contradictory (also forbidden in some of them) in orthodox Sunni circles and in the mosques; however, devotees' actions and bowing to the tomb transformed the Sunni space of the mosque into a Sufi *tekke* space. Shems' mosque was a great example of the meeting of the conservative Sunni and adaptable Sufi values that defined the multiplicities of Turkish Islam.

Such meetings also defined post-tariqa *Rifai* devotional life. Despite the lack of sleep and exhaustion, as soon as devotees left their beds, devotees' actions conveyed dedication and discipline. The room tended to be cold, thus, devotees prepared their daily outfits—pants, wool socks, sweaters, dervish cloaks, shawls and *tespihs* (wooden prayer beads)—ahead of time. The night before, devotees arrived at the room in exhaustion following the nights' singing and dancing *zikir* ritual activities and before going to bed, they placed their clothes on top of their bags to make sure that at 5 a.m., they could quickly get dressed to be on time for the morning *namaz* (which is an indispensable practice in conservative Sunni devotional life). As soon as a devotee got up, she left the bed or mattress and quickly walked into the bathroom, jumping from one empty spot to another to avoid stepping on floor mattresses and each other's bags. By the time everyone was ready to travel to the mosques, it tended to be still dark so female devotees wait for one another to make sure that no one was left behind by themselves. Once everyone was ready, devotees walked down the stairs, and as they did, doors opened and other devotees also stepped out of their rooms to walk to the mosque. By the time devotees reached the lobby, there were around ten to fifteen male and female devotees leaving the hotel together. Most of the devotees were sleepy, tired and cold, yet filled with the desire to walk to the mosque as a group.

The mosque was the first space devotees embodied their all-embracing values and inscribed their Sufi beliefs and values publicly in Konya. When devotees arrived, the mosque tended to be packed with their spiritual siblings and other individuals (devotees affiliated with other Sufi groups and non-Sufi Muslims). There were around thirty female and forty male devotees from the *Rifai* group who received a lot of attention as they arrived and took their seats in large groups, some wearing their black cloaks and large wooden *tespihs*. Devotees entered the mosque, bowed forward in the direction of the tomb and found seats on the floor. Then, devotees started performing *zikir* by moving the beads of their *tespihs* as they waited for the *imam* (Muslim religious leader in a mosque) to start the prayer.

While most of the people in the mosque arrived to perform their morning *namaz*, Sufi devotees after performing the *namaz* with everyone else continued their Sufi devotion by praying and performing *zikir* in the presence of Shems' tomb. Although performance of *namaz* also had a valuable role in some of the devotees' pious living, performing *zikir* in the presence of a Sufi tomb was perceived as the central worship activity in most of the post-tariqa *Rifai* group. Devotees began their morning worship by praying in the mosque with everyone when the *imam* started the collective *namaz* with a prayer. Everyone in the mosque (approximately two hundred people, most of them devotees from *efendi*'s *group* and other Sufi groups as well as non-devotee Muslims) stood up to pray and performed the prescribed actions along with the *imam*. In the beginning, everyone in the mosque stood in a row with their hands at their sides and silently recited their *niyet* (intention), in which they stated the name of the *namaz* and the number of *rekats* (units of prayer). Then, performing *tekbir getirmek* (meaning the pronouncement of "*Allahu Akbar*"—"God is Great"), they raised their hands to the level of their shoulders to begin the first *rekat*. Everyone stayed in *kiam* (the standing position), keeping their hands folded below the navel, in which position practitioners silently recite verses from the Quran. They then moved to *rükü*, bowing forward and placing their hands on their knees. After *rükü*, they went to *secde*, placing their knees on the floor, bringing their foreheads to the ground and completing the first *rekat*. The morning *namaz* is two *rekats* so that practitioners repeat these actions again and end the *namaz* with everyone offering *selam* (greeting) by turning their heads to the right and left.

Devotees' constant execution of remembrance continued after finalising their *namaz* cycle. There was not one moment that they released their practice of remembrance. They desired to make use of each moment to continue their devotion, concentration and meditation by performing silent *zikir* with their *tespihs* in their hands while other individuals prepared to leave. After the collective *namaz*, some devotees stayed in their final position to pray or perform silent *zikir*, while others left their seats to stand before Shems' tomb to pray on foot and to kiss the wooden fence-like piece behind which the tomb was placed. Devotees' actions, as they prayed in front of the tomb, bowed towards the tomb and kissed the wooden fence in front of the tomb, conveyed their beliefs and values. There were male and female devotees praying side by side. Considering that both, praying to saints by taking into consideration of a Sufi master's divinity and performing gender-mixed devotional acts in the main hall of the mosque, were in opposition of Sunni Islamic values, *Rifais*' embodiment of post-tariqa Sufi values was conveying a vivid picture of Turkish Islam that is in harmony with the secular values of Atatürk. When the devotees performed their devotion to the tomb by bowing, kissing the wooden screen of the tomb and walking backwards to the door of the mosque without turning their back to the tomb, their bodies were conveying an alternative Islamic devotion.

Presence of female devotees and their embodied actions in the mosque was especially regenerative of Sunni customs considering how each one of them walked in confidence towards Shems' tomb (which is located in the male praying area) to pray and perform *zikir*. As Sheemem Burney Abbas states:

> In the Islamic world, the mosque is primarily an arena for male activity, with little visible participation of women in the rituals. . . . Thus, the important spheres of religious and spiritual participation for women

are the Sufi shrines. There, women's input is visible and they are significant participants in the events.[24]

In 2013, *Tebrizli Şems*' mosque was more than a mosque. Devotees inscribed their values onto the space of the mosque and transformed it into a Sufi shrine.

In 2012, the *imam* of the mosque as anticipated, despite the lack of space in female sections, followed the rules and did not allow female devotees to perform in the same space with male devotees. However, in 2013, because the majority of devotees coming to pray in the mosque were female, the *imam* allowed female devotees to pray in the same space with men, asking male participants to move closer to the front section to give enough space for female devotees. Female devotees prayed right next to the tomb of Shems and their presence conveyed the Sufi idea of unity and importance of post-tariqa Sufi practice for female Muslims, who cannot usually perform *namaz* in the same space as the men. The female devotees' presence and their devotion to the tomb with male devotees also transformed the male-dominated Sunni space of the mosque turned into an adaptable *Rifai* space in which male and female devotees prayed together. The mosque, representing the one-sided values of the RAD (and their conservative Sunni teachings), became a site of Veli *efendi*'s multi-cultural beliefs, values and devotional acts. All of his students were performing his *Rifai* vision.

Travelling to, Within and Between Sufi Masters' Tombs: Embodying the Divine Meaning in the Buses and Making Shrines Alive With Sufi Devotion

After visiting Shems' tomb, devotees returned to their hotel to rest, had breakfast and prepared for the worship activities planned for each day. The morning rituals, performing *abdest*, walking to the mosque and performing *namaz* were just ninety minutes of the devotees' pilgrimage day in Konya and perhaps the least rigorous of all. Devotees returned to the hotel around 6:30 a.m. Some rested in their rooms, some performed meditation and some attended breakfast at 7 a.m. There were usually two free hours in which devotees could shower, rest and get breakfast. Around 9 a.m., two buses and a number of cars would wait for devotees in front of the hotel for devotees to travel to shrines in and near Konya.

Collective worship and sacralisation of spaces would continue in the buses. During their travel times, devotees tended to convey a sense of devotion at every step of the way, inspiring their values onto any space they occupied throughout this journey. In bus number one (which is Veli *efendi*'s bus), devotees continued worshipping by performing *sohbet* and *zikir* with the *efendi*, while the group in bus number two performed prayers and *zikir* with one of the *dedes*. Sometimes the buses stopped and the *efendi* moved to the other bus to perform *sohbet* there as well. The devotional acts in the buses were not planned. Sometimes they lasted for an hour and stop when the group got to one of the shrines. Sometimes they continued on and off along the way. Rituals performed in the bus tended to begin spontaneously, when someone asked a question or when the *efendi* meditating quietly felt the urge to speak or sing. At other times, most of the devotees in the bus stayed quiet, meditated and listened to their group's recorded *zikir* ceremonies in between collective rituals. Sometimes a group of devotees worshipped by playing their percussive instruments and vocalising liturgical songs in the back seats. At times, other devotees sang along, while others continued to quietly perform *zikir*. Also, some of the devotees read and shared religious poems, while others discussed Sufi teachings in groups of four or five.

In the *sohbets* that took place in the buses, devotees listened to the *efendi* speak about divine love, unity and the Sufi idea of *nefs*. He also discussed problems of the country or the world and answered devotees' questions. At times, while answering a question, he recited a religious poem or sang a liturgical song. Topics changed each day with current events, such as war, the economy and sickness. The *efendi* used a microphone, which allowed him to converse with the devotees in his soft tones. He spoke slowly, compassionately and kindly, allowing the sounds of each word to travel in the bus. As he talked about a topic, such as poverty or war, he hid his lament and made jokes about humanity's need for more material power. Once, after his talk, he wanted to pray for his devotees and humanity and performed *zikir*. As the devotees participated in the *zikir*, the bus started to feel like a travelling sacred bus shrine full of devotees who with their voices conveyed a sense of devotion, contentment and togetherness.

Devotion continued with the performance of collective *zikir* in the shrines, which tended to be physically demanding due to the cold weather in and around Konya. Some tombs were located outdoors, while others positioned in small stone structures. *Zikir* was performed louder and longer when a shrine was in an enclosed space and quieter when in a shrine located in a residential area. Devotees visited shrines of Sufi mystics—including Sadrettin Konevi, Ateşbaz Veli, Nasrrettin Hoca, Tavus Baba and Seyit Mahmut Hayrani—in the first three days, leaving Rumi's shrine for the final day, December 17. However, many devotees made use of their two-hour break to gather in small groups on the first and second days to visit Rumi's shrine, which was only a ten-minute walk from the *tekke* hotel.

Other shrines visited in the first three days were not as crowded as Rumi's shrine. Rather, most of them were empty or had approximately five or so visitors when devotees arrived to perform their *zikir* ritual as a group. When devotees arrived at the shrines, the courtyard of the isolated buildings conveyed a sense of detachment from the celebratory feeling that was sensed in and near Rumi's shrine. But when hundreds of devotees' recited God's names and prayed together, these isolated shrines became alive. Arriving at a shrine, devotees first surrounded the tombs, located in a small structure in an iron cage or behind a fence. Veli *efendi* and the *dedes* created the first circle around the tomb, male devotees surrounded the *dedes*, then the rest of the devotees surrounded the first and second circles, with female devotees usually forming the fourth circle. During pilgrimage, women freely performed the rituals in the same space with men; however, they stood behind male devotees. This, according to some of the devotees, did not reflect the gender dynamics in the *efendi*'s group. According to a devotee (Melda), the *efendi* followed such Islamic rules and principles to avoid conflict with strictly doctrinal groups and individuals who witnessed their ritual performances in public or as guests in their private spaces. Melda explained further that although there were a small number of both male and female devotees in the group who were conservative, the *efendi* constantly sought to create a balance with the ideas of strictly doctrinal individuals and individuals who believe that Sufi practice is about unity (as manyness of reality), equality and adaptation. As Sa'diyya Shaikh states it is possible to against the idea of women as "oppositional to spirituality, intellect, and rationality" in Islam and embrace "gender-egalitarian impulses."[25]

The *zikir* ceremonies at the shrines were demanding due to the cold weather in and around Konya. By the time devotees left each shrine, their faces would turn red and purple due to the cold weather, yet they would have tremendous motivation and excitement to continue their journey. Especially on the second day, due to the locations of the shrines, devotees walked on foot from one shrine to another in the village. The weather got exceedingly cold after 2 p.m. so that by the time we walked to the shrine to perform *zikir*, every part of our body was freezing. When I performed *zikir* at the shrine in the village with the devotees, I felt my body, including my face, hands and feet, hurting due to the cold. It was as if the wind was scratching my skin. Despite the temperature, devotees performed the *zikir* with dedication as if they were not disturbed by the cold. As Nur said, in the shrines, at first, "she experiences her aching hands and feet. Then as she performs the *zikir*, she feels motivated and connected to her devotion so that she forgets about the freezing weather." Yiğit also pointed out that he could feel his devotion in his aching body. He explained what he felt was a therapeutic pain. As Seyran said, first, she could not focus on her devotion but by the time she started to participate in the *zikir*, she forgot her discomfort. She did not know when or how her pain ended but she ultimately felt fine. Seyran said, "I just want to be there. Nothing else is important." Other devotees like Seyran, as they travelled to shrines and performed their *zikir*, transmitted a sense of motivation, confidence and dedication for their devotion because as Şale explained, as we participated *zikir*, the cold and deserted feeling in the shrine transformed. It did not get warm, but it did somehow feel warmer. Devotees' sense of otherworldliness increased during these visits. The shrines transformed as devotees performed *zikir* and carved the names of Allah into the cold stones that make up the shrines.

164　*Transforming*

Performing *Zikir* Outside the Walls of Rumi's Shrine

Performing *zikir* in Rumi's overcrowded shrine (located in the *Mevlana* Museum) was a different experience than visiting other mystics' isolated shrines. When devotees visited Rumi's shrine individually or in small groups on the first and/or second day of the pilgrimage (two or three days before Rumi's *urs*), they entered and prayed inside the lodge along with other visitors. However, on Rumi's *urs*, an interesting "doubling" occurred in the *Mevlana* Museum. A large crowd of visitors (non-devotee tourists, politicians and devotees from different Sufi groups) were inside the shrine watching a performance of *Sema* ceremony to honour Rumi's *urs*, while Veli *efendi*'s group of devotees were staying outside the walls of the shrine to perform collective *zikir* in the courtyard of the *tekke*, standing in lines in front of large windows that made the room with Rumi's tomb visible. In Veli *efendi*'s group, a dervish known to be an *evliya* (saint) from Rumi's bloodline was able to get permission from the mayor of Konya to use a section of the courtyard for their collective *zikir* gathering. Due to the recognition of the space as a museum, devotees modified their worship in Rumi's shrine. Muhittin *dede* shortened the collective *zikir* and did not allow it to last more than fifteen minutes, in which devotees repeated the Quranic names of God in a low tone as guided by the *dede*. While devotees performed collective *zikir* in the courtyard, inside the shrine, visitors attended the praying sessions organised every year by the mayor of Konya to honour Rumi's *urs*. As devotees performed in the courtyard, most of the visitors were already inside the building, participating in the worship ceremony organised by the government for Konya residents and tourists. While visitors witnessed the vocalisation of liturgical songs and performance of prayers inside the shrine building, devotees got the chance to perform their *zikir* in a bit of privacy outside. Although some of the visitors passed by the devotees performing *zikir* and stopped to watch and listen to them, witnessing their sense of privacy, most tended to leave quickly and did not interfere with the *Rifai* devotees' performance.

Performing *zikir* in the courtyard in public, devotees' bodies expressed a sense of privacy as they stood very close to one another chanting God's names in unison facing the building with their backs turned to visitors passing behind them. They were able to keep their focus on the repetitions during their worship in the courtyard even when they knew that there were people watching them. Aylin explained that it was the sense of love and joy that guided her to keep her focus:

> By the time we complete the *zikir* in Rumi's shrine, having visited a variety of shrines for four days and worshipping mentally and physically day and night, I feel more motivation, commitment, joy and energy that connects me to my devotion. I say "Thank you, *Hazret* [referring to Rumi as Holiness], thank you for having me in your presence." Then, I pray for a permanent experience of divine meaning.[26]

Devotees experienced the museum as a sacred space and with their sense of concentration and devotion gave the shrine converted into a tourist site the sacredness it deserved. To them, every moment, every thought and every action were journeys to experience and sacralise the museum into the space of Rumi's spirit. Tourists and tourist attractions were not distracting to the devotees, who were able to improve their focus through the actions they performed as part of their *zikir* ceremony.

Shaking the Dining Room of the Hotel With the Embodiment of Divine Energy on Rumi's *Urs* (December 17)

Having performed *zikir* in the presence of Rumi's tomb, devotees arrived at the *tekke* hotel to prepare for the evening *zikir* ceremony. Celebrating December 17 as the day Rumi passed away and united with his beloved God, devotees seemed committed to experiencing this day to the fullest. The gathering started around 7:30 p.m. right after the devotees have completed their rehearsals for the practice of liturgical songs, dinner, tidying of rooms and ablution, and ran until 1 a.m. or 2 a.m. Upon arrival at the *tekke* hotel, devotees changed their outfits to warm their bodies after being outside in the cold. Female chorus members and the orchestra (comprised of male and female devotees) met in one of the rooms to rehearse their liturgical songs, while other devotees prepared the dining room for the *zikir* gathering. They were determined and in a hurry to participate in all the activities to experience the love and unity Rumi had experienced. As mentioned earlier, all the tables and most of the chairs were taken out of the dining room and placed in the corridors of the hotel. The entire floor of the dining room was covered with large clothes so that devotees could comfortably sit as if they were in their prayer hall in the wooden *tekke*. Then, devotees attended dinner in the restaurant reserved only for the devotees and their guests. Most of them did not want to eat much because they did not want to perform the ceremony with a full stomach. Then, they returned to their rooms for final preparations to perform ablution and *namaz* (not obligatory) and get dressed.

Preparation for the evening was a special occasion for female devotees. Most of them wore clean clothes and put on their *mests* after ablution. Then they wore their dervish cloaks and colourful shawls on their heads; some put on earrings that match their shawls as well as little makeup. As soon as they were ready, they walked down the stairs to the dining room to take their positions as chorus members. Minutes before the gathering began, there was a celebratory feeling in the rooms, corridors and the prayer hall of the hotel. Groups of people staying in the other hotel reserved for devotees and their guests (who stayed in other Konya hotels) started to arrive at the *tekke* hotel to participate in the ceremony. The presence of female devotees taking their places as chorus members ready to sing their Sufi liturgical songs was conveying the *Rifai* groups' modern and flexible Islamic values to the guests waiting to witness and participate the ceremony of the *Rifai* devotees. I remember many guests, although most were also devotees of a variety of Sufi groups, were wondering about how the *Rifais*, whom they knew as howling dervishes, practised their *zikir*.

Each year, there were groups from the United States, United Kingdom, India, Italy and Egypt. Also, a Russian Sufi group participated in the gatherings and performed *zikir* with the devotees of the *efendi*'s group. There tended to be also individuals who were family members and friends of the *efendi* and the devotees as well as other devotees who chose to stay with their family or friends in the other hotel. Aside from the groups and individuals coming from the other hotel, there were also guests of the *efendi*'s and devotees who live in and near Konya as well as guests who were invited to meet with the *efendi*. By the time the prayer hall was filled with devotees and guests, the space turned into an international religious festival site with devotees and guests speaking in many different languages. As Cemal once said, "the diversity of God becomes visible in the room with everyone waiting for *efendi*'s arrival."

The evening *zikir* gatherings began with devotees' performance of liturgical songs, in which female devotees recited religious hymns for their *efendi*, *dedes*, devotees and guests. This was usually the time when the *efendi* arrived and sang along with the female devotees. With his arrival, everyone got up, bowed to him and returned to sitting position on the floor when the *efendi* took his seat. The *efendi* closed his eyes and listened to the songs (some composed and written by him) about God, Prophet Muhammed, and Sufi mystics' ideas of divine love and longing. At times, Veli *efendi* felt overwhelmed with joy and longing that he made a loud, deep sound, emphasising and extending the vowel sounds of the word "Allah." He was performing his sorrow and yearning to be with God. At times, he joyously howled "Allah," communicating his love and excitement to experience divine love with everyone else quietly repeating after him. In those moments, Veli *efendi* and the devotees conveyed their desire to be with God. The *efendi* continued to hum the songs with the female devotees while everyone in the room moved into a meditative state, either vocalising the hymns quietly along with female devotees or at times exhaling with the sound "*Hu*" (an Arabic suffix meaning He used to refer to God—also recognised as the last sound of the word Allah). When female chorus members said "Allah," "Muhammed," or the names of one of the mystics as part of the lyrics of the song, the sense of energy increased with the sounds such as humming and exhalations that came as a response to the lyrics. In such moments, everyone in the room placed their right hands on their hearts for a brief second and again said "*Hu*." Devotees performed these actions on their own. Such actions were not directed by the *efendi* or performed in unison. By the time the songs were over, everyone in the room seemed to convey a sense of readiness and longing to start the ceremony. This was visible in each devotee's act of helping each other willingly to reorganise the space. The chairs used by some of the orchestra and chorus members were quickly taken out of the prayer hall.

As soon as the chairs were removed, all the devotees positioned themselves in circles and lines around the first circle that surrounded the *efendi*. In the dining room converted into the prayer hall, not everyone was positioned in circles due to the recessed shape of the spaces and the columns that cut the space into two or three sections. However, despite this, the *efendi* was visible from every part of the dining room. Male and female devotees sat in lines filling the rest of the space. Then there was a brief moment of silence before *Sakin dede* (senior dervish) began the collective *zikir* ceremony with extensive readings of Quranic passages and *Salavatı Şerifs* (chants that praise Prophet Muhammed). Along with the *dede*, devotees in unison sought God's forgiveness and the *efendi* continued the ceremony by feeding the first phrase "*la ilaha illa Allah*." As in the *zikir* ceremony performed in the wooden *tekke*, the cycle of names and the rhythm changed with the *efendi*'s notifications. Keeping up with the sounds of the drums and chanting of God's names, the repetitive, sometimes fast-paced movements were at times a demanding physical and mental task. At the end of the first hour, the rapture increased in climatic moments, and devotees left their seats, stood up, and started moving with more energy. It was impossible not to see the sweat trickling down devotees' backs. Around this time, *Sakin dede* started reciting liturgical songs along with devotees performing vocal *zikir*. Two devotees accompanied *Sakin dede*'s vocalisation by playing their drums to keep the beat and rhythm going. As Kerem *dede* explained, with the songs, chants, drums and devotees' movements, every look, sound, movement, heartbeat and breath was performing *zikir*. Devotees' body language, their heads, eyes, hands and feet performed *zikir*.

The length of the *zikir* ceremonies could change with the *efendi*'s and *dedes*' guidance, but the ceremony on December 17 lasted approximately three to four hours. About one hundred men and women, young and old, facing the *kıble* (the direction of the Ka'aba in Mecca), delivered God's names with loud cries and forceful movements of the body. Also, as mentioned earlier, a Sufi group (around fifty men and women) that travelled to Konya from Russia every year to honour Rumi's *urs* arrived at the *tekke* hotel around 9:30 p.m. as the *Rifais* continued to perform *zikir*. When the group arrived, the devotees who were responsible for the entrance of the *tekke* hotel brought the Russian group into the prayer hall and senior dervishes positioned them in the space.

With their arrival, the prayer hall got very crowded with around one hundred and fifty people reciting God's names in unison. Occasionally, the *efendi* slowed the devotees down as a group for a few seconds of rest and continued the recitations and movements. In the moments of slowing down and rest, suddenly the *efendi* screamed new lines in a forceful tone so that the devotees' rhythm grew faster. At this time, it was as if something stormy occurred in the room. Devotees and guests filled with rapture continued *zikir* by bending their knees and leaning forward and back. Having moved to the rhythm for hours without a break, devotees "were feeling as if the room was moving."

Soon, when the *dede* changed the movement in the circle by turning the devotees right and left with their feet and shoulders, the devotees started to move along with him hand in hand. Then, after a while, movements changed again with the *dede* jumping in the circle as devotees held each other's hands and jumped in unison, moving their held hands up and down quickly and continuing to jump at such a pace with liveliness and happiness. The high level of energy embodied on Rumi's *urs* every year was exclusive to the night of Rumi's *urs*, with December 17 being the last day of the pilgrimage in which devotees conveyed a high state of rapture. It was possible to see devotees sweating, smiling and holding each other's hands tightly. With each jump, they were more committed and joyful.

Although devotees repeated the same movements, each moment seemed different, instinctive and spontaneous as the energy of the group and each individual grew. Each moment, each jump, as devotee was discovered in the moment. The vocal intonations were strong and were often accompanied by the most singular gestures, such as laughs and cries. As a participant performing the changing tones and cries, some of the devotees' "heartbeat started to change."[27] They discussed such experiences as " My breath was so fast that it was everything," " It was ecstatic," "I found something in that moment of pace," "I was one with my breath," "No more thoughts, just the breath." Some believed they found God's unity in such moments.

As Reynold Nicholson points out, "the name of Allah inscribed in the rhythms of the heart and breath is God, or divine knowledge."[28] Similar to Nicholson's analysis, devotees' physiological suggestions showed that they experience God in their heartbeat and breath. As Ceylin once explained, as she jumped, she felt her breath. It was as if she witnessed the divine meaning in her breath and heartbeat. She said,

> she inhales thinking God and exhales vocalising His name, and in that moment, she can sense a growing power and energy in her body. She says in those climatic moments that her mind is released of any thought or idea apart from God.

She explained how the exhaustion and togetherness experienced in the pilgrimage and the sensations she felt during the day in the presence of the Sufi mystics' tombs motivated Ceylin to worship with more power and energy and her breath reminded her of her non-existence in God. She sensed the mortality of her body and immortality of her spiritual self. This, she explains, "causes excessive liberation from the world as a material space. It is as if in the prayer hall devotees are beyond the space they see, touch, and smell."

A similar experience is also explained in detail by a young *halife* in Pnina Werbner's study. He explains the following:

> [T]here are seven points of energy in our body through which the spiritual power of Allah enters the body. If you do the *zikir* correctly, and

in my case it didn't take long, then your heart starts doing the *zikir* all the time, every moment of the day and night, even when a person is doing other things. Like now, when I'm talking to you.[29]

As Werbner asserts, the devotees perform *zikir* to unite their body with the cosmos and that is the means of purifying and transcending the spiritual self. The constant and continuous practice of *zikir*, as Werbner discusses in her analysis of Sufi devotees, "purifies, or 'opens,' the seven hidden *lata'if*, the light (or subtle) spots in a person's chest and body, to receive the light of Allah."[30] Performance of *zikir* helps the devotee to

open the curtains in front of the eyes and [move] on a journey toward an ultimate illumination, first of the shadows and reflections of the attributes of Allah, then of the attributes themselves and finally of God's very being or essence (*zat*).[31]

For *Rifai* devotees, this sense of presence was an experience that created a new understanding of the self and a reality beyond the physical space (world) and the body. All actions were performed to remember God, to experience divine meaning, and to feel a sense of liberation. Elif said, "we seek to move to a space beyond space and, as Rumi says, to embrace all and be part of all." Through different sounds and movements, Elif explained, how *Rifais* had a strong desire to experience God's unity.[32] While every movement and sound were performed as a journey within oneself and to God, devotees' actions also created a space in which devotion was lived and shared.

During the pilgrimage, devotees chanted, danced, prayed and meditated until they experienced intense physical and mental exhaustion. Devotees constantly embodied remembrance and reevaluated their relationship to the material world and to divine meaning at all times of their journey. When the ritual ended, devotees seemed to reenter ordinary life "just about where they went in"[33] and followed the routines of their daily life: phone calls, family arrangements and work obligations. However, as Nur explains, they returned to ordinary life, having embodied the divine meaning from moment to moment and from space to space. The pilgrimage experience became part of their perception of reality and everyday life because devotees carried their bodily memories and their physical and mental transformations to everywhere.

Ronald Grimes, in *The Craft of Ritual Studies*, argues how "functional definitions of religion sound a lot like definitions of spirituality."[34] To clarify his point, he refers to broader definitions of spirituality and references Paul Jones' analysis of spirituality.[35] Grimes states:

Spirituality is the manner in which a person is oriented in being, through which one's meaning is recognised, embraced, disciplined, and enhanced. Expressed more simply, spirituality is the way in which the whole of me responds to the whole of life.[36]

This definition draws attention to how devotees relate to their practice of *zikir*. Searching one's meaning in relation to everything in this world is the primary drive in this performance. Devotees ask questions as they experience high levels of concentration, ecstasy and unity. They ask, "How is this experience of joy is related to our perception of this universe? This, I desire to grasp."[37] *Zikir*, for devotees, is a way to dispute their role in this world.

In their view, Sufi devotion, whether practised in the form of prayer, fasting or *sohbet*, is aimed at performing *zikir* (remembering God) at all times. The *efendi* would advise his devotees to remember God in every moment, reminding them that *zikir* serves as a further remembrance of the goal towards which all spiritual practice is directed. As Werbner also examines, devotees "perform the *zikir* at all times of the day and night. Even as they work they perform the *zikir*."[38] For this reason, *Rifais* inscribe their values onto any space they walked on, any space they passed through.

Dwight Conquergood asks about the "conceptual consequences of thinking about culture as a verb instead of a noun, process instead of a product . . . as an unfolding performative invention instead of a reified system, structure, or variable."[39] Perceiving *Rifai* devotional life as a performatic invention, it is possible to describe how each devotee creates his or her own processual experience during and after the pilgrimage in the practice of everyday life. Each devotee perceives his or her pilgrimage experience as part of his or her life journey within oneself and to God. As Meriç, one of the devotees, explained,

> when she performs *zikir* silently at work, the sounds and rhythms that she experienced in evening *zikir* gatherings pop right back into her head. She immediately remembers the movements of her body and the sensations she experienced, such as energy and joy.

Remembering that experience of energy and unity, she felt content and free from the burdens of the material world.[40] Devotees explained that they experienced a move away from the material aspects of their specific work or home space. Sitting at her desk, Ceren "remembers the exhaustion and liberation she experienced in the collective *zikir* and then she recalls the sense of energy and power." In such moments, Meriç said, "her workspace transforms and she starts to perceive the world as a sacred space."

Remembering the sensations experienced in the performance of *zikir* in Konya, with kinaesthetic imagination, the individual continues to recall and embody contentment, joy, and energy in day-to-day interactions. The physicality of *zikir* in Konya, due to its pace, allows a deeper sensation. What happens during pilgrimage serves as a rehearsal for devotees to live in the material world with more awareness of divine meaning, the sense of otherworldliness. Having the chance to perform collective *zikir* every night in Konya, devotees return to their ordinary lives with a heightened awareness of their spiritual self and the physical world. As Ruya says, she "stays positive and less competitive with others during work and leisure time."[41] Devotees believe that through spiritual practice of *zikir*, whether collective, vocal, practical or silent, they heal their mind, body and soul and sacralise the urban spaces as sacred sites. The *tekke* hotel is a space of physical, mental and spiritual sensations, such as feeling one's heartbeat, sweat, aching muscles, sore throats, humidity, heat and vibrations as well as smelling incense; hearing changing sounds, tones, tinkles, screams, soft and harsh melodies; and witnessing the shaking floor from devotees' jumps. During pilgrimage devotees experience, any space they occupy in Konya as sacred. The experience of *zikir* inspires *Rifais* to perceive and organise their daily life, including their jobs and family tasks, as activities that are part of their spiritual training. With this intense pilgrimage experience, devotees embodied their perception of the world as a sacred space.

Transforming Minds and Hearts: Possession

It was one of the most crowded *zikir* gatherings, on December 15, 2012, two days before the *Şeb-i Arus* celebrations in Konya. There were around two hundred people in the dining room of the hotel that devotees transformed into a *semahane*. There were many guest pilgrims visiting the hotel to participate in the communal *zikir* ritual along with Veli *efendi*'s students. These were non-Turkish devotees visiting Konya from other countries. The night started with women vocalising Sufi hymns about their love and longing for their beloved God. With their tender vocalisations of the hymns, devotees conveyed a strong sense of peace in coming together to celebrate their unity and love. Their voices were full of desire and yearning for unity as they were articulating longing. They were closing their eyes as they sang, allowing themselves to let go of any thoughts other than their sense of worship, presence and, as one of the students (Rüya) explained, sense of "becoming one with the sounds of the *ney*." There was a sense of concentration and a meditative atmosphere in the room with the devotees listening quietly to the sounds of the drums when the *dede* started the *zikir* ceremony. This felt like one of the most joyous ceremonies I attended in the past three years. Devotees were repeating God's names with such strength and care, conveying their experience of love and passion for God. This was the night when the appellation "howling dervishes," used in the West for the *Rifai* devotees, made a lot of sense as they were singing in unison creating a powerful ritual performance.

As Ceylin and some other devotees explained, they were seeking to convey a sense of appreciation for their togetherness and the opportunity to worship. As the night wore on, the devotees had performed for almost two hours, dancing and singing, at times slowing down to change from one name of God to another. When the *dede* would be ready to call out a different name of God, the hymns accompanying the *zikir* would also change. While some dervishes were in the inner circle singing hymns, other devotees were continuing to repeat one of God's names in unison, bringing together the sounds of the hymns with repetitions of God's names in a choral performance. At times, as devotees would start to dance and sing faster and faster, it was as if the room was no longer a fixed physical space; it was as if it was moving, travelling, as one of the students explained, turning into a space out of this realm. As the dancing and singing became louder and faster, I heard someone crying out in such pain that my heart dropped.

This was an outcry coming from the female section of the room, behind the first line of the devotees I was performing with. But the voice was so coarse that I was not sure whether this was a female or a male ritual participant. Although the devotees were continuing the singing and dancing, some of us attempted to turn back to see what was going on. I also made an effort to look back, but one of the senior female dervishes informed me that I should not be looking and that I should continue to perform the ritual facing the first *zikir* circle. In this first attempt, I saw a lady moving on the floor as if she was in the throes of death, as if she was being stabbed or shot. Her screams continued and sounded as if she was experiencing an unimaginable torture. As I continued to dance, I was upset. I was scared. I was devastated but also curious, desiring to know what was happening. At that moment, because the screaming started to turn into words that made some sense, most of us in the room were singing in a lower voice to hear what words were coming out of her mouth. Then, I heard the *dede* leading the *zikir* circle, calling out, warning all of us to continue the ceremony, to not stop. He said what was happening should not stop the *zikir* ritual.

Everything was happening at once: the drums, people singing, the *dede* announcing his directions and the woman screaming and speaking at the same time. The words and sentences coming out of her mouth disoriented me even more. She was saying: "I will kill you." Also, she was cursing. As noted in my journal, "She was telling us to stop singing and dancing ... warning us that she will turn our lives into hell." What was more disturbing was the tone of her voice as she spoke. The coarseness and the depth of her voice as she spoke felt out of the ordinary. At this point, I was still trying to understand whether this was one or two people, but it was unclear. I was at a point at which I wanted to leave but with the number of people standing in line, filling the entire room, it was impossible to walk through the crowd. I stayed. Some of the devotees seemed more confident with what they were doing, committed to singing and dancing, but some seemed a bit more disoriented like me, dancing involuntarily just to conform to the group.

After a while, probably a couple minutes later, the woman stopped and started to snuffle, trying not to stay out of breath. I was looking for an opportunity to turn back and see her face but the dervishes standing behind me were closing off my view of her body, which was laying on the floor. I saw four dervishes, also on the floor, beside the lady, holding her arms and legs down (which I later found out was to protect her from hurting herself with unintentional severe movements). When the lady started to speak again, this time more quietly, I turned my back and saw her lying on the floor, with a face whiter than a sheet. I could almost see her veins and blood under her skin. But the most discomforting vision was her eyes. Only the white of her eyes was visible. She was trying to move on the floor as the dervishes were holding her arms and legs, she was whispering and saying things as if she was talking in her sleep. She seemed unconscious. I could not bear to look anymore and turned away, trying to stay calm, and continued breathing. The female devotee standing beside me held my hand and with her movements guided me to focus on the dancing and chanting again. With the dissolving of the woman's voice, the devotees started to perform with more commitment once again until the lady started to scream again: "You morons, stop the zikir, you bastards, you will do as I say." She added, "Or, I will turn your life into hell." Then she started to make other sounds that made no sense. Then the *dede*, leading the *zikir*, left the circle along with two other male dervishes and came to the female section of the floor. Now, it was another *dede* leading the ceremony. I was still in a state of shock as I tried to dance and sing along with the devotees standing next to me, not sure what was happening. Later, I saw the crowd near the stairs, moving to the sides trying to create a passageway for a group of male and female dervishes, who were carrying the lady out of the room.

The amount of attention created by the lady was as if a group of audience members were watching a very exciting circus performance with acrobats, trapeze artists or rope walkers making spectacular moves. People were trying not to look, but clearly all of the participants' focus shifted from the sounds of the *zikir* to the sounds of the lady. I was aware of how some participants standing around me were holding their breaths like me with a desire to understand what was happening in the room. The way the lady was delivering her messages was breathtakingly powerful when analysed in relation to theatricality. Her speech shifted the entire mood. The sense of joy and devotion conveyed by the devotees performing *zikir* was in competition with the lady screaming her words. Both the heightened performances of the howling dervishes (their voices and movement filling the entire space of room) and the one lady taking over the room (with her vocal range, screaming and speaking in different tones) were creating powerful focus points. For this reason, the *dedes* were able to continue the ritual performance for another fifteen to twenty minutes. That's when I heard one of the dervishes talking about spirit possession. Most of the devotees seemed calm and in control. One of the *dedes* was kind enough to tell me that there was nothing to worry about. He explained that the dervishes were going to take care of the sick lady and that she was going to be fine. Then, one of the dervishes invited me to speak with Veli *efendi*, who was sitting in the centre of the male section of the room. He offered me water and wanted to make sure I was feeling ok.

That night and the next few days, devotees' sense of focus continued to shift as they continued to visit the shrines and observed how a group of senior dervishes were taking turns to take care of the lady. That night, with four other dervishes in the room, I was able to sleep very little until the call for morning prayers. The next day, I did not see the woman and heard that the dervishes were taking turns to accompany her and that she was feeling better. The day after, when the lady started to participate in communal gatherings, dervishes were very supportive, some did not want to leave her side, making sure that she fully recovered from the incident. Two days after the incident, I witnessed devotees communicating with the lady as if she did not cause any distress. I saw some female dervishes sitting and eating by her side, holding her hands and trying to support her with love.

Later, I learned from the devotees that to them, this was not an act of tolerance. Devotees had explained to me more than once that they perceived the idea of tolerance as a destructive way of thinking. To be tolerant, according to Veli *efendi*, was perceiving oneself as better than the other. Devotees were showing compassion believing that this was an illness, a challenge, designed for the possessed and the witnesses of the experience. Veli *efendi* believed that if a student acted out of tolerance, that would mean she or he was not aware of the illusions of the egoic self. Such individuals, according to Veli *efendi*, lived in the shadows of certain societal logics such as human beings' urge to decide who was good or who was bad or who was deserving and who was not." Veli *efendi* explained to me that as part of training, the students sought to let go of such discriminatory mind activities (preconceived notions) such as learned ways of shaping oneself through thoughts that start with "I need to, should, can or can't be and/or do this or that." This, according to Veli *efendi*, was the practice of unity as manyness of reality.

This idea of tolerance was also available in Sadeq Rahimi's research on psychosis and Sufism. Rahimi explains how in Sufi knowledge, "there is no such thing as tolerance, you don't need to tolerate anybody, because you are not better than them anyway, they are just different, and all this difference is an illusion anyway."[42] The experience of "I" is an illusion "produced by ego, a dangerous illusion in fact, one which makes the person susceptible to the tricks of the Devil."[43] Sufi discourse includes ways of recognising the relationship of the illusory "I" and "the human soul, owing to the fact that in its structure it has reserved room for the Other within."[44] Ego is the devil that "lives within the cracks of the self, and the self is always already full of cracks, never to be taken as a stronghold."[45] In line with this perception, a psychotic patient may be affected by the persistent illusions of her or his cultural milieu. For this reason, she or he may be in need of a space, in which the nature of human comprehension is beyond the established societal ideas and judgements.[46]

This sense of practising certain ideas by behaving with compassion when interacting with one another was a significant part of Veli *efendi's nefs* training. Therefore, Veli *efendi* was content with how his students' focus shifted inspiring them to act along with the senior dervishes supporting the lady. The compassion between devotees was contagious. They were observing and restoring their actions and behaviours. Some explained later how Veli *efendi*'s and the senior dervishes' actions inspired them to become more empathetic towards people whose activities they perceived as not fitting to the normative behaviours of how one should speak or move in public. Veli *efendi* explained in one of his *sohbets* in the hotel that he wanted to teach his students alternative ways of understanding people with mental illnesses.

A *Sohbet*: Veli *efendi*'s Performatic Teachings

As discussed in Chapter 2, Veli *efendi*'s *sohbets* tended to be performatic, inspiring his students to embody his teachings. This *sohbet* was about comprehending people experiencing different mental states. As discussed earlier, *sohbets* were times when Veli *efendi*'s students scattered around him in the shape of a slightly crooked half-moon. In his *sohbets*, all of the devotees would sit and listen to him talk about many different subjects or experiences. They would sit and listen to him as long as he spoke. They admired his wisdom about life and existence. They admired his peaceful expressions when talking about the world issues, his compassion for all living things, his strength in the face of difficulties and his calm stance in the face of all kinds of challenges. To them, their teacher was an example of a wise human being, a *kamil insan*, who fully comprehended, felt and embodied unity as manyness of reality. He understood and felt compassion for all kinds of people. Among them were individuals who were social outcasts.

Focusing on the idea of healing oneself and others, Veli *efendi* was interested in creating spaces that function as worship centres for people perceived as social outcasts or simply not fitting into society. This way, even persons with mental illnesses could become part of a community that related to their conditions and expected them without or with less judgment. Veli *efendi* believed that as *Rifais*, they needed to move beyond general stereotyped views about people with mental illnesses. He often discussed how many people perceived the mentally ill as violent and dangerous, when in fact they were the ones in need of safe environments. In the residential, wooden and hotel *tekke*, I have met and conversed with a variety of individuals who have been experiencing a sense of isolation from their families and society due to certain physiological or psychological conditions. Some were experiencing a lack of belonging to the society or to their families due to specific issues that tend to be beyond their control such as certain addiction problems and mental illnesses. Others were dealing perhaps with less complicated issues that they were not ready to tamper with such as shyness and/or fear of speaking in public. One of these cases was especially significant regarding how devotees embody Sufi idea of unity as diversity and identify with their sacred homes as spaces inspiring devotees to move beyond societal judgements.

When I referred to my notes from Veli *efendi*'s private *sohbets*, I came across his ideas about healing people with mental illnesses. He explained how he works together with a psychiatrist for healing schizophrenia patients. He discussed that there were cases in which patients need both the assistance of Western medicine and the counselling of a Sufi teacher, who, under any

176 *Transforming*

circumstances, would take the patient to be mentally different rather than sick. Such ideas about bringing together science and spirituality in comprehending mental experiences appear in a variety of anthropological and psychological studies. Comparing mental illnesses and faith-related occurrences, anthropologist Raymond Prince states:

> Highly similar mental and behavioural states may be designated psychiatric disorders in some cultural settings and religious experiences in others. . . . Within cultures that invest these unusual states with meaning and provide the individual experiencing them with institutional support, at least a proportion of these individuals may be contained and channelled into socially valuable roles.[47]

In Sufi history, there are also accounts of sheikhs and dervishes serving as healers, practising specific rituals to treat a person whom devotees believe as possessed by a spirit. Such practices include reading the Quran, praying, playing music and dancing to free the possessed person from the spirit.[48] There is, however, evidence that seeks to depict how such healing methods, while useful for treating neurotic symptoms, are not effective in treating severe mental or physical illness.[49]

Analysis of such complex treatment methods is available in a study conducted by psychiatrists Simon Dein and Abdool Samd Illaie. Simon Dein and Abdool Samd Illaie state:

> The findings of empirical studies on jinn and mental health . . . have significant clinical implications. Mental health professionals should be aware of the explanatory models adopted by their patients and there is a need for these professionals to collaborate with imams.[50]

Therefore, clinical research focuses on the idea that both parties need one another to accomplish full recovery. Dein and Illaie also discuss that "attribution of misfortune to malevolent forces including jinn, witchcraft and the evil eye is widely described in the anthropological literature on Islam. This includes mental disorder which is often treated by exorcism of jinn spirits."[51] According to them, " Jinn are frequently held to cause both madness and epilepsy, ideas which go back to pre-Islamic Arabia."[52] They also discuss "holistic mental healthcare which incorporates biological, psychological and spiritual factors."[53] This belief is about how in such circumstances, "mental health professionals can teach imams to recognise mental illness" while "Islamic religious professionals can in turn educate health professionals about the importance of religious factors in psychiatric disorders."[54]

Another psychologist, David Lukoff argues that "In more recent years, religious institutions and the mental health field—especially in the West—have taken a more dichotomous view of spirituality and psychosis."[55] There are "contemporary clinicians and researchers" who observe that "psychotic episodes occasionally result in improvements in an individual's functioning."[56] Julian Silverman refers to Karl Menninger, who is "recognised as a founder of American psychiatry," and his notes as explaining how "Some patients have a mental illness and then get well and then they get Weller . . . they get better than they ever were. . . . This is an extraordinary and little-realised truth."[57] Having spent one year in Turkey, observing and interviewing schizophrenia patients, their families, and their clinicians, as well as collecting social and cultural data on schizophrenia, Rahimi explains that "When it comes to mental health and spirituality in the Muslim world, Tasawwuf, or Sufism as it is called in the West, stands as an automatic and obvious point of reference."[58] He is also aware how

> Sufism has become a loose tag over time, used and abused in a vast range of meanings and applications. So much so that one could raise the objection that it signifies too wide a range of thought and practices across various Muslim societies (say from North Africa to India), to be a useful concept.[59]

But as Rahimi's research shows,

> it is also possible to turn this problem around, and suggest that fluidity, that proverbial elusiveness so associated with Sufism, is indeed an important characteristic at the very heart of what makes Sufi discourse a wonderful space of refuge for subjective recovery.[60]

If both parties are well informed about each other's teachings, their knowledge may inspire them to choose best-suited partners in treating their patients.

Veli *efendi* cared tremendously about combining spirituality with scientific knowledge. He believed that post-tariqa Sufism is also about teaching his devotees to find courage to bring together their scientific trainings with their comprehension of self as a *kamil insan*. In his *sohbets*, Veli *efendi*'s introduction of such ideas about psychiatry and spirituality inspired devotees to be more open to differences and a variety of experiences, including spirit possession.

In Islam, possession means the entrance of a spirit into a person's body to control that person's actions. This, according to psychiatrist and anthropologist Roland Littlewood, can also be "a parahuman force," which takes charge of the person's body to change his or her identity.[61] Anthropologist Ioan Lewis discusses "two types of possession: central and peripheral, former being a valuable aspect of religious ceremonies worldwide, latter indicating an invasion of evil spirits.[62] Not all cases of possession are seen as signs of illness.[63] For example, "during Zar ceremonies in Egypt and Sudan, women become possessed by Zar spirits who speak through them. Such experiences in the West would likely be deemed pathological."[64] Anthropologist Emma Cohen further discusses while some possession experiences are healthy transformations, as in the case of Zar ceremonies, others such as jinn possession in Islam are related to illness and discomfort.[65] Islamic texts discuss a variety of spiritual beings "that populate the universe: *jinn* (spirits), *shaytaan* (satanic beings), *marrid* (demons), *bhut* (evil spirits) and *farista* (angels)."[66] Most popular in Turkish society is the fear of jinn, which has its origin "in pre-Islamic Arab societies, even prior to the arrival of Judaism and Christianity in the Arab peninsula. Pagan Arabs would refer to jinn as demon-like creatures."[67] These creatures, lower in ranking than angels, have become very popular in making children fear the dark and being alone. According to the Quran, "the jinn are made of a 'smokeless and scorching fire' and they have the physical property of weight."[68] While there are Islamic scholars that accept the possibility that jinn can possess people, some scholars disagree and argue that "jinn can only influence mankind and cannot literally take up physical space within a human's body."[69] However, it has not been my intention to examine how Veli *efendi*, *dedes* and devotees believe in such spiritual experiences. My intension has been to examine how Veli *efendi* and his devotees relate to a possessed individual and how such connections inspire the students to embody unity and create sacred spaces that are free from biases.

Veli *efendi* often articulated *Rifai* houses as spaces open to people dealing with mental illnesses because he also believed that madness was a sacred quality attributed to certain human beings. Veli *efendi* and his devotees often referred to the words of prominent Sufi poets such as Hafiz of Shiraz and Ibn Arabi to describe their relationship to madness as divine irrationality. Veli *efendi* sought to create a multifaceted vision of madness and invited his students to interact with love rather than merely reason. Ibn Arabi writes, "Reason strives to define and delimit God. . . . The heart frees God of all constraints and absolves Him of all limitations. The heart alone is able to perceive God's self-disclosures through the faculty of imagination."[70] Hafiz also discusses "the tension between love and reason, madness and rationality" in his divan and states: "O Hafiz, be content, and bear this pain in silence, that will have to be enough/Those who judge all by reason, will never understand the mystery of love."[71] Veli *efendi* also refers to how in Sufi literature, there are accounts of some Sufis visiting mental hospitals "to catch some insight" about the lives of people with mental disorders.[72] The imagined or real social isolation and suffering is a divine experience in which "the emotional and physical suffering displayed by renunciations" inspire "intimacy with God."[73] This type of relationship to madness, according to Veli *efendi*, may be a healthy experience that has the potential to inspire a human being to the path of divine wisdom.

Another aspect that informed Veli *efendi*'s teachings was the idea of studying the inner meaning of Islam. The Sufi path, according to Hafiz, is not about obeying societal logics to keep a good name but about the annihilation of the self. Hafiz criticises followers who solely practice the visible aspects of the religious law, such as praying, without trying to study their inner meaning, as insincere. Discontentment with the transformation of Sufi cultural beliefs into a doctrine-oriented practice in the ninth century was common among dervishes who desired to voice their opinions about how Sufism had become "a name without a reality, though it used to be a reality without a name."[74] A very well-known dervish, Hallac Mansur, warned one of his students stating:

> May God veil you from the exterior of the religious law, and may he reveal to you the reality of infidelity. For the exterior of the religious law is a hidden idolatry, while the reality of infidelity is manifest gnosis.[75]

To Mansur, trying to follow the religious law word by word was a fetishisation. One had to challenge the law in order to find unity. Mansur believed that the religious law was only one of the many methods in a devotee's spiritual journey. It was only an invitation into the world of God, nothing more.

Challenging law meant that there is an antipathy between *shariah* and *tariqa*. This conflict becomes clearer in Hafiz's ideas about "the figure of the "*rind* . . . a Persian noun that has been translated many different ways; it generally refers to a person of questionable character."[76] There are several definitions of the word: "sagacious, shrewd; a knave, a rogue; a Sufi; dissolute; a drunkard, one whose exterior is subject to censure, but who at heart is sound; a wanderer, traveler; an insolent, reckless, fear-nought fellow."[77] This was a way of life that the *qalandari* dervishes created "beginning in the second half of the . . . eleventh century."[78] Persian scholar De Bruijn points out, "The true follower of the Path of Love is equal to the *qalandar* dervish who is eager to sacrifice his good name as a pious Muslim for the sake of his total submission to the Beloved."[79] As Hafiz says, "I am a lover and a *rind* and a carousing wine-drinker, And all three offices I hold because of that enchanting beauty."[80] Hafiz is one of the Sufis whose teachings clearly show that one needs to move beyond the confines of any orthodoxy.

Veli *efendi* often talked about how orthodox Sufism is about obeying rules and meeting social requirements in order to look good, while the latter (post-tariqa or versatile Sufism) is about finding love and unity, reaching a state of complete harmony with the universe and letting go of societal judgements. Veli *efendi* explained this teaching by giving a specific example of how he guides one of his devotees. He describes that if a devotee finds so much acceptance, comfort and pride in helping other people, then he tells him to stop helping and performing any sort of kindness to others. This idea of the *rind* inspired devotees to move beyond their prejudices about how a person should be or what he or she should do to look good, feel good and fit into the society. Following the ideas of these masters, Veli *efendi* was not interested in pleasing others or gaining social acceptance. His teachings were contradictory to the dominant social and religious procedures in Turkey (RAD). Thus, his idea of madness was beyond certain discriminatory expressions such as senseless, worthless, violent, useless or hopeless. His teachings seemed to be contradictory to the Islamic law because he did not seek to produce a single type of believer. To him, each student had a different path in finding unity, not a single one as described in the law. In the gatherings, Veli *efendi* talked about Hafiz's and Ibn Arabi's messages in a way that deliberately sought to avoid any sense of harm or error in order to appeal to all his students, including the ones with difficulties understanding the idea of moving beyond the law. For instance, when talking about the law, he would explain how it is not the ultimate design and goal but only one of the vehicles to move to the greatest aspiration, that is, the *haqiqa* (the absolute truth).[81]

Veli *efendi* also perceived the law as a system that might have the potential to help a devotee discipline oneself through reading, praying five times a day and helping people in need. Most of the ones who had difficulties in understanding Veli *efendi*'s relationship to the law were either trained in religious schools of Islam (*imam hatip*) in Turkey or raised in a family that carried out conservative religious ideologies, perceiving law as the ultimate goal to a place in heaven. It was Veli *efendi*'s openness and compassion that brought together devotees who prioritised the law, devotees who perceived the law as one of the many steps, and devotees who read but did not follow the law.

Other Sufi concepts that Veli *efendi* often articulated to inspire the students to overcome their prejudices and to embody compassion to all living things and create sacred spaces beyond societal norms and judgements were *mecnun* and *meczup*. Veli *efendi* explained how in Sufism they had many terms and articulations that defined and cherished madness. Veli *efendi* explained *mecnun* as a person who experienced heightened and/or overpowering love for the Beloved God. The Sufi idea of madness is related to a variety of notions about love: "all the way from the spiritual or religious love for Allah to the masculine love for flesh-and-blood females."[82] According to Sadeq Rahimi, "It is in madness that the 'problem' of 'self' is fundamentally 'resolved' and Allah and the flesh finally unite."[83] Rahimi adds the two directions for landing at madness:

> [W]with earthly love it is a loss of the love object that leads to madness, on the heavenly side of the coin madness marks the consummation of the quest and the union with, or at least being touched by Allah.[84]

Veli *efendi* and the *dedes* conveyed multilayered ideas and actions about madness. Ali *dede* often explained that the cause of madness could simultaneously be spiritual and physiological. Veli *efendi* articulated how both medical treatments and Sufi healing methods were valuable when interacting with individuals who desire some sort of help. Madness caused by excessive love is examined as "a natural and desirable aspect of human existence."[85] For the devotees, to hear Veli *efendi* address one of the devotees as *mecnun* was a sign of accomplishment, almost an initiation without a ritual, because one who was *mecnun* was the one who was devoted to the path of unity.

Meczup was another concept through which devotees started to comprehend how *Rifai* devotees related to people with mental disorders. The Sufi idea of *meczup* as "an individual who experiences an overwhelming attraction to God" and loses "all interest in the outer, physical world" conveys similar attributes to a person experiencing clinical madness.[86] The *meczup*

> forgets all earthly things and follows only the internal call, living—so to speak—with his Caller. Being completely absorbed by his inner life, his outer existence is characterised by disconnected speech, repeating one and the same sentence, and roaming aimlessly in the streets or fields.[87]

In Turkish Sufi terminology, "the word *meczub* . . . implies a fatal attraction to Allah with the outcome of the loss of self [*nefs*] and the abandonment of the world of meanings."[88] Frembgen describes the *meczup* as "a special, but many-faceted ecstatic who is at the wilder end of the Sufi spectrum."[89] *Meczup* is a term that

> is employed with slightly varying nuances in different schools of Sufism, and it can have 'positive' (healthy, desirable state of selflessness) or 'negative' (associated with illness or possession) connotations from one school to another, but it always indicates a state that can safely be translated as 'madness.'[90]

I heard devotees articulate more than once that all are welcome: the wise ones, the mad ones, the curious ones, the sick ones, the startled ones, the loveless ones and the lost ones. By these descriptions, they meant all *meczups* that were in need of support were welcome in their *Rifai* houses to participate in the gatherings. Mystical experiences related to madness were also common among other religions: for instance, among "Biblical prophets and saints" who "have played an essential role in religion for thousands of years."[91] Divine madness was an experience in which human beings may experience a distance from their minds' reasoned activities and connect to a sense of pattern that brings out inspiration and creativity that extend the limits of common sense.[92]

It is this quality of divine madness that had parallels with the Sufi experience of *fana* (annihilation of the self, the egoic self) and then *baqa* (purity of consciousness), leading to the embodiment of unity between God and all that exists, including the mind's activities. Ibn Arabi discusses how "human beings may, through careful practice and contemplation, ascend the levels of existence to be reunified with their source."[93] This process requires one to study in detail and rule the mind's thoughts, images, questions and judgements.

Such rigorous spiritual journey of letting the self go, according to Rahimi, is very similar to the psychotic deprivation of self. Rahimi argues: "By pointing this out, however, I do not mean to imply 'sameness' of the Sufi experience of *fena* [*fana*] and the psychotic loss of self. Even though semiotic and structural similarities are striking."[94] He is "not arguing that the phenomenological and/or existential dimensions can be identified as the same."[95] In the *Rifai* post-tariqa training, madness conveyed spiritual lessons for each devotee. What seemed to be unconventional, discomforting, unpredictable behaviour to me was actually a significant part of the devotees' everyday lives and experience of Sufi meaning in ways that I was not able to fully comprehend in the first year. Dervishes told stories of spirits, and how they managed to overcome their fears and judgements. To them, such experiences were proof of Sufi spiritual wisdom. While some cherish such acts, others experienced tremendous discomfort about sharing and witnessing such experiences. Although they were aware of the fact that each devotee had different sets of beliefs and experiences in regard to such religious matters, instead of focusing on the differences, as guided by Veli *efendi*, they chose to focus on how to create a sacred space that inspires unity. Instead of labelling each other's differences, devotees talked about how to be free of such societal norms, limitations, judgements, fears, alienations and discriminations.

The focus created by the possessed lady and Veli *efendi*'s ideas were performatic in the sense that they transformed devotees' perception of Sufi space as a sanctuary for anyone who seeks to conduct himself or herself openly without marginalisation. Although I watched the kind of support devotees provided for one another in many instances throughout my fieldwork, I did not truly understand how many of them performed *Rifai* idea of unity until I witnessed the lady's healing journey with the support of the devotees. Veli *efendi* guided the students to relate to the possessed lady through the eyes of their spiritual teacher, not different from any human being going through a difficult time in life (such as people trying to adjust to new set of circumstances, such as change of school, divorce or losing a loved one). The students talked of the lady as any person with a psychological illness and did not seem afraid to speak to her. Instead, they seemed to interact with her with a desire to help her, to understand her experience and to support her. Devotees sought to understand that the lady's experience was one of the many conflicts of the self that each of them experience in different ways. The students also sought to encourage the lady to believe that she was not alone and that she was going to feel much better one day. Their representation of unity also provided the sense of trust that devotees needed in order to express their problems of depression or anxiety. As they shared personal life events, they reminded one another that despite their illusionary differences, they were one. As Veli *efendi* reminded often in the *sohbets*, human beings, animals, trees, oceans, insects and even objects such as a chair and a cloth are all one, parts of a whole as Ibn Arabi explains in his idea of *Vahdat al Vucud* (meaning oneness and/or unity of being).

Although I have not had a chance to converse with the lady (due to her shyness), one of the dervishes, Kaan, who was very active during the events and gatherings, helping Veli *efendi*, *dedes* and other devotees organise the space, shared his challenge with jinn possession. When I listened to him telling his story of possession the day after the event, I couldn't believe he also had such experiences because by the time he revealed his story, I had known him for four years.

One of our days in Konya, with a group of dervishes, I went to an old coffee shop in Konya, a very small place that was famous for its Turkish coffee. There, Kaan told me about a very difficult part of his life when he had to live in possession. He said he did not have a moment of peace. He could not sleep day or night because a spirit would communicate with him, disturb him and make him feel worthless. All he wanted was to be free, not see or hear from the spirit again. He was lost. He wanted to sleep. He wanted to socialise like everyone else. He needed friends. He explained that he tried every remedy and went to psychiatrists, *imams*, and spiritual teachers but could not get rid of the spirit, which would control his thoughts and his body. One day, he met a dervish at a gathering, who introduced him to Veli *efendi*. He talked about this moment as the end of his suffering, the day he found the sun, the beauty of nature, the butterflies and his friends.

Kaan was an open-minded devotee in the sense that he did not believe in the literal interpretation of the Quran and the law. He was interested in the controversial Sufi mystics such as Hafiz. His idea of Sufism, as he explained, was about love and unity. He was interested in poetry, research and music. In Kaan's experience, it was the sense of love and sharing that he experienced in the *Rifai* spaces that allowed him to move beyond his fears. He explained he was able to say goodbye to the spirit and learn to be useful to his friends in the lodge. As he started to spend more time at the wooden house and the residential building, he says he started to gain his peace back and transformed into a happier person, healthier than ever. He also shared how no one treated him as a desperate person dealing with mental illness.

Having listened to his story that day, I could not believe how a positive and healthy person like Kaan could experience possession. To Kaan, although his days of possession were the most difficult times of his life, they led him to the lodge, where he started to train with Veli *efendi*. Attending all the events and gatherings at the lodge, Kaan explained he learned to meditate and control his mind. To him, it was the sense of acceptance and support that he learned to embody in the *Rifai* sacred spaces that allowed him to find comfort and peace. Veli *efendi* believed that the human mind had endless capabilities, and it had to be the purpose of a *Rifai* devotee's life to remember to perform compassion every moment and direct the mind to the path of unity.

The relationship between this incident and *Rifai* sacred space production also shows how Veli *efendi*, with his embodied acts, seeks to create a healing space that is beyond societal norms and discernments. Veli *efendi* welcomes what he calls "people with different mental processes" (in clinical language, people with mental disorders such as psychological and/or developmental disorders like autism) to train together with the devotees. Veli *efendi* guides his devotees to move beyond labelling people with mental illnesses such as schizophrenia as destructive.

184 Transforming

In the *Rifai tekkes*, I came across a variety of individuals "with different mental processes."[96] Some had autism spectrum disorder; some were dealing with specific mental illnesses such as bipolar, schizophrenia, and depression; some had drug and alcohol problems; some were experiencing what Veli *efendi* calls a mixture of mental illnesses and spiritual experiences such as contacting evil spirits; and some were experiencing intoxication due to emotions caused by what devotees expressed as intense love and longing for God. What was common about these individuals was that they came to the lodge to find comfort, support and healing. *Dedes*', dervishes' and other devotees' relationship to such persons was a matter of how they perceived madness and how they sought to go against societal discriminations. *Rifai* devotees desired to perceive post-tariqa Sufi space as a sanctuary that was beyond the archetypes, limitations and discriminations of society (or what they call human beings' personal and collective consciousness) and how openness to diversity transforms *Rifai* training (embodiment of unity). Veli *efendi*'s training comprised the idea that the embodied acts of such persons were performatic transforming devotees' sense of society, inspiring them to experience the world as a sacred space by achieving a deeper comprehension of God's unity.

Notes

1 Ahmet Aktaş and Yakin Ekin, "Case Study 5: The Importance and the Role of Faith (Religious) Tourism in the Alternative Tourism Resources in Turkey," in *Religious Tourism and Pilgrimage Festivals Management: An International Perspective*, ed. Razaq Raj and Nigel D. Morpeth (Reading and King's Lynn: Biddles Ltd, 2007), 170–184.
2 Kevin Gould, "Konya, in a Whirl of its Own," *The Guardian*, April 9, 2010, http://www.theguardian.com/travel/2010/apr/10/konya-turkey-jelaluddin-rumi-dervish.
3 "Tourists rush to Konya's famous Mevlana Museum," *Hürriyet Daily News*, July 16, 2013, http://www.hurriyetdailynews.com/tourists-rush-to-konyas-famous—museum.aspx?pageID=238&nID=50737&NewsCatID=379.
4 "Tourists rush to Konya's famous Mevlana Museum."
5 Engin Özekinci, "Turkey: Mevlana Rumi museum drew 3.4M visitors in 2019," *AA*, February 19, 2020, https://www.aa.com.tr/en/culture/turkey-mevlana-rumi-museum-drew-34m-visitors-in-2019/1738375.
6 And, "The *Mevlana* Ceremony," 83–94.
7 Chambers, Du Toit, and Edelman, "Introduction," 13.
8 Since 2013, devotees have been able to perform silent *zikir*, meditate and pray in small sections renovated for devotees who seek to perform *namaz* and pray in the presence of Rumi's tomb.
9 Personal communication, December 17, 2013.
10 Personal communication, December 16, 2012.
11 Personal communication, December 16, 2010.
12 Since 2012, *Şeb-i Arus* tickets have been sold online due to the high demand. Before that, tourist agencies were the only places where people could purchase tickets.
13 "9 Days Rumi Commemoration Tours," accessed March 15, 2014, http://www.travelshopturkey.com/rumi_tours_konya/9_days_rumi_commemoration_tours_konya.asp.

World as Manyness of Reality   185

14 Tom Brosnahan, "Cultural Center, Konya," *Turkey Travel Planner*, accessed April 4, 2013, http://www.turkeytravelplanner.com/go/CentralAnatolia/Konya/sights/kultur_merkezi.html.
15 Kenneth Lymer, "Rags and Rock Art: The Landscapes of Holy Site Pilgrimage in the Republic of Kazakhstan," *World Archeology* 36, no. 1 (2004): 160–161.
16 Peña, *Performing Piety*, 148.
17 David E. Long, *The Hajj Today: A Survey of the Contemporary Pilgrimage to Makkah* (Albany: State University of New York Press, 1979), 122.
18 Robert R. Bianchi, *Guests of God: Pilgrimage and Politics in the Islamic World* (Oxford: Oxford University Press), 8.
19 Razaq Raj, "Case Study 1: The Festival of Sacrifice and Travellers to the City of Heaven (Makkah)," in *Religious Tourism and Pilgrimage Festivals Management: An International Perspective*, ed. Razaq Raj and Nigel D. Morpeth (Reading and King's Lynn: Biddles Ltd, 2007), 137.
20 Personal communication, November 4, 2012.
21 Personal communication, October 15, 2012.
22 Personal communication, December 1, 2011.
23 Peña, *Performing Piety*, 57.
24 Sheemem Burney Abbas, *The Female Voice in Sufi Ritual: Devotional Practices of Pakistan and India* (Austin: University of Texas Press, 2002), xvii.
25 Sa'diyya Shaikh, Sufi Narratives of Intimacy: Ibn 'Arabī, *Gender, and Sexuality* (Chapel Hill: University of North Carolina Press, 2012), 24–25.
26 Personal communication, December 12, 2011.
27 Personal conversation, January 5, 2014.
28 Reynold A. Nicholson, *Studies in Islamic Mysticism* (Cambridge: Cambridge University Press, 1967), 93.
29 Werbner, "Stamping the Earth with the Name of Allah and the Sacralizing of Space Among British Muslims," 322.
30 Werbner, "Stamping the Earth with the Name of Allah and the Sacralizing of Space Among British Muslims," 322.
31 John A. Subhan, *Sufism: Its Saints and Shrines* (Lucknow: Lucknow Publishing House, 1960), 61–66.
32 Personal communication, December 12, 2011.
33 Richard Schechner, "Performers and Spectators Transported and Transformed," *The Kenyon Review* 3, no. 4 (1981): 91.
34 Ronald Grimes, *The Craft of Ritual Studies* (Oxford: Oxford University Press, 2014), 323.
35 W. Paul Jones, *Trumpet at Full Moon: Introduction to Christian Spirituality as Diverse Practice* (Louisville: Westminster John Knox Press, 1992), 8.
36 Grimes, *The Craft of Ritual Studies*, 323.
37 Personal conversation, January 12, 2014.
38 Werbner, "Stamping the Earth with the Name of Allah and the Sacralizing of Space Among British Muslims," 311.
39 Dwight Conquergood. "Rethinking Ethnography: Towards a Critical Cultural Politics," in *The Sage Handbook of Perfomance Studies*, ed. D.S. Madison and J. Hamera (Thousand Oaks, CA: Sage, 2006), 351–365. Also, the article can be found on http://www.open-frames.net/pdf/145-Conquergood_19xx__rethinging_ethnograohy.pdf.
40 Personal communication, May 12, 2011.
41 Personal communication, June 17, 2012.
42 Rahimi, "Intimate Exteriority," 409–421. Rahimi, "Intimate Exteriority," 419.
43 Rahimi, "Intimate Exteriority," 419.
44 Rahimi, "Intimate Exteriority," 419.
45 Rahimi, "Intimate Exteriority," 420.

46 Swami Tapasyananda, *Srimad-Bhagavad-Gita: The Scripture of Mankind* (Chennai: Sri Ramakrishna Math, 2005), 60.
47 Raymond H. Prince, "Religious Experience and Psychopathology: Cross-Cultural Perspectives," in *Religion and Mental Health*, ed. J.F. Schumacher (New York: Oxford University Press, 1992), 289, 281–290.
48 A. Al-Krenawi and J.R. Graham, "Spirit Possession and Exorcism in the Treatment of a Bedouin Psychiatric Patient," *Clinical Social Work Journal* 25 (1997): 211–222, https://doi.org/10.1023/A:1025714626136.
49 S.M. Razali, "Conversion Disorder: A Case Report of Treatment with the Main Puteri, a Malay Shamanastic Healing Ceremony," *European Psychiatry* 14, no. 8 (1999): 470–472, https://doi.org/10.1016/S0924-9338(99)00218-7. For a companion of Western and Eastern cultural perspectives, refer to Mumtaz F. Jafari, "Counseling Values and Objectives: A Comparison of Western and Islamic Perspectives," *The American Journal of Islamic Social Sciences* 10 (1993): 326–339.
50 Simon Dein and Abdool Samad Illaiee, "Jinn and Mental Health: Looking at Jinn Possession in Modern Psychiatric Practice," *The Psychiatrist* 37, no. 9 (2013): 293, https://doi.org/10.1192/pb.bp.113.042721.
51 Dein and Illaiee, "Jinn and Mental Health: Looking at Jinn Possession in Modern Psychiatric Practice," 293.
52 Dein and Illaiee, "Jinn and Mental Health: Looking at Jinn Possession in Modern Psychiatric Practice," 293.
53 Dein and Illaiee, "Jinn and Mental Health: Looking at Jinn Possession in Modern Psychiatric Practice," 293.
54 Dein and Illaiee, "Jinn and Mental Health: Looking at Jinn Possession in Modern Psychiatric Practice," 293.
55 David Lukoff, "Visionary Spiritual Experiences," in *Psychosis and Spirituality*, ed. Isabel Clarke (Sussex: Wiley and Blackwell Publishing, 2010), 216.
56 Lukoff, "Visionary Spiritual Experiences," 216.
57 Julian Silverman, "Shamans and Acute Schizophrenia," *American Anthropologist* 69 (1967): 21, https://doi.org/10.1525/aa.1967.69.1.02a00030.
58 Rahimi, "Intimate Exteriority," 409.
59 Rahimi, "Intimate Exteriority," 409.
60 Rahimi, "Intimate Exteriority," 409.
61 Roland Littlewood, "Possession States," *Psychiatry* 3, no. 8 (2004): 8–10, https://doi.org/10.1383/psyt.3.8.8.43392.
62 Ioan M. Lewis, *Ecstatic Religion: A Study of Shamanism and Spirit Possession* (New York: Routledge, 1989).
63 Dein and Illaiee, "Jinn and Mental Health: Looking at Jinn Possession in Modern Psychiatric Practice," 290.
64 Dein and Illaiee, "Jinn and Mental Health: Looking at Jinn Possession in Modern Psychiatric Practice," 290.
65 Emma Cohen, "What is Spirit Possession? Defining, Comparing, and Explaining Two Possession Forms," *Ethnos* 73, no. 1 (2008): 101–126, https://doi.org/10.1080/00141840801927558.
66 Dein and Illaiee, "Jinn and Mental Health: Looking at Jinn Possession in Modern Psychiatric Practice," 291.
67 Dein and Illaiee, "Jinn and Mental Health: Looking at Jinn Possession in Modern Psychiatric Practice," 291.
68 Dein and Illaiee, "Jinn and Mental Health: Looking at Jinn Possession in Modern Psychiatric Practice," 291.
69 Dein and Illaiee, "Jinn and Mental Health: Looking at Jinn Possession in Modern Psychiatric Practice," 291.
70 Chittick, *The Sufi Path of Knowledge: Ibn al-'Arabi's Metaphysics of Imagination*, 107.

71 James R. Newell, "The Wisdom of Intoxication: Love and Madness in the Poetry of Hafiz of Shiraz," in *Creativity, Madness and Civilization*, ed. Richard Pine (Cambridge: Cambridge Scholars Publishing, 2007).
72 Laury Silvers, "Early Pious, Mystic Sufi Women," in *The Cambridge Companion to Sufism*, ed. Lloyd Ridgeon (Cambridge: Cambridge University, 2014), 24–52; Michael W. Dols, *Majnun: The Madman in Medieval Islamic Society* (Oxford: Oxford University Press, 1992), 391–392, 388–422, Oxford Scholarship Online, 2011, http://doi: 10.1093/acprof:oso/9780198202219.001.0001.
73 Silvers, "Early Pious, Mystic Sufi Women," 44.
74 Carl Ernst, *Words of Ecstasy in Sufism* (Albany: State University of New York, 1985), 2.
75 Ernst, *Words of Ecstasy in Sufism*, 3.
76 Newell, "The Wisdom of Intoxication," 206.
77 Newell, "The Wisdom of Intoxication," 206.
78 Thomas Rehder, "Hafiz: An Introduction," PhD dissertation, Princeton University, 1970, 253.
79 Johannes Thomas Pieter Bruijn, *Persian Sufi Poetry: An Introduction to the Mystical Use of Classical Poems* (Richmond: Curzon Press, 1997), 80.
80 Bruijn, *Persian Sufi Poetry*, 311.
81 He would explain the importance of understanding the differences between *şeriat* (shariah), *tarikat* (path or way), *marifet* (gnosis) and *hakikat* (truth).
82 Sadeq Rahimi, *Meaning, Madness, and Political Subjectivity: A Study of Schizophrenia and Culture in Turkey* (London: Routledge, 2016), 182.
83 Rahimi, *Meaning, Madness, and Political Subjectivity*, 182.
84 Rahimi, *Meaning, Madness, and Political Subjectivity*, 182.
85 Dols, *Majnun*, 12.
86 Newell, "The Wisdom of Intoxication," 208.
87 Dols, *Majnun*, 417–418.
88 Rahimi, *Meaning, Madness and Political Subjectivity*, 138.
89 Jürgen Wasim Frembgen, "The *Majzub* Mama Ji Sarkar: A Friend of God Moves from One House to Another," in *Embodying Charisma: Saints, Cults and Muslim Shrines in South Asia*, ed. Pnina Werbner and Helen Basu (London: Routledge, 1998), 144.
90 Rahimi, *Meaning, Madness and Political Subjectivity*, 138. A detailed account of *meczup* cases is available in the British physician Dr. William Donkin's research on the work of Indian spiritual leader Meher Baba. William Donkin, *The Wayfarers: Meher Baba with the God-Intoxicated* (South Carolina: Sheriar Foundation, 2001).
91 Lukoff, "Visionary Spiritual Experiences," 205–216.
92 Eric R. Dodds, *The Greeks and the Irrational* (Berkeley: University of California Press, 1951), 20.
93 Tamara Sonn, *Islam: A Brief History* (Sussex: Blackwell Publishing, 2010), 68.
94 Rahimi, *Meaning, Madness and Political Subjectivity*, 192.
95 Rahimi, *Meaning, Madness and Political Subjectivity*, 192.
96 Personal communication, October 15, 2012.

Conclusion

Will it be possible to continue creating a post-tariqa Sufi practice that is in harmony with the secular values of the Turkish State? In the socio-political environment of today's Turkey, many *Mevlevis* and *Rifais* discussed in this book ask themselves this question. Many post-tariqa groups disbanded or took a break from organising ritual gatherings. These devotees hope that they will continue to restore their vision for a versatile Sufi practice without having to confront oppression in Turkey. As many writers, artists and minority religious groups, who challenge the Islamist agenda in Turkey, *Mevlevis* and *Rifais* know that more oppression might mean lack of freedom. However, most seem to find comfort in their faith similar to the senior dervishes that had experienced the closing of all the *tekkes* during the Turkish revolution (as discussed in Chapter 1). These devotees believe that as long as Turkey manages to preserve its secular and democratic values, there is hope.

As discussed throughout, *Mevlevis* and *Rifais* use their embodied acts to create sacred spaces. Devotees, with or without knowing, used performance's ability to restore Sufism, transmit their core spiritual values and transform themselves and the spaces they occupied. Schechner's idea of "restored behaviour as living behaviour" informed my comprehension of how devotees seek to restore their practice of remembrance (*zikir*) by rearranging and reconstructing their practice of *zikir* in a variety of private and public spaces. Drawing from the idea that to perform an action is to recreate that action, it is possible to comprehend how devotees restored their devotional lives by repeating and recreating their idea of *zikir*. What informed *Mevlevi* sense of restoration is embedded in the paradox of repetition "with critical difference."[1] It is this "paradox of the mechanism of repetition inherent in all performances" that led the way to comprehending devotees' actions and behaviours as newness and change. Through processes of restoration, devotees produced temporary or permanent sacred sites and learned to perceive the universe as a sacred space.

Pnina Werbner points out, Sufism "beyond the transformation of the person" is "a movement in space that Islamicizes the universe and transforms it into the space of Allah."[2] Taking Werbner's idea even further, this book sought to show how devotees used their embodied acts to sacralise

Conclusion 189

their minds and bodies to perceive the universe as God's unity. *Mevlevi* and *Rifai* organisation of spiritual practice showed that post-tariqa Sufism is about merging the religious with the secular vision. As a result of social and political changes, devotees raised in the secular society of Turkey sought to mobilise post-tariqa Sufism as a devotional life that is in conformity with the secular values of Atatürk. As most of the devotees explained, they embraced Atatürk's idea of *laïcité*, explaining it as the separation of state and religious affairs, while also expressing themselves as religious individuals. Their idea of Islam is similar to Brian Silverstein's analysis of moderate Islam as a living tradition that can "change through engagement with the received."[3] Embracing both secular and religious values, devotees modified their systems of worship and produced public and private spaces to continue their devotional living, including the social roles (such as supporting the poor or the mentally ill) that are significant to their religious practice.

The way devotees produced their Sufi beliefs and values in various spaces also conveyed how post-tariqa Sufism has been becoming more and more about commitment to scientific as well as religious knowledge. As John Voll points out, "Sufi saints and their devotional paths (*tariqas* [tarikat]) with their popular followings have frequently been identified with rural, village, and tribal societies, in contrast to the religious mode of the literate scholars of the cities."[4] As we have seen in the case of Saygın and Narin *dede*'s group and the *Rifai* order, devotees are working professionals, academics, doctors, lawyers, bank workers, entrepreneurs and artists who participate in everyday Sufi living in a variety of ways. Even those who devote almost all their spare time to their spiritual teacher are able to make choices regarding their personal, professional and even religious lives. As in the case of the devotees in the *Rifai* order, secular education and the ability to think critically about their actions and behaviours is a significant component of their devotional practice (transformation of self). Examining the everyday life in the *Rifai* order, I discussed why and how devotees value modern ways of communication and reasoning.

Claire Marie Chambers, Simon Du Toit and Joshua Edelman examine Jürgen Habermas' ideas and point out that

> the root of the desire to exclude religion from the public sphere is the fear of its return as a proto governmental voice, one that is unresponsive to the demand of enlightened rationality that all human beings must be equal in dignity under the law.[5]

Chambers, Du Toit and Edelman highlight Habermas' view further, stating that "The demand for equality is framed as a rational principle, and therefore, there is a terrifying prospect that religiously based forms of authority and government may not recognise it."[6] Further, Habermas says, "Each side must accept an interpretation of the relation between faith and knowledge from its own perspective, which enables them to live together in a self-reflective manner."[7] Habermas' ideas illuminate how, like secular Turks who feared the dominance of religion and the fundamentalist refusal to communicate, Sufi individuals, like Narin *dede*'s student Yiğit, also felt threatened by individuals who were unresponsive to the rational and democratic demands of Turkish society. Devotees of the *Rifai* order, as educated working professionals with their own ideas about divine unity, have formed alternative religious visions and called their practices as post-tariqa Sufi devotional living, a phrase that has been more acceptable in the eyes of secular society. In the post-tariqa *Mevlevi* practice, devotees from different ethnic, religious and economic backgrounds returned to Sufi teachings to seek inner peace, to move closer to divine meaning, and to become aware of what devotees identify as their true selves. As working-class individuals, some devotees, while seeking to adapt to the needs of money-oriented modern everyday life, also sought to be less dependent on their desires relating to the material world. Devotees sought inner detachment from worldly needs and desires, while continuing to perform their responsibilities outside their places of worship. Guests attending these gatherings became participants/observers, witnessing the ideas and teachings of Sufism and having the chance to communicate their everyday problems and ask questions about Sufi spiritual life. Each gathering I participated in with *Mevlevis* and *Rifais* offered living examples of the cultural processes of Sufi devotees, who somehow have been seeking ways to restore a multi-cultural post-tariqa Sufi practice in Turkey.

While devotees in these groups continued to influence, guide and challenge each other regarding their educational needs, they also continued to challenge any overarching analysis of what constitutes Sufi tradition. Devotees studied foreign languages, received access to online databases and discussed Sufi tradition as versatile, open to renewal and adaptation. Devotees, as I discussed throughout, valued deeply the examples, discussions and ideas of their past saints and took their words and way of living as a model for their spiritual elevation. However, devotees were also aware that their commitment to studying the past did not mean that what is available in the teachings of Sufi masters is absolute. As Silverstein examines, "discussions about correct practice are always evolving, and the judgements reached are constantly changing."[8] Devotees influenced each other to think about their beliefs and values as continuously expanding or evolving. Silverstein argues, "Stasis is not a characteristic of tradition."[9] Similar to Silverstein's analysis, devotees actually sought to perceive their idea of self-transformation as a living tradition that can be preserved while evolving with each devotee's need. With the participation of new devotees from various cultural, religious and national backgrounds, Sufism transformed and became more diverse and active. Participating in Sufi devotional living, devotees learned and sought to embody the idea that all human beings are different, yet united in God. Devotees' embodiment of Sufi beliefs and values transmitted the knowledge that there is an alternative way of practising faith that is in line with secular and democratic values. Due to these devotees' efforts, post-tariqa Sufism in Turkey has been in constant transformation, resisting any conclusive definition due to each devotee's or group's experience with producing temporary and permanent lodges, ritual spaces, community gathering spaces and educational spaces. Devotees desire to restore, formulate, revive and transmit their beliefs and values by converting museums, shrines, dervish lodges, cultural centres, hotels, offices and private homes into sacred sites for devotional living through face-to-face interaction, sharing, teaching and performing rituals.

To research post-tariqa Sufi devotional living in Turkey, this book focused on a site-specific analysis, "one that simultaneously privileges the production of space and the production of the sacred,"[10] to show how Sufism is in constant transformation. Following Elaine Peña's idea "that space is not absolute, that the process of sacred space production embraces both religious and secular elements, often in unison,"[11] I showed how devotees consecrated both Sufi and non-Sufi spaces to generate Sufi devotional living. Focusing on Werbner's analysis that Sufi Islam is simultaneously a journey within the body and person, a journey towards God, and a journey in space,[12] I have also depicted how *Rifais* sought to maintain the sites they occupy with their embodied acts while practising self-transformation.

This book shows how Sufi devotional living is a performative intervention that is beyond the rules, principles, structures and systems of religion inside and outside the sacred sites.[13] The devotees I have discussed are multicoded individuals, in the sense that they simultaneously embody modern, secular and religious knowledge, continuously wanting to learn, discuss and become part of social progress. As Joshua Edelman states in his discussion of performing religion in the public sphere, religion can be "a dynamic, lived, and fluidly embodied set of actions, practices, gestures, and speech acts at specific points in time and space."[14] Taking Edelman's idea further that religions exist because devotees perform their beliefs and values through ritual, prayer and meditation, I examined how post-tariqa *Mevlevi* and *Rifai* practice is also about the embodiment of divine meaning in everyday interactions in urban social contexts.

As Hermansen points out, there is a Sufi practice that is alternative "to mainstream religious institutions . . . that have come to be viewed by many as no longer offering intense and personally meaningful experiences of spiritual community."[15] It was ideas such as "western Sufism," "universal Sufism" and "new-age Sufism" that informed the position of minority post-tariqa Sufism in Turkey. These theories show that Sufism is neither a relic of the past nor generally Islamist. As in every religious institution, there are groups and individuals that dishonour what genuine believers seek to achieve. Through the efforts of *Mevlevi* and *Rifai* devotees that genuinely worked hard to restore post-tariqa Sufism, this may continue to change. Nicholas Birch states, "Many secular Turks used to respond to the word *tarikat* [Sufi order] with a grimace of distaste . . . however, since the 1990s, secular fears have increasingly centred on political Islam."[16] Today, many secular Turks, raised with Atatürk's ideas, experience piety through Sufi teachings and rituals, perceiving Sufism as an alternative to the strictly doctrinal practice of Islam. In the post-tariqa cases discussed in this book, experiencing Sufism, it is important to create an egalitarian environment in which male and female devotees lived and trained together. For the female devotees I encountered, the free environment of Sufi spaces was an opportunity for them to practice all aspects of Sufism, including the participation of *sohbets* and ceremonies with male devotees, which is not possible in strictly doctrinal Sufi orders. The residential building and the wooden house that *Rifais* converted into a *dergah* were spaces where women could make music, sing, dance and discuss their beliefs and values freely. Examining the practice of everyday life of these female devotees inside and outside of the *dergah* spaces, I came to understand how a Sufi teacher can be willing to generate spaces in which male and female devotees live beyond the rigid values of Islam. Female devotees from different ages and educational backgrounds continuously sought to find a balance between their family lives with their husbands and children and their devotional practice in the secluded *Rifai* spaces. Although their husbands and children may not be interested in becoming devotees, female devotees, as guided by their teacher, found ways to plan their family lives around the long hours they spend in the *Rifai* houses. Each female devotee had different ways of operating according to their family life, job and number of children. These female devotees' practices of everyday life require extensive research to show how women, while becoming active participants in the Sufi houses, manage to perform their second or third social roles as lawyers, pharmacists, mothers and wives.

Considering the life within the Sufi groups, there is still limited research about gender and sexuality. The scope and character of women's participation in the ritual, social and intellectual dimensions of Sufism require broader research by comparing specific case studies because gender dynamics change from group to group. These teachers challenge the modernist image that presents Sufi masters as strictly doctrinal individuals. Women perceive Sufi devotional living as a safer form of religion as opposed to fundamentalist movements that threaten the democratic order of society. It would also be a significant contribution to the study of Sufism and gender to compare the embodied acts of female devotees in strictly doctrinal Sufi groups with Sufi groups that perceive that Islamic law, like tradition, needs reviving according to the needs of modern Turkish society. Also, more research is necessary on Cemalnur Sargut, a female *mürşit*, who, with her female students, practise Sufism by collaborating with her devotees in writing Sufi books, giving seminars and organising *sohbets*. She has played a significant role in the mobilisation of Sufism as a way of living that is a synthesis of religious and secular values.

The most effective way to engage in and comprehend post-tariqa Sufi culture in present-day Turkey has been to follow the analytical directions provided in performance theory and methodology. The study of religion through performance, as Catherine Bell explains, has been "indispensable for the articulation of specifically cultural dynamics involved in religious activity, thereby recognising religious life as more than a functional expression of conceptual beliefs."[17] Peña alerts us to see "the places and times where power wordlessly changes hands—interactions that often define a community. Recognising the contingency of boundaries and connections is what the study of everyday and extraordinary performances renders."[18] One must take the embodied acts of devotees as an object in which to evaluate the struggles, conflicts and needs of each individual from one space or time to another. Following performance as a methodology compelled me as a researcher into an embodied engagement with the complexity of Sufi culture. Such an engagement requires "an understanding of the knowledge of the body in the culture, a clear sense of what has been embodied in the corporeality of the people who participate in religious practice, what their tongues, skin, ears, 'know.'"[19] Learning with and through action "is not a task that we can accomplish by reading textbooks, merely observing ritual practices, or participating sometimes."[20] It is vital for a researcher to place his or her body in a given setting and coperformatively witness the practice of everyday life. Sharing rooms, cooking, cleaning, praying and sleeping alongside devotees in their sacred sites as opposed to simply conducting interviews with them allowed me as a researcher to share the individual and group struggles, thirsts, exhaustion and fears that shape post-tariqa Sufi devotional practice in contemporary Turkey. Practising everyday life and performing their rituals regularly with the devotees in the *Rifai* group, I also witnessed how each seeker has come to perceive the idea of performing an action as a process of learning and self-transformation. I have encountered devotees who showed me that although based on Islamic teachings, Sufi devotion is not only about the study of theological texts and the performance of rituals and prayers in sacred spaces. Sufi devotion is also about acting for change and renewal, as well as learning to adapt to the given circumstances of hectic urban everyday life. It is coming together to practice divine meaning through education, networking, music, whirling, praying, meditating, cleaning, cooking and inventing ways to blend their embodiment of divine meaning in the Sufi spaces with their practice of everyday life in the non-Sufi places.

Coperformatively witnessing the everyday life of *Rifai* devotees while they witnessed mine, we cooked and cleaned together. We organised the houses for gatherings. We shared our struggles with friends and family who are critical of or against the practices of Sufi groups. We witnessed each other's interactions with non-Sufi and non-Muslim guests and audiences. We shared food. We heard and created music together. We woke up early in the morning to travel to shrines in Konya to pray. We shared dormitories, even when we were ill due to the cold weather and a hectic schedule in Konya. We had discussions about life and death. We performed collective *zikir* rituals in private and public spaces. We supported each other regarding work and education. We sang hymns, socialised outside the houses, visited each other's living spaces and listened to each other's problems with coworkers and family members. We had ideas and lifestyles that were very different from one another. It was Veli *efendi*'s performatic training that taught the devotees the idea of unity as manyness of reality.

194 *Transforming*

Notes

1. Drewal, *Yoruba Ritual: Performers, Play, Agency*, 3–5.
2. Werbner, "Stamping the Earth with the Name of Allah: Zikir and Sacralising of Space Among British Muslims," 323.
3. Silverstein, "Sufism and Modernity in Turkey," 40.
4. John O. Voll, "Sufism in the Perspective of Contemporary Theory," *Sufism and the 'Modern' in Islam*, edit. Martin Van Bruinessen and Julie Day Howell (London: I.B. Tauris, 2007), 281.
5. Chambers, Du Toit, and Edelman, "Introduction," 10.
6. Chambers, Du Toit, and Edelman, "Introduction," 13.
7. Jurgen Habermas, *Europe: The Faltering Project* (Cambridge: Polity, 2009), 77.
8. Silverstein, "Sufism and Modernity in Turkey," 40.
9. Silverstein, "Sufism and Modernity in Turkey," 40.
10. Peña, *Performing Piety*, 4.
11. Peña showed how "Key texts in the study of geography, especially after 1970, have shown us that 'absolute' space is a positivist ahistorical fallacy." Peña, *Performing Piety*, 4. Also, for related discussions about space, refer to Lefebvre, *The Production of Space*; Michel Foucault, "Of Other Spaces," *Diacritics* 16, no. 1 (1986): 22–27; David Harvey, *The Urbanization of Capital: Studies in the History and Theory of Capitalist Urbanization* (Baltimore, MD: Johns Hopkins University Press, 1985); David Harvey, *Spaces of Hope* (Edinburgh: Edinburgh University Press, 2000); Yi-Fu Tuan, *Space and Place: The Perspective of Experience* (Minneapolis: University of Minnesota Press, 2001); Dolores Hayden, *The Power of Place* (Cambridge, MA: MIT Press, 1995); and Setha Low and Denise Lawrence-Zúñiga, *The Anthropology of Space and Place: Locating Culture* (Malden, MA: Blackwell Publishing, 2001).
12. Pnina Werbner, "Stamping the Earth with the Name of Allah and the Sacralising of Space Among British Muslims," *Cultural Anthropology* 11, no. 3 (1996): 76.
13. Dwight Conquergood, "Rethinking Ethnography: Towards a Critical Cultural Politics," *Communication Monographs* 58 (1991): 190, Open-Frames.net, EBSCO Publishing, http://www.open-frames.net/pdf/145-Conquergood_19xx__rethinging_ethnograohy.pdf.
14. Chambers, Du Toit, and Edelman, "Introduction," 2.
15. Marcia Hermansen, "Introduction," in *Varieties of American Sufism: Islam, Sufi Orders, and Authority in a Time of Transition*, ed. Elliott Bazzano and Marcia Hermanse (Albany: State University of New York Press, 2020), xi.
16. Nicholas Birch, "Sufism in Turkey: The Next Big Thing," *Eurosianet.org*, June 22, 2010, http://www.eurasianet.org/node/61379.
17. Catherine Bell, "Performance," in *Critical Terms for Religious Studies*, ed. Mark C. Taylor (Chicago: University of Chicago Press, 1998), 208.
18. Peña, *Performing Piety*, 147.
19. Bell, "Performance," 208.
20. As Margaret Thompson Drewal suggests in her critical evaluation of research in Africa, "Performance participants can self-reflexively monitor their behaviour in the process of doing. Therefore, more than simply observing that performance is emergent, it is crucial to examine the rhetoric of performers situated in time and place. For performance as a mode of activity is often tactical and improvisational." Drewal, "The State of Research on Performance in Africa," 19. As Peña notes, "Thompson Drewal's intervention advocates for a relationship based on reciprocity, one that is focused on the performer's agency, how these communities continually theorise their traditions, the temporal and spatial components of their performances, and on the researcher's role as co-actor and interpreter." Peña, *Performing Piety*, 190.

Bibliography

Abbas, Sheemem Burney. *The Female Voice in Sufi Ritual: Devotional Practices of Pakistan and India*. Austin: University of Texas Press, 2002.
Abu Rabi, Ibrahim. *Islam at the Crossroads*. Albany: State University of New York, 2003.
Afzaal, Ahmed. "Sufism." In *The Encyclopedia of Religion and Nature*, ed. Braun Taylor and Jeffrey Kaplan, 1605–1606. Oxford: Oxford University Press, 2005.
Akdeniz, Doğukan. "Evolution of JDP's (Adalet ve Kalkınma Partisi) and Recep Tayyip Erdoğan's View on Human Rights in Turkey." Master's thesis. Université Libre de Bruxelles, 2016. http://doi.org/10.13140/RG.2.2.29407.66723.
Akman, Kubilay. "Sufism, Spirituality and Sustainability/Rethinking Islamic Mysticism through Contemporary Sociology." *Comparative Islamic Studies* 6, no. 4 (2010): 47–55.
Aktaş, Ahmet and Yakin Ekin. "Case Study 5: The Importance and the Role of Faith (Religious) Tourism in the Alternative Tourism Resources in Turkey." In *Religious Tourism and Pilgrimage Festivals Management: An International Perspective*, ed. Razaq Raj and Nigel D. Morpeth, 170–184. Reading and King's Lynn: Biddles Ltd, 2007.
Alantra, Toni. *Contemporary Kemalism: From Universal Secular-Humanism to Extreme Turkish*. London: Routledge, 2014.
Alavi, Karima Diane. "Pillars of Religion and Faith." In *Voices of Islam: Voices of Tradition*, ed. Vincent J. Cornell, 5–42. Westport: Praeger Press, 2007.
Al-Krenawi, Alean and John R. Graham. "Spirit Possession and Exorcism in the Treatment of a Bedouin Psychiatric Patient." *Clinical Social Work Journal* 25 (1997): 211–222. https://doi.org/10.1023/A:1025714626136.
Almond, Ian. *Sufism and Deconstruction: A Comparative Study of Derrida and Ibn 'Arabi*. London: Routledge, 2004.
Al-Sarraj, Abu Nasr. *The Kitab al-Luma'fi'l-tasawwuf*. ed. Reynold Alleyne Nicholson. Leiden: E.J. Brill and London: lUZACS, 1914.
Altunışık, Meliha Benli and Özlem Türk. *Turkey: Challenges of Continuity and Change*. New York: Routledge, 2005.
Alvi, Anjum. "Concealment and Revealment: The Muslim Veil in Context." *Current Anthropology* 54, no. 2 (2013): 177–199. http://www.jstor.org/stable/10.1086.
And, Metin. *A Pictorial History of Turkish Dancing: From Folk Dancing to Whirling Dervishes, Belly Dancing to Ballet*. Istanbul: Dost Yayınları, 1976.
———. "The Mevlana Ceremony [Turkey]." *TDR: The Drama Review* 21, no. 3 (1977): 83–94.

Bibliography

Anjum, Tanvir. "Sufism in History and its Relationship with Power." *Islamic Studies* 45, no. 2 (2006): 221–268.

An-Na'im, Abdullahi Ahmed. *Islam and the Secular State: Negotiating the Future of Shari'a*. Cambridge: Harvard University Press, 2008.

Arberry, Arthur John. "Introduction." In *Muslim Saints and Mystics: Episodes from the Tadhkirat al-Auliya (Memorial of the Saints)*, ed. Farid al-Din Attar, trans. Arthur J. Arberry, 1–19. London: Routledge and Kegan Paul, 1979.

Asad, Talal. *Formations of the Secular: Christianity, Islam, Modernity*. Stanford: Stanford University Press, 2003.

———. "The Idea of an Anthropology of Islam." *Qui Parle* 17, no. 2 (2009): 1–30.

Ashcraft, W. Michael. *A Historical Introduction to the Study of New Religious Movements*. London: Routledge, 2018.

Aslan, Seyfettin ve Müslüm Kayacı. "Historical Background and Principles of Kemalism." *New World Science Academy* 8, no. 1 (2013): 16–32.

Atacan, Fulya. *Sosyal Değişme ve Tarikat: Cerrahiler [Social Change and Tarikats: Cerahhis]*. İstanbul: Hill Yayın, 1990.

Atay, Tayfun. *Batı'da Bir Nakşi Cemaati: Şeyh Nazım Kıbrısi Örneği [A Nakşi Congregation in the West: Şeyh Nazım Kıbrısi Case]*. İstanbul: İletişim Yayınları, 1996.

Austin, John Langshaw. *How To Do Things with Words*. Cambridge: Harvard University Press, 1962.

Ayata, Sencer. "Patronage, Party, and the State: The Politicization of Islam in Turkey." *Middle East Journal* 50, no. 1 (1996): 40–56.

Ayverdi, Semiha. *Ken'an Rifai ve Yirminci Asrın Işığında Müslümanlık*. Istanbul: Hülbe, 1983.

Babb, Lawrence and Susan Wadley. *Media and the Transformation of Religion in South Asia*. Philadelphia: University of Pennsylvania Press, 1995.

Badone, Ellen, ed. *Intersecting Journeys: The Anthropology of Pilgrimage and Tourism*. Urbana: University of Illinois Press, 2004.

Balibar, Etienne. "Dissonances within Laicite." *Constellations* 11, no. 3 (2004): 353–367.

Barber, X. Theodore. "Four Interpretations of Mevlevi Dervish Dance, 1920–1929." *Dance Chronicle* 9, no. 3 (1986): 328–355. http://www.jstor.org/stable/10.2307.

Barker, Chris. *The Sage Dictionary of Cultural Studies*. London: Sage Publication, 2004.

Barkey, Henri J. and Yasemin Çongar. "Deciphering Turkey's Elections: The Making of a Revolution." *World Policy Journal* 24, no. 3 (2007): 63–73.

Barks, Coleman. *Rumi: The Big Red Book*. New York: Harper Collins, 1995.

Barth, Fredrik. *Principles of Social Organization in Southern Kurdistan*. Oslo: Universitets Etnografiske Museum, 1953.

Başgil, Ali Fuat. *Din ve Laiklik [Religion and Laicism]*. Istanbul: Kubbealti Negriyati, 1998.

Başkan, Filiz. "The Fethullah Gülen Community: Contribution or Barrier to the Consolidation of Democracy in Turkey?" *Middle Eastern Studies* 41, no. 6 (2005): 849–861.

Bausani, Alessandro. "Modern Religious Trends in Islam." *East and West* 4, no. 1 (1953): 12–18. http://www.jstor.org/stable/10.2307.

Baykan, Toygar Sinan. *The Justice and Development Party in Turkey: Populism, Personalism, Organization*. Cambridge: Cambridge University Press, 2018. http://doi.org/10.1017/9781108570725.

Bedding, James. "Istanbul, European Capital of Culture 2010: City Highlights." Accessed January 9, 2010. http://www.telegraph.co.uk/travel/festivalsandevents/6946035/Istanbul-European-Capital-of-Culture-2010-city-highlights.html.

Bell, Catherine. "Performance." In *Critical Terms for Religious Studies*, ed. Mark C. Taylor. Chicago: University of Chicago Press, 1998.

———. *Ritual Theory, Ritual Practice*. Oxford: Oxford University Press, 2009.

Benningsen, Alexander. *Mystics and Commissars: Sufism in the Soviet Union*. London: Hurst, 1985.

Berkes, Niyazi. *The Development of Secularism in Turkey*. New York: Routledge, 1998.

Bermek, Sevinç. *The Rise of Hybrid Political Islam in Turkey: Origins and Consolidation of the JDP*. London: Palgrave Macmillan. https://doi.org/10.1007/978-3-030-14203-2.

Bhargav, Hemant, Aarti Jagannathan, Nagarathna Raghuram, T.M. Srinivasan, and Bangalore N. Gangadhar. "Schizophrenia Patient or Spiritually Advanced Personality? A Qualitative Case Analysis." *Journal of Religion and Health* 54 (2015): 1901–1918. https://doi.org/10.1007/s10943-014-9994-0.

Bianchi, Robert R. *Guests of God: Pilgrimage and Politics in the Islamic World*. Oxford: Oxford University Press, 2004.

Biçer, Birol. "Tasavvuf'un Dönüşü Muhteşem Oldu [Tasavvuf's Coming Back Has Been Spectacular]." *Aktüel* 209 (2010): 16–22.

Biegman, Nicolaas. *Living Sufism: Sufi Rituals in the Middle East and Balkans*. Cairo: American University in Cairo Press, 2009.

Birch, Nicholas. "Sufism in Turkey: The Next Big Thing." *Eurosianet.org*, June 22, 2010. http://www.eurasianet.org/node/61379.

Blair, Sheila S. "Sufi Saints and Shrine Architecture in the Early Fourteenth Century." *Muqarnas* 7 (1990): 35–49. http://www.jstor.org/stable/10.2307.

Bourdieu, Pierre. *The Logic of Practice*, trans. Richard Nice. Stanford: Stanford University Press, 1980.

Bozdoğan, Sibel and Reşat Kasaba. *Türkiye'de Modernleşme ve Ulusal Kimlik [Modernization in Turkey and National Identity]*. İstanbul: Tarih Vakfı Yurt Yayınları, 1998.

Brockett, Gavin D. "Collective Action and the Turkish Revolution: Towards a Framework for the Social History of the Atatürk Era 1923–1938." *Middle Eastern Studies* 34 (1998): 44–66.

Brosnahan, Tom. "Cultural Center, Konya." *Turkey Travel Planner*. http://www.turkeytravelplanner.com/go/CentralAnatolia/Konya/sights/kultur_merkezi.html.

Brown, Jonathan. *Hadith: Muhammad's Legacy in the Medieval and Modern World*. Oxford: Oneworld, 2009.

Brown, Michael F. "Safeguarding the Intangible." 2013. scholarworks.iu.edu/journals/index.php/mar/article/view/3167/2998.

———. "Heritage Trouble: Recent Work on the Protection of Intangible Cultural Property." *International Journal of Cultural Property* 12, no. 1 (2015): 40–61. https://doi.org/10.1017/S0940739105050010.

Browning, Barbara. *Samba: Resistance in Motion*. Bloomington: Indiana University Press, 1995.

Bruijn, Johannes Thomas Pieter. *Persian Sufi Poetry: An Introduction to the Mystical Use of Classical Poems*. Richmond: Curzon Press, 1997.

Burckhardt, Titus. *An Introduction to Sufi Doctrine*. Lahore: Sh. M. Ashraf, 1959.

Butler, Judith. "Performativity Acts and Gender Constitution: An Essay in Phenomenology and Feminist Criticism." *Theatre Journal* 40, no. 4 (1988): 519–531.
Çağaptay, Soner. "Race, Assimilation and Kemalism: Turkish Nationalism and the Minorities in the 1930s." *Middle Eastern Studies* 40, no. 3 (2004): 86–101.
———. *The Rise of Turkey: The Twenty-First Century's First Muslim Power*. Lincoln: Potomac Books and Imprint of University of Nebraska Press, 2014.
Çağlıyan-İçener, Zeyneb. "The Justice and Development Party's Conception of 'Conservative Democracy': Invention or Reinterpretation?" *Turkish Studies* 10, no. 4 (2009): 595–612.
Can, Şefik. *Fundamentals of Rumi's Thought*. Lanham: Tughra Books, 2006.
Cantlie, Audrey. "Divine Madness: Tantric Ascetics on the Cremation Ground in Tarapith, Birbhum District, West Bengal." In *Insanity and Divinity: Studies in Psychosis and Spirituality*, ed. John Gale, Michael Robson, and Georgia Rapsomatioti. London: Routledge, 2014.
Carlson, Marvin. *Performance: A Critical Introduction*. New York: Routledge, 2018.
Castañeda, Quetzil E. "The Invisible Theatre of Ethnography: Performative Principles of Fieldwork." *Anthropological Quarterly* 79, no. 1 (2006): 75–104.
Çelebi, Celaleddin Bakır. "Hz Mevlanaya Göre Sema [Sema According to Mevlana]." *Analiz Aylık Sektörel, Kültürel ve Siyasal Dergi* 1 (2008): 24–25.
Çepni, Ozan. "Güneydoğu Nurculara Kaldı [Southeast is in the Hands of Nurcus]." *Cumhuriyet*, February 13, 2018. http://www.cumhuriyet.com.tr/haber/egitim/925998/.
Çevikoğlu, Timuçin. *Sema'nın Sadası [Sema's Sound]*. İstanbul: Türkiye Finans Katılım Bankası Kültür Yayınları, 2008.
Chambers, Claire Marie, Simon W. Du Toit, and Joshua Edelman, eds. *Performing Religion in Public*. New York: Palgrave Macmillan, 2013.
Chattopadhyay, Saayan. "From Religion to Culture: The Performative Puja and Spectacular Religion in India." In *Performing Religion in Public*, ed. Claire Marie Chambers, Simon W. du Toit, and Joshua Edelman, 194–208. New York: Palgrave Macmillan, 2013.
Chih, Rachida. "What is a Sufi Order? Revisiting The Concept Through a Case Study of the Khalwatiyya in Contemporary Egypt." In *Sufism and the "Modern" in Islam*, ed. Martin Van Bruinessen and Julia Day Howell, 21–38. London: I.B. Tauris, 2007.
Chittick, William C. "The Perfect Man as the Prototype of the Self in the Sufism of Jami." *Studia Islamica* 49 (1979): 135–136.
———. *Sufi Path of Love: The Spiritual Teachings of Rumi*. Albany: State University of New York Press, 1983.
———. *Sufi Path of Knowledge: Ibn al-'Arabi's Metaphysics of Imagination*. Albany: State University of New York Press, 1989.
———. *Imaginal Worlds Ibn al-'Arabı and the Problem of Religious Diversity*. Albany: State University of New York Press, 1994.
———. *Me and Rumi: The Autobiography of Shams-i Tabrizi*. Louisville: Fons Vitae, 2004.
Çıtak, Zana. "Nationalism and Religion: A Comparative Study of the Development of Secularism in France and Turkey." PhD dissertation. Boston University, 2004.
———. "The Transformation of the State–Religion Relationship Under the Akp: The Case of the Diyanet in Turkey's New State in the Making." In *Turkey's New State in the Making: Transformations in Legality, Economy and Coercion*, ed. Pınar

Bedirhanoğlu, Çağlar Dölek, Funda Hülagü, and Özlem Kaygusuz. London: Zed Books, 2020.
Çıtlak, M. Fatih and Huseyin Bingul. *Rumi and his Sufi Path of Love*. Somerset: Light, 2007.
———. *40 Mektup [40 Letters]*. İstanbul: Sufi Kitap, 2010.
Cizmeci, Esra. "World as Sacred Stage for Sufi Ritual: Performance, Mobilization and Making Space with the Act of Whirling." *Dance, Movement & Spiritualities* 3, no. 3 (2016): 203. https://doi.org/10.1386/dmas.3.3.199_1.
Clarke, Morgan. "Cough Sweets and Angels: The Ordinary Ethics of the Extraordinary in Sufi Practice in Lebanon." *The Journal of the Royal Anthropological Institute* 20, no. 3 (2014): 407–425. http://www.jstor.org/stable/43907697.
Clifford, James. "Introduction: Partial Truths." In *Writing Culture: The Poetics and Politics of Ethnography: A School of American Research Advanced Seminar*, ed. James Clifford and George E. Marcus. Berkeley: University of California Press, 1986.
Çobanoğlu, Yavuz. *"Altın Nesil" in Peşinde: Fethullah Gülen'de Toplum, Devlet, Ahlak, Otorite [In Pursuit of "Golden Generation": Fethullah Gülen's Understanding of Society, State, Morality, Authority]*. Istanbul: İletişim, 2012.
Cohen, Emma. "What is Spirit Possession? Defining, Comparing, and Explaining Two Possession Forms." *Ethnos* 73, no. 1 (2008): 101–126. https://doi.org/10.1080/00141840 801927558.
Coleman, Simon and John Eade, eds. *Reframing Pilgrimage: Cultures in Motion*. London: Routledge, 2004.
Conquergood, Dwight. "Performing as a Moral Act: Ethical Dimensions of the Ethnography of Performance." *Literature in Performance* 2, no. 5 (1985): 1–13.
———. "Between Experience and Meaning: Performance as a Paradigm for Meaningful Action." In *Renewal and Revision: The Future of Interpretation*, ed. Ted Colson, 47–48. Denton: NB Omega, 1986.
———. "Health Theatre in a Hmong Refugee Camp." *TDR: The Drama Review* 32 (1988): 174–208.
———. "Rethinking Ethnography: Towards a Critical Cultural Politics." *Communication Monographs* 58 (1991): 179–194. Open-Frames.net, EBSCO Publishing, http://www.open-frames.net/pdf/145-Conquergood_19xx__rethinging_ethnogr aohy.pdf.
———. "Life in Big Red: Struggles and Accommodations in a Chicago Polyethnic Tenement." In *Structuring Diversity: Ethnographic Perspectives on the New Immigration*, ed. Louise Lamphere, 95–144. Chicago: University of Chicago Press, 1994.
———. "Performance Studies: Interventions and Radical Research." *TDR: The Drama Review* 46 (2002): 145–156.
———. "Rethinking Ethnography: Towards a Critical Cultural Politics." In *The Sage Handbook of Perfomance Studies*, ed. D.S. Madison and J. Hamera, 351–365. Thousand Oaks, CA: Sage Publication, 2006.
"The Constitution of the Republic of Turkey." http://www.hri.org/docs/turkey/con2b.html.
Cornell, Svante. "The Rise of Diyanet: The Politicization of Turkey's Directorate of Religious Affairs." *The Turkey Analyst*, October 9, 2015.
Correspondences, Dahiliye Vekili to Recep Peker, April 20, 1935, Türkiye Cumhuriyeti Arşiv Genel Başkanlığı [Republic of Turkey General Directorate of State Archives], 38.

Bibliography

Correspondences, Dahiliye Vekili to Recep Peker, May 4, 1935, Türkiye Cumhuriyeti Arşiv Genel Başkanlığı [Republic of Turkey General Directorate of State Archives], 38.

Correspondences, Dahiliye Vekili to Recep Peker, May 9, 1935, Türkiye Cumhuriyeti Arşiv Genel Başkanlığı [Republic of Turkey General Directorate of State Archives], 38.

Correspondences, Vilayet Idare Heyeti to Yüksek Genel Katipliğine, May 18, 1935, Türkiye Cumhuriyeti Arşiv Genel Başkanlığı [Republic of Turkey General Directorate of State Archives], 38.

Correspondences, Dahiliye Vekili to Recep Peker, January 1, 1936, Türkiye Cumhuriyeti Arşiv Genel Başkanlığı [Republic of Turkey General Directorate of State Archives], 38.

Correspondences, Dahiliye Vekili to Recep Peker, January 14, 1936, Türkiye Cumhuriyeti Arşiv Genel Başkanlığı [Republic of Turkey General Directorate of State Archives], 38.

Correspondences, Başvekil to Milli Müdafaa Vekilliği, December 5, 1941, Türkiye Cumhuriyeti Arşiv Genel Correspondences, Başkanlığı [Republic of Turkey General Directorate of State Archives], 318.

Csordas, Thomas J. "Embodiment as a Paradigm for Anthropology." *Ethos* 18, no. 1 (1990): 5–47.

De Certeau, Michel. *The Practice of Everyday Life*. Berkeley: University of California Press, 1984.

De Jong, Frederick. "The Sufi Orders in Nineteenth and Twentieth-Century Palestine: A Preliminary Survey Concerning Their Identity, Organizational Characteristics and Continuity." *Studia Islamica* 58 (1983): 149–181. http://www.jstor.org/stable/10.2307.

De Jong, Frederick and Bernd Radtke, eds. *Islamic Mysticism Contested: Thirteen Centuries of Controversies and Polemics*. Leiden, NL: Brill, 1999.

de Meyerovitch, Eva. *Rûmî and Sufism*. Sausalito: Post-Apollo Press, 1987.

Deflem, Mathieu. "Ritual, Anti-Structure, and Religion: A Discussion of Victor Turner's Processual Symbolic Analysis." *Journal for the Scientific Study of Religion* 30, no. 1 (1991): 1–25.

Dein, Simon and Abdool Samad Illaiee. "Jinn and Mental Health: Looking at Jinn Possession in Modern Psychiatric Practice." *The Psychiatrist* 37, no. 9 (2013). https://doi.org/10.1192/pb.bp.113.042721.

Delibas, K. "Conceptualizing Islamic Movements: The Case of Turkey." *International Political Science Review* 30, no. 1 (2009): 89–103.

Demirağ, Yelda. "Osmanlı İmparatorluğunda Yaşayan Azınlıkların Sosyal Ve Ekonomik Durumları [Social and Economic Conditions of Minorities of the Ottoman Empire]." *OTAM (Ankara Üniversitesi Osmanlı Tarihi Araştırma ve Uygulama Merkezi Dergisi)*, no. 13 (2002): 32. http://doi:10.1501/otam_0000000481.

Demiralp, Seda. "The Rise of Islamic Capital and the Decline of Islamic Radicalism in Turkey." *Comparative Politics* 41, no. 3 (2009): 315–335.

Deren, Seçil. "Kültürel Batılılaşma." In *Modern Türkiye 'de Siyası Düşünce-Modernleşme ve Batıcılık [Political Thought in Modern Turkey: Modernisation and Westernism]*. Istanbul: İletişim, 2004.

Derrida, Jacques. "Signature Event Context." In *Margins of Philosophy*, trans. Alans Bass. Chicago: University of Chicago Press, 1982.

Dickerman, Watson B. "Whirling Dervishes." *Theatre Arts Monthly* 18, no. 1 (1934): 67–72.

Dillon, Michele. "The Authority of the Holy Revisited: Habermas, Religion, and Emancipatory Possibilities." *Sociological Theory* 17, no. 3 (1999): 290–306.

Dodds, Eric R. *The Greeks and the Irrational*. Berkeley: University of California Press, 1951.

Dols, Michael W. *Majnun: The Madman in Medieval Islamic Society*. Oxford: Clarendon Press, 1992.

Dominguez-Diaz, Marta. *Women in Sufism: Female Religiosities in a Transnational Order*. London and New York: Routledge, 2014.

Donkor, David. "Performance, Ethnography and the Radical Intervention of Dwight Conquergood." *Cultural Studies* 21, no. 6 (2007): 821–825.

Dossey, Larry. "Deliberately Caused Bodily Damage." *Alternative Therapies in Health and Medicine* 4, no. 5 (1998).

Drewal, Margaret Thompson. "The State of Research on Performance in Africa." *African Studies Review* 34, no. 3 (1991): 1–64.

———. *Yoruba Ritual: Performers, Play, Agency*. Bloomington: Indiana University Press, 1992.

Durgun, Gonca Bayraktar and Emrah Beriş. "Civil Society and Perspectives on Turkish-American Relations." In *Turkish-US Relations: Perspectives from Ankara*, ed. Ralph Salmi and Gonca Bayraktar Durgun. Boca Raton, FL: Brown Walker Press, 2005.

Durkheim, Emile. *The Division of Labor in Society*, trans. George Simpson. Mansfield Centre: Martino Publishing, 2012.

El-Aswad, El-Sayed. "Spiritual Genealogy: Sufism and Saintly Places in the Nile Delta." *International Journal of Middle East Studies* 38, no. 4 (2006): 501–518.

Eligür, Banu. *The Mobilization of Political Islam in Turkey*. Cambridge: Cambridge University Press, 2010.

Emre, Yunus. *The Drop that Became the Sea: Lyric Poems of Yunus Emre*, trans. Kabir Helminski and Refik Algan. Boston: Shambhala, 1989.

Ergene, M. Enes. *Geleneğin Modern Çağa Tanıklığı: Gülen Hareketinin Analizi [Tradition Witnessing to the Modern Age: Analysis of the Gülen Movement]*. İstanbul: Yeni Akademi Yayınları, 2005.

Ergüner, Kudsi. *Journeys of a Sufi Musician*. London: Saqi, 2005.

Erman, Tahire and Emrah Göker. "Alevi Politics in Contemporary Turkey." *Middle Eastern Studies* 36, no. 4 (2000): 99–118.

Ernst, Carl W. *Words of Ecstasy in Sufism*. Albany: State University of New York, 1985.

———. *The Shambhala Guide to Sufism*. Boston: Shambhala Press, 1997.

———. *Following Muhammad: Rethinking Islam in the Contemporary World*. Chapel Hill: University of North Carolina Press, 2003.

Ernst, Carl W. and Bruce B. Lawrence. *Sufi Martyrs of Love: Chishti Sufism in South Asia and Beyond*. New York: Palgrave Macmillan, 2002.

Esposito, John L. and Natana J. DeLong-Bas. *Shariah: What Everyone Needs to Know*. Oxford: Oxford University Press, 2018.

Ete, Hatem and Coşkun Taştan. *The Gezi Park Protests: A Political, Sociological and Discursive Analysis*. Ankara: SETA Foundation for Political, Economic and Social Research, 2014.

Ewing, Katherine. "The Politics of Sufism: Redefining the Saints of Pakistan." *Journal of Asian Studies* 42, no. 2 (1983): 251–268.

Eyüboğlu, Sabahattin. *Yunus Emre*. İstanbul: Cem Yayınevi, 1975.

Fadiman, James and Robert Frager. *Essential Sufism*. San Francisco: Harper San Francisco, 1997.
Fedman, Walter. "Structure and Evolution of the Mevlevi Ayin: The Case of the Third Selam." In *Sufism Music and Society: In Turkey and the Middle East, Part III: Structure and Evolution, Swedish Research Institute in Istanbul Transaction*, ed. Andres Hammarlund, Tord Olsson, and Elisabeth Özdalga. London: Routledge and Curzon Press, 2001.
Findley, Carter V. *Turkey, Islam, Nationalism, and Modernity: A History, 1789–2007*. New Haven: Yale University Press, 2010.
Fischer-Lichte, Erika. *The Transformative Power of Performance*, trans. Saskya Iris Jain. London: Routledge, 2009.
Flyvbjerg, Bent. "Habermas and Foucault: Thinkers for Civil Society?" *The British Journal of Sociology* 49, no. 2 (1998): 210–233.
Foley, Sean. "The Naqshbandiyya-Khalidiyya, Islamic Sainthood, and Religion in Modern Times." *Journal of World History* 19, no. 4 (2008): 521–545.
Foster, Susan Leigh. "Walking and Other Choreographic Tactics: Danced Inventions of Theatricality and Performativity." *SubStance* 31, no. 2/3 (2002): 125–146.
Foucault, Michel. "Of Other Spaces." *Diacritics* 16, no. 1 (1986): 22–27.
Fox, Jonathan. "Do Democracies Have Separation of Religion and State?" *Canadian Journal of Political Science/Revue Canadienne De Science Politique* 40, no. 1 (2007): 1–25.
Fraser, Nancy. "Rethinking the Public Sphere: A Contribution to the Critique of Actually Existing Democracy." In *Habermas and the Public Sphere*, ed. Craig J. Calhoun, 109–142. Cambridge: MIT Press, 1992.
Freeland, Felicia. *Recasting Ritual Performance, Media, Identity*. London: Routledge, 1998.
Frembgen, Jürgen Wasim. "The Majzub Mama Ji Sarkar: A Friend of God Moves from One House to Another." In *Embodying Charisma: Saints, Cults and Muslim Shrines in South Asia*, ed. Pnina Werbner and Helen Basu. London: Routledge, 1998.
Friedlander, Shems. *Rumi and the Whirling Dervishes*. New York: Parabola Books, 2003.
Frishkopf, Michael. "Authorship in Sufi Poetry/الشعر في الصوفي/المؤلف الشعر في." *Alif: Journal of Comparative Poetics*, no. 23 (2003): 108–178. http://www.jstor.org/stable/10.2307.
Fuchs, Ebaugh and Helen Rose. *The Gülen Movement: A Sociological Analysis of a Civic Movement Rooted in Moderate Islam*. London: Springer, 2010.
Fuchs, Elinor. "Staging the Obscene Body." *TDR: The Drama Review* 33, no. 1 (1989): 33.
Fuller, Robert C. *Spiritual but Not Religious: Understanding Unchurched America*. Oxford: Oxford University Press, 2001.
Gaborieau, Marc. "What Is Left of Sufism in Tablîghî Jamâ'at?" *Archives De Sciences Sociales Des Religions* 51, no. 135 (2006): 53–72. http://www.jstor.org/stable/10.2307.
Gardner, Katy. *Global Migrants Local Lives: Travels and Transformation in Rural Bangladesh*. Oxford: Clarendon Press, 1995.
Geaves, Ron, Markus Dressler, and Gritt Maria Klinkhammer, eds. *Sufis in Western Society: Global Networking and Locality*. London and New York: Routledge, 2009.

Geaves, Ron and Theodore P.C. Gabriel, eds. *Sufism in Britain*. New York: Bloomsbury Academic, 2013.
Geertz, Clifford. *The Interpretation of Cultures: Selected Essays*. New York: Basic Books, 1973.
———. "The Pitfalls of Cultural Analysis." In *The Interpretation of Cultures*. New York: Basic Books, 2000.
Gellner, Ernest. *Muslim Society*. Cambridge: Cambridge University Press, 1981.
Genn, Celia A. "The Development of a Modern Western Sufism." In *Sufism and the "Modern" in Islam*, ed. Martin Van Bruinessen and Julie Day Howell, 257–278. London: I.B. Tauris, 2013.
Gharavi, Lance. *Religion, Theatre, and Performance: Acts of Faith*. New York: Routledge, 2012.
Gilsenan, Michael. *Saints and Sufis in Modern Egypt: An Essay in the Sociology of Religion*. Oxford: Clarendon Press, 1973.
———. *Recognizing Islam: An Anthropologist's Introduction*. London: Croom Helm, 1982.
Glasse, Cyril. *The New Encyclopedia of Islam*. Lanham: Rowman & Littlefield Publishers, 2008.
Goffman, Erving. *The Presentation of Self in Everyday Life*. Edinburgh: University of Edinburg, 1956.
Gohrab, Ali-Asghar Seyyed. "Sufism in Classical Persian Poetry." In *Routledge Handbook on Sufism*, ed. Lloyd Ridgeon. New York: Routledge, 2020.
Goldberg, Roselee. *Performance Art from Futurism to the Present*. New York: H.N. Abrams, 1988.
Göle, Nilüfer. *The Forbidden Modern, Civilization and Veiling*. Ann Arbor: University of Michigan Press, 1996.
———. "Secularism and Islamism in Turkey: The Making Elites and Counter-Elites." *Middle East Journal* 51, no. 1 (1997): 52–53.
———. "Civilizational, Spatial, and Sexual Powers of the Secular." In *Varieties of Secularism in a Secular Age*, ed. Michael Warner, Jonathan Van Antwerpen, and Craig J. Calhoun, 243–264. Cambridge: Harvard University Press, 2010.
Gölpınarlı, Abdülbaki. *Mevlana'dan Sonra Mevlevilik [Mevleviyeh after Mevlana]*. Istanbul: İnkilap Kitabevi, 1953.
Gordon, Mel. "Gurdjieff's Movement Demonstrations: The Theatre of the Miraculous." *TDR: The Drama Review* 22, no. 2 (1978): 32–44. http://www.jstor.org/stable/10.2307.
Gould, Kevin. "Konya, in a Whirl of its Own." *The Guardian*, accessed July 5, 2013. http://www.theguardian.com/travel/2010/apr/10/konya-turkey-jelaluddin-rumi-dervish.
Green, Doris. "The African Corner: Drum Talk." *Attitude Magazine* 8, no. 4 (1992).
Green, Nile. "Geography, Empire and Sainthood in the Eighteenth-Century Muslim Deccan." *Bulletin of the School of Oriental and African Studies* 67, no. 2 (2004): 207–225.
Gregg, Heather Selma. *The Path to Salvation: Religious Violence from the Crusades to Jihad*. Lincoln: Potomac Books, University of Nebraska Press, 2014.
Gribetz, Arthur. "The Samā Controversy: Sufi vs. Legalist." *Studia Islamica* 74 (1991): 43–62. http://www.jstor.org/stable/10.2307.
Grigoriadis, Ioannis N. "Islam and Democratization in Turkey: Secularism and Trust in a Divided Society." In *Religion and Democratizations*, ed. Jeffrey Haynes. London: Routledge, 2011.

Grimes, Ronald. *The Craft of Ritual Studies*. Oxford: Oxford University Press, 2014.
Gülalp, Haldun. "Globalization and Political Islam: The Social Bases of Turkey's Welfare Party." *International Journal of Middle East Studies* 33, no. 3 (2001): 433–448.
Gürbilek, Nurdan. *The New Cultural Climate in Turkey: Living in a Shop Window*. London: Zed Books, 2011.
Gurdjieff, G.I. *Views from the Real World*. New York: Dutton, 1973.
Habermas, Jurgen. "Religion in the Public Sphere." *European Journal of Philosophy* 14, no. 1 (2006): 1–25.
———. *Europe: The Faltering Project*. Cambridge: Polity, 2009.
———. *An Awareness of What is Missing: Faith and Reason in a Post-Secular Age*, trans. Ciaran Cronin. Cambridge: Polity, 2010.
———. "'The Political': The Rational Meaning of a Questionable Inheritance of Political Theology." In *The Power of Religion in the Public Sphere*, ed. Eduardo Mendieta and Jonathan Van Antwerpen, 15–33. New York: Columbia University Press, 2011.
Habibis, Daphne. "Change and Continuity: A Sufi Order in Contemporary Lebanon." *Social Analysis: The International Journal of Social and Cultural Practice*, no. 31 (1992): 44–78. http://www.jstor.org/stable/10.2307.
Haeri, Shaykh Fadhlalla. *The Elements of Sufism*. Longmead: Element Books, 1990.
Hagen, G. "Dina Le Gall, A Culture of Sufism: Naqshbandis in the Ottoman World, 1450." *Journal of Semitic Studies* 52, no. 2 (2007): 412–414.
Hall, Howard. "Sufism and Healing." In *Neuroscience, Consciousness and Spirituality*, ed. Harald Walach, Stefan Schmidt, and Wayne B. Jonas, 263–278. Dordrecht, Netherlands: Springer, 2014.
Halman, Talat Sait and Metin And. *Mevlana Celaleddin Rumi and The Whirling Dervishes*. Istanbul: Dost Yayinlari, 2005.
Hammarlund, Anders, Tord Olsson, and Elisabeth Özdalga, eds. *Sufism, Music and Society in Turkey and the Middle East: Papers Read at a Conference Held at the Swedish Research Institute in Istanbul, November 27–29, 1997*. Istanbul: Swedish Research Institute in Istanbul, 2001.
Hammer, Olav. "Sufism for Westerners" In *Sufism in Europe and North America*, ed. David Westerlund. London: Routledge and Curzon Press, 2004.
Harmless, William. *Mystics*. Oxford: Oxford University Press, 2008.
Harrison, Rodney. "Multicultural and Minority Heritage." In *Understanding Heritage and Memory*, ed. Tim Benton, 164–201. Manchester: Manchester University Press, 2010.
Harvey, David. *The Urbanization of Capital: Studies in the History and Theory of Capitalist Urbanization*. Baltimore, MD: Johns Hopkins University Press, 1985.
———. *Spaces of Hope*. Edinburgh: Edinburgh University Press, 2000.
Hashmi, Sohail H. "The Problem of Poverty in Islamic Ethics." In *Poverty and Morality: Religious and Secular Perspectives*, ed. William A. Galston and Peter H. Hoffenberg. Cambridge: Cambridge University Press, 2010.
Hatina, Meir. "Religious Culture Contested: The Sufi Ritual of Dawsa in Nineteenth-Century Cairo." *Die Welt Des Islams* 47, no. 1 (2007): 33–62.
Hayden, Dolores. *The Power of Place*. Cambridge, MA: MIT Press, 1995.
Heath, Pamela Rae. *The PK Zone: A Cross-Cultural Review of Psychokinesis (PK)*. Jefferson: iUniverse, 2003.

———. *Mind-Matter Interaction: Historical Reports, Research and Firsthand Accounts*. Jefferson, NC: McFarland, 2010.
Heck, Paul L. "Mysticism as Morality: The Case of Sufism." *The Journal of Religious Ethics* 34, no. 2 (2006): 253–286. http://www.jstor.org/stable/10.2307.
———. "Sufism—What is It Exactly?" *Religion Compass* 1, no. 1 (2007).
Hefner, Robert W. "Public Islam and the Problem of Democratization." *Sociology of Religion* 62, no. 4 (2001): 491–514.
Hegland, Mary Elaine. "Shi'a Women's Rituals in Northwest Pakistan: The Shortcomings and Significance of Resistance." *Anthropological Quarterly* 76, no. 3 (2003): 411–442.
Hendrich, Béatrice. "Contemporary Sufism and the Quest for Spirituality Transgressing Borders, Transgressing Categories." *European Journal of Turkish Studies Social Sciences on Contemporary Turkey* (2011). https://doi.org/10.4000/ejts.4523.
Heper, Metin. "Islam, Polity and Society in Turkey: A Middle Eastern Perspective." *Middle East Journal* 35, no. 3 (1981): 345–363. http://www.jstor.org/stable/10.2307.
———. "Islam and Democracy in Turkey: Toward a Reconciliation." *Middle East Journal* 51, no. 1 (1997): 32–45.
Hering, Doris. "The Whirling Dervishes of Turkey." *Dance Magazine* 71, no. 5 (1997): 76.
Hermansen, Marcia. "What's American about American Sufi Movements?" In *Sufism in Europe and North America*, ed. David Westerlund. London and New York: Routledge and Curzon Press, 2004.
———. "Introduction." In *Varieties of American Sufism: Islam, Sufi Orders, and Authority in a Time of Transition*, ed. Elliott Bazzano and Marcia Hermanse. Albany: State University of New York Press, 2020.
Hodgson, Marshall. *The Venture of Islam 1: Conscience and History in a World Civilization*, 3 vols. Chicago: University of Chicago Press, 1974.
Hoffman, Valerie J. "Eating and Fasting for God in Sufi Tradition." *Journal of the American Academy of Religion* 63, no. 3 (1995): 465–484. http://www.jstor.org/stable/10.2307.
Howell, Julia Day. "Sufism and the Indonesian Islamic Revival." *Journal of Asian Studies* 60, no. 3 (2001): 701–729.
Hurd, Elizabeth Shakman. "Negotiating Europe: The Politics of Religion and the Prospects for Turkish Accession." *Review of International Studies* 32, no. 3 (2006): 401–418.
Hutson, Alaine S. "Women, Men, and Patriarchal Bargaining in an Islamic Sufi Order: The Tijaniyya in Kano, Nigeria, 1937 to the Present." *Gender and Society* 15, no. 5 (2001): 734–753. http://www.jstor.org/stable/10.2307.
"In Turkey, Sufi Music is Used to Decrease Patient Stress." Accessed September 30, 2013. http://www.pri.org/stories/2012-04-27/turkey-sufi-music-used-decrease-patient-stress#.
İnalcık, Halil. "Tarihsel Bağlamda Sivil Toplum ve Tarikatlar." In *Global-Yerel Ekseninde Türkiye*, ed. Fuat Keyman and Ali Yasar Sarıbay. Istanbul: ALFA Press, 2005.
———. *Doğu Batı: Makaleler I [East West: Articles I]*. Ankara: Doğu Batı Yayınları, 2006.
İnan, Abdülkadir. *Eski Türk Dini Tarihi*. Istanbul: Kültür Bakanlığı, 1976.

İnan, Mert. "Mevleviler 'Stajyer Postnişin'e Tepkili." *Milliyet*, July 28, 2020. https://www.milliyet.com.tr/gundem/mevleviler-stajyer-postnisine-tepkili-6269897.
İnançer, Ömer Tuğrul. *Sohbetler [Conversations]*. İstanbul: Keşkül Yayınları, 2006.
İnançer, Ömer Tuğrul and Kenan Gürsoy. *Gönül Gözü [Heart's Eye]*. Istanbul: Sufi Kitap, 2006.
İnançer, Tuğrul. "Rituals and Main Principles of Sufism During the Ottoman Empire." In *Sufism and Sufis in Ottoman Society: Sources, Doctrine, Rituals, Turuq, Architecture, Literature and Fine Arts, Modernism*, ed. Ahmet Yaşar, 123–182. Ankara: Atatürk Supreme Council for Culture, Language and History, 2005.
"İnançer'in Sözleri Meclis Gündeminde." *Hürriyet*, Eylül 24, 2013. http://www.hurriyet.com.tr/gundem/24768154.asp.
Ingram, David. "Between Political Liberalism and Postnational Cosmopolitanism: Toward an Alternative Theory of Human Rights." *Political Theory* 31, no. 3 (2003): 359–391.
Iqbal, Afzal. "Mevlānā Rūmī on the Perfect Man." *Islamic Studies* 30, no. 3 (1991): 353–384. http://www.jstor.org/stable/10.2307.
Işık, Emin. *Belh'in güvercinleri: Mevlana Celaleddin Rumi*. İstanbul: Ötüken, 2008.
———. *Aşkı Meşk Etmek*. Istanbul: Sufi Kitap, 2010.
Izutso, Toshiko. *Hy*. Berkeley: University of California Press, 1983.
Jackson, Michael. "Knowledge of the Body." *Man* 18, no. 2 (1983): 327–345. http://www.jstor.org/stable/10.2307.
Jafari, Mumtaz F. "Counseling Values and Objectives: A Comparison of Western and Islamic Perspectives." *The American Journal of Islamic Social Sciences* 10 (1993): 326–339.
Jones, Joni L. "Performance Ethnography: The Role of Embodiment in Cultural Authenticity." *Theatre Topics* 12, no. 1 (2002): 1–15.
Jones, W. Paul, *Trumpet at Full Moon: Introduction to Christian Spirituality as Diverse Practice*. Louisville, KY: Westminster and John Knox, 1992.
Jowett, Benjamin. *The Dialogues of Plato*, vol. 1. Oxford: Clarendon Press, 1871.
Jung, Carl G. *The Red Book, Liber Novus*, ed. Sonu Shamdasani, trans. Sonu Shamdasani, John Peck, and Mike Kyburz. New York and London: Norton and Company, 2009.
Kafadar, Cemal. "Self and Others: The Diary of a Dervish in Seventeenth Century Istanbul and First-Person Narratives in Ottoman Literature." *Studia Islamica* 69 (1989): 121–150. http://www.jstor.org/stable/10.2307.
———. "The New Visibility of Sufism in Turkish Studies and Cultural Life." In *The Dervish Lodge: Architecture, Art and Sufism in Ottoman Turkey*, ed. Raymond Lifchez, 307–322. Berkeley: University of California Press, 1992.
Kapferer, Bruce. *A Celebration of Demons: Exorcism and the Aesthetics of Healing in Sri Lanka*. Bloomington: Indiana University Press, 1983.
Kaplan, M. *Türk Edebiyatı Üzerinde Araştırmalar: Tip Tahlilleri [Research on Turkish Literature]*. İstanbul: Dergah Publications, 1985.
Karabulut, Savaş. "A Comparative Study on Asceticism in Buddhism and Islam." Master's thesis. Seoul National University, Seoul, South Korea, 2008.
Karamustafa, Ahmet T. *God's Unruly Friends: Dervish Groups in the Islamic Later Middle Period, 1200–1550*. Salt Lake City: University of Utah Press, 1994.
———. *Sufism: The Formative Period*. Berkeley: University of California Press, 2007.
Karasipahi, Sena. "Comparing Islamic Resurgence Movement in Turkey and Iran." *Middle East Journal* 63, no. 1 (2009): 87–107.

Kasapoğlu, M. Aytül and Mehmet C. Ecevit. "Culture and Social Structure: Identity in Turkey." *Human Studies* 27 (2004).

Kaya, Emir. *Secularism and State Religion in Modern Turkey: Law, Policy-Making and the Diyanet*. London and New York: I.B. Tauris, 2018.

Kazmi, Yedullah. "Faith and Knowledge in Islam: An Essay in Philosophy of Religion." *Islamic Studies* 38, no. 4 (1999): 503–534. http://www.jstor.org/stable/10.2307.

"Kemalism." *OED Online*, 2013. http://www.oed.com/view/Entry/102863?redirectedFrom=kemalist.

Keyman, Emin Fuat. *Global/Yerel Ekseninde Türkiye*, 1st ed. İstanbul: ALFA, 2000.

Keyman, Emin Fuat and Berrin Koyuncu. "Globalization, Alternative Modernities and the Political Economy of Turkey." *Review of International Political Economy* 12, no. 1 (2005): 105–128.

Kia, Mehrdad. *The Ottoman Empire: A Historical Encyclopedia*, vol. 2. Santa Barbara: ABC-CLIO, LLC, 2017.

Kili, Suna. "Kemalism in Contemporary Turkey." *International Political Science Review* 1, no. 3 (1980): 381–404.

Kılınç, Nirgül. "Mevlevi Sema Ritual Outfits and Their Mystical Meanings." *New World Sciences Academy* 6, no. 4 (2011): 814.

Kim, Heon Choul. "The Nature and Role of Sufism in Contemporary Islam: A Case Study of the Life, Thought and Teachings of Fethullah Gulen." PhD dissertation. Temple University, 2008.

King, James Roy. "Religious and Therapeutic Elements in Sufi Teaching Stories." *Journal of Religion & Health* 27, no. 3 (1988): 221–235.

Kinzer, Stephen. *Crescent and Star: Turkey Between Two Worlds*. New York: Farrar, Straus and Giroux, 2001.

Kirshenblatt-Gimblett, Barbara. "Theorizing Heritage." *Ethnomusicology* 39, no. 3 (1995): 367–380.

———. *Destination Culture: Tourism, Museums, and Heritage*. Berkeley: University of California Press, 1998.

Kısakürek, Necip Fazıl. *Konuşmalar [Conversations]*, 82–128. İstanbul: Büyük Doğu Yayınları, 1999.

Knysh, Alexander. *Al-Qushayri's Epistle on Sufism*. Reading: Garnet, 2007.

———. *Sufism: A New History of Islamic Mysticism*. Princeton: Princeton University Press, 2017.

Koç, Doğan. *Strategic Defamation of Fethullah Gülen: English vs. Turkish*. Lanham: University Press of America, 2012.

Kocaman, Recep Ender. *Ariflerin Gül Bahçesi, Rahmanın Konusu [Rose Gardens of Wise Men, Subject of The Compassionate]*. İzmir: Dizgi Montaj Baskı, 1993.

Kolawole, Ositola. "On Ritual Performance: A Practitioner's View." *TDR: The Drama Review* 32, no. 2 (1988): 31–41.

Köni, Hakan. *Transformation of Political Islam in Turkey: Causes and Effects*. Newcastle upon Tyne: Cambridge Scholars Publishing, 2019.

Köprülü, Mehmet Fuat. *Osmanlı İmparatorluğunun Kuruluşu [Establishing of the Ottoman Empire]*. Ankara: Türk Tarih Kurumu Publications, 1929 (1972).

Küçük, Hülya. "Sufi Reactions After Turkey's National Struggle." In *The State and The Subaltern: Modernization, Society and the State in Turkey and Iran*, ed. Touraj Atabaki, 123–143. London: I.B. Tauris, 2007.

Kuhn, Thomas S. *The Structure of Scientific Revolution*. Chicago: University of Chicago Press, 1996.

Kuran, Timur. "Islam and Underdevelopment: An Old Puzzle Revisited." *Journal of Institutional and Theoretical Economics* 153, no. 1 (1997): 41–71. http://www.jstor.org/stable/10.2307.

Kuru, Ahmet T. "Globalization and Diversification of Islamic Movements: Three Turkish Cases." *Political Science Quarterly* 120, no. 2 (2005): 253–274.

Kuru, Zeynep Akbulut and Ahmet Kuru. "Apolitical Interpretation of Islam: Said Nursi's Faith-Based Activism in Comparison with Political Islamism and Sufism." *Islam and Christian-Muslim Relations* 19, no. 1 (2008): 99–111.

Kutlu, Sönmez. "The Presidency of Religious Affairs' Relationship with Religious Groups (Sects/Sufi Orders) in Turkey." *The Muslim World* 98, no. 2–3 (2008): 249–263.

Kuzmanovic, Daniella. *Refractions of Civil Society in Turkey*. New York: Palgrave Macmillan, 2012.

Laan, Nina Ter. "Performing Dhikr above a Nightclub: The Interplay of Commerce and Spirituality at the Fez Festival of Sufi Culture." *Performing Islam* 1, no. 1 (2012): 161–170.

Lapidus, I.M. "State and Religion in Islamic Societies." *Past & Present* 151, no. 1 (1996): 3–27.

Leask, Josephine. "Ecstatic Rituals." *Dance Theatre Journal* 13, no. 3 (1997): 138–139.

Lefebvre, Henri. *The Production of Space*, trans. Donald Nicholson Smith. Oxford: Basil Blackwell, 1991.

Leonardo, Micaela Di. "Dwight Conquergood, Political Economy, Performance Studies." *Cultural Studies* 21, no. 6 (2007): 810–814.

Levine, Michael P. *Pantheism: A Non-Theistic Concept of Deity*. New York: Routledge, 2014.

Levtzion, Nehemia and John O. Voll. *Eighteenth-Century Renewal and Reform in Islam*. Syracuse: Syracuse University Press, 1987.

Lewis, Bernard. *The Emergence of Modern Turkey*, 2nd ed. Oxford: Oxford University Press, 1968.

———. "The Faith and the Faithful." In *The World of Islam: Faith, People, Culture*, ed. Bernard Lewis, 1–24. London: Thames and Hudson, 1992a.

———. *The World of Islam: Faith, People, Culture*. New York: Thames and Hudson, 1992b.

———. *The Middle East: A Brief History of the Last 2,000 Years*. New York: Scribner, 1995.

Lewis, Franklin D. *Rumi, Past and Present, East and West: The Life, Teaching and Poetry of Jalal Al-Din Rumi*. Oxford: Oneworld, 2001.

Lewis, Ioan M. *Ecstatic Religion: A Study of Shamanism and Spirit Possession*. New York: Routledge, 1989.

Lichte, Erika. *The Transformative Power of Performance: A New Aesthetics*. New York: Routledge, 2008.

Lifchez, Raymond, ed. *The Dervish Lodge: Architecture, Art, and Sufism in Ottoman Turkey*. Berkeley: University of California Press, 1992.

Littlewood, Roland. "Possession States." *Psychiatry* 3, no. 8 (2004). https://doi.org/10.1383/psyt.3.8.8.43392.

Long, David E. *The Hajj Today: A Survey of the Contemporary Pilgrimage to Makkah*. Albany: State University of New York, 1979.

Lord, Ceren. *Religious Politics in Turkey: From the Birth of the Republic to the AKP*. Cambridge: Cambridge University Press, 2018.

Low, Setha and Denise Lawrence-Zúñiga. *The Anthropology of Space and Place: Locating Culture*. Malden, MA: Blackwell, 2001.
Lughod, Lila. *Veiled Sentiments: Honor and Poetry in Bedouin Society*. Berkeley: University of California Press, 2000.
Lukoff, David. "Visionary Spiritual Experiences." In *Psychosis and Spirituality*, ed. Isabel Clarke. Sussex: Wiley and Blackwell, 2010.
Lymer, Kenneth. "Rags and Rock Art: The Landscapes of Holy Site Pilgrimage in the Republic of Kazakhstan." *World Archeology* 36, no. 1 (2004): 158–172.
MacKenna, Christopher. "Jung's Divine Madness." In *Insanity and Divinity: Studies in Psychosis and Spirituality*, ed. John Gale, Michael Robson, and Georgia Rapsomatioti. London: Routledge, 2014.
Madison, D. Soyini. *Critical Ethnography: Method, Ethics and Performance*. Los Angeles: Sage Publications, 2011.
Magnat, Virginie. "Theatricality from the Performative Perspective." *SubStance* 31, no. 2/3 (2002): 147–166.
Mahmood, Saba. "Rehearsed Spontaneity and the Conventionality of Ritual: Disciplines of Salat." *American Ethnologist* 28, no. 4 (2001): 827–853.
Malamud, M. "Gender and Spiritual Self-Fashioning: The Master-Disciple Relationship in Classical Sufism." *Journal of the American Academy of Religion* 64, no. 1 (1996): 89–117.
Malik, Jamal and Saeed Zarrabi-Zadeh, eds. *Sufism East and West: Mystical Islam and Cross-Cultural Exchange in the Modern World*. Leiden and Boston: Brill, 2019.
Mantran, Robert. *İstanbul Tarihi [History of İstanbul]*. Istanbul: İletisim, 2001.
Mardin, Şerif, ed. *Religion and Social Change in Modern Turkey: The Case of Bediuzzaman Saidi Nursi*. Albany: State University of New York Press, 1989.
———. "The Nakşibendi Order in Turkish History." In *Islam in Modern Turkey: Religion, Politics and Literature in a Secular State*, ed. Richard Tapper. London and New York: I.B. Tauris, 1991a.
———. "Religion and Secularism in Turkey." In *Atatürk: Founder of a Modern State*, ed. Ali Kazancıgil and Ergün Özbudun. London: Archon Books, 1991b.
———. *Din ve İdeoloji*. İstanbul: İletişim Publishing House, 1995.
———. "Turkish Islamic Exceptionalism Yesterday and Today: Continuity, Rupture and Reconstruction in Operational Codes." *Turkish Studies* 6, no. 2 (2005): 145–165.
———. *Türkiye, İslam ve Sekülarizm: Makaleler 5 [Turkey, Islam and Secularism: Articles 5]*. İstanbul: İletişim Yayınları, 2011.
Markoff, Irene. "Introduction to Sufi Music and Ritual in Turkey." *Middle East Studies Association Bulletin* 29, no. 2 (1995): 157–160. http://www.jstor.org/stable/10.2307.
Marks, Alexandra. "Persian Poet Top Seller in America Rumi Revival." *The Christian Science Monitor*, November 25, 1997. http://www.csmonitor.com/1997/1125/112597.us.us.3.html.
Marshall, Douglas A. "Behavior, Belonging, and Belief: A Theory of Ritual Practice." *Sociology Theory* 20, no. 3 (2002): 360–380.
Martin, Emily. "The Potentiality of Ethnography and the Limits of Affect Theory." *Current Anthropology* 54, no. 7 (2013): 149–158.
Massignon, Louis. *Essay on the Origin of the Technical Language of Islamic Mysticism*, trans. Benjamin Clark. Notre Dame, Indiana: University of Notre Dame Press, 1997.

Mcauley, Gay. "Interdisciplinary Field or Emerging Discipline? Performance Studies at the University of Sydney." In *Contesting Performance: Global Sites of Research*, ed. Jon McKenzie, Heike Roms, and C.J.W.L. Wee, 37–50. Basingstoke: Palgrave Macmillan, 2010.

Mcconachie, Bruce. "An Evolutionary Perspective on Play, Performance, and Ritual." *TDR: The Drama Review* 55, no. 4 (2011): 33–50.

McKernan, Bethan. "Erdoğan Leads First Prayers at Hagia Sophia Museum Reverted to Mosque." *The Guardian*, July 4, 2020. https://www.theguardian.com/world/2020/jul/24/erdogan-prayers-hagia-sophia-museum-turned-mosque.

Melchert, Christopher. "Origins and Early Sufism." In *Cambridge Companion to Sufism*, ed. Lloyd Ridgeon. New York: Cambridge University Press, 2015.

———. *Before Sufism: Early Islamic Renunciant Piety*. Berlin: De Gruyter, 2020. https://doi.org/10.1515/9783110617962.

Mendieta, Eduardo and Jonathan Vanantwerpen, eds. *The Power of Religion in the Public Sphere*. New York: Columbia University Press, 2011.

Meschonnic, Henri, Gabriella Bedetti, and Alice Ottis. "Modernity Modernity." *New Literary History* 23, no. 2 (1992): 401–430.

"Mevlevi Leaders Move to Reclaim the Order." *Daily Sabah*, December 13, 2014. https://www.dailysabah.com/turkey/2014/12/13/mevlevi-leaders-move-to-reclaim-the-order.

Micozzi, Marc S. *Common Pain Conditions: A Clinical Guide to Natural Treatments*. St. Louis, MO.: Elsevier, 2016.

Micu, Andreea S. *Performance Studies: The Basics*. London: Routledge, 2022.

Minareci, Semih. "Search for Identity: Turkey's Identity Crisis." *SSRN Electronic Journal* (2008). http://dx.doi.org/10.2139/ssrn.1297378.

Mirza, Umair, *Hafız of Shiraz: Thirty Poems*, trans. Peter Avery and John Heath-Stubbs. London: John Murray, 1952.

Mitchell, Colin Paul. "A Culture of Sufism: Naqshbandis in the Ottoman World, 1450–1700." *Journal of Near Eastern Studies* 67, no. 4 (2008): 316–317.

Mitra, Royona. "Living a Body Myth, Performing a Body Reality: Reclaiming the Corporeality and Sexuality of the Indian Female Dancer." *Feminist Review* 84, no. 1 (2006): 67–83.

Morady, Farhang and İsmail Şiriner. "Islamism, Globalization and Development in Iran and Turkey." In *Political Economy, Crisis and Development*, ed. Ismail Şiriner, Farhang Morady, Janusz Mika, Murat Aydin, Şevket Alper Koç, Hakan Kapucu, and Emrah Doğan. London: IJOPEK Publication, 2011.

Muedini, Fait. *Sponsoring Sufism: How Governments Promote Mystical Islam in their Domestic and Foreign Policies*. Palgrave Macmillan US, 2015. https://doi.org.10.1057/9781137521071.

Mulacz, Peter. "Deliberately Caused Bodily Damage (DCBD) Phenomena: A Different Perspective." *Journal of the Society for Psychical Research* 62 (1998): 434–444.

Murray, Ros. *Antonin Artaud: The Scum of the Soul*. London: Palgrave Macmillan UK, 2014.

Naqvi, Ayeda Husain. "The Rose of Istanbul." *Cemalnur Sargut*. http://www.cemalnur.org/contents/detail/the-rose-of-istanbul/716.

Nasr, Seyyed Husein, ed. *Islamic Spirituality: Manifestations*. New York: Crossroad, 1991.

———. *Sufi Essays*. Chicago: ABC International Group, 1999a.

---. "What does Islam Have to Offer to the Modern World?" In *Sufi Essays*. Chicago: ABC International Group, 1999b.
---. "Preface." In *Rumi and the Whirling Dervishes*, ed. Shems Friedlander, Seyyed Hossein Nasr, Annemarie Schimmel, and Nezih Uzel. Sandpoint, ID: Morning Light Press, 2003.
"Nasreddin Hoca UNESCO Listesine Girmeye Hazırlanıyor [Nasreddin Hodja is Preparing to Enter the UNESCO List]." *Cumhuriyet*, Nisan 24, 2013. https://www.cumhuriyet.com.tr/haber/nasreddin-hoca-unesco-listesine-girmeye-hazirlaniyor-417866.
Nereid, C.T. "Kemalism on the Catwalk: The Turkish Hat Law of 1925." *Journal of Social History* 44, no. 3 (2011): 707–728.
Netton, Ian Richard. *Sufi Ritual: The Parallel Universe*. Richmond: Curzon Press, 2000.
Neuman, Gerald L. *Human Rights in a Time of Populism: Challenges and Responses*, ed. Gerald L. Neuman. Cambridge: Cambridge University Press, 2020.
Newell, James R. "The Wisdom of Intoxication: Love and Madness in the Poetry of Hafiz of Shiraz." In *Creativity, Madness and Civilization*, ed. Richard Pine. Cambridge: Cambridge Scholars Publishing, 2007.
Nicholson, Reynold Alleyne. *Studies in Islamic Mysticism*. Cambridge: Cambridge University Press, 1967.
---. *The Mystics of Islam*. London: Routledge, 1963.
Norris, Harry T. *Popular Sufism in Eastern Europe: Sufi Brotherhoods and the Dialogue with Christianity and "Heterodoxy"*. Oxon: Routledge, 2006.
"O Kişi Sahte Mevlevi Şeyhi." *Vatan*, January 20, 2020. http://www.gazetevatan.com/-o-kisi-sahte-mevlevi-seyhi—1297534-yasam/.
O'Fahey, R.S. and Bernd Radtke. "Neo-Sufism Reconsidered." *Islam* 70, no. 1 (1993): 52–87.
Ocak, Ahmet Yaşar. *Türk Sufiliğine Bakışlar [Perspectives in Turkish Sufism]*. İstanbul: İletişim, 1996.
---. *Türkler, Türkiye ve İslâm [Turks, Turkey, and Islam]*. İstanbul: İletişim, 1999.
---. *Sufism and Sufis in Ottoman society: Sources, Doctrine, Rituals, Turuq, Architecture, Literature and Fine Arts, Modernism*. Ankara: Atatürk Supreme Council for Culture, Language and History, 2005.
---. *Osmanlı Sufiliğine Bakışlar [Perspectives on Ottoman Sufism]*. İstanbul: Timaş Yayınları, 2010.
Oğuzhan, Özlem. "Re-Reading Nasreddin Hodja as an Opportunity for 'Intercultural Contact'." *Bilig* (2017): 249–267. https://dergipark.org.tr/tr/download/article-file/807322.
Öncü, Ayşe. "Becoming 'Secular Muslims': Yaşar Nuri Öztürk as a Super-subject on Turkish Television." In *Religion, Media, and the Public Sphere*, ed. Birgit Meyer and Annelies Moors. Bloomington: Indiana University Press, 2006.
Oring, Elliot. "Anti Anti-'Folklore'." *Journal of American Folklore* 111, no. 441 (1998): 328–338.
Otto, Rudolf. *The Idea of the Holy*, trans. John W. Harvey. Oxford: Oxford University Press, 1923.
Özdalga, Elisabeth. "The Alevis—A 'New' Religious Minority? Identity Politics in Turkey and Its Relation to the EU Integration Process." In *Religion, Politics and Turkey's EU Accession*, ed. Dietrich Jung and Catharina Raudvere. Basingstoke: Palgrave Macmillan, 2008.

———. "Transformation of Sufi Based Communities in Modern Turkey: The Nakşibendis, Nurcus, and the Gülen Community." In *Turkey's Engagement with Modernity*, ed. Celia J. Kerslake, Kerem Öktem, and Philip Robins. New York: Palgrave Macmillan, 2010.

Özekinci, Engin. "Turkey: Mevlana Rumi Museum Drew 3.4M Visitors in 2019." *AA*, February 19, 2020. https://www.aa.com.tr/en/culture/turkey-mevlana-rumi-museum-drew-34m-visitors-in-2019/1738375.

Öztürk, Ahmet Erdi. "Turkey's Diyanet under AKP Rule: From Protector to Imposer of State Ideology?" *Southeast European and Black Sea Studies* 16, no. 4 (2016): 619–635. https://doi.org/10.1080/14683857.2016.1233663.

Öztürkmen, Arzu. "Staging a Ritual Dance out of Its Context: The Role of an Individual Artist in Transforming the Alevi Semah." *Asian Folklore Studies* 64, no. 2 (2005): 247–260. http://www.jstor.org/stable/10.2307.

Özyürek, Esra. *Nostalgia for the Modern: State Secularism and Everyday Politics in Turkey*. Durham: Duke University Press, 2006.

———. "Christian and Turkish: Secularist Fears of a Converted Nation." In *Secular State and Religious Society: Two Forces in Play in Turkey*, ed. Berna Turam. New York: Palgrave Macmillan, 2012.

Paloutzian, Raymond F. and Crystal L. Park. *Handbook of the Psychology of Religion and Spirituality*. New York: Guilford Press, 2005.

Pals, Daniel L. "Reductionism and Belief: An Appraisal of Recent Attacks on the Doctrine of Irreducible Religion." *Journal of Religion* 66 (1986).

Papas, Alexandre. "Toward a New History of Sufism: The Turkish Case." *History of Religions* 46 no. 1 (2006): 81–90.

Parker, Andrew and Eve Kosofsky Sedgwick, eds. *Performativity and Performance*. London: Routledge, 1995.

Patterson, Ruairi. "Rising Nationalism and the EU Accession Process." *Turkish Policy Quarterly* 7, no. 1 (2008): 132.

Pavis, Patrice. *The Intercultural Performance Reader*. London: Routledge, 1996.

Peacock, James. "From Ritual to Theatre: The Human Seriousness of Play. Victor Turner." *American Anthropologist* 87, no. 3 (1985): 685–686.

Peña, Elaine A. "Beyond Mexico: Guadalupan Sacred Space Production and Mobilization in a Chicago Suburb." *American Quarterly* 60, no. 3 (2008): 721–747.

———. *Performing Piety: Making Space Sacred with the Virgin of Guadalupe*. Berkeley: University of California Press, 2011.

Perlmutter, Dawn. *Investigating Religious Terrorism and Ritualistic Crimes*. London: CRC Press, 2004.

Picken, Gacin N. "Al-Ḥārith Al-Muḥāsibī and Spiritual Purification Between Asceticism and Mysticism." In *Routledge Handbook on Sufism*, ed. Lloyd Ridgeon. London: Routledge, 2020.

Pinto, Paulo G. "Mystical Bodies/Unruly Bodies: Experience, Empowerment and Subjectification in Syrian Sufism." *Social Compass* 63, no. 2 (June 2016): 197–212. https://doi.org/10.1177/0037768616628791.

Piraino, Francesco and Mark Sedgwick. "Introduction." In *Global Sufism*, ed. Francesco Piraino and Mark Sedgwick. London: Hurst & Company, 2019.

Pope, Nicole and Hugh Pope. *Turkey Unveiled: A History of Modern Turkey*. Woodstock: Overlook Press, 1997.

Poulton, Hugh. *Top Hat, Grey Wolf, and Crescent: Turkish Nationalism and the Turkish Republic*. New York: New York University Press, 1997.

Prince, Raymond H. "Religious Experience and Psychopathology: Cross-Cultural Perspectives." In *Religion and Mental Health*, ed. J.F. Schumacher. New York: Oxford University Press, 1992.
Quinn, Charlotte A. and Frederick Quinn. *Pride, Faith, and Fear: Islam in Sub-Saharan Africa*. Oxford and New York: Oxford University Press, 2003.
Raban, Jonathan. *Arabia: A Journey Through a Labyrinth*. New York: Touchstone Books, 1991.
Rabi, Ibrahim Abu. *Islam at the Crossroads*. Albany: State University of New York Press, 2003.
Radtke, Bernd. "Sufism in the Eighteenth Century: An Attempt at a Provisional Appraisal." *Die Welt des Islams* 3 (1996): 326–364.
Rahimi, Sadeq. "Intimate Exteriority: Sufi Space as Sanctuary for Injured Subjectivities in Turkey." *Journal of Religion and Health* 46, no. 3 (2007): 409–421.
———. *Meaning, Madness, and Political Subjectivity: A Study of Schizophrenia and Culture in Turkey*. London: Routledge, 2016.
Rahman, Fazlur. *Islam and Modernity: Transformation of an Intellectual Tradition*. Chicago: University of Chicago Press, 1982.
Raj, Razaq. "Case Study 1: The Festival of Sacrifice and Travellers to the City of Heaven (Makkah)." In *Religious Tourism and Pilgrimage Festivals Management: An International Perspective*, ed. Razaq Raj and Nigel D. Morpeth, 127–139. Reading and King's Lynn: Biddles Ltd, 2007.
Raudvere, Catharina. *The Book and the Roses: Sufi Women, Visibility, and Zikir in Contemporary Istanbul*. Lund, Sweden: Bjarnums Tryckeri, 2002.
Raudvere, Catharina and Leif Stenberg, eds. *Sufism Today: Heritage and Tradition in the Global Community*. London and New York: I.B. Tauris, 2009.
Razali, Salleh Mohd. "Conversion Disorder: A Case Report of Treatment with the Main Puteri, a Malay Shamanastic Healing Ceremony." *European Psychiatry* 14, no. 8 (1999): 470–472. https://doi.org/10.1016/S0924-9338(99)00218-7.
Redmond, John. "Turkey and the European Union: Troubled European or European Trouble?" *International Affairs* 83, no. 2 (2007): 305–317.
Reed, Howard. "Revival of Islam in Secular Turkey." *The Middle East Journal* 8, no. 3 (1954): 267–282.
Rehder, Thomas. "Hafiz: An Introduction." PhD dissertation. Princeton University, 1970.
Reinelt, Janelle. "Rethinking the Public Sphere for a Global Age." *Performing Publics, Performance Research* 16, no. 2 (2011): 124–131.
Reinhertz, Shakina. *Women Called to The Path of Rumi: The Way of the Whirling Dervish*. Prescott: Hohm Press, 2001.
Reischer, Erica and Kathryn S. Koo. "The Body Beautiful: Symbolism and Agency in the Social World." *Annual Review of Anthropology* 33, no. 1 (2004): 297–317.
Reynolds, Dee. "A Technique for Power: Reconfiguring Economies of Energy in Martha Graham's Early Work." *Dance Research* 20, no. 1 (2002): 3–32.
Rifai, Kenan. *Sohbetler [Talks]*. İstanbul: Hülbe, 1991.
———. *Seyyid Ahmed Er-Rifai*, ed. Mustafa Tahralı and Müjgan Cunbur. İstanbul: Cenan Kültür Eğitim ve Sağlık Vakfı İktisadi İşletmesi, 2008.
Roach, Joseph R. *Cities of the Dead: CircumCircum-Atlantic Performance*. New York: Columbia University Press University Press, 1996.
Robins, Philip. "Turkish Foreign Policy since 2002: Between A Post-Islamist Government and a Kemalist State." *International Affairs* 83, no. 2 (2007): 289–304.

Rodriguez, Carmen, Antonio Avalos, Hakan Yilmaz, and Ana I. Planet. *Turkey's Democratization Process*, ed. Carmen Rodriguez, Antonio Avalos, Hakan Yilmaz, and Ana I. Planet. New York: Routledge, 2014.

Rouget, Gilbert. *Music and Trance: A Theory of Relations Between Music and Possessions*. Chicago: University of Chicago Press, 1985.

Rubenstein, Jeffrey. "Purim, Liminality, and Communitas." *AJS Review* 17, no. 2 (1992): 247–277.

Rubin, Jeffrey B. "A New View of Meditation." *Journal of Religion and Health* 40, no. 1 (2001): 121–128.

Rudie, Ingrid. "Making Persons in a Global Ritual? Embodied Experience and Free-floating Symbols in Olympic Sport." In *Recasting Ritual: Performance, Media, Identity*, ed. Felicia Hughes-Freeland and Mary Crain, 113–134. London: Routledge, 1998.

Rumi, Mevlana Celaleddin. *Fih-i Mafih [Discourses]*. Konya: Konya ve Mülhakatı Eski Eserleri Sevenler Derneği, 2001.

———. *Fih-i Mafihi [Discourses of Rumi]*, trans. A.J. Arberry. Ames, IA: Omphaloskepsis. Accessed October 30, 2020. http://rumisite.com/Books/FiheMaFih.pdf.

———. "Rumi's The Mathnawi, Vol. 5 and Vol. 6." In *Internet Archive*, trans. Reynold A. Nicholson. Accessed November 30, 2020. https://archive.org/stream/RumiTheMathnawiVol5Vol6/Rumi_The-Mathnawi-Vol-5-Vol-6_djvu.txt.

Rutherford, Tristan. *National Geographic Traveler: Istanbul and Western Turkey*. Washington: National Geographic, 2011.

Ruthven, Malise. *Islam in the World*. Oxford: Oxford University Press, 2006.

Rutz, Henry and Erol M. Balkan. *Reproducing Class: Education, Neoliberalism, and The Rise of the New Middle Class in Istanbul*. New York: Berghahn Books, 2010.

Sakallıoğlu, Ümit Cizre. "Rethinking the Connections Between Turkey's 'Western' Identity Versus Islam." *Critique* 13, no. 3 (1998): 18.

———. "Parameters and Strategies of Islam-State Interaction in Republican Turkey." *International Journal of Middle East Studies* 28 (2006): 231–251.

———. *Secular and Islamic Politics in Turkey: The Making of the Justice and Development Party*, ed. Ümit Cizre Sakallıoğlu. New York: Routledge, 2008.

Salemink, Oscar. "Embodying the Nation: Mediumship Ritual and the National Imagination." *Journal of Vietnamese Studies* 3, no. 3 (2008): 261–290.

Samarrai, Ibrahim. *Es-Seyyid Ahmed Er Rifai Hayati ve Eserleri [Life and Teachings of Es-Seyyid Ahmed Er Rifai]*, trans. Münir Atalar. Bağdat: Esad Matbaasi, 1988.

Şapolyo, Enver Behnan. *Mezhepler ve Tarikatler Tarihi [History of Denominations and Orders]*. İstanbul: Elif Kitabevi Milenyum Yayıncılık, 2013.

Sargut, Cemalnur. *Sohbetler [Talks]*, ed. Arzu Eylül Yalçınkaya. İstanbul: Nefes Yayınları, 2013.

Sarıkaya, M. Saffet. "Cumhuriyet Dönemi Türkiye'sinde Dini Tarikat ve Cemaatlerin Toplumdaki Yeri [Religious Orders and Congregations During the Republican Era of Turkey]." *SDÜ Fen-Edebiyat Fakültesi Sosyal Bilimler Dergisi* 3 (1998): 93–102.

Sarıtoprak, Zeki. "Fethullah Gülen: A Sufi in His Own Way." In *Turkish Islam and the Secular State: The Gülen Movement*, ed. M. Hakan Yavuz and John L. Esposito. New York: Syracuse University Press, 2003.

Savova, Nadezhda Dimitrova. "Heritage Kinaesthetics: Local Constructivism and UNESCO's Intangible-Tangible Politics at a *Favela* Museum." *Anthropological Quarterly* 82, no. 2 (2009): 547–585.

Schechner, Richard. "Performers and Spectators Transported and Transformed." *The Kenyon Review* 3, no. 4 (1981): 91.
———. *Between Theater and Anthropology*. Philadelphia: University of Pennsylvania Press, 1985.
———. *Performance Studies: An Introduction*. London: Routledge, 2020.
Scher, Philip W. "UNESCO Conventions and Culture as a Resource." *Journal of Folklore Research: An International Journal of Folklore and Ethnomusicology* 47, no. 1–2 (2010): 197–202.
Schimmel, Annemarie. *Mystical Dimensions of Islam*. Chapel Hill: University of North Carolina Press, 1975.
———. "Sufism and Spiritual Life in Turkey." In *Islamic Spirituality: Manifestations*, ed. Seyyed Hossein Nasr. London: Publisher, 1987.
———. "Mystical Poetry in Islam: The Case of Maulana Jalaladdin Rumi." *Religion & Literature* 20, no. 1 (1988): 67–80. http://www.jstor.org/stable/10.2307.
———. *Rumi's World: The Life and Work of the Great Sufi Poet*. London: Shambhala, 1992.
———. *Deciphering The Signs of God: A Phenomenological Approach to Islam*. Albany: State University of New York Press, 1994.
Scott, Joan Wallach. *Politics of the Veil*. Princeton: Princeton University Press, 2008.
Sedgwick, Mark. "The Reception of Sufi and Neo-Sufi Literature." In *Sufis in Western Society: Global Networking and Locality*, ed. Ron Geaves, Markus Dressler, and Gritt Maria Klinkhammer. London: Routledge, 2009.
Sedgwick, Mark. *Western Sufism: From the Abbasids to the New Age*. Oxford: Oxford University Press, 2016.
Seleny, Anna. "Tradition, Modernity, and Democracy: The Many Promises of Islam." *Perspectives on Politics* 4, no. 3 (2006): 481–494.
Shaikh, Sa'diyya. *Sufi Narratives of Intimacy: Ibn 'Arabī, Gender, and Sexuality*. Chapel Hill: University of North Carolina Press, 2012.
Shankland, David. "Islam and Politics in Turkey: The 2007 Presidential Elections and Beyond." *International Affairs* 83, no. 2 (2007): 357–371.
Shannon, Jonathan H. "Sultans of Spin: Syrian Sacred Music on the World Stage." *American Anthropologist* 105, no. 2 (2003): 266–277.
Sharify-Funk, Meena. William Rory Dickson, and Merin Shobhana Xavier. *Contemporary Sufism: Piety, Politics, and Popular Culture*. New York: Routledge, 2018.
Shiloah, Amnon. "The Status of Traditional Art Music in Muslim Nations." *Asian Music* 12, no. 1 (1980): 40–55. http://www.jstor.org/stable/10.2307/833797?ref=search-gateway:ec2d61fc922276b0cb014c69db951a83.
Shils, Edward. *Tradition*. Chicago: University of Chicago Press, 1981.
Shively, Kim. "Sufism in Modern Turkey." In *Routledge Handbook on Sufism*. London: Routledge, 2020.
Siegel, Marcia B. "Liminality in Balinese Dance." *TDR: The Drama Review* 35, no. 4 (1991): 84–91.
Silverman, Julian. "Shamans and Acute Schizophrenia." *American Anthropologist* 69 (1967). https://doi.org/10.1525/aa.1967.69.1.02a00030.
Silvers, Laura. "Early Pious, Mystic Sufi Women." In *The Cambridge Companion to Sufism*, ed. Lloyd Ridgeon. Cambridge: Cambridge University, 2014.
Silverstein, Brian. "Islam and Modernity in Turkey: Power, Tradition, and Historicity in the European Provinces." *Anthropological Quarterly* 76, no. 3 (2003): 497–517.

———. "Islamist Critique in Modern Turkey: Hermeneutics, Tradition, Genealogy." *Comparative Studies in Society and History* 47, no. 1 (2005): 134–160.

———. "Sufism and Modernity in Turkey: From the Authenticity of Experience to the Practice of Discipline." In *Sufism and the "Modern" in Islam*, ed. Martin Van Bruinessen and Julie Day Howell. London: I.B. Tauris, 2007.

———. "Sufism and Governmentality in the Late Ottoman Empire." *Comparative Studies of South Asia, Africa and the Middle East* 291, no. 2 (2009): 171–185.

Singh, Karan. "Istanbul: Dance of the Dervishes." *India International Centre Quarterly* 30, no. 3–4 (2003): 169–173. http://www.jstor.org/stable/10.2307.

———. "Sufism and Modernity in Turkey: From the Authenticity of Experience to the Practice of Discipline." *Sufism and the "Modern" in Islam*, ed. Martin Van Bruinessen and Julia Day Howell, 39–60. London: I.B. Tauris, 2007.

Skora, Kerry Martin. "The Pulsating Heart and Its Divine Sense Energies: Body and Touch in Abhinavagupta's Trika Śaivism." *Numen* 54, no. 4 (2007): 420–458.

Slavs and Tatars. *Molla Nasreddin: Polemics, Caricatures & Satires*, ed. Slavs and Tatars. London: I.B. Tauris, 2017.

Smith, David. "Networking Real-World Knowledge." *AI & Society* 21 (2007): 421–428. https://doi.org/10.1007/s00146-007-0105-6.

Smith, Margaret. *Readings from the Mystics of Islām*. London: Luzac & Co, 1972.

———. *Studies in Early Mysticism in the Near and Middle East*. Oxford: Oneworld, 1995.

Sonn, Tamara. *Islam: A Brief History*. Sussex: Blackwell Publishing, 2010.

Spielmann, Katherine A. "Feasting, Craft Specialization, and the Ritual Mode of Production in Small-Scale Societies." *American Anthropologist* 104, no. 1 (2002): 195–207.

Stoddart, William and R.W.J. Austin. *Sufism: The Mystical Doctrines and Methods of Islam*. Wellingborough: Thorsons Publishers, 1976.

Subhan, John A. *Sufism: Its Saints and Shrines*. Lucknow: Lucknow Publishing House, 1960.

"Sufism, Sufis, and Sufi Orders: Sufism's Many Paths." 2013. http://islam.uga.edu/Sufism.html.

Summer Boyd, Hillary and John Freeley. *Strolling Through Istanbul: The Classic Guide to the City*. London: I.B. Tauris, 2009.

Szuchewycz, Bohdan. "Evidentiality in Ritual Discourse: The Social Construction of Religious Meaning." *Language in Society* 23, no. 3 (1994): 389–410.

Tabi-Farouki, Suha. *Beshara and Ibn Arabi: A Movement of Sufi Spirituality in the Modern World*. Oxford: Anqa Publishing, 2007.

Tanman, M. Baha. "Settings for the Veneration of Saints." In *The Dervish Lodge: Architecture, Art and Sufism in Ottoman Turkey*, ed. Raymond Lifchez. Berkeley: University of California Press, 1992.

Tapasyananda, Swami. *Srimad-Bhagavad-Gita: The Scripture of Mankind*. Chennai: Sri Ramakrishna Math, 2005.

Tapper, Richard. *Islam in Modern Turkey: Religion, Politics, and Literature in a Secular State*. London: I.B. Tauris, 1991.

———. "'Islamic Anthropology' and the 'Anthropology of Islam'." *Anthropological Quarterly* 68, no. 3 (1995): 185–193. http://www.jstor.org/stable/10.2307.

Tarhanlı, İştar B. *Müslüman Toplum "Laik" Devlet: Türkiye'de Diyanet İşleri Başkanlığı [Muslim Society "Laic" State: Religious Affairs Directory in Turkey]*. Istanbul: AFA Yayınları, 1993.

Taylor, Charles. "Two Theories of Modernity." *The Hastings Center Report* 25, no. 2 (1995): 24–33.

———. *Seküler Çağ [A Secular Age]*. Istanbul: Türkiye İş Bankası Kültür Yayınları, 2009.

Taylor, Diana. *The Archive and the Repertoire: Performing Cultural Memory in the Americas*. Durham: Duke University Press, 2003.

Ter-Matevosyan, Vahram. *Turkey, Kemalism and the Soviet Union: Problems of Modernization, Ideology and Interpretation*. London: Palgrave Macmillan, 2020.

Tezcür, Güneş Murat. "Constitutionalism, Judiciary, and Democracy in Islamic Societies." *Palgrave Macmillan Journals* 39, no. 4 (2007): 479–501.

Tharoor, Ishaan. "The Trouble with Making Hagia Sophia a Mosque Again." *The Washington Post*, July 13, 2020. https://www.washingtonpost.com/world/2020/07/13/hagia-sofia-mosque-erdogan/.

Tierney, Robin. "Lived Experience at the Level of the Body: Annie Ernaux's Journaux Extimes." *Substance* 35, no. 3 (2006): 113–130.

Timothy, Dallen J. and Gyan P. Nyaupane. "Heritage Tourism and Its Impacts." In *Cultural Heritage and Tourism in the Developing World: A Regional Perspective*, ed. Dallen J. Timothy and Gyan P. Iyaupane, 56–70. London: Routledge, 2009.

Tobias, Toni. "Whirling Dervishes." *Dance Magazine* 53 (1979): 114–115.

Tombuş, H. Ertuğ. "Reluctant Democratization: The Case of the Justice and Development Party in Turkey." *Constellations* 20, no. 2 (2013): 312–327. http://doi.org/10.1111/cons.12037.

Toprak, Binnaz. "Secularism and Islam: The Building of Modern Turkey." *Macalester International* 15 (2005): Article 9. http://digitalcommons.macalester.edu/macintl/vol15/iss1/9.

"Tourists Rush to Konya's Famous Museum." *Hürriyet Daily News*. Accessed October 25, 2013. http://www.hurriyetdailynews.com/tourists-rush-to-konyas-famous-museum.aspx?pageID=238&nID=50737&NewsCatID=379.

Toynbee, Arnold J. and Kenneth P. Kirkwood. *Turkey*. New York: Charles Scribner's Sons, 1927.

Trimingham, J. Spencer. *The Sufi Orders in Islam*. Oxford: Oxford University Press, 1998.

Tuan, Yi-Fu. *Space and Place: The Perspective of Experience*. Minneapolis: University of Minnesota Press, 2001.

Tugal, Cihan Z. "The Appeal of Islamic Politics: Ritual and Dialogue in a Poor District of Turkey." *The Sociological Quarterly* 47, no. 2 (2006): 245–273.

Tunagöz, Tuna. "The Divine Attributes in Mawlānā Jalāl Al-Dīn Al-Rūmī." *Journal of Turkish Studies* 8, no. 8 (2013): 583–608.

Tunaya, Tarik Zafer. *Turkiye'de Siyasal Gelişmeler [1876–1938] [Political Developments in Turkey (1876–1938)]*. Istanbul: Bilgi Universitesi Press, 2002.

———. *İslamcılık Akımı [Islamist Movement]*. Istanbul: İstanbul Bilgi University Press, 2003.

Tunca, Elif. "Reed Flute Players, DJs Perform to Recount *Mevlana*'s Life." *Today's Zaman*, June 4, 2012. story://www.todayszaman.com/newsDetail_openPrintPage.action?newsId=114331.

"Turkey's 4 Cultural Values on Way to UNESCO Intangible Heritage List." *Daily Sabah*, April 5, 2020. https://www.dailysabah.com/arts/turkeys-4-cultural-values-on-way-to-unesco-intangible-heritage-list/news.

"Turkish Humanism and Anatolian Muslim Saints (Dervishes)." December 12, 2013. http://www.kultur.gov.tr/EN,35148/turkish-humanism-and-anatolian-muslim-saints-dervishes.html.

Turner, Terence. "Social Body and Embodied Subject: Bodylines, Subjectivity, and Sociality among the Kayapo." *Cultural Anthropology* 10, no. 2 (1995): 143–170.

Turner, Victor. *The Ritual Process: Structure and AntiStructure.* Chicago: Aldine, 1969.

———. *Dramas, Fields, and Metaphors: Symbolic Action in Human Society.* Ithaca: Cornell University Press, 1974.

———. *From Ritual to Theatre: The Human Seriousness of Play.* New York City: Performing Arts Journal Publications, 1982a.

———. "Introduction." In *Celebration: Studies in Festivity and Ritual,* ed. Victor Turner. Washington, DC: Smithsonian Institution Press, 1982b.

———. "Body, Brain and Culture." *Performing Arts Journal* 10, no. 2 (1986): 26–34.

———. *The Anthropology of Performance.* New York: PAJ Publications, 1987.

Turner, Victor and Edith Turner. *Image and Pilgrimage in Christian Culture: Anthropological Perspectives.* New York: Columbia University Press, 1978.

Türsan, Huri. *Democratisation in Turkey: The Role of Political Parties.* Bruxelles: PIE–Peter Lang, 2004.

Ulusoy, K. "The Changing Challenge of Europeanization to Politics and Governance in Turkey." *International Political Science Review* 30, no. 4 (2009): 363–384.

UNESCO. "Intangible Cultural Heritage: What is Intangible Cultural Heritage?" Accessed July 19, 2011. http://www.unesco.org/culture/ich/?pg=00003.

UNESCO. "Mevlevi Sema Ceremony." 2011. http://www.unesco.org/culture/intangible-heritage/39eur_uk.htm.

UNESCO. "What is Intangible Cultural Heritage?" 2011. http://www.unesco.org/culture/ich/?pg=00003.

Üzel, Nezih. *Aşıklarin Dünyası: Yenikapı Mevlevihanesi [World of Lover: Yenikapı Mevlevi Lodge].* Ankara: Republic of Turkey Ministry Directorate General of Foundation, 2010.

Van Bruinessen, Martin and Julia Day Howell, eds. *Sufism and the 'Modern' in Islam.* London: Tauris, 2007.

Van Der Veer, Peter. "Playing or Praying: A Sufi Saint's Day in Surat." *Journal of Asian Studies* 51, no. 3 (1992): 245–564.

Van Gennep, Arnold. *The Rites of Passage.* Chicago: University of Chicago Press, 1960.

Vásquez, Manuel A. and Marie F. Marquardt. *Globalizing the Sacred Religion across the Americas.* New Brunswick: Rutgers University Press, 2003.

Verney, Susannah, Anna Bosco, and Senem Aydın-Düzgit. *The AKP Since Gezi Park: Moving to Regime Change in Turkey,* ed. Susannah Verney, Anna Bosco, and Senem Aydın-Düzgit. New York: Routledge, 2020.

Vicente, Victor Amaro. "The Aesthetics of Motion in Musics for the Mevlana Celal Ed-Din Rumi." PhD dissertation. University of Maryland, 2007.

Vicini, Fabio. *Reading Islam: Life and Politics of Brotherhood in Modern Turkey.* Boston: Brill, 2020.

Villalón, Leonardo A. "Sufi Rituals as Rallies: Religious Ceremonies in the Politics of Senegalese State-Society Relations." *Comparative Politics* 26, no. 4 (1994): 415–437. http://www.jstor.org/stable/10.2307.

Voll, John O. "Renewal and Reform in Islamic History: Tajdid and Islah." In *Voices of Resurgent Islam,* ed. John C. Esposito, 32–47. Oxford: Oxford University Press, 1983.

———. "Contemporary Sufism and Current Social Theory." In *Sufism and the "Modern" in Islam*, ed. Martin Van Bruinessen and Julia Day Howell, 281–298. London: I.B. Tauris, 2007.

———. "Neo-Sufism: Reconsidered Again." *Canadian Journal of African Studies* 42, no. 2/3 (2008): 314–330. http://www.jstor.org/stable/10.2307.

Volm, Florian. "The Making of Sufism: The Gülen Movement and Its Efforts to Create a New Image." In *Global Sufism*, ed. Francesco Piraino and Mark Sedgwick. London: Hurst & Company, 2019.

Volpi, Frédéric. "Pseudo-Democracy in the Muslim World." *Third World Quarterly* 25, no. 6 (2004): 1061–1078.

Warner, Michael. *Publics and Counterpublics*. New York: Zone Books, 2002.

Warner, Michael, Jonathan Van Antwerpen, and Craig J. Calhoun, eds. *Varieties of Secularism in a Secular Age*. Cambridge, MA: Harvard University Press, 2010.

Watenpaugh, Heghnar Zeitlian. "Deviant Dervishes: Space, Gender, and the Construction of Antinomian Piety in Ottoman Aleppo." *International Journal of Middle East Studies* 37, no. 4 (2005): 535–565.

Webster, Donald Everett. *The Turkey of Atatürk, Social Process in the Turkish Reformation*. Philadelphia: American Academy of Political and Social Science, 1939.

Weismann, Itzchak. "The Forgotten Shaykh: 'Īsā Al-Kurdī and the Transformation of the Naqshbandī-Khālidī Brotherhood in Twentieth-Century Syria." *Die Welt Des Islams* 43, no. 3 (2003): 373–393.

———. "Sufi Brotherhoods in Syria and Israel: A Contemporary Overview." *History of Religions* 43, no. 4 (2004): 303–318.

Werbner, Pnina. "Stamping the Earth with the Name of Allah: Zikir and Sacralizing of Space Among British Muslims." *Cultural Anthropology* 11, no. 3 (1996): 309–338.

———. *Embodying Charisma Modernity, Locality, and Performance of Emotion in Sufi Cults*. London: Routledge, 1998.

———. *Pilgrims of Love: The Anthropology of a Global Sufi Cult*. Bloomington: Indiana University Press, 2003.

Westerlund, David. *Sufism in Europe and North America*. London and New York: Routledge and Curzon Press, 2004.

Wetzsteon, Ross. "The Whirling Dervishes: An Emptiness Filled With Everything." In *What is Dance? Readings in Theory and Criticism*, ed. Roger Copeland and Marshall Cohen. Oxford: Oxford University Press, 1983.

William, M. Hale and Ali Çarkoğlu. *The Politics of Modern Turkey: Major Issues and Themes in Contemporary Turkish Politics*. London and New York: Routledge, 2008.

Winnicott, Donald W. *Psycho-Analytic Explorations*, ed. Clare Winnicott, Ray Shepherd, and Madeleine Davis. London: Karnac Books, 1989.

Wolper, Ethel Sara. *Cities and Saints: Sufism and the Transformation of Urban Space in Medieval Anatolia*. University Park: Pennsylvania State University Press, 2003.

Xavier, Merin Shobhana. *Sacred Spaces and Transnational Networks in American Sufism: Bawa Muhaiyaddeen and Contemporary Shrine Cultures*. London: Bloomsbury Publishing, 2018.

Yavuz, M. Hakan. *Islamic Political Identity in Turkey*. Oxford: Oxford University Press, 2005.

———. *The Emergence of a New Turkey*. Salt Lake City: Utah University Press, 2006.

———. *Secularism and Muslim Democracy in Turkey*. Cambridge: Cambridge University Press, 2009.

———. *Nostalgia for the Empire: The Politics of Neo-Ottomanism*. Oxford: Oxford University Press, 2020.

Yavuz, M. Hakan and Ahmet Erdi Öztürk. "Turkish Secularism and Islam under the Reign of Erdoğan." *Southeast European and Black Sea Studies* 19, no. 1 (2019): 1–9. https://doi.org/10.1080/14683857.2019.1580828.

———. *Islam, Populism and Regime Change in Turkey: Making and Re-making the AKP*, ed. M. Hakan Yavuz and Ahmet Erdi Öztürk. New York: Routledge, 2020.

Yazaki, Saeko. "The Transformation of Muslim Mystical Thought in the Ottoman Empire: The Rise of the Halveti Order, 1350–1650, John J. Curry." *British Journal of Middle Eastern Studies* 39, no. 3 (2012): 420–422.

Yesil, Bilge. "Press Censorship in Turkey: Networks of State Power, Commercial Pressures, and Self-Censorship: Press Censorship in Turkey." *Communication, Culture & Critique* 7, no. 2 (2014): 154–173. http://doi.org/10.1111/cccr.12049.

Yürekli, Zeynep. "A Building Between the Public and Private Realms of The Ottoman Elite: The Sufi Convent of Sokollu Mehmed Pasha in Istanbul." *Muqarnas Online* 20, no. 1 (2003): 159–185.

Zakaria, Fareed. "Islam, Democracy, and Constitutional Liberalism." *Political Science Quarterly* 119, no. 1 (2004): 1–20.

Zaman, Amberin. "Erdogan's Order Making Hagia Sophia Mosque Brings Cheers, Mourning." *Al-Monitor*, July 10, 2020. https://www.al-monitor.com/pulse/originals/2020/07/turkey-hagia-sophia-church-mosque-erdogan-divide-pompeo.html#ixzz6est3NNwC.

Zamir, Syed Rizwan. "'Tafsir al-Quran bi'l Quran': The Hermeneutics of Imitation and 'Adap' in Ibn-i Arabi's Interpretation of the Quran." *Islamic Studies* 50, no. 1 (2007): 16–17.

Zarruq, Ahmed, Zaineb Istrabadi, and Hamza Yusuf Hanson. *The Principles of Sufism*. Bristol: Amal Press, 2008.

Zilfi, Madeline C. *The Politics of Piety: The Ottoman Ulema in the Postclassical Age 1600–1800*. Minneapolis: Bibliotheca Islamica, 1988.

Zinnbauer, B.J., K.I. Pargament, and A.B. Scott. "The Emerging Meanings of Religiousness and Spirituality: Problems and Prospects." *Journal of Personality* 67 (1999): 889–919.

Zubaida, Sami. "Turkish Islam and National Identity." *Middle East Report* 199 (1996): 10–15. http://www.jstor.org/stable/10.2307.

Zürcher, Erik Jan. *Turkey: A Modern History*. London: I.B. Tauris, 2005.

Index

AA (Anadolu Agency) 150
Abbas, Sheemem Burney 160–161
Adalet ve Kalkınma Partisi (Justice and Development Party-JDP) 1
And, Metin 56, 57, 60, 118, 150
An-Na'im, Abdullahi Ahmed 52
Arabi, Ibn 178, 180, 182
Archive and the Repertoire: Performing Cultural Memory in the Americas, The (Taylor) 5–6
Artaud, Antonin 142
Atacan, Fulya 103
Atatürk, Mustafa Kemal 13–14, 38, 114; critics of 49; *laïcité* idea of 189; modernisation ideas of 41–42; radical reforms, causes for 42–43
Austin, John Langshaw 8
Ayasofya 38; *see also* Hagia Sophia
Ayata, Sencer 41
Ayşe, female devotee whirling in public 117–120

Baba, Tavus 162
Barks, Coleman 149
Basu, Helena 60
Bedding, James 55
Bell, Catherine 192–193
Benhabib, Seyla 23
Benli, Yusuf 150
Bermek, Sevinç 48
Bhabha, Homi K. 9
Bianchi, Robert 154
Birch, Nicholas 191
body and mind, sacralisation of 127–146; *burhan* and 138–143; overview of 127–128; renunciation practices and 143–146; wooden house and 128–131; *Zikir* ceremony gatherings and 131–138
Bourdieu, Pierre 24–25
Brown, Michael 120
Bruijn, Johannes Thomas Pieter 179
burhan ritual performance 8, 138–143
buses, collective worship/sacralisation of spaces and 161–163
Butler, Judith 8

Cağatay, Soner 52
Carlson, Marvin 9
Çelebi, Faruk Hemdem 109–110
Çelebi, *pir* Adel 55, 56
Cengiz Bey 105–106
Chambers, Claire Marie 189
Chattopadhyay, Saayan 119
Chelebi, *pir* Adel 118
Chih, Rachida 20
çile training 70, 72–73
Cities and Saints: Sufism and the Transformation of Urban Space in Medieval Anatolia (Wolper) 21–22
Çıtak, Zana 47
Çıtlak, Fatih 108, 110, 118
Clarke, Morgan 142
Cohen, Emma 177–178
Conquergood, Dwight 9, 11–12, 75, 76, 170
coperformative witnessing 11–13, 75
Craft of Ritual Studies, The (Grimes) 169–170
cultural closure 120

Danforth, Nicholas 38
de Certeau, Michel 19, 61
Dede Efendi, Hamamizade İsmail 37; House 112–113

Dein, Simon 176
de Lefebvre, Michel 82
Deniz (female devotee) 59, 62, 90
dergahs, Sufi importance of 98
Derrida, Jacques 8, 23
dervish: becoming one with God 77–80; defined 79
devotees, Sufi 4–5, 7–8, 10; coperformative witnessing with 11–13; migration of, to Europe and North America 14–15; role-playing 10–11; separation and 17; *see also* post-tariqa *Mevlevi* devotion
Dickson, William Rory 18
Din Valed, Baha al- 151
Drewal, Margaret Thompson 10, 75, 86, 133
Du Toit, Simon 189

Edelman, Joshua 189, 191
edep practice, described 86–87
embodied acts 10–11
Erbakan, Necmettin 48
Erdoğan, Recep Tayyip 37–38
Ergüner, Kudsi 44, 45
Eski Evleri Koruma Derneği 112
European Recovery Program 45

Fatih Sultan Mehmet Vakıf University 38–39
Feldman, Walter 118
Fethullahçıs 50
Fraser, Nancy 120
Frembgen, Jurgen Wasim 181

Galip, Sheikh 37
Genn, Celia 20
Geylani, Abdulkadir 128
global war on terror 13
God 20, 38, 110–111, 190–191; *burhan* and 8–9; dervishes becoming one with 77–80; devotees and 7–8; *hizmet* and 54–55, 83–84; *Mevlevi* gatherings and 105–106; *nefs* stages and 84–85; Quranic names/attributes of 111–112, 132; *sema* and 61–62, 137; Veli *efendi* ritual performances and 72–76; *zikir* performance and 4–6, 24, 135–137
Goffman, Erving 10, 82–83, 90
Goldberg, Roselee 142

Göle, Nilüfer 23, 24, 48
Gould, Kevin 149
Green, Nile 16
Grimes, Ronald 169–170
Guardian, The 149
Gülen, Fethullah 50
Gurdjieff, George Ivanovich 116

Habermas, Jürgen 119, 189–190
Hafız of Shiraz 178, 179–180
Hagia Sophia 37–38; reclassifications in Turkey and 38, 39
Halveti Cerrahi order 71
Hayrani, Seyit Mahmut 162
Heper, Metin 50
Hermansen, Marcia 15, 191
hizmet 54–55; Veli *efendi* devotees performing 73
Hoca, Nasrrettin 162
Hoffman, Valerie J. 143
Howell, Julia Day 18
howling dervishes 2, 13, 70, 171; *see also Rifai*
Hunter, Shireen 18
Hürriyet Daily News 150

Illaie, Abdool Samd 176
Illuminated Rumi, The (Barks) 149
İnançer, Tuğrul 97, 101, 103
insan 4
International Mevlana Foundation 109
Islam: mobilising, as social force 48; perceptions of 13
Islam and the Secular State (An-Na'im) 52
Islamist Welfare Party (WP) 49, 50
Istanbul-European Capital of Culture 2010 55, 62

Jalal ad-Din Muhammad Balkhi 115
jinn, fear of 178
Jones, Paul 169
Journeys of a Sufi Musician (Ergüner) 44
Justice and Development Party 51–52
Justine, Byzantine Emperor 38
Just Order *(Adil Düzen)* 49

kader (fate) 78
Kafadar, Cemal 41
kamil insan (mature or perfect human being) 4, 5, 85
Kapferer, Bruce 134
Karabulut, Savaş 143

Karamustafa, Ahmet 16
Karasipahi, Sena 47, 50
kinaesthetic imagination 133–134
kinesis, representation as 10
Kirshenblatt-Gimblett, Barbara 45
Kılınç, Nirgül 57
Kısakürek, Necip Fazıl 48
Knysh, Alexander 16
Kolawole Ositola 88
Konevi, Sadrettin 162
Konya, Turkey experience 149–154
Konya Turkish Sufi Music Ensemble 152
Küçük, Hülya 41

Lefebvre, Henri 21
Lewis, Franklin 108, 115, 116
Lewis, Ioan 177
Lifchez, Raymond 98
Littlewood, Roland 177
lokma yapma 130
Lukoff, David 176
Lymer, Kenneth 153

Malik, Jamal 18
Mansur, Hallac 179
manyness of reality 4, 81, 127, 149–184; buses and collective worship/sacralisation of spaces 161–163; hotel conversion into *tekke* 154–158; Konya experience 149–154; overview of 149; performing *zikir* outside Rumi's shrine 164–165; possession 171–175; Rumi's *Urs*, celebrating 165–171; *Tebrizli Şems*' mosque 158–161; Veli *efendi*'s *sohbets* 175–184
Mardin, Şerif 48
master Veli *see* Veli *efendi* (master Veli)
McAuley, Gay 7
meczup 180–181
Mehmet II, Sultan 38
Melchert, Christopher 16
Melih *dede* 52, 53
Menninger, Karl 177
Meschonnic, Henri 24
meşk 76
Mevlana Cultural Center 152
Mevlana's students *vs.* tarikatçiler 106–112
Mevlana Türbesi (the tomb of Rumi) 151–152

Mevlevi dervishes 1–2; performed as tourist attraction and worship 1; practice of remembrance 56–63
Mevlevi lodge 1–2; reclassification of 1
Mevlevi ritual gatherings 1
Mevlevis 3, 18, 19; *çile* training 70, 72–73; embodied acts 3–4; by heart 104–106; locating 53; post-tariqa, positions 13; restoration process 39–40, 188; *vs.* tarikatçiler 106–112
Micu, Andreea 9–10, 141
mimesis, representation as 10
modernity 24
Muhammed, Prophet 56, 101, 108, 115, 131, 166, 167
Muslims in Turkey 2

Nakşibendi order 19, 48, 49, 51
Naqshbandi-Halidi groups 19
Narin *dede* 39, 52–53, 112–117
National Order Party 48
National Salvation Party 48
nefs-i ammara stage 84–85
nefs-i lavvama stage 85
nefs-i mardiyya stage 85
nefs-i mulhima stage 85
nefs-i mutmainna stage 85
nefs-i raddiya stage 85
nefs-i safiyyali kamiliye stage 85
nefs training 4–5; self, restoring 82–93; stages of 84–85
Netton, Ian Richard 76–77
Nicholson, Reynold 168
Nitsch, Hermann 142
non-worship time 3
Nurcus 19, 49
Nurettin Cerrahi *tekke* 97–104; performatic shift and doubling 103; tourist audience at 101–102; whirling dervishes 101–104; women at 99–101
Nur movement 49–50
Nursi, Said 49–50

Ocak, Ahmet Yaşar 16
Ottoman Sufi lodges, names for 98
Özyürek, Esra 23

Pane, Gina 142
Parker, Andrew 8
Peña, Elaine A. 12, 24–25, 61, 139, 153, 157, 191, 193

224 Index

performance 3–5; *burhan* 8, 138–143; centered restoration 44–46; coperformative witnessing and 11–13; Drewal on 10; embodied acts and 10–11; as kinesis 9; Micu on 9–10; as object of study 4–11; religious studies through 192–193; Taylor on 8; wooden house and 128–131; of *zikir* 5, 131–138
performatic shift and doubling 8, 24, 103, 120
performativity 9
Piraino, Francesco 14, 15
possession, mind/heart transformation and 171–175
post-tariqa communal Sufi training, designing spaces for 70–93; becoming Veli *efendi's* student 77–80; co-performance participation and 74–76; overview of 70–74; restoring self (*nefs* training) 82–93; Rifai site organization 76–77; sacred sites for *çile* training 80–82; *see also* Veli *efendi* (master Veli)
post-tariqa *Mevlevi* devotion 37–63; *Mevlevi* practice of remembrance 56–63; overview of 39–40; performance-centered restoration 44–46; reclassified lodges as museums and 37–40; revolution, Sufism and 40–44; secularism, political Sufi groups and 47–54; *Sema* ceremony, commodification of as tourist attraction 44–46; Sufism in Turkey and 13–16; Yenikapı *Mevlevi* lodge 54–56
post-tariqa Sufism: body and mind, sacralisation of 127–146; historical perspectives 37–63; introduction to 1–4; manyness of reality, world as 149–184; *Mevlevi* and *Rifai*, comprehending 13–16; *Mevlevi* devotion 37–63; performance described 4–11; training, designing spaces for 70–93; whirling 97–120; *see also* manyness of reality; post-tariqa *Mevlevi* devotion
prayer time 3

Prince, Raymond 176
public spheres 120

Radtke, Bernd 16
Rahimi, Sadeq 174, 177, 180, 181
Raj, Razaq 154
Raudvere, Catharina 101, 103–104
reclassified lodges as museums 37–40
Reinhertz, Shakina 83–84
Religious Affairs Directorate (RAD) 17–18, 38, 43, 51; devotional spaces of secluded groups and 71–72
renunciation practices 143–146
representation 10
restored behaviour as living behaviour 188
revolution, Sufism and 40–44
Rifai 2; dervishes 70, 79; *nefs* training 73
Rifai, Kenan 41
Rifais 3, 19; embodied acts 3–4; post-tariqa, positions 13
rind, figure of 179
Risale-i Nur (Epistle of Light) (Nursi) 49
Roach, Joseph 8, 133–134
role-playing, described 10–11
Rouget, Gilbert 140
Rumi, Mevlana Celaleddin-i 128, 142, 144; teachings 106–112; *Urs*, celebrating 165–171
Rumi Commemoration Tours 152

Sakallıoğlu, Ümit Cizre 14
Salemink, Oscar 91, 135
Sargut, Cemalnur 57, 192
Saygın *dede* 47, 50, 74, 92, 99, 101, 104; Ayşe's performances and 120; case study 39–40; permanent spaces and devotional practices 70–71; Yenikapı *Mevlevi* lodge and 54, 55–63
Schechner, Richard 5, 6, 8, 10, 86, 135, 188
Schimmel, Annemarie 43
Scott, Joan 23
Şeb-i Aruz (Rumi's *urs*) ceremonies 45, 153–154
secularism 23–24; political Sufi/Sufi-esque groups and 47–54
Sedgwick, Eve Kosofsky 8
Sedgwick, Mark 14, 15
self (*nefs* training), restoring 82–93

self-mutilation 144
Sema 1, 7, 15; ceremony, commodification of 44–46
semahanes 17, 127–128, 129
semazens 1–2
Şemseddin, Mehmed 41
separation 17
Shaikh, Sa'diyya 163
Sharify-Funk, Meena 18
Shems of Tebriz mosque 158–161
Silverman, Julian 177
Silverstein, Brian 18, 22, 189, 190
Sirriyeh, Elizabeth 18
Smith, David 109–110
Smith, Margaret 16
sohbets 11, 12; Veli *efendi*'s 175–184
spirituality, defined 169
"State of Research on Performance in Africa, The" (Drewal) 133
Sufi practice in Turkey: devotional living and 191–192; etymological sources of word 73; gender/sexuality research about 192; introduction to 1–4; Islam and perceptions of 13; performance and 4–11; politics and 19
Sufi ritual gatherings 1
Sufism: as moderate alternative to mainstream Islam 18–19; music/dance and 137–138; revolution and 40–44
Süleymancıs 19
symbolic capital 24–25
synagogue, described 2

Tanman, Baha 98
Taylor, Charles 24
Taylor, Diana 5–6, 8, 11, 24, 103, 114–115, 120
Tebrizli Şems' (Shems of Tebriz) mosque 158–161
tekkes 17, 97; hotel conversion into, manyness of reality and 154–158
teslimiyet (submission) 78
Tezcür, Güneş Murat 47, 51
theatricality 9
theatrical performance 8–9
tolerance 174
Tourism and Promotion Projects of Istanbul 2010 European Capital of Culture Program 55
Turkey Travel Planner 152

Turkish Adalet ve Kalkınma Partisi (AKP) 51–52
Turkish War of Independence 43
Turner, Bryan 16
Turner, Victor 12, 86, 92, 135–136, 141
"Two Theories of Modernity" (Taylor) 24

UNESCO World Intangible Cultural Heritage 14, 44, 55
urban Sufi space 19–25

Vahdat al Vucud (Ibn Arabi) 181
Van Bruinessen, Martin 18
Veled, Sultan 118
Veli, Ateşbaz 162
Veli *efendi* (master Veli) 70, 71; *burhan* ritual 73–74, 138–143; *çile* adaptation use by 84; devotee journeys with 86–93; *edep* practice 86–87; female students and 88–90; meeting with 74–76; *nefs* training 83–85; performatic practices 72–73, 127–128; place of worship 72; renunciation practices 143–146; *Rifai* site organization and 76–77; sacred sites for *çile* training 80–82; schooling and teachings of 76; *sohbets* 175–184; student, becoming 77–80; student perceptions of 77; wooden house 128–131; *zikir* ceremony 73–74, 131–138; see also post-tariqa communal Sufi training, designing spaces for
versatile Sufism 12, 120
Voll, John 20, 189

Wahhabism 13
Werbner, Pnina 12, 60, 133, 168–169, 170, 188, 191
whirling dervishes 1–2, 13, 44, 97–120; female devotee Ayşe 117–120; Mevlana's students *vs.* tarikatçiler 106–112; Mevlevi gatherings 104–106; Narin *dede* 112–117; at Nurrettin Cerrahi *tekke* 97–104; see also Mevlevi dervishes; *Sema*
Wolper, Ethel Sara 21–22
wooden house, performatic 128–131

226 *Index*

World Intangible Cultural Heritage 14, 18, 44, 55
WP *see* Islamist Welfare Party (WP)

Xavier, Merin Shobhana 18, 59–60

Yavuz, Hakan 44, 47
Yenikapı *Mevlevi* lodge 37–38, 54–56; reclassification of 38–39

Zarrabi-Zadeh, Saeed 18
zikir 1, 4, 5, 7, 10; mixed-gender, ceremonies 129; performatic 131–138; performing, outside Rumi's shrine 164–165; restoration of, practice 70; Veli e*fendi* performatic practices of 72–73, 79
zuhd, practitioners of 143–144
Zürcher, Eric Jan 14